HEADS OR TALES

BY THORNTON CLARK

ISBN: 978-0-692-05145-0

Printed in the United States of America

Cover design by Phil Scarsbrook

Oil painting on cover “ *Storm Cloud at Sunset*” by the author

"HEADS OR TALES "

HEADS OR TALES

INTRODUCTION

These are all true stories, many about friends and events that I stumbled across in life. A lot of the stories and some useful information results from my having been to seven continents and more than a hundred countries, all the major ones in Europe, Asia and South America many times each. Plus, of course, Canada, Central America and all 50 states of the U.S.

This book is about journeys. The biggest was the abrupt transition from a public high school in Montgomery to Harvard in 1955. The most snow I had seen before that was a quarter of an inch in 1945. The longest journeys were by plane, chalking up more than two million miles and having many unusual experiences. Many stories involve boats, from canoes and sailboats to huge yachts and cruise ships. Pat and I sailed more than 15,000 miles, most of the time with just the two of us. This includes four times up and down the entire east coast of the United States from the Canadian border to Key West and all the way down the Bahamas, many times in the Virgin Islands and along the marvelous coast of Maine, sailing the length of the Caribbean down to Grenada, from Jost van Dyke to Bermuda and some sailing boats we chartered in Thailand, and the Dalmation Coast of Croatia. Of course, everyone makes the journey from childhood to old age, but I bet most did not encounter so much excitement (especially life-threatening danger), face more challenges or meet more important people than I did. I came very close to being murdered twice.

Dozens of people are named. Because of concerns, friends suggested I call this book fiction or just change all the names. In many cases the person involved is what makes a story interesting. If I am sued, in all cases there is another witness to verify the story and, if not, I will be pleased to take a lie detector test (that is, if you will pay for it).

A well-respected expert on the history of my town, Mary Ann Neely, told me an old story that probably fits the problem this book faces. She told me that many years ago a writer was going to charge $25 (which was a whole lot of money back when this occurred) for a person to be included in his book, but charge $50 if they wanted to be left out. Maybe I should try that (at a somewhat higher price). I did, in a few cases, use an initial instead of the name of girls whose husbands might be less than appreciative of a story.

My sister, Carolyn, was born in 1916 when my mother was 21, at the time an accepted age for baring your first child. Shortly thereafter mom had what a century ago was considered an extremely dangerous late-term miscarriage. Her doctor cautioned her that she could not have any more normal children. *I guess that proved to be true.* Dad was born in 1890 and Mom in 1895.

My mother's relatives were in shock when she became pregnant and was due to deliver 21 years after Carolyn was born. The close relatives all came to Montgomery to be with my mother when she died. They had no doubt that they would be there for her death. Only in late 2017 did a friend, Julie Crane, bring an article from the Montgomery newspaper dated July, 1937 (a week before I was born), that read:

> "Captain and Mrs. John W. Persons, their daughter Juliette and Mrs. M.M. McLendon arrived recently from Washington, D.C. to visit Mr. and Mrs. Thornton Clark."

This was not a joke; they were very sad. The newspaper article did not say why they had come to Montgomery, but it did give me the names. In those days at her age, death would certainly be the outcome for my mother. Now that I am 82, having a child that late in life is common, but as you can read it was definitely unusual in many respects eighty years ago. She lived to be 96.

Because it is where I went to college, there are stories about Harvard. Meeting so many interesting people was the result of living in New York, Boston and Munich and travelling to so many countries, an experience that made it difficult to adjust to living back where I grew up. There is one sad story about sexual abuse.

I was one of the very few people who traveled the world so much that the US State Department allowed me to have two current U.S. passports. I traveled so frequently to so many esoteric countries that there was usually not enough time for fairly-costly visa service companies in Washington, DC to take one passport from embassy to embassy to acquire the long list of visas required for many of my business trips. This was in addition to the fact that you could not have a customs stamp in your passport from Israel if you wanted to enter most Arab countries.

In the years in which I was having to do so much travel, US passports were valid for only five years, half of what they are today. Even so, my primary passport filled up so quickly that I had to get the State Department to glue "extra pages" into that passport. Extra pages are essentially an accordion fold of "pages," each the size of a passport, that are issued one at a time, attached and officially sealed to one edge of a page in the passport so that the pages can fold evenly back into the passport. The extra pages pull out to provide room for a few dozen extra visas and entry and exit stamps on the front and back sides of each page of each extender. At the height of my travel, my primary passport had four such extra foldout pages attached, providing room for many dozens of visas and all the entry and exit customs-control stamps, and that was during just five years of travel, not counting the pages of the original passport or the one for Arab countries.

If I had put all of the best stories at the start of the book, your interest would decline steadily and you would quit reading. I couldn't save all of the best stories till the end, because readers would never get that far. Chronological order made no sense, and I do not remember many of the dates anyway. Stories about State Street Bank, American Express, Harvard University, boating, the travel industry and football games are spread throughout the book so you don't get too much of one subject at one time. So that they are easy to find, subjects within chapters are identified by sub-headings. Pat complained recently about a book she was reading that was repetitious. This one is intentionally repetitious, so that each chapter can stand alone and be understood without having to have read a full chapter on the company, club or event that is the preface to a story.

These stories are almost all fairly short. Some extremely short ones are combined into chapters called "Tidbits," that are scattered throughout the book. All these stories have been told, where pauses, accents and inflection can greatly impact the effect. You can't create a pregnant pause in writing. Written stories are nowhere-near as much fun as telling tales. It is also not as effective for the audience. Until beginning to recall and then list the various stories, I would never have believed the sheer quantity, 403 stories sorted into 98 chapters. At the end, chapters 86, 87 and 88 are about travel, so you can skip them if you are not interested in travel.

Jobs, usually thought of as nothing but work, are sad. Work can be very interesting, challenging, rewarding and exhilarating, even though a lot of hard work has to fit into the equation. One of the interesting results of my work was a great deal of knowledge about a lot of places in the world. I didn't make anywhere close to as much money as hundreds of millions of people did, but my life was enjoyable, exciting, challenging and, in many cases, amusing. Yes, today I regret having failed to focus enough on making money. That was probably my most important and unfortunate mistake. A million and a half dollars seemed like a lot until you no longer have earned income and have to rely upon it.

As the English language continues to be mongrelized, I am becoming more and more cognizant of poor grammar. Way back when I was in grade school you had to learn how to diagram sentences. Today dreadful grammar is widespread and will get worse now that newspaper and magazine writers get away with using bad English. Not just poor....bad. It was distressing to read in December of 2017 that texting in cell phones is leading to the demise of the apostrophe. It is certainly eliminating the hyphen. How will texters every write meaningfully.

Just like the case with accents being replicated by those who hear them all the time, bad English in publications and broadcasts will result in the dissemination of the problem. I was always amused by Winston Churchill's famous quote about how ending a sentence with a preposition is something "up with which I will not put." It may have been correct, but it sure sounds funny. I bet most people don't even know that saying "something I won't put up with." is bad English. My version of that sentence is "I was taught that a gerundive phrase such as "when you see me going to town" (sic) always had to be preceded by the possessive case, that an infinitive was something you were not supposed to ever split (sic, again) and a preposition was something you should never end a sentence with (sic, the last time). You may catch a few mistakes, but I have attempted to avoid all of those errors. Regarding that gerund, (in case you don't know) it means you should not say "he observed me driving to work." It is "*my* driving." A gerundive phrase must be preceded by the possessive case. I'm sure you knew that, but I had to explain it for the majority who don't. Sorry, I admit to being stuffy and old fashioned.

Because of my job for ten years as President of what became the most respected company specializing in business travel worldwide, I got to stay for free in the best suites in many of the finest hotels in the world, ones that now have single room prices starting at over a thousand dollars a night. Several of the suites I stayed in are now over $15,000 per night. I just wish that could have been after I was married instead of just getting to sleep in them by myself. My secretary could make a call and get me a free first-class ticket on most any airline in the world with the routing I needed on the day I needed it. It may have been my job, and it was work, but I was badly spoiled.

Finally, I could not resist some chapters that are nothing but my opinions, especially about art and music.

Hope you find the stories amusing and the information useful.

Thornton Clark

1 TERROR

Coming Too Close

One of the toughest things about organizing all these stories was which to put first. I came close to dying a few times, but I am starting with the story that was by far the most terrifying. You can expect much shorter ones farther along. After many years go by, you cannot relive or explain being terrified. Terror is probably like pain…you can remember how it was at the time, but the feeling is completely gone.

It started with a meeting of State Street Bank officers in Munich regarding the Boston bank's first foreign office. I had been assigned responsibility for picking the country and then the city in which the bank would locate its first foreign office. It was a fabulous assignment, but I gained lots of weight, eating all my meals in European restaurants. To my amazement the bank is now in 23 countries. Bud Page, a partner at Peabody and Arnold, was the bank's counsel in this area of business. Because the bank's meeting was in early July, Bud and I decided it would be fun to go to the Riviera for the Fourth of July weekend, before flying back to Boston. Our drive was on the night of July 3, 1969.

It appeared that the best way was to fly from Munich to Turin, a heavily industrialized city in northwestern Italy, pick up a rental car at the airport and drive south to the Mediterranean and then down the coast to Cannes. We decided to rent a little two-seater Fiat Spider 124 for the trip; it would be fun to have a good-looking little convertible sports car with the top down during our days on the Riviera. Because I was accustomed to driving my two-seat Jaguar XKE in Massachusetts, I drove. We landed at Turin's airport, picked up our car, and started the drive south through downtown after dark. This was before the days of GPS in cars or excellent highway bypasses around major cities.

A WRONG TURN….REALLY WRONG

We were driving southwest down a main street until we made a wrong turn onto a wide boulevard with a landscaped median running down the middle. Years later when I was back in Turin on business, I prowled around in the daytime trying to find the street. It was Corso Traiano. I remember that it was eerily dark, suddenly realizing it was pitch black; no street lights and no lights. There were not even any other cars.

Suddenly we were slowed by people in the street, all heading in the north-westerly direction. Soon the crowd was so thick it was blocking our way. The mob began to run, accompanied by lots of screaming. Later we learned that their chant, "Cosa volete? Tutto! Quando? Subito!" in Italian translated to "What do we want? Everything!, When do we want it? Now!" For several minutes we inched along and, luckily, our presence in the middle of all this commotion somehow went unnoticed for a remarkably long time.

The median on our left was long and, even in the dark, we could see it was full of trees, monuments and benches. A hundred feet ahead of us the street was suddenly lighted by bright orange flames leaping high into the sky. We had seen the mob push over onto its side a large gasoline tanker truck and set it ablaze. I think I am correct in remembering it was Mobil. We needed to get out of there, fast, but there was nowhere to go other than by running over people in front of us or driving through the trees and people in the median. Needless to say, by this time we knew we were in extremely serious danger. That was without even knowing until reading in the papers days later that it had been a communist and student-led anti-Fiat and anti-American riot that became known as "The Battle of Corso Traiano." At that time, the press reported that there were something on the order of 5.5 million workers on strike in Italy and most of them were in Turin. In their notices to workers, the labor leaders called their associates "comrades" and the riot was anti-American because they considered the United States to be the principle opposition to their beloved Communism. The press said the rioters erected barricades in major streets and fought the police into the night.

We stood out "like a sore thumb." Not only were we in an expensive bright-red sports car with the top down; but also we were still in our grey pin-striped suits from the meeting in Munich and we didn't understand or speak Italian. To make matters worse, our car was a Fiat, made in the huge plant nearby and the mob's primary target. I could not accelerate without mowing down lots of people. Even though it was dark, I could see the gang in the rearview mirror and hear their threats over all of the noise being made by the angry mob. I panicked. We simply had to get out of there and get out of there very fast. I bet we were the only Americans in the middle of the rioting mob.

ESCAPE

Our only choice was to jump the curb immediately and wind our way through the bushes, trees and people in the median in order to reach the side of the boulevard headed in the other direction, away from the center of the riot. We had to dodge trees and the people who must have been quite surprised to see a car with a pickup truck in pursuit weaving through the median. The pickup truck had it much easier, having the benefit of our lights and being able to follow us through the melee. I had to avoid hitting people and trees while picking our route, and I had to try to keep driving faster. This was now sheer terror. I thought we could easily be caught and beaten to death. There were a few moments when the thugs could have jumped out of the truck and caught us on foot.

At this point, being a trained high-speed driver in the fast and maneuverable sports car was a big advantage. We still had no idea where we were or in which way we should be heading; we just knew we had to escape our pursuers. Once across the median and off of the main boulevard, the smaller streets off to the right opened up. It was still pitch-black dark, but we could speed down streets that were no longer blocked by people and, luckily, void of automobile traffic. After cornering dangerously fast around tight turns we were able to elude the thugs behind us. A sign pointed us toward the city of Cuneo, about 50 miles away. We stopped at a store and purchased a double bottle of Italian red wine. Having no glasses, we just took turns drinking from the bottle.

COL DE TENDE

Today computer driving systems and beautiful new highways result in the recommended route south to the Riviera's passing far to the east through Savona. That night we just planned to head due south on the narrow road through Tende, a city known for its high mountain pass, the Col de Tende.

Between Cuneo and Ventimiglia, both in Italy, there is a long bulge of France that extends eastward into Italy. The actual boundary is to the east of Tende, but because the mountain ridge is inaccessible, it appeared as if the border was the valley down which we drove. We reached a point where we had to pull out our passports and leave Italy. We crossed a bridge to the other side of the valley and had to stop at customs to enter France. After a short while we came to a customs stop where we had to go through the passport routine in order to leave France and re-enter Italy. I don't know how many times we stopped, but the process repeated several times. The highway made its way down the valley by crossing the river over and over again, each time changing countries. A few days later, when we read about the riot in the International Herald Tribune, we knew we would have been a prime target of the mob.

DANGER TOO MANY TIMES

I traveled so much that I was bound to run into danger in numerous places. In the 1970s I had *Sail* magazine for a client at Heritage Travel. *Sail's* editor, Bernie Goldhirsh, wanted to organize a trip for advertisers, major U. S. boating industry executives, to go to the London and Paris Boat Shows. The first was in London's large Earl's Court Exhibition Center southwest of downtown London. On January 5, 1974, Irish terrorists set off two bombs in London, the day after our group arrived from Boston. The bombs in two locations went off less than three minutes apart.

The one at Earl's Court had been placed inside a motor cruiser in the boat show, staffed by a man who was a friend of most of the boating industry people in our group. It blasted the boat into neighboring displays in all directions. The show had to remain closed for the day while they cleaned up the mess. We got out because the Irish terrorists gave warning before setting off the bomb, so the large crowd, as I recall something like 30,000, was rushed out the exits before the bomb went off. A bomb had gone off a few minutes earlier in Madame Tussard's Wax Museum. Luckily, there were no casualties. In contrast, Islamic terrorists today focus on maximizing the number of dead.

ENCORE
In all of those millions of miles of traveling I all too often found myself in the middle of danger. This time it was Hamburg, Germany, where my wife, Pat, and I were attending a large, international travel conference at the Congress Center Hamburg (CCH) on Tiergartenstrasse. The CCH was at the southern end of the park named the Moorwiede and our hotel was at the northern end of the park.

Heading from CCH back to the hotel we had to walk through that park. It was full of tough-looking young Germans yelling anti-American chants. We had heard that, under George H. W. Bush the US had just invaded Iraq. This time it was clearly justified given Hussein's invasion and then destruction of Kuwait, but the German youth were still furious at the United States. The crowd had congregated in the park to protest because the US Consulate was nearby. Our American accents would have been easily detectable as we took the long pathway through the park. At least we didn't say a word.

SCARED AGAIN
In the mid 60s, I lived on the top floor of 45 Pinckney Street on Boston's Beacon Hill. The place had a living room overlooking Pinckney, a small bath and kitchen in the middle and the bedroom in the rear, overlooking the trees in the space between my bedroom and the buildings facing Myrtle Street. One night I was awakened in the middle of the night by a dreaded problem; my room was aglow in brightly-flickering orange flames. My immediate reaction was that my building was on fire. With the flames coming up in my building, I was in deep trouble on the top floor. Jumping out of bed, I looked out the window and saw the building behind me ablaze. There were huge flames spiraling up from the first floor, quickly consuming the entire building. I never went around and checked, but from the satellite picture today it looks as if the rear of the building on fire was 35 feet from my bedroom window, close enough to make my spot quite hot. There was no way a fire truck could get at the back of the building, so it stayed ablaze for a long time. Didn't make for a good night's sleep.

ANOTHER FIRE
Years later, I had an apartment at 7 Mt.Vernon Place, a little private alley off of Joy Street. It was on the second floor, with a large roof deck in back with a fantastic view of the State Capitol (in Boston language, called the "State House") just 77 feet away. One evening we were drinking while cooking steaks on the charcoal grill on the deck. At some point we heard sirens approaching and then saw a hook and ladder fire truck stop in Joy Street. When we looked to see where the problem was we realized it was us. The ladder was being raised up and turned to reach my roof deck. I guess it was a good thing that someone had seen fire and called the fire department and it added a good bit of excitement to our evening.

DESSERT

My favorite dessert is Cherries Jubilee, not the plain old, but delicious, kind, I liked the spectacle of a flaming waterfall of brandy poured from up high into a bowl on the dining room table in front of all the guests in a darkened room. It is a very memorable dessert. Using a lot of brandy and pouring from too high caused problems twice. Once in Jim Heald's home at the entrance to the harbor of West Falmouth, on Cape Cod, I held the flaming pan of brandy too high and left soot on the ceiling.

The second time was at my ski house in Vermont. The girl I was dating at the time, Brenda Lee Landry, had on a black and white fuzzy-wool skirt and was seated on my left. Before I learned the importance of using large straight sided and flat bottomed bowls into which to pour the flaming brandy, I held the large skillet up high and poured the burning brandy so that it went into the right side of the bowl, across the bottom and up the left side, into the air, landing in Brenda's lap, setting her skirt on fire. At least it was extinguished quickly and she was not injured. It did make for an exciting dinner.

AND YET ANOTHER FIRE

Even today, people do not pay attention to the warnings about things to avoid while pumping gasoline, especially smoking a cigarette or using your cell phone while pumping gas. One night while leaving Harvard's Fox Club at 44 JFK, Cambridge, I saw the Gulf gas station across JFK at the southern corner of what is now Winthrop Square explode in flames. The flames from the gasoline pumps went very high into the sky. I think it was a Gulf gas station. It burned for a long time. You wouldn't want to be in the middle of that. People may be warned, but too many use their cell phones while pumping gas.

ONE FINAL FIRE

Writing this has made you wonder if I have "a thing" about fire. It just happened that there are several. Mom and Dad had accepted an invitation to dinner on February 7, 1967. At the last minute, Dad became too sick to go, so they cancelled. The dinner was to be in Dale's Penthouse Restaurant on top of a building overlooking Montgomery.

The reports said that the fire had started in the coat closet, started by a carelessly discarded cigarette. To keep from disturbing the customers, an employee tried to put out the fire. Then smoke came out of the coat room door, filling the restaurant, causing panic. Some rushed and made it to the elevator, many died in the far corner of the dining area, but a few were able to smash out windows and bravely climb carefully out onto a narrow ledge ten stories up in the air in 25-degree weather. Twenty five died in the fire.

When you live in Boston, you frequently hear about the famous Coconut Grove fire, largely because of hundreds who died. It led to laws governing exits and their signage, especially for revolving doors. Most people don't know that the Dale's Penthouse Fire led to many new fire regulations nationwide, the most recognizable being the millions of signs that throughout the country read "In case of fire, use stairs." My parents were 77 and 72 at the time, so they almost certainly would not have survived. Just remembered, there is one more fire, but this one is in a separate chapter

WANTED, DEAD OR ALIVE

Pat and I had purchased furniture from Northgate Gallery so, when we sold our house in Massachusetts, we had lots of things to sell. David Paterson at Northgate sent a truck to pick up stuff for auction. Northgate's large four-color catalogues usually involved the sale from an estate and showed a picture of the home and the name of the deceased.

When the catalog with our stuff came out, it had on its cover a picture of our house in Dover and the words "From the Estate of Thornton Clark." When an old friend, Hugh Frazer, a Northgate customer, saw the catalog he knew I had died. en years later when we moved from Savannah to Montgomery another classmate, Paul Sweatt, hosted a "welcome home" party for us. Of course, you must have guessed it, Hugh was there. When I walked in his jaw dropped. He had to be seeing a ghost; an old ghost at that. David laughed and apologized about his catalog's cover.

ANOTHER WRONG PLACE AT THE WRONG TIME

I can't remember where I had flown from that evening, but I had landed in Rapid City, South Dakota about 9pm on Friday night, June 9. It was raining worse that the proverbial cats and dogs. I was in the type of plane that parked on the tarmac so that you had to go down the steps in the rain and walk into the terminal. At least I made my connecting flight out at 10 and got away before the dam broke. 238 people died and 1,335 homes in Rapid City were destroyed. It was the second deadliest flood in U.S. history, second only to the famous Johnstown Flood on May 31, 1989 that killed 2,209 people in Pennsylvania. You frequently hear about the Johnstown Flood but rarely about the one that wiped out Rapid City. Glad I got out of Rapid City that night. At least I dodged a bullet.

HALIFAX, NOVA SCOTIA

There is another example of my being in the wrong place, this time at the wedding of my college roommate, John Frith of Bermuda. I ended up being an usher in 39 weddings and this was one of them. The unusual part was the march down the aisle. Ushers usually reach their spots first, walking out from the side, followed by the bridesmaids' walking up the aisle one at a time. Finally, the dad escorts his daughter down the aisle.

In this beautiful church the practice was backward. The bride, the most important person, walked first, the ushers last. John had an odd number of ushers who walked down the aisle in pairs, so as the tallest, I walked alone at the end. It was a very strange feeling.

2 TIDBITS

School Days

A number of kids experimented with making small, very primitive, bombs. One kid, a well-known name I reluctantly agreed not to use, brought one of his bombs to school and put it in his locker at Sidney Lanier High School. It must have been much more sophisticated than the ones my other friends made because his cousin told me, he had been told to expect something to happen at a specific time that morning.

The bomb had been set to go off at a time when everyone would be in their classrooms. The culprit apparently had not taken into account the possibility of someone's walking down the hall to the restrooms, each of which were reached through doors in the locker areas. One teacher had to leave class and head down the hall to the lady's room At the moment of the explosion she was close enough to be terrified, but luckily not injured in the blast. It was ridiculously easy to identify the locker that was the location of the explosion, so the culprit was easily and immediately identified.

GUNS

David Crosland was a friend from childhood. He had gone on to head the Immigration and Naturalization Service in Washington and appeared on the evening TV news many times when we were experiencing the Iranian Hostage Crisis and everybody wanted to know where all of the Iranians in the U.S. were located. In 2019, he still works for the Department of Justice, where he oversees many of the Federal judges responsible for immigration courts, a very busy specialty at this time.

David told me a story I simply had not remembered about our building a pistol. A grip I had made, fashioned from wood and attached to a piece of pipe, with a cap screwed to the back and having a hole through which a fuse could be passed. The pipe was loaded with explosive, filled with buckshot and tamped tight with wadding. David says he won the coin toss to get to fire the "pistol" first but wisely elected to just stand it up in the dirt, light the fuse and run. Had he been holding the pistol when it exploded, he would not have been around to tell the story. I am very happy that he "won" the toss.

THE GREAT VIEW

Most of the Montgomery YMCA parties for the kids were at Camp Rotary on Lake Jordan, about an eleven-mile drive north of town. With less frequency, we used to go to Camp Belser, a few miles east of Montgomery. It was close enough that we ran hayrides out to the camp.

There was an interesting design problem with the bathrooms, probably just to save money on construction. The flat-topped concrete block walls around the building and between the boys' and the girls' restrooms was open to the peaked roof. The strong guys could stand on a bench, reach the top of the wall and then pull themselves up high enough to look over the wall into the girls' showers and dressing area. I recall there being about six or eight guys in a row hanging up there on the wall. They somehow went unnoticed. I wished I had grown up stronger.

DOGS

Our family has a tradition of owning dogs, almost all Scotties, and naming them after public officials, usually elected officials from Alabama. My uncle, Major General John W. "Bill" Persons, had a Scotty that flew with him in bombers. "Angus" is buried under a granite stone bearing his name at the end of a runway at Langley Field, Virginia. One Scotty was named for Governor Gordon Persons, one was named "Rose" for the wife of Governor Kilby and one, that belonged to my sister, was "Ronnie" for Ronald Reagan.

When in 2004 we received, through a strange series of events, our West Highland Terrior, she was a girl, and at that time the only well-known female government official was somebody named Hillary. We did not want to inflict that name on our dog.

The name we thought most appropriate was another female, prominent in politics, and actually from Alabama. That is why our lovely dog is named Condoleezza, "Condi" for short. We have had a beautiful Augusta National Golf Club green jacket made for her, including Masters buttons we had purchased more than ten years ago when we were lucky to be given tickets to The Masters for at least the Wednesday practice round that allowed you to walk close to the players, take pictures, and watch the exciting and amusing Par 3 tournament in the late afternoon. We keep hoping that someday we can take a picture of our Condi with her namesake.

THE GOVERNOR

When I was a kid in grade school living at 921 E Fairview Avenue, our house (since torn down) had a screen porch all the way across the front. You entered up some steps at the west end of the porch. There was a ceiling fan over where you stood waiting at the door.

My sister, for some reason I would rather not know, was asked out by Big Jim Folsom, aka "Kissin Jim." This would have been sometime in 1947, so I would have been about ten years old. He was very tall, but also a dreadful, low-class bum. One day, when he came to pick up my sister, I saw him at the door, flipped on the fan switch so the ceiling fan hit him in the head. My sister was not happy (and neither was he). Unfortunately, he was not injured.

The funniest often-told story about Kissin Jim took place outside a motel room in Montgomery where the press had gathered, having been alerted he had spent the night with a black prostitute. Back in those days, prostitution was bad enough but the thought of a white screwing a black was much worse. When the governor walked out with the prostitute that morning a reporter yelled at him in an incredulous tone "Did you sleep with the woman?" Jim's great response was "I didn't sleep a wink."

RADIO

When I was 15, I was asked to host a radio program on WAPX (no longer in business) interviewing people and talking about high school news. It was sponsored by what might at the time have been Montgomery's only sporting goods store, May and Green on South Court Street. The shows were recorded five at a session in one afternoon so they could be played back during the week.

It was fun having a date in my old two-door Ford (cost $50), being able to turn on the radio and have her hear me talking. Only once in three years did I make a dreadful mistake, having the recording include my saying "Hi" to my date only to have it broadcast when the girl in the car was someone other than the one I had planned. That was, to say the least, very awkward. Sixty years later I learned that the Manager with whom I had dealt at May and Green was the father of a good friend, Frank Rosa.

When I arrived at college, I saw signs soliciting volunteers to work at the country's oldest college radio station, WHRB, Harvard Radio Broadcasting. I filled out an application and they produced a tape of my reading copy. I was told I had more radio experience than anybody they had had, but with that thick Southern accent they could not use me.

In 1956, I applied for a summer job back home at WAPX. Their answer was amusingly similar. They knew me and knew I was familiar with the station but, with that Yankee accent I had acquired, they could not use me. For seven years in the 80s, I was on WCBS, New York, and WEEI, Boston, every weekday afternoon during rush hour. Advertising Weekly had a small article, commenting that my voice and style reminded them of Franklin Delano Roosevelt's "Fireside Chats" on the radio assuring the American people during World War II.

EPILOGUE

Sometime, probably in the late 80s, I was at a travel convention in Atlanta. A father and son, who owned a limousine company, were manning their booth in the exhibition hall when I walked up and began to speak with them. Both immediately said "We know you." I did not know them and had no clue. They literally began to argue with each other about it. They were sure that they knew me from somewhere. Only after a lot of discussion and argument did one of them exclaim he knew the answer. The father and son had for years listened to my talking about business travel on WCBS while driving home from work every afternoon. They did get a good laugh out of it.

3 THE CAMBRIDGE HYATT

The World's Most Expensive Breakfast For Two (by far)

When I was President of the travel company called Woodside, we had just completed construction of our large computer Central Reservations Office at Woodside's headquarters on two large floors of 131 Tremont Street in Boston. The systems connected all of the North American offices and many of those outside the US. We decided that a grand opening would generate good publicity and have most of the airline, hotel and car rental companies see the complex operation. One objective was to get the senior executives of those companies that had *not* installed their system to see that they were being left out and move quickly to give theirs to us.

We invited people to the dinner on June 6. 1978. It was quite a show. I remember that I was seated at the table with Bob Crandall, CEO of American Airlines; Dick Ferris, CEO of United, and Bill Marriott (you can guess what company he was with). Charles Benisch, owner of the top travel agency in New York, Don Travel, and current Chairman of the Board of Woodside. The 422 guests made it a wonderful evening.

THE SPEECHES

At the dinner on opening night, one of the speakers, a Member of the British Parliament, had been invited by Trevor Wagstaffe of Woodside's London Office. Helping him get his speech started was a mistake we had made.

On one large wall of the dining room behind the speakers we had arranged the flags of all the nations in which Woodside had offices. The flags were positioned on the wall in the form of a world map, with each country's flag in its proper place. The heavy trim with the attachment holes was, correctly, on the left side of every flag. In his opening sentence, the British speaker questioned our indicating that Great Britain was in serious trouble. Actually the official word applicable to this story is "distress." Until he explained, I bet not one single person in the large room understood the problem.

A flag flown upside down on a ship is the universally accepted signal of distress, dating back to the days before radios. He said we had the Britain's Union Jack upside down, signaling distress. I bet many Englishmen and essentially all Americans do not know how to tell when a British flag is right side up or upside down.

The flag of the Great Britain looks almost exactly the same whether it is right-side up or upside down. There are white stripes diagonally between the four corners of the flag. When the holes by which the flag is attached are on the left, the larger diagonal white stripes are *above* the smaller white stripes nearest the flagpole and on the right (away from the flagpole) the wider diagonal white stripes are *below* with red stripes. If someone really was in distress you could very easily notice when an American flag is upside down, but you would have to know to look quite closely, even when the flag is not flying, to detect that the British flag is upside down.

In his opening comments, the President of American Airlines, Bob Crandall, chided his competitor Richard Ferris, President of United, for having an inferior computer system (which he did). In retaliation, the head of United, which at the time owned Western International Hotels (later Westin, and finally part of Starwood), chided Crandall for having an inferior hotel chain. Americana Hotels (no longer in business) did not hold a candle to Westin. Both CEOs were correct, but they said it in a very amusing manner.

DINNER

The problem was with the dinner. We had paid a lot of money to provide the best dinner possible for the VIP guests. The meal, as it turned out, was lousy. Not just fair or poor….it was *truly* lousy. The expensive steaks were simply cold and relatively tasteless. I was, to say the least, irritated and embarrassed.

Immediately following the dinner, Joe Kordsmeier, Senior VP Sales of Hyatt, accosted me complaining about my having chosen a menu that the hotel obviously could not prepare well for such a large group. He was embarrassed that his excellent hotel chain had been made to look bad for such an important audience. Luckily, I was able to say that we had been talked into that entrée by Hyatt's Director of Sales and their Director of Food and Beverage at the hotel we were in. They had bragged about their large convection ovens that could deliver 400 steaks in fine shape, all nice and hot, at the same time. Only problem was that this time, they had failed badly.

AND NOW TO THE REASON FOR THE TITLE OF THIS CHAPTER

In the seventies, Braniff had been one of the most interesting airlines in the country. They made lots of innovative moves, especially in the area of style. They began to paint aircraft in bright colors, culminating in an extremely strange looking paint job in bright blobs of color, designed by an artist most famous for his mobiles, Alexander Calder.

Switching from the traditional, stodgy dark blue uniforms common in the airline industry, Braniff went with multi-colored dresses for their stewardesses designed by leading Parisian high-fashion powerhouse, Emilio Pucci. Braniff's elegant headquarters in Dallas were illustrative of Braniff's image, and some corporate customers took exception to Braniff's elite attitude. Unfortunately, airline deregulation led Braniff's CEO at the time, Harding Lawrence, to believe that this was a unique opportunity for rapid expansion, adding flights on routes to many international destinations.

Most people in the industry don't even remember that, in addition to Air France and British Airways, Braniff once flew the Concorde. Actually, 16 airlines had taken options to purchase Concordes, but they backed out when hit by the fuel crisis of 1974. Another forgotten fact is that the Concorde flew routes from Europe to Singapore, Bahrain and Rio de Janeiro. Braniff Concordes flew Dallas to Washington and on to Europe. The planes could fly at two times the speed of sound over the Atlantic, where the sonic boom created by the sonic boom would not disturb residents below.

Such was not the case between Dallas and Washington, where the speed had to be kept below the speed of sound. The Concorde was an expensive experiment for British Airways and Air France, but a financial disaster for Braniff. My wife, Pat, happened to fly on Braniff's final Concorde flight which that day flew only from Dallas to Washington, D. C. She says the pilot cheated and bumped it up past Mach 1 (the speed of sound) during the flight. Because speed was of such interest to passengers on Concordes, the planes had a Machmeter on the right bulkhead facing the passengers so you could read when your plane had broken the sound barrier.

Now how in the world does this fit in with a meeting at the Hyatt in Cambridge? A man I had dealt with at United, Howard Putnam, had been in charge of sales at United and moved to become CEO of Braniff. It would have been an impossible task no matter who took it on, and Braniff began to sink into dire financial straits.

A SCARY PHONE CALL

Months later, Bill Marriott called and told me I owed him a lot of money. As I recall, it was about three million dollars. Thankfully, he was kidding. Bill told me that, on the morning after the dinner in the Hyatt, Howard Putnam had walked up to Bill's table and asked if he could join Bill for breakfast. Howard had apparently been hiding, waiting to see when Bill Marriott came off the elevators.

In those days, Marriott was by far the largest supplier of in-flight meals to airlines, meals that in those days were quite edible; some in first class on international flight were truly delicious, served with top-rated wines and liqueurs. Braniff was far behind on its payments to Marriott for inflight meals, and someone at Marriott had notified Howard that no more meals would be provided unless a very large payment was made toward the overdue bills. Bill had gone on to say that Howard, at that breakfast, had talked him into giving Braniff an additional 90 days credit. Braniff had to be able to serve meals to its passengers. Of course, Braniff abruptly ceased flying, declaring bankruptcy. Of course, this was not before running up an even higher debt to Marriott. It was an incredible way to go under. Passengers already onboard Braniff planes for departures were simply told to leave the plane, the airline had ceased to exist.

Bill said that his was the most expensive breakfast ever. He reduced the "debt" I owed him by two million when he called a year or so later for advice and I strongly urged him *not* to invest in an airline that planned to offer only first-class service between New York and Los Angeles. I pointed out several major problems, not the least of which was frequency of flights and backup planes at each end of the route when needed because of mechanical problems or just routine maintenance. If your meeting ran late or the traffic was bad, causing you to miss your flight on a major carrier, you could usually just catch that airline's next flight. This was not going to be an option with the new all-first-class carrier. Also, frequent flyer programs were beginning to lead many business travelers to take as many flights as possible on their preferred carrier, amassing millions of frequent flyer miles that enabled them to earn very valuable free vacation travel for their families. Low cost carriers might succeed, but high-priced operations were not a good bet, especially when it was to operate on just one route. Bill must have listened because he did not invest and thanked me.

BOATING

For decades, a memory of Bill Marriott still prompted me to be careful whenever I started a gasoline engine in a boat. Many boaters know about the caution sign for inboard gasoline engines, but don't bother running the engine room blower long enough to be sure there are no explosive gas fumes in the enclosed engine area before pressing the starter button. At Bill's summer home on the northeastern shore of Lake Winnipesaukee in New Hampshire, he once made the mistake of failing to run the blower long enough, resulting in an explosion and serious injury to him, which luckily was not fatal.

"I NEED A HOTEL ROOM"

My only other Marriott experience was one that made for a great story. Bill's dad, J. Willard Marriott (the founder of the hotel chain), was about to undergo major surgery at Massachusetts General Hospital and was expected to be there for about a month. Marriott owned five beautiful hotels in downtown Boston and along Route 128 in the outskirts, but Bill's mother wanted to be in the Holiday Inn on Cambridge Street, which at the time was the only hotel adjacent to the hospital.

Someone at Marriot had called for a reservation and been turned down (the hotel was booked full), but Marriott called to ask for my assistance. Luckily, I knew the manager fairly well and got through to him quickly. When I said I was asking for a room for Mrs. Marriott, the manager of the hotel did not pause for even an instant; Mrs. Marriott was welcomed in their best suite and stayed there for about a month while her husband recuperated nearby.

POLITICS

Living in Alabama during the presidential campaign of 2008, it was discouraging having to listen to Republicans of the Christian Right complain about Mitt Romney's being a Mormon. Mitt, for whom Pat and I campaigned when he ran for Senator against Teddy Kennedy in Massachusetts in 1992 (we knew him because Pat was a manager for Bain), probably would have had a better chance at beating Obama except for the fact that too many on the Christian Right considered Mormonism a cult and refused to support him because of his religion. We observed that attitude up close in Montgomery.

One of the most wealthy, respected and generous businessmen in Montgomery at a dinner in Mark Anderson's home, when asked if he preferred Obama, said "I could never vote for a Mormon." I had not expected this from someone so intelligent. I suspect he would have preferred Mitt to Obama by a mile. Bill Marriott, a devout Mormon, was one of the most honest people in the business world, with a superb reputation. At least Bill never made me pay for his costly breakfast.

"WE, TOO, NEED HOTEL ROOMS"

When on business in London, most senior executive travelers liked to stay in the old, prestigious hotels, at the time this was usually the Ritz, the Dorchester, the Connaught, and to a lesser extent The Grosvenor House (but it was at the time very convenient to the US Embassy) London is usually not hot in the summer, so most of the old hotels did not have air conditioning. We tried to direct business to the chain that was our first hotel client, Sheraton, but had to honor requests for the more expensive hotels. When a heat wave struck London and continued for days, Heritage Travel was besieged with calls from London pleading with us to get executives out of the "deluxe" hotels and into the air conditioned Sheraton. This time, we needed hotel rooms and could not get them.

4 TWO NIGHTS AT THE THEATER
Hot Times on Boston's Boylston Street

Back in the mid 1980s, I was dating a girl named Eileen Prose who was the host of a TV Show, "Good Day," every weekday morning in Boston for 12 years. It was syndicated in 71 markets throughout the US and in parts of Canada. She had been a Second Runnerup Miss America in 1966, having won the Talent portion of the competition with her outstanding voice. She got to interview a wide variety of interesting people, including writers, actors, actresses, singers, songwriters and some who became politicians.

One day, Eileen asked if I would like to go to see the premier of a new movie with Alan Alda. I said sure. It was to be the premier, for some reason on Boylston Street in Boston, probably because the movie had been filmed in New England. The Paramount theater was quite close to the point on Boylston, where the finish line is set up each year for the Boston Marathon, close to where the infamous bombs were exploded in 2013.

THE MOVIE

The movie was written by, directed by and had as the actor playing the lead role, Alan Alda. If you are old enough, you may remember the plot in "The Four Seasons." It was about four couples. The four wives were close friends. One of the guys left his wife and the remaining three women were not about to accept his new young girlfriend. When the group chartered a sailboat in the Caribbean, the three wives fumed while the man they detested made lots of noise screwing his stewardess girlfriend, amidst many loud squeals of excitement (or whatever you call it.....ecstasy, I guess) from the girl.

One evening on a ski trip, the wives were even more brutal in their ostracism of the new girlfriend. She, having become too tired of the exclusion, screams out her exasperation and runs out of the ski house into the cold darkness. Her boyfriend, on crutches from a skiing accident, starts to rush out the door to search for her in the dark. Alan Alda grabs him to stop him, telling him he should let her go; he certainly should not be going out at night in snow and pitch-black darkness. The boyfriend announces that Alan does not understand, he must find her because she is pregnant. Alan then stated quite loudly "You could not have gotten her pregnant, you're 43 years old."

Being 43 at the time and taking offence (amusingly) at that comment, both written and spoken by Alan, I put my hands around his neck and jokingly pretended to choke him for the insult to 43-year-old men throughout the world. I had thought that when Eileen had mentioned going to the movie "with Alan Alda" that it just meant he was in the movie. Boy, what a surprise. His two daughters were in the movie, so they were there, too, along with his wife. The movie and the people made for a fabulous and highly-memorable evening. The next day on the "Good Day" show Alan complained (laughingly) about his host's boyfriend's attempting to strangle him the night before.

ALMOST TOO HOT

The other funny occurrence in a theater with Eileen was while we were sitting in the front row of the Shubert Theater on April 21, 1981, for a performance of "They're Playing Our Song," a hilarious comedy made even more funny (at least in my opinion) by the events of the evening. The play was a very amusing comedy, quite similar to the well-known "Noises Off."

At some point, I heard a loud rustling sound and muffled voices behind us. Even in the darkened theater, the light from the stage enabled me to see that everyone in the balcony was scrambling and pushing, trying to reach the aisles and exits. Smoke was rising from the electrical fire in the spotlight cluster attached to the front center of the balcony.

There is that old First Amendment rule that freedom of speech does not include the right to shout "Fire" in a crowded theater. I jumped up and called out for someone backstage to turn up the house lights. The actors were shocked to have their parts so rudely interrupted in the middle of a scene. Without being able to use the word "fire," it was difficult trying to convince the manager backstage to turn up the house lights while the play was underway. The best I could think of was to say there was an emergency in the audience. It took a long time before I could get action.

I turned around and quite forcefully asked the audience to remain calm while I repeatedly asked for the house lights. You could now clearly see the smoke, the more than half empty balcony and the last people still pushing to get out of their rows and into the two aisles to flee the building. Finally, the actors on stage recognized the seriousness of the problem and why they had been so rudely interrupted.

After electricians, hanging over the balcony rail, had stopped the fire, solved the problem and the people had returned to their seats, the actors attempted to restart where they had been interrupted. Every time the actors tried to restart their lines, someone would flub their lines and the whole cast would start laughing. They couldn't stop; it happened over and over again. The more times they muffed their lines, the more they couldn't stop laughing. The laughter resulted in one of the actors' saying it was not their fault, it was the fault of that guy who had interrupted them. It must have taken four or five restarts for the actors to get back in character. Their uncontrollable laughter, ad libs and inability to restart became one of the most amusing parts of the hilarious show.

As before, that night got talked about on TV the next day, this time by Eileen, reviewing what her date had done the night before. She was a brilliant and charming TV show host.

5 LIABILITY

Try To Pin It on Somebody…Anybody

PAN AM 103

Pan Am's Flight 103 was blown up by a terrorist bomb over Lockerbie, Scotland on December 21, 1988. Writing this, it is hard to believe that was thirty years ago. The bomb killed 243 passengers, 16 crew and 11 on the ground when the plane disintegrated. Years later blame was pinned on Libya and the government paid millions in claims.

Of all of the innocent people killed that day, the best known was Nicholas Bright of Brookline, Massachusetts. He had been in Europe on business for Bain and Co., well known years later for its Executive VP, later President of Bain Capital, Governor of Massachusetts and 2008 US presidential candidate, Mitt Romney. I became involved because Bain was a client of Heritage Travel, and Mr. Bright's wife, Eleanor, was the leader of the group that called themselves the "Victims of Pan Am 103."

Mr. Bright had finished his business in London and was returning home to the States for Christmas. Mrs. Bright claimed that Bain and Heritage were liable for forcing Mr. Bain to fly on Pan Am. In those days, many companies instituted policies requiring their employees to fly on designated carriers when a carrier on a route offered a contract for a discount on travel by employees of that specific company. In addition to trying to blame Bain, Mrs. Bright tried to claim that his being on Pan Am 103 was also the fault of Heritage Travel, because we owned and operated a branch, dba Bain Travel, in Bain headquarters in downtown Boston and had booked the original reservation.

The story became even more complicated because, by the time everything was getting examined and sorted out two months later, the woman who was at the time my fiancé, Pat, was now employed by Bain as their Travel Manager, responsible for managing the Bain employees in Bain's travel office upstairs in Copley Place. The key legal question was "Why was Nick Bright on Pan Am 103?" The answer was extremely complicated.

First, Nicholas had "double booked," something you were not supposed to do but which was common practice in those days. Actually, we discovered later had *20* booked. He was holding multiple reservations, most booked by Heritage's office. He had also made a long list of changes, each shown in technical computer language.

To counter the claim against us, I studied the computer record of Mr. Bright in Heritage's records, converted the actions into layman's language and delivered it to the judge and the plaintiff's lawyer in the case. It was very complicated. In those days, a computer printout of a reservation usually fitted on one perforated 8-inch-long computer-printout paper. Mr. Bright's record was just over six feet long and every bit of the complex computer language had to be translated into plain old English.

As it turned out, in addition to three sets of reservations on several carriers, Bright had changed the reservations over and over again while in London, finally deciding to fly on British Airways. At the last minute, he had learned that a close friend would be flying home for Christmas on Pan Am and switched flights to join him. My translation of the technical computer record into an English language description of each step of the reservation record was an arduous task. Mr Bright had made the final and deadly change himself.

A MISSED OPPORTUNITY, OR WAS IT A HOAX?

Lockerbie occurred more than a decade before 9/11, when US security was dramatically increased when reaction to threats, perceived or real, grew exponentially. There was one fact in the Pan Am 103 crash that was overlooked by the news. A few weeks before the bombing, the FAA issued a security bulletin stating that on December 5 an Arab man had called the U.S. Embassy in Helsinki, alerting them that in a few weeks a passenger aligned with the Libyan terrorist organization would carry a bomb on board a Pan Am flight from Frankfurt via London to the U.S.

The State Department had taken the threat seriously and notified its embassies in Europe as well as US airlines. The warning was overlooked until the investigation following the crash. This warning did have one effect.... numerous government employees in several embassies had read the warning and changed their flights home, leaving many seats available for sale to those unwitting passengers who died as a result. The SEC might claim this was acting on "insider information" but the info was public.

Pan Am officials later tried to claim that the call to the embassy had been a hoax and that the close relationship to the actual events was just a "coincidence." Some coincidence: The origin, the route and the airline matched exactly and the date was only off by a few days. Could that really have been just a coincidence? Not likely. In my opinion, the claim by Pan Am was ridiculous. The threat was real, the warning was real and the result was another successful attack against the United States, killing many Americans.

A SAD AND SURPRISING EPILOGUE

When the tragedy at Lockerbie occurred, the press did not include a list of passengers. Typically, in this type of situation, the list does not get published in many places at all, and in those where it does appear, it is usually weeks if not months later. You read the news when it was "news," and did not continue after a few weeks. I would not have read the list anyway. I had no idea that I knew anyone on the plane.

Twenty-two years after the terrorist attack, I was trying to get a phone number for my college roommate, Roberto Juan van Tienhoven. When I Googled his name I did not find it, but I found loads of references to a van Tienhoven who had been is seat 2B of Pan Am 103. This portion of the plane that stayed attached to the cockpit and nose that were in all the crash pictures.

Tom van Tienhoven, Robby's younger brother, had been en route home for Christmas, planning to meet his oldest brother in New York for a drink before heading on to Buenos Aires for the holidays with his family. The name van Tienhoven was rare enough, but when I saw his residence listed as Buenos Aires I knew it had to be Robbie's brother. Even coming so many years later, the news of Tom's death in the horrific terrorist attack came as a shock. Especially having spent so much time on the subject of one passenger's involvement it was incredible that so many years passed before I learned that I had known someone on the plane that day.

HYATT, KANSAS CITY

On July 17, 1981, several walkways high up in the atrium lobby of the Hyatt Regency, Kansas City, Missouri, collapsed into the hotel lobby, killing 114 people and injuring more than two hundred others among the two thousand who had gathered for a tea dance in the lobby of the hotel. Spectators filled the three walkways that were up in the air above the lobby. The fourth-floor walkway, built like a bridge over the lobby, collapsed under the weight of so many people and carried with it the walkway below it into the lobby, killing people who had been on the bridges as well as those in the lobby.

The hotel, which opened July 1, 1980, was part of a master plan designed by internationally known architect, Edward Larrabee Barnes, and was the tallest building in Missouri. A small, but fatal, change in the engineering design had been made by Havens Steel Company that doubled the load on the fourth-floor walkway. A structural engineer hired by the Kansas City Star after the tragedy discovered the change and won a Pulitzer Prize for his story in 1982.

I answered the call Heritage Travel received a call from the press about our "involvement" in the catastrophe. I had answered the call from the obnoxious writer. All we had done was book one reservation in that hotel at the time. The person complaining so vehementlycould not accept that we had been so stupid as to book someone into that hotel without having checked its structural integrity. He argued that we had certainly been negligent and were, therefore, liable.

It was a terrifying example of how the press can attack you and cause irreparable damage without any opportunity to rebut their pronouncements, no matter how absurd. How could anyone, even the most aggressive lawyer, think that every travel agency could or should check the design and construction of a hotel, much less the millions of hotels into which travelers are booked? The problem at the Hyatt was not even identified in the construction stage by those expert engineers and steel contractors who should have known what they were doing. It was another example of claims of liability gone wild. If we experienced these two examples, how many more must there be out there every day? Again, the only appropriate word is "ridiculous."

MCDONALDS

It is not unlike the millions of dollars a court awarded to a lady because her coffee, served by McDonalds, was hot. She had picked it up at Drive Through and spilled it in her own lap. Given all the places where companies have to print and post warning signs, it is ludicrous to blame a fast food place for serving hot coffee. I am surprised that this event did not result in cups having to be labeled "Warning, the contents of this cup of coffee may be hot." Once again, "ridiculous."

GETTING THEIR JUST DESSERTS

After a gunman murdered 12 people and injured 70 in an Aurora, Colorado theater, in 2012, some of the families of victims sued the theater, claiming negligence and security lapses, primarily failure to have an armed guard on duty. Several families settled because they were aware of the Colorado law that if you sue and lose you can be required to pay the winner's reasonable costs, primarily legal fees. Other states should follow that lead.

Some chose to sue, an expensive example of greed. The theater won and then submitted their bill for $699,187.13. As the chapter is titled, try to pin it on somebody. This time the bad guys lost.

6 BLOODY MARYS

For Internal Consumption Only

My mother (with the good old southern double given name Eva Mae Clark) founded the Montgomery Women's Golf Association about 90 years ago. She was always called Eva Mae, never just Eva. There was a story about the founding meeting in her Fairview Avenue home in the local newspaper, the *Montgomery Advertiser.*

Mom had grown up on Clayton Street, close to the end of Sayre Street where Zelda Sayre's parents lived in a stately Victorian, sadly torn down, leaving an empty lot on Sayre Street. Of course, Zelda become famous when she married F. Scott Fitzgerald. Mom played golf well and managed to keep playing for many years, winning a number of local championships but doing poorly when she played in major amateur events, including a tournament I got to watch in Texas in the late 1940s, a tournament won by Babe Didrickson Zaharias, arguably the greatest female athlete of all time. I still cherish the Babe's autograph that I had asked her for when she was playing in Montgomery. I also have a beautiful silver tray inscribed "WWGA" denoting the organization that hosted that tournament, the Women's Western Golf Association.

Years earlier there had been a long article with an amusing picture of Mom and Dad in their golf attire, long pants (knickers, once called "plus fours" for my dad). long all-white skirt, stockings and skirt with long sleeves for Mom. Mom was also wearing a wide-brimmed white hat, Dad wore a tie…..*not* the way people dress for golf these days The newspaper article included comments about Mom's having brought as her guest F. Scott Fitzgerald to play the Montgomery Country Club course when he was near the height of his literary career. Mom was lots of things, a consummate hostess, an amusing character and a good organizer. Wish I had a picture of the two-some playing golf.

Over the years, Mom organized matches in which the women would play in teams representing the various clubs around the city and the matches were held at a different club each week. The matches were held in the morning, followed by a luncheon at someone's home. In those days, women were only allowed to play on weekdays because the men, the only members of the families who worked in those days, needed to use the courses on the weekends.

According to the stories (I was only there for one, and then because it was at my house on Woodley Road), alcoholic beverages were served at these luncheons, sometimes *lots* of them. One of Mom's best friends was the matriarch in a family that owned a major manufacturing company in Montgomery, Kershaw Manufacturing, producer of huge machines for maintaining railroad tracks. Their machines were capable of riding slowly down the tracks while lifting the rails, replacing the grey rocks in which the crossties sat and, at the rear end of the machine, putting everything back in place. I think until the day she died, Miriam Kershaw dyed her hair almost-day-glow orange. It was *not* just red.

Another lady at the luncheon that day was Eunice Davis, who also lived overlooking the Montgomery Country Club's golf course on Allendale Road, a few doors down the street from the Kershaws. Eunice's husband, Tine Davis, was a VP of Winn Dixie grocery stores and the Davis family were the largest stockholders.

As I had learned from listening to the story from several of the ladies who were there that day, Eunice, made a comment about Miriam's blazing red, actually orange, hair. Miriam was pissed and proceeded to pour her Bloody Mary over Eunice's head, so she, too, could have red hair. Eunice was, to say the least, reported to be somewhat less than happy about this action so she picked up the entire pitcher of Bloody Marys and poured it over Miriam's head. I think I remember correctly that Eunice never drank, so she would not have had a Bloody Mary other than the big pitcher on the bar.

The women's golf luncheons had to be canceled for weeks so things could down. I was caught in the middle, answering the numerous phone calls from each of the "pourers" and frequently listening to their initial blasts before turning the phone over to my mother. I also overheard Mom's side of the discussions that eventually calmed down her two friends.

It was almost a month before Mom was able to get the weekly lady's golf tournaments and luncheons going again.

7 MANCHESTER BY THE SEA

No, Not The 2016 Movie

A good friend in New York, an investment advisor named Alex Arnold, had a summer home in Marblehead, Massachusetts. I was still single, but he was married. Alex had a client he and his wife, Jane, wanted me to meet. I normally avoided blind dates, but as he had described (an is so rarely the case with blind dates) Audrey della Russo was very good looking, wealthy and great fun. She dressed in New York high-fashion style, in contrast to what was then the antithesis of fashion, the typical attire for ladies in Boston.

My uncle, Lewis Clark, had worked as a career diplomat for the US State Department, serving in several countries, most notably China in the late 1940s as Consul General, attaining the rank of Ambassador. My mother related the story of Lewis' having been quite mad at my dad for wearing a dark blue suit to a formal affair in Washington. Lewis felt Dad embarrassed him by being the only person there not in a tux. His wife, my aunt, Ann Covington Clark, was the sister of Harry Covington, the name in the prestigious DC law firm, Covington and Burling.

Despite having rarely heard from Lewis during my childhood and college years, I received a call in the inviting me to a luncheon. It was to be a Sunday lunch at the home of his old friend, John Moors Cabot, who lived in a great home overlooking the Atlantic Ocean from a cliff just west of the entrance to the harbor of Manchester, Massachusetts in an area called Tucks Point. The Cabots were old, highly respected and extremely wealthy. The old line about the power of these two elite Massachusestts families was that "The Lowells speak only to Cabots, and the Cabots speak only to God."

The beautiful rocky coastline of Manchester by the Sea includes some of the grandest old mansions along the coast of New England. Being invited to the Cabot home for a small luncheon was a great honor and I felt very privileged to be included.

At the time I was dating Audrey, who was great to look at, but I was concerned about the atmosphere at the luncheon and what would be considered proper attire. Audrey usually wore very attractive high fashion.... sexy, even by Manhattan standards. Knowing my uncle and the importance of this luncheon to him, I knew I had to be extremely careful. Of course, I was going to be in coat and tie. Audrey was cautioned over and over again about the need to appear something she clearly was not: conservative.

LUNCH

The day of the luncheon arrived and Audrey appeared dressed from neck and ankles in black. The outfit even had long black sleeves that went all the way down to her wrists. All black. Does this sound extremely conservative, possibly a little too formal, if not funereal, for a Sunday lunch, even in Manchester by the Sea? Even at the Cabots? I was in shock. The outfit may have been all black and all covering, but all too much of it was "see through." Her great figure made it much worse (Under other circumstances, I would say "much better").

Audrey's outfit was at once black and all covering while at the same time being one of the sexiest outfits ever seen, and Audrey had the figure and good looks to show it off to the max. She saved money on her bra; at least it was very small. The conservative, much-older men at the luncheon appeared to be in awe; their eyes were so big that they probably had to go see their ophthalmologists the next day, that is if they survived their wives' fury when they arrived home that evening.

I remember little about the lunch other than the eyes of the men and the unhappy looks on the faces of their wives. That is an inaccurate statement; I certainly remember the way Audrey looked.

Lewis was obviously displeased with me, but did not say anything. I never heard from my uncle again. In 2106 there was a movie named after this town. Unfortunately, the movie had little to do with the beautiful town, Manchester by-the-Sea. The movies that do have lots of scenes in Manchester are "Profile" and "State and Main."

8 A VERY BAD DAY IN THE ATLANTIC
And At A Party In Manchester By The Sea

July 31, 1968 started off as a normal day. For non-sailors, this story requires several definitions and explanations, so sailors please bear with me.

In the sixties, the three largest yacht clubs in Marblehead, Massachusetts hosted a series of races that ran a whole week during late July. It has since, sadly, been reduced to a few days and the participation is far from what it had been. One of my crew this day was a neighbor, Ann Hastings, whose husband was the Chairman of the Corinthian Yacht Club's Race Committee, which was running that day's races. Also aboard my boat were Jerry Moulton (Ann's brother), and Carl Hiam.

We were in my beautiful 33-foot-long sloop (one mast about a third of the way from the bow to the stern) called an International One-Design and named "Tango." In the old days when ships used flags to communicate, when Tango was flown at a mooring it was a request for transportation and, more importantly when racing, meant "Do not pass ahead of me." International One-Designs, constructed beginning in 1936, are still considered among the most beautiful sailboats in the world. To focus on the skill of the helmsman rather than the money spent on designing a fast boat, the boats were all identical, including fleets on the Atlantic and Pacific coasts of the United States, in Bermuda and Northern Europe. I served ten years as World President of the IOD Class.

The effort to keep the boats the same began with their being constructed in Frederickstad, Norway, building each wooden boat on the same frame so that the dimensions would be identical. The keels were cast in lead, using the same mold for each, so they would all weigh the same. When the Nazis occupied Norway in World War II, the construction forms were buried underground in the boatyard so that the Germans could not damage them.

THE INTERNATIONAL ONE-DESIGN CLASS

The IOD class carried the identical boat process one important step farther than other "one-design" racing classes. A fleet bands together, selects a sailmaker and orders sails that will be as close as possible to identical. The sails are piled together and each owner "draws" from the pile which sail would be theirs. Owners are also prohibited from making even minor changes to their sails without an explanation of the reason a change is needed and an examination before approval by the local fleet is obtained. Boat owners were absolutely prohibited from purchasing additional sails. The hulls, the masts and the sails are as close as possible to identical. The class goes to a lot of trouble to make the racing as much as possible based upon the skill of the crew, not who has the most money to buy sails or a faster hull.

Sailboat racing normally involves starting into the wind (on what is called a "beat,") sailing frequently two legs of the course upwind, the first and the sixth. The second and third legs were reaches (with the wind blowing from one side and then from the other side), and the fifth was usually a run (sailing with the wind blowing from almost directly behind you.) A reach is sailing with the wind blowing from the side of the boat, results in the fastest speeds (sailors, yes, I know that is an oversimplification, but most people simply do not know the terminology). When the wind is strong, it can be an exhilarating experience (frequently exiting, and especially in San Francisco, terrifying).

On this day we had done well. 19 boats were on the unusual final leg, a reach, headed for the finish line on starboard tack. We were happy because one of the very best sailors, Jon Wales, was just ahead of us and a frequent world champion, Bill Widnall, was just astern. In a sailboat race, the biggest opportunity to gain on your opponents is on the beat, where you have to "tack" a number of times, knifing into the wind by switching back and forth from having the wind blow onto the boat from the right (starboard tack) and then from the left (port tack). Under normal conditions, it is relatively rare for positions to change during a reach, so we were heading confidently toward the finish line, feeling secure in our position in the race. The wind was still blowing strong from the southeast and during the day had resulted in higher than average waves breaking on the shore. More on that subject later.

When on a close reach, the leading edge of a spinnaker has to be held off to one side of the boat, with its leading edge held essentially straight ahead by a long and strong spinnaker pole. On a beam reach, when the pole is straight in front of the boat, a strong wind puts an enormous strain on the "guy" (sailor's name for a rope, when used in this manner). This rope runs through the end of the pole and holds the forward corner of the spinnaker out in front of the bow of the boat. The guy then passes through a "block" (a large pulley) on the stern and then forward to a large winch (I hate having to give definitions, but non-sailors need to know this to understand sailboat racing).

THE ACCIDENT

The sheet (also a rope), was wrapped around a metal drum (called a winch) with a handle that provides the boat's crew with a large mechanical advantage to pull in the sail.

When reaching in a strong wind, the crew, in this case four of us, huddle on the side of the boat to counteract the wind's tendency to heel the boat over. We were all out on the starboard (right) side of the boat, with me in the last position, nearest the stern of the boat, holding with my left hand the tiller that connected to the boats rudder for steering.

To ensure safety, I had invested in extra-large stainless-steel blocks where the strain of the spinnaker would be greatest. The steel blocks were each 7,000 lb. test. Most people don't understand the effect of a pulley on pressure. If you hang a 4,000 weight on one end of a rope, run it over a pulley at the top of your boat's mast, and hold it down, the downward pressure is doubled, bringing it to 8,000 pounds.

The block on Tango exploded under the strain. I was positioned in what amounted to the middle of a very large slingshot. The heavy steel pulley (remember it's called a "block") hit me in the left forearm. I had on a very heavy wool sweater and foul weather gear (those yellow jackets that keep sailors dry), but even with that padding the hit hurt like hell and fifty years later I still have the scar. The crew immediately debated taking the spinnaker down, but we were determined to keep Bill Widnall 50 feet astern of us. We led the spinnaker guy directly to the starboard wench amidship, which was not designed to take this kind of strain. Luckily it was bolted securely to the deck and it held.

My left arm hurt, but I stayed at the helm until Ann (Moulton) Hastings had gone below and, upon emerging from the cabin, saw lots of blood in the bilge (the inside bottom of the hull of the boat) and running down and covering my left hand, which was still holding the tiller to steer. She screamed. I had been focusing on the water and the trim of the sails ahead and had not seen the blood. Again, the crew suggested dropping the spinnaker, but continuing to race as fast as we could was the quickest way to get me ashore.

Ann's husband at the time, Bob Hastings, was the Chairman of the Corinthian Yacht Club's Race Committee at the finish line. Her call to him as we crossed the line resulted in an ambulance being at the Corinthian when we sailed back into the harbor and arrived at the dock. As soon as we finished the race, I was feeling increasingly weak enough that I agreed to lie down on the stern of the boat for the sail back into the harbor. It was very embarrassing being carried on a stretcher with blood all over the place from the dock up the ramp and into the ambulance. A crowd had gathered on the dock to see what the hell was going on. Ann went with me in the ambulance to Salem Hospital, where the doctors insisted upon cutting off my Harvard Class ring (not repairable), before stitching up my arm and tying it to me in a sling. When they finished stitching me up, the doctors told me not to use the arm, keep it in the sling, and not do anything strenuous for two days.

GETTING MY BOAT BACK TO ITS MOORING

Marblehead Harbor is beautiful, historic and packed with boats at moorings. The last count I heard was that in the middle of the summer season, there are more than 3,000 boats in that harbor, all at moorings. In a motorized sailboat, you lower the sails, enter the harbor and approach a mooring very slowly under power. This is relatively quite simple. When you have no motor it is much more challenging. You sail on a reach downwind from the mooring, judge how far the boat will coast and at the right moment turn directly into the wind so that the boat coasts forward into the wind, wait till someone on the bow has grabbed the mooring pennant (one more word for rope, in this case a very large one) and then let the sails flop to stop all forward movement .

It is much more complicated and can be exciting in a sailboat with no motor, trying to grab a mooring that sits in the water surrounded by boats. When the wind is blowing hard, as it was that afternoon after the race, a boat ahead to windward pulls back on its mooring, usually making the stern of that boat very close to the empty mooring that has to be grabbed for the boat coming in.

It takes lots of practice to judge how far away you need to be from the mooring, when to stop using the wind to drive the boat ahead, and turn into the wind toward the mooring fast enough to coast to the mooring but not so fast that you "overshoot" the mooring. You can't just put the engine in reverse or step on the brakes in a sailboat.

Having dropped me off at the dock, Jerry was at the helm and Carl was on the bow to grab the mooring. As you may have guessed, Jerry misjudged the boat's speed and Tango's very-sharp, pointed bow drove all the way through the beautiful varnished mahogany transom of a powerboat whose mooring was just ahead. It was not a glancing blow. The powerboat's stern was wide with almost no curvature. Tango hit it squarely and Tango's bow punched a nice hole through the wood, including the boat's name which was in gold leaf across its stern.

It ended up being a very expensive day.

THE PARTY

Nevertheless, I felt obligated (foolishly) to all the gang planning to sail to a great beach party that night. The party had been organized by a then 13-year-old club called the Sitzundjibers, derived from the description of a long-out-of date ski turn called a Sitz Turn, the German "und" for "and," and jibers from jibing downwind in a sailboat. The words combined to be Sitzundjibers. There is whole chapter on this club. Most of the early members of the club were skiers, sailors or both. The beach party that evening was to be at the home of John Parker and his wife, Libby. They lived in a beautiful mansion overlooking the Atlantic in Manchester-by-the-Sea (at the time it was still named just Manchester). There was a beautiful swimming pool surrounded by classic columns of stone about halfway up the climb from the beach to their home. Their beach is just west of Graves Island, a fairly big island just off the coast at that point.

One of the men on the boat that evening, John Hamilton, was dating one of King Simonds' daughters, so he got permission to borrow the Simonds' Boston Whaler for the evening. Our plan was to tow the small boat with outboard engine behind the sailboat and use it to ferry passengers to the beach and back.

Our first problem was anchoring. When I purchased it, my boat had come with an old-style folding anchor which was rusted so badly that it took at least half an hour's struggling just to get it open and usable.

We didn't know how close we dared anchor to the beach because the waves were pounding and we had not bothered to check whether the tide would be coming in or going out (making the water shallower). An old friend recently wrote that he suspected "adult beverages" were being consumed during the process, and that was admittedly the case.

For some reason (I think some of the girls needed to get to a restroom) the decision was made to have John take all the girls into shore first, then come back out and pick up their dates. John motored in to shore, unloaded the girls, but did not return for all the rest of us on the sailboat.

A LONG WAIT

We began to get irritated. Calls of "Come get us" were carried to shore in the wind, but we could not make out the "Sail back to Marblehead" response, and certainly did not want to do so when we finally understood what was being yelled back at us. He was fairly far away, but we could see John working on the motor on the stern of the Boston Whaler, but did not know what problem he was attempting to solve. We later learned that, as the boat was approaching the beach, it was caught by a big wave that swamped the engine and John was unable to get it back running.

After a half hour of this, a somewhat heavyset (that's a polite way of saying it) guy on our boat, Steve Wolfe, decided he was tired of waiting and was going to swim to shore. I came up with the idea of attaching the end of a string of ropes (which served as what are known as sheets and lines on a boat) so he could pull the line to shore, attach it to the bow of the Boston Whaler so we could pull the boat back out to Tango, get aboard, let the line out so the waves would carry the Whaler back to the beach and finally once the party was over use the rope to pull ourselves off the beach and back to the sailboat.

Steve still had on his jockey shorts. His claim today that he was nude does make the story better, but it was not true. Steve did not get urged to swim ashore. It was his idea. When he insisted, we made him wear two life preservers because it did not look as if one would have been enough to hold him up. It also meant the rope would be tied to one of the life preservers so that it could not be dropped. Dick Kirk, now deceased, was the principle person strapping Steve in for his swim.

As Steve swam toward shore, we tied sheet after sheet together, including five sets of spinnaker sheets (even the very small very light-air sheets, the medium light sheets, the light sheets and the heavy sheets. Each was 66 feet long, so these alone resulted in a 528 foot length. We added the main sheet, the one used for the mainsail, which got us to about 642 ft. We gave out of lines to add and ended up with just barely enough for Steve to reach the shore. We would have been out of line if the shore had been 25 feet farther away.

Steve stayed awhile in the water near shore trying to get someone to hear him, realize he was at the beach and bring him something he could put around himself before he walked up onto the beach.

When Steve finally reached shore and tied the line to the bow of the Whaler, he turned it around and we pulled it back to Tango uneventfully. After the empty Whaler reached us, I took all of the line and coiled it carefully in the bow of the Whaler, so I could let it out and avoid the risk of a tangle that would have gotten us stuck between my sailboat and the shore. We made it to the beach.

HOMEWARD BOUND

At the end of the party, some of the girls (the smarter ones, actually it ended up being all of them) elected not to attempt the Saturday night sail home and accepted rides back to Marblehead or Boston. Getting through the breakers on the beach was going to be the only tough part of the pull back to Tango. It would have been better to make two trips out to Tango, but nobody wanted to be risk being in the second boat.

When we got the Boston Whaler turned with its bow into the waves and everyone back aboard, I sat in the bow and started to pull hard on the rope (using both hands, as I had been ordered by the doctors not to do).

There were too many people and the waves were too big. When the boat got thrown by a big wave, I found myself swimming in the Atlantic, in the pitch black dark, having had a lot of drinks, with one arm tied to me. It was not one of my favorite moments.

When we finally got settled and through the waves breaking on the beach, the pull out against the waves to Tango took a long time. The waves had remained in the ocean long after the wind had died down and the wind had abated so much that it took us almost all night to sail the seven miles back to Marblehead, but at least we could sleep late the next morning.

Several names and phrases were used as the story was related to others. The nickname for Steve that stuck was "Fishbait," and he answers to that to this day. We had been "fishing" with Steve as the bait on the end of the line.

PLEASURE ISLAND

Sitz had many enjoyable parties over the years. One of the most memorable was Saturday night, September 14, 1963 when we took over for the evening an amusement park just north of route 128 outside of Boston. The place, a poor-but-fun attempt to be a little like a miniature Disneyland (there was no Disney World back in those days. It was called "Pleasure Island" and, amusingly, the exit off of 128 still bears that name at what is now the Edgewater Office Park. It had special interest to me because I chaired that party, one that several members still claim was the club's best party ever.

It was early fall, so it should have been warm enough to have an outdoor party with booze, a band and the ability to enjoy all of the rides. When you were on the boat ride a big plastic whale jumped out of the water beside the boat. Things like this were made even more scary in the dark. The most popular ride was the train on the "Old Smokey Railroad" that looped around the outer edge of the park.

The party started off well with everyone enjoying the late afternoon. When the sun went down it got cold…not just chilly…cold. The band was having a problem because the valves in the wind instruments began to stick so the music became really bad. The party moved inside the Wild West Saloon where the atmosphere could not have been more appropriate and the band filled the place with loud music.

About a half-dozen guys somehow got bandanas to tie over their lower faces, stopped the train, climbed on board and proceeded to "rob" the passengers. One time, when the boat passed under the train, some passengers poured their drinks on the people below in the boat. The most expensive act was by the man who somehow got into the Haunted House, pushed the mechanical skeleton that normally played the piano off the piano stool and was playing away when the ride full of passengers came through. The club got charged six-hundred dollars for the damage to the mechanical skeleton. That would be about $4,600 today. Expensive, but it had been a helluva fun night.

"Pleasure Island," the amusement park, was used in the 1968 movie, "Charly" and the Academy Awards gave the Oscar for "Best Actor" to Cliff Robertson, who played Charly.

9 MORE TIDBITS
No Category, Just Funny

THE MASSACHUSETTS INSTITUTE OF TECHNOLOGY
There is a long-standing tradition in Cambridge, Massachusetts of stunts executed by MIT students. It is always something done to be discovered later, with the identities of the perpetrators neither present nor identified later. The focus of several of the annual stunts has been the large “Great Dome” of the engineering library that faces the Charles River and Boston across the water. By far the most famous such stunt took place in 1994. As I was driving down Memorial Drive to work that morning I emerged from the short tunnel under Massachusetts Avenue and saw a bunch of people pointing to my left.

Sitting atop the Great Dome was a Cambridge Police car. No, they had not somehow lifted it up there. They had disassembled the vehicle, stripped out all but the shell of the body and constructed connections so that the parts could hoisted up and be reassembled in the dark 140 feet up in the air.

The car had its blue lights blinking; you could see that from far away. What was not discovered until the dome was ascended and closer inspection could be conducted was the presence of a dummy in the uniform of a Cambridge policeman sitting behind the steering wheel. At the time people said that this was appropriate because most of Cambridge’s police officers were dummies. Because of the widespread reputation of policemen, there was a box of Dunkin Donuts on the seat beside the officer

ILLEGAL BOOZE
It made the news all over the country that Alabama had banned a California wine. It was because the label (an advertising poster published in 1895 by a French bicycle manufacturer named "Cycles Gladiator") was unacceptable because the lady riding the bicycle was nude.

It was a pretty good Cabernet Savignon and the stylized lady with long flowing red hair was not sexy, much less pornographic. The story appeared nationwide and the winery said that the ban had increased sales substantially. The winery also sold things like T-shirts and bumper stickers that read "Banned in Bama." At the time, the head of the Alabama Beverage Control Board was former long-time Mayor of Montgomery, Emory Folmar, who had been a friend of my parents.

Pat at the time was working for McDowell Lee, the long timenand highly-respected Secretary of the Alabama State Senate. I urged her not to, but she gave him a bottle. Given the law, I thought that a little risky, especially when Mac laughed and said he couldn't wait to show it to Emory. Two weeks went by before I went to answer the phone and was terrified by the name on to caller ID: "Emory Folmar." We were in big trouble. Illegal wine and untaxed when brought into the state.

I breathed a huge sigh of relief when the voice said she was Anita Folmar, Emory's wife, who was calling me because she was an artist and member of the Montgomery Art Guild and I was President.

THE TOMATO WARS

You probably didn't study these wars in school. Also, most people don't even know of battles fought between the opposing forces of New York City and Boston, beginning in the 1950. It grew into a major rite of spring.

Skiers, eager to get underway with ski season, began holding a battle in upstate Vermont every year on Columbus Day weekend. It evolved from a two-person incident into a major event with lots of rules. Good tomatoes would have been too expensive and hard, so large quantities of slightly rotten tomatoes were purchased cheaply from vendors in the Fulton Market section of downtown New York City.

Even if you got hit by a tomato, you could go to a "Medical Tent" for surgery that would allow you to reenter the fray. Needless to say, some imbibing of liquids was concurrent with the battle, which was essentially an adult and more complex version of Capture the Flag mixed with Dodge Ball..

In the 1970s I introduced a variant on this theme, held in the spring in lieu of an Easter Egg Hunt. Here again, it was for adults, and it was held in the yard of our ski house at Sugarbush, Vermont. It was named "The Martini Hunt," with chilled martinis in small plastic cups hidden under bushes or behind trees throughout the front yard. People had to get down on their hands and knees to hunt and, if very successful in locating and drinking the tinis, occasionally ended up on their hands and knees from that point on.

Sadly, the Tomato Wars, although they continued into the 21st Century, deteriorated into battles between two designated teams. I guess New Yorkers were not as eager to have fun as Bostonians because the battle declined to the point where there were nine times as many Boston fighters as there were from New York.

THE FACTS

Kids can be led to believe something just because they are told it by an elder who supposedly knows the facts.

My wife, Pat, worked as a guide giving tours of the historic Alabama State Capitol. The capitol building has many areas and items of interest. The House of Representatives has special importance to me because of my grandfather's having been elected Speaker of the House in 1894. His chair is still there, protected by fancy ropes to prevent sitting.

Several organizations give tours of the Capitol. Pat worked for the Senate, being available for interesting tours of the various points of interest. In addition to school groups of all ages, Senators who had constituents arrive to call on them could call upon her to provide an appropriate tour for them. Pat had to know a lot of history and be able to talk about it accurately, every tour had to be customized to fit the audience. Talks varied enormously depending up the age or area of interest of the group, frequently requiring treading very gently on the subjects of the Confederacy and the Selma to Montgomery March.

The guides who were employed by the Senate and the House of Representatives had to be outstanding in knowledge, adaptability and delivery. Others working for tour companies were less knowledgeable and less concerned about sticking with the facts. One in particular loved to interject himself into stories, in many cases telling tales that simply could not be true.

The funniest one had to do with a question from a person in a group he was leading through the Capitol. The South has loads of beautiful old homes that survived the Civil War. Because they were built prior to the Civil War, the term normally applied to them is "ante bellum"…which, in Latin, simply means "before the war."

One day a tour participant asked about the term "ante bellum." The guide went into a long story about how a woman with very good taste in architecture had started a movement to build these stately old homes, almost invariably painted white with large two-story columns across the front. The man went on to say that the style began to be named after her…..Auntie Bellum. She must have been quite a lady.

AMERICA'S FUNNEST HOME VIDEOS

Pat and I are far from being regular watchers of the TV show, America's Funniest Home Videos, but occasionally we have stumbled across it and watched. Most are pretty funny and, although some appear to have been staged, most appear to be accidents that occurred when someone had their video camera working. You are ready for the next story.

JUST ROLLING ALONG

In Montgomery, as is true in many cities, trash and garbage are put into a plastic thing with a hinged cover and wheels so you can push it out to curb of the street for pickup. The cover is hinged in such a way that it can fold all the way to vertical behind the "Curbie," leaving the handlebar exposed and top of the garbage-container open.

I usually close the lid before starting down the driveway. For some reason I started to roll our Curbie down our driveway with the lid left open and hanging straight down behind the container part of the Curbie. On the flat driveway, the hinged flap did not reach the ground. As I went from flat to the start of the hill the hinged top flap remained vertical while the main part of the Curbie was tilted back on its wheels rolling down the driveway ahead of me. As the wheeled main part of the Curbie moved ahead, the flap that was hanging down touched the concrete and was dragged back toward me.

One of my feet stepped on the edge of the flap, abruptly stopping it, but the main part of the Curbie kept rolling downhill. Holding onto the handle and suddenly standing on the flap with the garbage container continuing downhill, I fell headfirst into the garbage with my feet waving in the breeze behind me. The Curbie continued downhill until it finally crossed the sidewalk and stopped in the street.

It would have looked hilarious to anyone who saw it, but it was not fun riding with my head in the garbage. Lucky I didn't hit by a car. It would have made a really strange newspaper story. Man riding in garbage gets killed by another "vehicle."

SHOWING "OFF"

When we were living in Dover, Massachusetts a utility worker became quite a celebrity, having his picture appear in the papers. It was less than the frequently cited "15 minutes of fame," but he will certainly never forget it. The guy was working on top of a telephone pole near our home when he slipped and fell, remaining held upside down by his safety belt. His only problem was that when he fell, the safety harness that had been around his waste pulled his pants and underpants to his ankles and held him by his feet so that he couldn't pull himself back up or pull his pants back to his waist.

The neighborhood had loads of laughs and the ladies got many good pictures, including interesting " details." At least the newspapers used pictures of his rear, funny, but not the whole story. Most of the "ladies" took pictures of his "front." The poor guy must have been pretty embarrassed when the news coverage began.

TSA

Once, going through security at Boston's Logan Airport, I was in a wheelchair and had tickets reading "TSA Pre check" that usually resulted in a quick trip through security. After waiting in the line on the left, when I told them I had a pacemaker the agent said their X ray machine. or whatever you call the body scanner, was not working and the Delta lady had to wheel me to the other longer line to the right. Ahead of me, Pat did not know what was happening.

Even though old people no longer have to take their shoes off, they do have to remove everything from their pockets (not just metal) and their belts to enter the scanner. This left my pants quite loose at the waist, so I had to move very carefully in the body scanner, in which you have to put your arms up over your head. When I emerged, the TSA man said he still had to pat me down. I warned him about my pants with no belt, but he ran his blue-gloved hands down each side of my legs, you guessed it, pulling my pants to my ankles. All of the people in line behind me howled laughing. At least no one caught it on camera.

HOW MUCH IS A DOLLAR WORTH?

My boss and several others from State Street Bank were working in Munich August 15, 1971, when Nixon announced the dollar would no longer be tied to a fixed gold price....essentially devaluing the dollar. We needed cash, but nobody in Munich would accept U.S. dollars, claiming they did not know how much a dollar was worth. We had to rent a car from Auto-Sixt and drive into Switzerland to change money. It was a very awkward day for American bankers in Europe.

UP AGAINST THE JUSTICE DEPARTMENT

This is another example of a story that doesn't fit anywhere else. It is a short bit, but for me extremely scary. When airline deregulation became law my company, Woodside, which had negotiated car rental and hotel room rates, looked at the airlines. Air travel was by far the largest share of dollar volume in business travel. We asked the major airlines in writing what prices they would offer us if we could direct business to them.

TWA filed a complaint with the Justice Department against Woodside, and me individually, for organizing a "group boycott," something our lawyers had made quite clear was illegal. We had never given any indication that we even thinking about, a "boycott" of any carrier. We had asked for proposals from all major US carriers, including TWA.

It is very scary having to have your staff load up many boxes of files, including all letters and minutes of board meetings and stockholder meetings going back years. Dozens of boxes of my files were copied and shipped to the Justice Department. Nothing ever came of it, but TWA continued for a while as a weak carrier and eventually went under. They deserved it for falling so far behind the competition when airlines were deregulated.

You should avoid having the Justice Department come after you. It is not fun.

10 MURDER SHE WROTE

I Lived And My Mother Was Acquitted

As a little kid, I was sick all the time, and it never got much better. When you go to see a new doctor, you usually have to fill out a form listing your medical history. I could never remember all the things wrong with me, so I had to prepare and print the list of 39 surgeries and hospitalizations. When you buy a new car and have lots of problems with manufacturing defects it is referred to as having bought "a lemon." I was a human lemon, and Dr. Brannon Hubbard told my mother this when I was born. Less than a day old, I can't remember this, but am told it is true. Looking at my incredibly flat feet, Dr. Hubbard had said "Eva Mae, you don't ever have to worry about his getting drafted."

DRAFTED

When I received my draft notice in 1960, I had to report to the Boston Army Base, where several funny things happened. First, you took a written intelligence test and then stripped naked to go through a long series of medical exams. You moved from station to station, at which doctors checked different things.

At the end of the day, with more than a hundred guys standing naked around an indoor basketball court, the head doctor, standing in the middle of the court, called out my name. It was very awkward because he called no other name. I was scared about what it could mean and embarrassed to have to walk out to the center. Somehow, I kept my balance when he reached down grabbed me by the ankle and held my foot up for everyone to see. Because it was so short, I remember his exact words: "For all of you who have letters from your doctors claiming you should be 4F because of flat feet, *THESE* are flat feet." I had not brought a letter from a doctor; I didn't even know it would exempt me from draft.

I got even when the group got dressed and reassembled, seated in the meeting room at the end of the day. The guy in charge started calling out lists of names of people to stand. When he finished each group, he would tell those people what draft category they had been assigned. I was not surprised to be in the 4F group, ineligible for service. It was interesting that the great sports stars, the Cleary brothers (Bob and Bill), who had played hockey at Harvard, gone on to great success in the Olympics, and coached winning U.S. Olympic teams were deemed to be 4F that day because of asthma, something that did not affect them on the ice. Bill and Bob were star athletes, but 4F.

JUST DESSERTS (Part One)

When the man in charge got to the end of the list of categories, he paused a few seconds and then called out my name. I stood, once again, alone, but he didn't say anything except that I could be seated. Some of my college classmates started to call out derogatory comments, such as saying I must be the one with VD, etc.

This became bad enough and went on to the point where the man had to say why I had been asked to stand. The guys shut up when he said he had just wanted to see the person who had gotten the highest score on the written exam of anybody in the two years he had been there doing this job, announcing the results to thousands of kids. This nice result was because, in addition to normal education, I had studied things like 3 years of woodworking in junior high school, so I must have been able to identify on the test the purpose of tools, pictures of which required you to identify the use of each tool. I had gotten correct answers to things the others knew nothing about.

AND NOW WE GET TO THE REASON FOR THE TITLE OF THIS CHAPTER
Throughout all of my childhood, severe Asthma left me very weak and unable to play any sports. At the time, the group of doctors who specialized in the treatment of asthma were on the coast of Mississippi in Gulfport. They operated under their names. Both were named Dr. Gay. It had no unusual meaning in those days, but I went for asthma treatment to "The Gay Clinic."

They treated me with a liquid medicine, a tablespoon of which had to be swallowed morning and night a half hour before eating. The liquid was pink. We had not been told why, but we had been instructed that you had to shake the glass bottle hard before taking it to ensure that the white powder that settled at the bottom of the bottle was spread throughout the liquid. The amount of powder increased gradually over the years that I had to take the medicine.

THE MISTAKE
One morning my mother came in with bottle, woke me up and had me swallow the medicine. A few minutes later I was in agony lying on the living room floor. At least I threw up. Had I not, I would not have lived. The pain was excruciating. We could not figure out what was wrong until my mother went in the kitchen and discovered she had mistakenly given me a tablespoon full of rat poisoning. Had this happened today, we would have sued, and clearly won lots of money.

The neighborhood pharmacy, on Fairview Avenue in Montgomery across from what is now the Capri Theater, had sold the rat poisoning. The inexcusable fact was that the owner/pharmacist mixed up a batch of poison, did not keep track of what he had put in the mix, sold it in what was then a standard clear-glass prescription-shaped bottle, and simply typed the words "RAT POISON" on the prescription label. This was in normal typewriter-size letters with no accompanying skull and crossbones or any indication, other than the two typed words in black, that the bottle was deadly poison. Beyond belief (but true) the clear glass prescription bottle containing the poison was the exact same size and shape as my asthma medicine and the color of the liquid was an identical shade of pink with the same white powder at the bottom of the bottle. It was easy to see how my mother had made the mistake, but inexcusable that the drug store had sold rat poison in this manner.

When rushed to the doctor, Dr. Jane Day (more on her in another chapter) I learned the awful meaning of pumping out your stomach. I was forced to swallow two quarts of water fast and then wait for the hose to be forced down my throat. After my stomach had been pumped out, I had a few seconds to rest before the process was repeated. This went on over and over again.

Now, here is the incredible, lifesaving coincidence. The local doctors tested my medicine, discovering that the white powder in the prescriptions I had been taking for years from the asthma doctor had been arsenic, and the steadily-increasing percentage of arsenic over the years in the medicine had gradually resulted in a high tolerance for the deadly poison. By this extremely strange coincidence, I had developed the ability to tolerate arsenic far beyond what a regular person would have been able to survive.

It is that ability to develop tolerance for arsenic that has led to two great books about people who murdered someone and escaped suspicion by putting arsenic in their own drink instead of just putting it in the drink of their victim. They appeared to have been given arsenic the same as had been given to their victims. Arsenic comes out in your scalp, where it can be detected quite easily.

Anyway, I lived, and Mom was *extremely* apologetic. The big apology, which never came, should have been from Easterling's drugstore.

EPILOGUE

In April of 2014 the results of research on arsenic by Professor Amy Schwartz at the University of New Hampshire were reported in the media. Her study indicated that even extremely minute amounts of arsenic found in some tap water would reduce a person's IQ by about six points.

I hate to think of how many dozens of tablespoons of arsenic I had ingested over the years. I would guess there were about three tablespoons of arsenic at the bottom of each bottle of the medicine, so about 30 tablespoons over the years. That's a lot of arsenic.

For some reason, both she and the Professor she said had led the study refused to make any comment about my accident.

11 STICKING IT TO AMERICAN EXPRESS

David (in this case Steve) Takes On Goliath….And Wins!

In the late eighties, First Bank Visa began to specialize in taking corporate accounts away from American Express, not a large number, but the loss of accounts was enough to irritate Amex. First Bank had developed specialized accounting programs to aid in travel cost control, making their Visa much more attractive to corporations than the standard consumer-oriented version of the Visa card.

At the time, fees charged businesses by Visa and MasterCard were in the 1.5% to 2% range, while Amex was way up around 3% to 4%.

Leadership of a small group of Boston area restaurant owners fell to Steve DiFillippo, who was owner of Davios, a very good and quite successful restaurant that has now expanded to Philadelphia and, in 2008, opened a new Davios in Foxboro, Massachusetts in the stadium used by the New England Patriots. To my amazement, he now has Davios in Manhattan, Philadelphia, Atlanta and King of Prussia. Incredible. I can't wait to try the one in Atlanta or in Boston the next time we are there.

Steve was the figurehead in this story, but he attributed the idea to three well-known Boston restaurant owners, Lydia Shire, Jasper White, and Roger Berkowitz (well known for his Legal Seafood).

GROUP BOYCOTT

The group of restaurant owners met and made the mistake of agreeing they would all get together and begin refusing to accept the American Express card. Amex simply took too big a percentage and almost everybody who had an Amex card also had a Visa or Mastercard they could use. Their complaint and their action hit the press and TV crews showed up at Davios the morning after DeFillippo's picture appeared in the Boston Herald cutting up an American Express card. Under US law, you and your business can boycott anyone you want, but a "group boycott" is illegal.

You may wonder how many people know the derivation of the term "Tea Party." as the ultra-conservative political movement that began in 2009 throughout the United States. I suspect that anyone likely to be reading this knows that the tea party name was given to the Pre-Revolutionary War revolt in Boston against the British tax on tea. Bostonians, dressed as Indians, attacked a vessel in Boston Harbor and through loads of tea into the water. It quickly became, known as the "Boston Tea Party." The revolt against American Express' high fee was immediately nicknamed by the media to be "The Boston Fee Party"

At the time, my wife was the Boston sales rep for First Bank Visa, the only Visa bank that was making an extra effort to provide the statistical analysis that big corporations needed. Pat's boss, Rob Abele, and his boss, Steve Putney, were concerned about what Steve DiFillippo's group was doing. They flew to Boston and Pat set up lunch for the three of them with Steve DiFillippo to discuss things. The existence of this luncheon became known and Amex seized on it to claim that First Bank Visa was behind the whole illegal group boycott of American Express. This version of the story, to my knowledge, has never been corrected.

Pat knew that what happened was the exact reverse of what Amex was claiming. First Bank Visa wasn't just not behind the boycott, First Bank Visa's Putney at that lunch had strongly cautioned the boycott's leader about the action by the group of restaurants and advised DiFillippo in no uncertain terms that they better get a lawyer, heed the lawyer's advice and immediately cease the boycott.

The Boston Fee Party quickly spread to several hundred restaurants throughout the country. Although quite reluctant to do so, Amex did finally respond, but kept it quiet. The restaurant's actions did have a desirable effect, at least for the restaurants. Amex made the decision to phase in lower percentage fees, saving restaurants throughout the world many hundreds of millions of dollars.

Amex percentage fees have climbed back to levels even higher than they were 30 years ago, but I figure that what Pat's luncheon saved restaurants worldwide massive amounts of money and therefore they should all offer her free meals for life. That didn't happen.

12 "THE GAME"
Harvard vs. Yale

Yes, be prepared; this is the longest chapter in the book because it is convoluted with many twists.

When you live in Alabama and see the incredible amount of attention paid to collegiate football, especially when Alabama or Auburn play for the National Championship, you wonder about the Harvard-Yale game's being called "The Game." There is a great old tradition and, despite the deterioration of interest in Ivy League football, even among the students, this event at the end of each season still evokes great interest. Even the stadium itself has a place in history, as you can read in the chapters on its construction and its role as a major force in the evolving rules governing football.

My wife, Pat, and I have been to many games throughout the country, watching teams that have been major competitors for decades, including such names as Oklahoma, USC and Ohio State, plus special events such as the Fiesta Bowl, the Rose Bowl, the Orange Bowl and the Super Bowl. Alabama is truly fanatic about its football. In the first year of Nick Saban's coaching, Alabama filled their stadium in Tuscaloosa with 92,000 people and turned away 8,000 others, not for a game, this was just for an intra-squad spring scrimmage. The saying that "Football is King in Alabama" is not an exaggeration.

The Super Bowl is quite a show, but for tailgating before the game we have not seen anything come close to the annual intra-state rivalry in Alabama between the University of Alabama and Auburn University. The number of huge bus-size RVs, set up days before the event and the number of tailgating parties and their elaborate preparation and execution, is quite something to see. At Auburn's home games the flight of the eagle from high in the stands around the stadium before landing in the middle of the field is a great moment before each game.

The sad decline of football in the Ivy League began in the hippie days of the sixties, but some games still attract a lot of attention. The 1968 season was highly unusual, with Harvard and Yale both approaching their final encounter undefeated. This was the first time since 1909. At least in New England, the hype almost reached SEC proportions (that's an exaggeration, but not by much) weeks before the game. When it appeared the final match-up in late November would be a battle between two undefeated teams for the Ivy League Championship, interest in the game grew to never-seen-before levels.

AND NOW TO THE GAME
Much earlier, I had been appointed Chairman of my class' first event of the big Harvard 10th Reunion. This post-football-game party in the fall of 1968 was the kickoff of all of

the events leading up to Harvard's commencement the following spring, 1969. After college, I was not interested in football enough to have purchased season tickets, but if I was to chair the big reunion party after the game, I certainly wanted to go to the game.

Season ticket holders had their seats, but all other tickets for all games were distributed by the Harvard Athletic Department on the basis of seniority a few weeks before each game. Normally, Harvard football games are poorly attended and getting a seat is not a problem, it just meant the most recent graduates got the lousy seats down near the goal line. The older the class in which you had graduated, the better your assigned seat. For most games, it was highly unlikely that anyone would be seated behind the end zone. In 1968, it was a totally different situation.

GETTING TICKETS

With tickets assigned on the basis of seniority, the school ran out of tickets with the Class of '49, meaning that the many thousands of people who had graduated after 1949 could not get tickets. As luck would have it, the President of State Street Bank (for which I worked at the time), George Rockwell, was the Chairman of the Class of '49 reunion and his class was the last allowed to buy tickets.

Luckily, a man who worked in my department at State Street Bank, Frank Napoli, was the son of the owner of the large ticket agency located in the subway kiosk in the middle of Harvard Square. I had to have a ticket. Frank's dad came up with two tickets for $100. That was an awful lot of money back then, probably the equivalent of about $736 fifty years later. It was a stretch, but I paid for the tickets and asked a date to the game and the reunion party to follow after the game across Storrow Drive in Newell Boathouse, only a few hundred yards from the stadium.

Arriving at the gate in the fence that surrounds the stadium area, I presented my tickets and was admitted. Entering the stadium through another set of gates, I showed the tickets again and was directed up the steps to the row we were assigned. By luck, the tickets I had purchased were on the Harvard side of the field, albeit far from the fifty-yard line. The seats were several dozen rows in front of most of my classmates who had season tickets together.

A NASTY SURPRISE!

When we reached our row and showed the tickets, my elbows were grabbed from behind and held by a large Boston Policeman (Harvard College is in Cambridge, but the stadium is just across the river in Boston). There were two additional officials there, one of whom notified me that he was FBI and that I was under arrest for a federal offence because I had stolen the tickets from the US Mail. The third, and least pleasant officer, was a Cambridge policeman, where the tickets had been stolen. It may sound unusual for people who attend football games these days, but I was in a grey pin-stripe suit, complete with tie, because where we were going to dinner that night required it. I tried to convince the officials that I had purchased the tickets from the well-known ticket agency located in Harvard Square.

Most people were already seated, so our group of five was quite visible standing in the aisle. Everyone could see my arms were being pinned behind me by the policeman in uniform and that I was being confronted by two more men. My date, on our first date, was in shock. Seeing what was going on, my supposedly-good friends higher up in the stands began to chant "Throw the bum in jail, throw the bum in jail," a chorus which picked up volume when more people in the stands saw what was happening.

I convinced the officers to let go of one wrist and allow me to reach in my suit coat pocket. I pulled out the reunion invitation, which showed the reunion committee with me listed at the top as chairman. From my shirt pocket, it helped a lot to have a business card showing that I was a Vice President of State Street Bank, clearly one of the most conservative and respected businesses in Massachusetts (the 13th largest bank in the country). Both items matched the picture on my driver's license in my wallet, which was being held by one of the officers.

It turned out that someone had stolen the tickets from a student's mailbox, but the officers were finally convinced that I was clearly not the culprit. The nice people in the long row in which we were to have been seated offered to squeeze together so that my date and I could sit there. The student whose tickets had been stolen had received a voucher for the seats he had been assigned and he was amused to learn what had transpired. The "thief" ended up sitting next to his victim.

A SAD GAME

The game got underway. Yale had two superstar players, Brian Dowling at quarterback and Calvin Hill at end, players who would end up playing in the NFL. Because both schools had numerous powerful and extremely wealthy graduates who had not succeeded in purchasing tickets, there were a number of small planes circling above the field during the game, not a great spot from which to watch, but better than nothing. They could at least say "I saw the game." Although the planes were all flying counterclockwise above the stands, two pilots' looking down at the field did cause some excitement when they swerved to avoid a collision. It wasn't close, but close enough to be dangerous and cause a loud gasp from the people who saw it. If two planes had fallen into the stands, the news reports of the game would have been quite different. At least, the near miss occurred over the Yale side of the stadium.

Anyway, Yale moved into the lead… *far* into the lead. As the end of the fourth quarter approached with Yale leading by 16 points, it became obvious who was going to win. All hope for Harvard was lost. Several members of my reunion party committee came down the aisle, urging me to join them and head on over to get the party set up to receive the crowd in a few minutes. We did need to get to the party location early, but I hung on until Jim Doty, a class of '59 friend and a member of the reunion committee, came down the steps and convinced me to leave when there were only two minutes left to play.

After we had left the stadium and run across Soldiers Field Road, we heard a big roar from the crowd. We had no clue as to what was happening. Harvard had taken their first string quarterback out of the game early, replacing him with a backup quarterback, Frank Champi, Incredibly, this relatively-inexperienced player completed several passes, moving his Harvard team down the field. Champi was tackled and fumbled at the Yale 38. It was an outstanding fumble. The ball was picked up by a teammate, Fritz Reed, who ran 25 yards to the Yale 15.

Despite the excitement, Harvard had obviously lost when they were trailing by 16 points with only 43 seconds left to play. It was clearly impossible to get two six-point touchdowns and add on two two-point conversions to each touchdown with just 43 seconds left. Yale was called for holding, so Harvard got an unexpected first down, followed by another long pass. Going into those final minutes Champi had completed just four of twelve passes all afternoon. He began to do a lot of scrambling around in the backfield, eluding the grasp of Yale players over and over again.

Yale supporters were still not the least bit nervous because a team, no matter how good and how lucky, could not get sixteen points in just 43 seconds. Once again, over in Newell Boathouse, we heard a tremendous cheer emanating from the stadium. What in the world could it be? We were already getting nervous about what we were missing.

Harvard had gotten its touchdown, leaving just 42 seconds left in the game, tried for the two points, and succeeded. The Harvard supporters were going wild. Across the street we sat there bewildered. There was no TV and this was before the days of cell phones. It had to be something wild, but we had no way of knowing. Harvard still trailed by 8 points, so with just a few seconds left and Harvard having to kick off to Yale, Yale wins the game!!! The crowd on the Yale side of the stadium resumed their traditional waving of white handkerchiefs so Harvard fans could wipe away their tears.

NOT JUST YET

It was obvious that Harvard would try to get possession of the ball again with an on-side kick. Trying to get the ball on your own team's kickoff is extremely difficult under any circumstances, but even more unlikely when the receiving team is expecting the attempt.

It wasn't just that Yale expected a short kick, everyone in the place knew that was what was going to happen. For an on-side kick to be successful, the kicker tries send the ball bouncing the minimum required ten yards before a Harvard player could touch it.

The defending team takes out its usual heavy linemen and puts its players with the "best hands" up front so they can grab and control the ball. Harvard would have to run those ten yards and grab the ball before a Yale player, standing there ready had caught it. Yale did not have to think about a runback, they just needed to grab the ball and fall down, allowing their team to run out the clock and win the game. For some strange and inexplicable reason, Yale failed to rearrange their players. Thank you, coach.

It was shocking, as I later found out from those who had stayed. The odds were highly against it, but the ball bounced low as planned, slowly moving the ten yards toward the line of Yale players. Harvard's players raced the ten yards. A Yale player, Brad Lee, had tried to leap onto the ball and appeared to have succeeded, but another Yale player accidentally tripped on Lee's helmet, causing a fumble, which was recovered by Harvard. Incredible!!!! Harvard got to continue on offense, but they were way out at midfield with half the field to go and very few seconds left to accomplish anything.

Champi came back into the game. On first down he tried to pass, couldn't find a receiver, eluded several would-be tacklers and ran around left end, gaining 14 yards all the way to the Yale 35, earning Harvard a first down. A Yale player accidentally grabbed Champi's facemask, resulting in a 15 yard "unsportsmanlike conduct "penalty that moved the ball all the way down to the Yale 20. It is remarkable that this all transpired in just 10 seconds of playing time since Harvard's previous touchdown.

Now, with only 32 seconds left in the game, Champi threw to the end zone trying for a touchdown, but his pass was incomplete. It was third down and Harvard still trailed by 8 points. Gus Crim ran a draw play to the Yale 6 yard line. On the next play, Champi ran around dodging tacklers, having several close calls before getting tackled for a two-yard loss. There are now just 3 seconds left in the game and Harvard still trailed by 8 points. It had gotten exciting but, obviously, Yale has won the game. A team simply could not score 8 points in 3 seconds. Though highly unlikely, the Yale fans were, at last, getting nervous; still confident, but nervous. Maybe Harvard would score, but they certainly could not get another two point conversion. After all, there were now just 3 seconds left. The fans had already climbed down out of the stands and were pushing right up to the lines that marked the end zone of the field where Harvard was trying to score. The officials, with quite a lot of difficulty, got the crowd to move back a few feet. Champi scrambled around again before getting off a pass to Vic Gatto in the end zone for the touchdown. Time has run out, the game clock showed zero seconds remaining, the game was over and the crowd flooded out onto the field. Harvard had lost by two points. It had been close, but Yale had won. It may have been by just two points, but they had still won. Time had run out. The Yalies were jubilant. The game was over and they had managed to hang on and win. Fantastic!!!!

This time the cheer was so loud that those of us at the boathouse across the street could not believe it. We had been there at Newell Boathouse for what seemed like an hour thinking the game would be have been over in a couple of minutes. We were incredulous. Despite all the exciting theatrics, Harvard had still lost. The entire football field was full of people. The Yale crowd was celebrating victory, although it had been terrifying at the end. Yale had hung on and won. Small problem. According to the rules (which few in the crowd knew), a football game cannot end on a touchdown without the scoring team's having a chance to kick the extra point or, in this case, try for two points. The clock may have showed zero, but the game was not over. The referees knew the game must go on, but the crowd did not, and there was no effective way of communicating amid all of the bedlam.

YOGI BERRA

How in the world does a baseball player fit into this chapter? Finally, the loudspeaker system overcame the noise on the field, the situation was explained and the crowd told to leave the field. The process was slow. People did not want to climb all the way back up into their seats in the stadium, so they stayed packed into the area of grass between the stands and the playing area of the field. It took a long time before the officials could clear the field. In 1968 the stadium had no lights and it was beginning to get dark. There was enough daylight to see, but you couldn't see much. Games were not supposed to last this long, and late November was just a month before the shortest day of the year.

The crowd clustered twenty deep around the field, toes still right up at the sidelines. Having been the first such concrete stadium ever built, the stands in Harvard Stadium were designed quite close to the field, leaving very little room for the players and the crowd along the sidelines. It took a long time to push everyone back to where they stood lined up around the field packed right up against the sidelines.

After what seemed like an eternity (certainly for those of us across Storrow Drive at the party site who still did not have any clue about what was happening), the game could finally be resumed. As you may by now have guessed, Ciampi completed another pass, this time to Pete Varney, scoring the necessary two points. A newspaper headline the next morning read "Harvard beats Yale 29-29." Dowling and Hill and the entire Yale offense had stood on the sidelines in shock, watching their defense give up the final 16 points without Yale's offense ever getting back on the field. For a tie, the celebration by Harvard was little short of incredible. As Yogi was famous for saying: *"It ain't over 'til it's over."*

13 ADAMS HOUSE

Another Harvard Story

At the end of freshman year at Harvard, we organized a bunch of friends and all applied to Adams House, catapulting it from last place in 1955 to first in one year. It continued to rank high on the sought-after list for many years. Adams had lots of advantages, not the least of which was its location on Plympton Street, just a block downhill from Massachusetts Avenue, where many of the stores, restaurants and bars were located, and by far the closest to classes which were spread out on the north side of Mass. Ave. Adams had been the residence of a guy who became President of the United States, Franklin Delano Roosevelt. Over the years there were also such notables as Buckminster Fuller, Henry Kissinger, Aaron Copeland, William Randolph Hearst, Jr., John Lithgow and Cardinal Bernard Law. For many years, students lived in Adams B-17, which looked like any other room in the building. In 2010 it was restored to the way it would have looked a hundred years ago and set aside as a memorial to FDR.

Harvard's other Houses (dormitories for upperclassmen) had their food delivered by underground tunnels from a central kitchen. Adams had its own kitchen, and the best food of any at the college. Adams House was old and relatively elegant, offering large rooms with antique wood doors and door frames plus fireplaces in many of the rooms.

Unlike the other "houses" where students heading to their rooms had to go past an office, usually staffed at night by a night watchman, Adams House, consisting primarily of converted apartment buildings, had a dozen separate entrances. C Entry was the only entry that required you to pass by the house offices to reach the stairway to your room. We picked E, and got the room we had chosen. I claimed the single because I had organized the deal and because I snored so loudly that nobody wanted to be in the same room with me. We picked E-32 because it was high enough to be away from the street noise and had a piano in the large living room.

In those days, the college had "Parietal Hours," those times when girls were allowed to be entertained in your room. On weekdays, these ended at 8pm, and you could not be caught with a girl in the stairway, much less in your room after hours.

PINCKNEY STREET

Having an apartment off campus was another offense subject to expulsion if caught. I lined up 7 guys to pay the rent and got Porter Anderson, the good friend from Montgomery who was attending the Harvard Medical School, to be the name on the lease of an apartment on Beacon Hill in downtown Boston. Graduate students were allowed to rent premises off campus, but not undergraduates. There is a chapter about Porter later.

One of my basic principles, later used in ski houses in Vermont and summer houses overlooking Marblehead Harbor, was that anything divided by enough people became financially feasible. Our rent for the Beacon Hill apartment was $70 per month, so just $10 each. I hate to think of what it rents for today. The apartment had two entrances, one on Mrytle Street and one entrance on Revere Street. The Beacon Hill apartment was our entertainment center. One unfortunate fact about Beacon Hill is that, with almost all houses having been built so long ago, very few have room to add an elevator. Our apartment required climbing three flights of stairs.

ADAMS HOUSE E-32

The even numbered side of E Entry was interesting because the single bedrooms had fire doors on every floor opening from the single bedroom to the F Entry staircase. I decided to take the lock out of the metal fire door in the back of my bedroom and take the lock to have a key made. A professor lived in E-22 and used the E staircase, so you could not risk bringing a girl up that E Entry staircase at night, plus the E stairway had windows that made the stairway viewable from out across a courtyard. With the key in hand, I would have a way of coming up the back staircase (F Entry) that was much less visible through its windows than the E staircase. The fire door had always been an escape-with-a-date route if campus police came to the front door, but the key allowed entrance from the rear hall into my bedroom.

Late one night, my date, Elyn, (as they used to say in those days) was hot to trot. She had to be home at Radcliffe College (nine blocks away) by their curfew so we creeped as quietly as we could up the F Entry staircase. The Bow Street Entrance to this portion of Adams House is downhill from my usual entrance on Plympton Street, so the rooms in E Entry are up one more floor than those in F.

I made the mistake of counting up from the street level entrance on Bow Street, forgetting that we needed to go up that one extra flight. We went up two flights to what I thought was the back door to E-32. The metal fire doors did not have any room or floor numbers. The key opened the door and I held the door while my date headed into the dark room and sat down on the bed. There was a sudden, quite loud, exclamation from the bed. Obviously, we had forgotten to climb the extra flight of stairs to E-32 and my date had ended up in the bed of a very proper (should I say stuffy?) guy, Professor Stephen Graubard, who must have been sound asleep in his bed.

Luckily, the room was pitch black dark and we were able to get out and scramble down the stairs before he could turn on his light. Graubard was a highly-regarded professor of modern intellectual history. I am sure he never knew how the girl had gotten into his bed. Needless to say, we did not tell. The key that I had had made was obviously a master key that opened all the doors in Adams House. It was a very close call.

14 "ONE IF BY LAND AND TWO IF BY SEA"

No, This Is Not About Paul Revere

Children are frequently told by their mothers that they can't do something. That becomes close to impossible when the kid, in this case me at age 16, was planning to do in 1954 what his Dad had done in 1911 with his cousin and best friend, Mills Thornton: canoe from Montgomery to Mobile.

In those days, both 1911 and 1954, there were no dams on the Alabama River, which is now almost entirely converted into lakes created by dams constructed by US Army Corps of Engineers. Before the three dams, there was a current to speed up the 340-mile trip down the Alabama, Mobile, Tensaw, Middle, Apalachee and Blakeley Rivers and three little creeks to Daphne, a small and beautiful little town on the eastern shore of Mobile Bay.

Bill Chandler, who was then the head of the Montgomery YMCA, agreed to let us borrow an aluminum canoe from Camp Rotary on the eastern shore of Lake Jordan. The canoe was small, just twelve feet long, designed for two people. It would have been full had there been just two of us. With three of us and supplies for two weeks, the boat was dangerously overloaded. Our diet consisted of Spam and Vienna Sausage and Sardines. Would you believe there is a Museum of Spam in Austin, Texas? At least the stuff did not have to be cooked.

Today, most paddling organizations require that life preservers be worn at all times. We didn't even carry them with us. When we got down to the river in the evening of August 20, 1954 and filled up the canoe, we discovered that there was nowhere near enough room, so we offloaded lots of stuff. We wore bathing suits for the entire voyage, so you can imagine how tanned we were at the end.

A FULL BOAT

Even leaving out a lot of gear, the boat was terrifyingly overloaded. Sterling Culpepper took a seat in the bow and Porter Anderson in the middle, on top of the supplies and we remained in those positions for the duration of the trip. Porter was then, and is now, a tall man. The gear filled up the center of the boat, so he was perched above the gunwale (pronounced gun'-uhl). This made the canoe extremely top heavy and, instead of riding on top of the water, it was so deep in the water that there were only five inches of freeboard (that's the part of the hull above water) left showing. Canoes normally are expected to glide along on top of the water, not down in it. In addition, we were delayed getting underway and started out so late in the evening that it was near dark when we climbed aboard and got underway.

A SCARY START

After just eight and a half miles, we ran into our first big problem, and the words "ran into" are most appropriate. In the dark, we could see a large bridge ahead. There is very little traffic on the Alabama River today; there was close to none back in those days. A green light identifying the center of a channel is usually under bridges over navigable waterways. Apparently, they didn't bother about aids to navigation; certainly there would be no boats in this area at night.

On the Highway 31 bridge that night there was no light, but we didn't need to worry about passing through the deepest water in the center of the channel because we were in a canoe and the water would be plenty deep enough anywhere.

Too late, we discovered that work was being done on the bridge and large planks extended on either side of the bridge, across the river just a few inches above the surface of the water. When to bow touched the wood, the strong current carried us sideways into the planks, pinning us against the wood and coming close to tipping us over for an ignominious start to our venture.

It was also, quite dangerous. If the water had been two feet lower the canoe would have been carried under and we would all have been struck head on by the big wooden planks. Pushing the canoe sideways against the current to get away from the planks, we slowly made it to the opening under the bridge. Even this was terrifying because the pressure against the hull kept the canoe pinned against the planks until the moment when the current's force against the bow suddenly reached the strength necessary to twist the bow suddenly downstream and the stern up into the current. All this in the pitch black dark.

THE LONG WAY AROUND

There is a huge bend in the river called Durant Bend. Looking at a map the strip of land between to two paths of the river appears so small that you would be tempted to get out and portage your canoe and supplies to the other side. It is, however, 1,027 feet across and the river's route is 5.4 miles. We hated having to go 25 times as far, but had to do so.

BLOODY SUNDAY

At Selma, you pass under the Edmund Pettus Bridge, sadly made famous during the Civil Rights Movement. The confrontation on the bridge precipitated the Civil Rights Voting Act and became the starting point of the Selma to Montgomery March a few weeks later. If you are driving or walking over the bridge, it conjures up bad memories of how blacks were beaten on "Bloody Sunday." It is sad that more people do not get to see it from the water, because the bridge's large graceful arch is beautiful from below, and the old, largely abandoned, brick buildings that sit on the cliff above the water are interesting even though they are in sad need of restoration.

ALABAMA STATE CAPITAL

In my handwritten-in-pencil diary of the trip, I wrote about our arrival in Cahaba, the early capital of Alabama seventeen miles downstream from Selma, where I wrote the "the entire population" showed up to welcome us ashore. The only problem is that my next sentence read "The entire population showed up to welcome us. He said…" You may need to read those last sentence fragments again.

When people see pictures of White Bluff, 25 miles downstream from Selma, they find it hard to believe that the high limestone cliffs they are seeing are in the largely-flat land of south Alabama. There is a dirt road along the top, but no way to reach a spot on the other bank where you can see the cliffs from below. The bluff is spectacular now, but was much more so before the dam downstream made the water much higher.

THE DELTA

Unlike today, when you see lots of houses, some boats and many people along the river, we saw hardly a soul for nine days. The river was very interesting (it still is today, although less so than it was then) and deserted. During the second week we reached the large area known as the Delta. It is claimed to be the second largest Delta in the country, second only to that of the Mississippi River. It is about 28 miles long and about 6 miles wide at its widest point. Navigation is tricky because the river keeps being joined by other rivers and then splitting into many more rivers and little creeks as it flows down into Mobile Bay and finally into the Gulf of Mexico. At one point I tried to go ashore and found myself stuck in thick mud up to my knees. Trying to get unstuck and back into the still-overloaded and very tippy canoe (no pun intended, Mr. Tyler) proved to be quite challenging.

LIFTOFF

At some point later, Sterling had to go to the bathroom. Without having to get overly graphic, it was not something that could be done from the canoe. We finally spotted on the left a small patch of what appeared to be dry ground, about 20 feet long and maybe 15 feet wide. I aimed the canoe's bow up onto the shore and Sterling climbed out. As luck would have it, there was a large log conveniently lying across the small strip of land, so Sterling dropped his pants and sat down with his bare ass hanging out over the log. A few seconds later, I remember seeing him leap like a rocket into the air. He went in an instant from sitting down to having his feet a foot off the ground. No, the log was *not* an alligator, but lurking behind the log was a coiled-up snake.

Porter, being the naturalist and renowned medical scientist that he became, killed the snake. I have a picture of Porter's holding the snake by the tail with his left hand. The snake looked strange, with all sorts of bulges in his body so Porter, in his inimitable fashion, proceeded to dissect the snake. Lo and behold, the autopsy revealed that the snake had been unable to move because it had, apparently quite recently, devoured a much larger snake, weighting the winning snake down.

In those days, the rule for treating snakebite was that someone had to make crosswise cuts at the point of the bite and suck the venom out. Our immediate response was that, had this been required, Sterling would have been a dead man because we were at least a full day's travel from the nearest civilization. Despite the overloaded canoe, we entered Mobile Bay, canoed east along the shoreline and pulled out at Daphne, Alabama on August 29, nine days after leaving Montgomery.

THE ALABAMA SENIC RIVER TRAIL

It is interesting to note that, in October of 2008, a kayaker named Ardie Olson from Cumming, Georgia made it from the Georgia state line up near Atlanta all the way down the seven rivers and three creeks to the Gulf of Mexico, 631 miles, in just 12 ½ days. The previous record had been 42 days. This route is what in June of 2008 became known as "The Alabama Scenic River Trail." My first cousin's husband, Charlie Doster, had offered a prize of $10,000 to the paddler who would make the fastest time over the entire route of the Trail. I had designed the Trail's intricate route through the beautiful narrow and totally natural Delta and served as Vice President.

As Ardie neared the end of his trip, he needed to be sure he followed the complex route I had selected for the ASRT to wind its way through all of the small and beautiful creeks in the Delta instead of the several big uninteresting rivers, one of which, the Mobile River, carries big ships. He had no cell service in this area, but his wife could communicate from her car to him via VHF radio. I sat at my computer in Montgomery, where I was able to follow his path down through the Delta on a great satellite system at www.findmespot.com, I could see exactly where he was, tell his wife by cell phone, so his wife could tell him by radio to do something like "about five hundred feet ahead, turn right into Bottle Creek."

It was eerie to see the dots on my computer as they showed his progress through the delta. I could see him reach the point and turn into the correct creek over and over again. The original ASRT 631-mile route includes seven rivers: the Coosa, Alabama, Mobile, Tensaw, Middle, Appalachee, and Blakeley Rivers and three beautiful little creeks: Bottle, Little Lizard and Big Lizard. This findmespot system, available on an annual subscription basis, has saved many lives and anyone planning a trip into the wilderness or any route where they might require rescue should pay to get it. It could save your life.

15 THE WRONG PLACE
At The Wrong Time (Twice)

When Pat and I first purchased the 55 foot long sailboat we lived on for a year and a half, *"Eagle,"* we had a frantic first couple of days. We had just sold our house in Dover, Massachusetts, and purchased the boat in Ft. Lauderdale, hiring crew for a fixed-date departure. Our house contained a huge amount of stuff, but Pat is a superb packer. As we were preparing to get our belongings boxed up for the movers, Pat's best friend died. She had to leave immediately and fly to Florida for the funeral, leaving me in shock. It came time to leave and I was far from finishing the job, but I had to head out. We met in Ft. Lauderdale and made the shopping trip to get food for five people for what was likely to be at least 10 days at sea. We may have set some sort of record, leaving the supermarket with 11 shopping carts, each piled high with stuff.

NORTHWARD BOUND
We sailed out of Fort Lauderdale, changed our course to intersect the Gulf Stream and headed north up the coast in the Atlantic. We were sailing on a broad reach on starboard tack which, when added to the current of the Stream, meant we could cover about 13 miles per hour. It is 166 miles up the coast to Cape Canaveral. The Kennedy Space Center is located just north of the tip of the Cape. The sailing charts of the area clearly show in purple a large restricted area in the ocean east of the Space Center.

About 2pm, as we were passing Cape Canaveral, we looked toward land and saw a large military helicopter flying very low to the water headed straight at us. It could not have been headed for anything but us. The copter, flying only about 15 feet above the water, circled our boat, dropping down close astern where they could read the name of our boat. In a few seconds a voice called out "Eagle, Eagle. This is Charley 4, do you copy?" I responded in the affirmative. The man announced that we were in a restricted area. We had thought we were well outside the area clearly shown on our chart. When I said that, he advised that the restriction was extended much farther out to sea when there is a Shuttle launch scheduled and there was one due to lift off right now. It was scheduled for about 2:15 so we apparently had caused mission control to put the countdown on hold.

The man on the radio then asked for our speed, destination and bearing. He certainly could tell both from his instruments, but he asked anyway. When I replied he told me to hold for a minute while he talked with Mission Control. A few minutes later he ordered us to hold our current course and speed. Moments later we saw the enormous blast of the shuttle lifting off the launch pad. I had seen a nighttime launch from NASA's viewing station, but this was a perspective few get to see. The Shuttle curved southeast into the air above and slightly behind us. We relaxed and kept sailing, but soon learned why we were a concern. There were two extremely loud bangs when the Shuttle's 153 foot long external fuel tanks, weighing 66,000 pounds each even when empty, hit the water.

We had a beautiful sail up the coast, going in the IntraCoastal Waterway from Beaufort, North Carolina to Norfolk, Virginia (avoiding having to round Cape Hatteras), then back out in the Atlantic direct to Newport, Rhode Island, through the Cape Cod Canal, reaching Marblehead, Massachusetts (17 miles north of Boston) in just 7 days. Even with stops in Beaufort and Newport, we averaged 213 miles per day. The most remarkable moment was getting a cell phone call about 100 miles offshore as we passed New York on a direct course from Norfolk to Newport. It paid to have an antenna 69 feet in the air.

AGAIN, THE WRONG PLACE AT A REALLY BAD TIME

My wife had to play in a state tennis championship in Macon, Georgia and borrowed my large Mercedes 420SEL sedan to take some of her teammates, leaving me with her tiny Mazda RX7. It was a two seater, but a really small and light one.

One night after a concert, I had to host a going away party for our excellent Associate Conductor, Scott Peck, who was leaving us to be conductor of the Mobile Symphony in Alabama (where he still is at the time of this writing). The party was in my old favorite Garibaldi Restaurant, on Congress Street at City Market in downtown Savannah. It was a fun evening and the party ran on and on. It was midnight before we shut down and I headed home. From Congress Street I took the first right onto Jefferson and as I approached the intersection with the main street, Broughton, I discovered the intersection and the part of Broughton to my left were blocked by at least a hundred young black men who must have been in the nightclub a hundred feet away to my left on Broughton.

I couldn't drive into or over them. Several started toward me. My doors were locked and they did not appear threatening. My heart began to beat a lot faster when they simply lifted the car up in the air and began to rock it side to side. At least they were laughing and finally put me back down. The next day I learned that a man had been shot and killed at in that area at 2:30am that night.

YOUV'E HEARD ABOUT DRIVERLESS CARS

Pat was playing a match in Macon, having parked my car with the sunscreen blocking the windshield. She had parked it, but had forgotten to put it in "Park." The lady in the tennis center office said she looked out and saw this car driving through the parking lot with the windshield blocked. It curved downhill and crashed backward into another car. There was no damage to my big heavy car, but the cost of the repairs to the Toyota belonging to the friend of Pat's was $1,200.

16 A CLOSED MOUTH

Gathers No Feet (not quite The Rolling Stones)

All during my childhood in Alabama, my family owned about half of a large building in the first block of Dexter Avenue, the main street in the middle of downtown Montgomery. I inherited my first share, a sixth, when my aunt died. The Weil family owned almost all of the other half. A small share had been purchased by Bill Nicrosi and Irving Winter, thinking they were getting a bargain.

The two-story building was large, stretching all the way through the block from Dexter Avenue to Washington Street. These days it is always referred to as the old Belk department store building. During my early childhood the tenant was F. W. Woolworth, a company that today is hard to imagine because their focus was on items that sold five or ten cents; hence the name "Five and Dime Store."

When Woolworth moved out, my Dad succeeded in getting Belk, a southern chain of department stores, as the tenant. They had been there for years, and when they wanted to expand, dad had a contractor excavate what became the basement. Our rent had a base, plus a percentage of sales, so adding space would benefit us in the long run. I don't know how they did it, but the contractor was able to dig out the large space directly underneath, somehow allowing Belk to stay in business on the first and second floors while his team was excavating and constructing the basement. When my Dad died in 1972 at the age of 82, the store became a major source of income for my mother. We were nervous because only a couple of years remained on the lease, businesses had begun to flee downtown Montgomery and shopping malls had just begun to sprout up in the suburbs.

I don't remember exactly, but the share owned by Irving Winter and Bill Nicrosi (one of my Godfathers) was quite small. Irving said he wanted his money out and tried to get us to buy their share. Their asking price was not much too high and we were not about to pay it. Bill and Irving went to court and got a ruling that the entire building was to be "sold by division." I don't think that title is a good description of a law that states if a person owns a minority interest and the other owners refuse to buy him out, the court can order that the entire building be sold at auction

What should we do? What could we do? At least I knew that there was a high risk that Belk would move out when their lease expired and that, if they did, we would be left with an empty building, one into which we had recently put a lot of money. I also knew that the insurance on an empty building was much more expensive than on an occupied one. I felt that my mother simply could not afford the risk of higher expenses and no rental income. I flew to Montgomery so Mom and I could meet with our lawyer, John Mathews (who was, incidentally, my other Godfather), to discuss the situation and develop a course of action. If we bought the entire building, we would have to come up with a good bit of cash and run the risk of owning an empty building.

THE SALE

On the appointed day, March 4, 1976, John Mathews went down and stood on the old Montgomery County Courthouse steps to represent Mom and me at the auction. A lawyer representing the Weil family was there, and Irving Winter was there on his own behalf, accompanied by his son. The court-ordered auction got underway, and Irving was bidding. Here was somebody that had to have his money out of his small share of the ownership bidding to buy the whole thing. It was obvious that he was attempting to drive the price up, so that he would realize as much from the sale as he could.

The bidding stopped. We were told by John that Irving had a classic look of panic on his face. The classic words "Going, going, gone,…sold to Irving Winter" were announced. John told us that Irving's son was quite mad at his dad and jumping up and down.

As it happened the Weil family had determined that they would not bid beyond amount that the Clarks had, through no collusion, decided upon the exact same amount. What a coincidence. Belk did close down and the building sat there empty for almost four decades….a lot of insurance, property tax and maintenance cost and no income whatsoever. Years later, Irving told me at a party at Joan Loeb's that Bill Nicrosi had gone in on the purchase with him, but Bill 's share meant he owed the bank $50,000 that he didn't have. Irving ended up having to pay the entire amount. We think he got his just desserts (yes, I know I have already used those words, but I will use them one more time much later). Years later the building was purchased by an old friend, John Bowman. Downtown is beginning to make a strong comeback, but there are lots of empty buildings and until 2019 this was still one of the largest. At long last, it is returning to use, with commercial space on the ground floor and apartments above.

You may be amused to know that the source of the title for this chapter dates all the way back to a proverb in 1546, "A rolling stone gathers no moss." In 1948, a *"Rolling Stone"* became a Muddy Waters song, and was later, and most famously, used by Brian Jones in naming his group comprised of himself, Mick Jagger and Keith Richards.

The truth of the matter is my family owed Irving a huge debt of gratitude. We had not been thinking of selling the building and would not have faced this question had Irving and Bill not forced us to do so. We would have lost a lot of money. Irving, we owe you a belated "Thank you.

17 THE BOX

A Gift From Home

Harvard University, with a few exceptions such as The Business School and the Medical School, is squeezed into Cambridge, Massachusetts, a close-in suburb of Boston. Freshmen at Harvard live in antique brick dormitories that surround the old original area of the college, "Harvard Yard," usually referred to by students as simply "The Yard." Founded in 1636, Harvard is the oldest college in the United States, and the historic area is quite crowded by current campus standards. With the exception of The Yard, there is almost none of what a less-historic college would consider a campus. It is almost entirely comprised of buildings packed tightly around narrow old city streets, crowded with parked cars.

Cambridge was so far left politically that my friends and I frequently referred to it as "The People's Republic of Cambridge." When asked to list the major communist governments in the world the typical answer was the Soviet Union, China, Cuba and Cambridge. Sadly, at least to me, Cambridge and Harvard have drifted much farther to the extreme left, as personified by Elizabeth Warren.

FRESHMEN

There are two small freshman dorms that sit off the main area of The Yard in a small grassy corner of the freshman dorm area, with the buildings just 20 feet from the heavy traffic on Massachusetts Avenue. Upon arrival at the start of my freshman year, I was assigned to one of these: Lionel Hall B-31, which meant it was on the third floor of the B entrance, one of the building's two entrances. The other of the pair of twin dorms was Mower, which also had two entrances, but had a basement in which the superintendent's office was located.

As a naïve young kid from Alabama, I did not know to arrive and check in at the earliest possible time on the first day allowed and claim one of the two single rooms in B-31. As a result, I got last choice and had to share a double. Also, because of arriving last, I was stuck with the upper bunk.

My roommates were a great bunch of guys. Pete Bragdon was an avid hockey player from Exeter who went on to become the headmaster of an excellent prep school, Governor Dummer (bad name, it was for smart kids, and the school eventually shortened the name). Roger Peirce was a handsome, active (and highly successful) girl chaser, who went on to become a partner of a major CPA firm in Milwaukee. Dave Davidson, my roommate, went to California. I used to enjoy watching him play the violin on his brother's annual Christmas TV Special, which included all of John Davidson's family.

Coming from a public high school in Montgomery, Harvard may not have been terrifying, but it certainly was intimidating. I was suddenly injected into the midst of hundreds of guys who had gone to top-rated private prep schools and, as a result, already had many friends who were also in the freshman class. Many had family names that made it obvious they were from some of the richest families throughout the country. Almost all were extremely smart.

MAIL DELIVERY

Mail for residents of Lionel was put in mailboxes at each entrance, one small mailbox for each room. The arrival of packages was noted by recipient's name on a piece of paper posted on a bulletin board near the mailboxes. Not expecting a package, I did not look at the list and nobody bothered to alert me that my name had been on the list for weeks.

One day there was very loud banging on the door. It was the Superintendent and he was hopping mad. I guess the better words would be "uncontrollably furious." "Livid" might be the best word. He was so agitated that it was difficult to understand what he was screaming about. When he calmed down enough to be understood, he demanded to know why I had not picked up my package and ordered that I get it immediately. This did not make sense. So, what if I was late picking up my package? I knew why once Dave Davidson and I reached the package pickup point in the basement of Mower Hall.

Boxes for people in Mower A and B were in the basement on the floor against the wall straight ahead, followed to the right by boxes for students in Lionel A and finally B, with my stairway's packages assigned to the spot closest to the door into the Superintendent's office.

When we opened the outside door into the basement of Mower, the stench was bad. When we got downstairs the smell was really unbelievable. It was the single worst smell I encountered in my entire life. We saw that a good portion of the brick wall between the hallway and the Superintendent's office had been smashed down. There were bricks all over the place. We were told that the buildings maintenance team had sledge hammered down part of the wall, starting at the door. The superintendent told me that they assumed there must be a dead animal in the wall. After knocking down a few feet of wall, they had to move the Lionel B boxes and, when they moved mine, the stench moved with it.

Ordered to do so, I started from upstairs, took a deep breath, ran down, grabbed the package addressed to me and rushed up the stairs to the open air. It is important to note that this horrendous smell was somehow making its way out of a sealed cardboard box. When I tried to carry it, the box was below my nose and there is no way that the written word can describe how bad it was. I carried the box, sat it down in the small courtyard between Holden Chapel and Harvard Hall and ran away twenty feet or so before inhaling.

After taking a few deep breaths, I ran back, picked up the package and, for some reason I don't remember, decided to move it out into the middle of the main Yard, on a crosswalk in front of the statue of John Harvard. This trip required deep breaths and running back and fourth. During those movements, I managed to read that the box was correctly addressed to me and that the name and return address was that of my mother in Alabama. I could not figure out what in the world she could have sent me.

The box looked innocuous enough. We later learned that this was intended to make me believe it was a gift from home. Under the circumstances, I am not sure why I decided that I had to open the box. It was going to be awful, but I had to know what my mother could have sent that would cause the smell. I cut open the cardboard box and folded the top flaps open. If the stench was awful with the box closed, it was beyond belief once the contents were exposed to the air. Sorties to the box began to require running farther away from it.

A Harvard Policeman arrived but did not want to stand very close. He did begin to direct people to other crosswalks.

THE CONTENTS

I knew it was bad when I saw a snake curled up on the top of what appeared to be a box of horrible looking gooey yellow cheese. Digging a bit (again between runs for air) I determined that the box contained a bunch of badly-decomposed large dead rats that had been disguised under what had originally been a layer of cookies. The intent had been for me to open the box from my mother, see the cookies and not even discover until later the rats hidden below. The campus policeman pulled out his radio and called for a Buildings and Grounds Department truck to come pick up the box, a request that took some explaining on his part. By this time, the pedestrian traffic through The Yard had increased substantially, the cause of which was discovered later.

THE TRUCK

After what seemed like an eternity, the gate at the north end of The Yard opened, a truck with high sides drove into the Yard and stopped near Harvard Hall, slightly uphill and directly across from where the odiferous box sat. The policeman walked up and talked to the driver, who told him to have me toss the box into the back of the truck.

It took about three moves to get the box up the hill. When I reached the truck, the driver told me to throw the box over the high side of the flatbed truck. My guess is the top of the side was about eight feet above ground, so it was very scary trying to make the toss. I did not want to miss the top of the truck and have the rats splash back down onto me.

With a huge heave, the box rose into the air, coming apart as the gooey mess passed over the top rail of the truck. I managed the toss without out getting any of the contents on me. The driver, having no idea what was in the box, had not bothered to mention that there was a guy sitting in the back of the truck. As the horrendous mess fell into the truck, the man cleared the other side in one leap, landing hard but uninjured on the pavement. Needless to say, he was quite furious. We wondered how he got home or wherever he had to go to get washed up first.

A CONFESSION

I do not remember how we determined the guilty party who had sent the box from Montgomery, but we did. There was at least one obvious suspect. That was a good guess and it proved to be correct. Some friends had gone out shooting rats in the city dump and thought it would be cute to send them to me. They put them in the box and covered them with cookies so, when opened, it would look like a gift.

The primary culprit was a man who became extremely successful as a medical research scientist, Dr. Porter Anderson, and his close friend, Sterling Culpepper, who I knew was a co-conspirator, claim to this day that they did not put the small snake in the box. He must have been swallowed alive by one of the rats, climbed out after the rat was shot and placed in the box, and then died after a while in the box. It was fifty years later that a third person, Jim Scott, admitted that he had been out shooting rats that night.

MOWER HALL

Weeks later, Harvard billed my parents for rebuilding the wall. The bill was $800, which does not sound like much today, but in today's dollars it would be $7,644. It was, at the time, a large bill. As neither I nor my parents had caused the problem and the damages, we ended up not having to pay.

ANOTHER GIFT?

Don't give up yet; there is a sequel. A year later a very small box addressed to me arrived in the mail. It is three inches long and less than an inch wide and deep. We were suspicious. As sophomores, Roberto Juan van Tienhoven, Doug Carver and I were now living in E Entry of an upperclassmen's dorm, Adams House. We opened the small box, but could not figure out what was inside. At least there was no smell.

The object was hard, round (about three quarters of an inch in diameter) and about three inches long. No, it is not what you are thinking. After a thorough inspection, we determined that the part on one end was a fingernail. Porter, at that time studying at the Harvard Medical School, had, literally, given me the finger. He had removed it while studying a corpse. Nice gift! Gives new meaning to "Giving somebody the finger." I did not send him a thank you.

EPILOGUE
We had a telephone in our room, as did almost everyone we knew. The cheap guys on the floor below us in F Entry (out of the back door of my bedroom) wanted to share the cost and put one phone in the stairway between their two rooms. They put the phone on a small table on the landing. This meant the people who slept in the rear single rooms of E Entry and all in F Entry got to listen to the phone whenever it rang and, too many instances had to listen to the conversations that ensued.

I decided that the best use of the finger was to give it to these guys. I snuck down the stairs in F and placed the fingertip in the dial of their telephone. Hope readers are old enough to remember when there were circular dials with holes, before touch buttons. The only name I remember in that room was David Papermaster. We never said anything, but we always wondered if they had figured out we had given them the finger. It certainly gave new meaning to the act.

JIM SCOTT
One of the culprits, Jim Scott, became a very successful lawyer and real estate developer in Montgomery, but he is best known for his incredible gardens overlooking Lake Martin. His magnificent and whimsical gardens have been featured on national TV and in about a dozen magazines. This was not just mentions in magazines, there were long articles with loads of pictures. The large gardens are a unique mix of beautiful plants, many bridges and, complex design and a good sense of humor.

Jim's wife, Vivian, who died a few years ago, had been a high school classmate of mine and a good friend. Jim admits that for his first date with Vivian he had taken her out to the city dump to shoot rats. How many young girls do you know would appreciate that? Jim had a fun evening but doubted she would want to go out with him again. He got up his nerve and asked. She said she had enjoyed Jim's company, so with some trepidation she agreed to go, but with just one condition.....that it not involve shooting rats again.

WHEN DID THIS HAPPEN?
The rat event was Thursday, December 1,1955, identifiable because it was the day the Harvard Freshman Union building where we had our meals, had suffered a large fire. I knew that the foot traffic in the yard picked up substantially that afternoon.

MEMORY
Despite the fire, it will always be remembered by me as "The Day of the Rats."

THE HASTY PUDDING CLUB
Yes, I know, but I could not find any other place to put this story. It just is here with the one about rats and fingers at Harvard.

The club, whose full name is The Hasty Pudding Institute of 1770, is the oldest college social club in the country and is located near Harvard Square at 12 Holyoke Street. It was the first club at Harvard to allow women as members and it is by far the largest club. One very interesting feature as you enter and start up the stairs is a wall covered with pictures of the five club members who had gone on to become Presidents of the United States. The most recent was JFK.

Long before Heritage Travel became the official agency for Harvard University, we handled the travel of Hasty Pudding Theatricals. At the end of their hilarious annual show's run in the clubhouse theater, the show moved for a few performances.

The sets were shipped to Bermuda and the manager filled out the country's forms that, in order to avoid paying the heavy import duty, required him to swear that they would be taken back out of the country. At the end, he thought they could save on shipping back to the US by just sending them to the garbage.

On the phone, the manager told me he figured that they would not be charged for "importing" anything into the country because the stuff had been destroyed. Being unable to prove the sets were being taken out of the country, as the letter of the law required, the Club had to pay the duty. He called me in Massachusetts but I could not help.

Expensive mistake.

18 TIDBITS
Miscellaneous

ARRESTED FOR MURDER
Certainly, if you live in Boson you remember the infamous serial killer who was nicknamed "The Boston Strangler." He strangled a dozen women throughout Boston. Albert di Salvo was finally caught and convicted, but the city had lived in terror for a year while the murders continued.

One of the last murders was committed upstairs in an apartment over the Paramount Deli on the west side of Charles Street between Chestnut and Mt. Vernon. Two days after that murder was discovered, I was walking the girl I was dating, Linda Hansen, back to her apartment a block north on the other side of Charles Street. She had to stop and pick up something at a market and I had gone ahead, climbed the stone steps from the street and, because I wanted to wait inside, I rang the door buzzer for her apartment.

A roommate was home. When I buzzed, she pushed the button to unlock the main door, letting me into the building. I waited for Linda. When I didn't come up the stairs the roommate panicked, chained her apartment door shut, climbed down the fire escape in the rear onto West Cedar Street and called the police. Linda came home and we climbed the stairs to her apartment. She used her key and unlocked the door, but we were stuck in the hallway because the door was chained from the inside. Linda called through the door to her roommate but got no response.

We had not been there but a few minutes before we heard the downstairs door open and saw eight Boston policemen come charging up the stairs. They grabbed me (fairly hard I might add). They thought they had finally caught the infamous serial killer. It took a while, but they finally realized with Linda standing there beside me, it did not take long for them to accept the fact that their hopes of catching the mass murderer were not coming true.

Sorry I was such a disappointment to the Boston police. It was several more months before they caught Di Salvo.

SLEEPING WITH ME AND I DIDN'T KNOW IT?
Shortly after moving back to Montgomery, Pat and I were talking to a group of people standing in a circle at a party. One of them was a prominent Montgomery resident, Carol Ballard, who is married to Major General Bowen Ballard.

To my shock, Carol told the whole group that she bet that she had "spent more nights in Thornton Clark's bedroom than anybody but Pat." People were in shock, but I knew the reason. Carol's parents, the Willises, had purchased the house I had grown up at 915 East Fairview Avenue in Montgomery. She had been assigned to "my bedroom." She got some laughs once everybody recovered from shock.

SAILING IN BOSTON HARBOR

Boat designer Ray Hunt is best known for his great design known as The Boston Whaler, an almost unsinkable outboard powerboat that has been around for more than 50 years.

Before that, Ray had designed two medium-sized racing sailboats, the 110 Class and the 210 Class, both taking early advantage of plywood construction. They were excellent "one design" racing boats, meaning every hull had to be as close as possible to identical. The skill of the skipper determined the winners, not the amount of money they had to buy the fastest boat.

Every year in the fall, the South Boston Yacht Club hosted the McKee Trophy, a series of races held in Boston Harbor for 210s. The series became very popular, attracting participants from up and down the Massachusetts coast. My friend, Dick Kirk, offered to help me sail my boat from Marblehead 19 miles down the coast and through Boston Harbor to the yacht club.

We had a pretty late-afternoon sail down the coast past Boston Light and into the harbor, but then the wind died. We still had five miles to go and it was getting dark. Boston Harbor has numerous aids to navigation, floating marks primarily delineating the main channel for the large cargo ships that go in and out frequently. A century ago shallow water was filled in to build Logan Airport, now one of the busiest airports in the country. The shipping channel wraps around the airport.

Our sailboat had no engine and no lights, so we were at risk of getting run over by a ship if we were in the channel when one came along. We had been expecting to reach our destination well before dark, so we didn't even have a flashlight. We could barely see and, early in my racing years, I was not the least bit familiar with the large and complex harbor. We could not read our chart in the dark. A chart is like a map, showing you the location of floating navigation marks and the numbers and colors that identified them.

The water close to the southeastern corner of the airport is not dredged for ships and we had no idea how deep it was, but we gradually worked our way over near the end of runway 33 (meaning the direction of planes landing on the runway is 330 degrees), where planes were landing from the southeast. Planes at a busy airport always seem to land frequently, but that night it took forever between planes. We would hold the chart up in the air and try to study the marks in the few seconds when we benefited from the landing lights of each plane as it passed close overhead.

We still had to venture out into the shipping lane and we were barely moving. Getting to the yacht club was a whole lot more exciting than the racing, but the racing did have two interesting developments.

The top 210 skipper in Boston, Mark Bromfield, had a big lead in one of the races. A freighter was passing the skyline of downtown Boston, turning and heading out of the harbor. Mort had to try to get across the bow of the ship or turn back toward his competitors, give up all of his lead and cross astern of the ship. He gambled....and lost.

No, he wasn't hit by the ship, but the freighter had to go into reverse, blare its horns to signal collision imminent, and let Mort cross its bow. The ship's captain radioed the Harbor Police who radioed the yacht club's race committee and Mort was disqualified.

The really-strange event occurred during the next day's race when my boat's co-owner, Larry Burckmyer, was at the helm as we raced on port tack eastward past Spectacle Island on our starboard side. Our other crew, Kitty Sides (later Mrs. Charles Flather) and I were sitting high up on the portside deck. Beating to weather and sitting on the high side, we were looking down into the water on the starboard side.

Kitty and I both gasped as we saw pass right beside our boat what appeared to be a man's body floating face down in the water. It was only in view for a second and we were not sure of what we had seen, but when the race was over and we got to a radio, we notified the harbor police. A short while later they pulled the body out from close to Spectacle Island where we had seen it.

ALABAMA SHAKESPEARE FESTIVAL

This one doesn't involve me, but it is funny, even for those who don't live in Montgomery. Red Blount was a major contractor worldwide, heavily in the Middle East, who served as US Postmaster General. He donated tens of millions in cash and beautiful land on Vaughn Road for the Blount Cultural Park which includes the beautiful Alabama Shakespeare Festival building and the Montgomery Museum of Fine Arts.

I do have a special interest in the ASF because me first cousin, Juliette Persons Doster, had been President of the festival when it was in Anniston, Alabama had had gotten Carolyn Blount on her board of directors, leading to the magnificent park. Juliette was been on the ASF board for 47 years until her death.

For some reason, Red wanted to have black swans in the park's ponds and dispatched his second in command at Blount Construction to go to England and try to locate and purchase some black swans. The man he sent, Joe McInnis, flew to England to talk with the expert, who asked Joe why he had come to England seeking black swans when the leading breeder of black swans with Black Swans for sale was right there in Alabama.

Juliette's daughter, Juliette the third, was an outstanding runner, finishing third in the Stockholm, Sweden Marathon on August 15, 1981.

ONE OF MY MANY MISTAKES

Back in fall of 1969 a good friend, Tom Kershaw, called and asked me to come see a building he was interested in buying. He was looking for investors, only needing $5,000 from each. I went to look.

It was an extremely nice looking four-story private residence with a basement, where the bar was to be and a beautiful roof deck overlooking Boston's Public Garden (famous for its popular rides in Swan Boats). It was a truly marvelous location on Beacon Street. When I was given the tour of the place it was easy to see the potential. I was tempted but I knew Tom and his partner, Jack Veasy, had been roommates at the Harvard Business School and I thought that, if there were any profits from the bar, those two would drink them up. At the time, I did not know how much they had matured and settled down. The pub opened on December 5, 1969. Of course, as you may have guessed by now, the bar became "Cheers" and the rest is history. The bar had become a great neighborhood hangout for me and it truly lived up to the line in the "Cheers" TV's opening song: "where everybody knows your name." The Hampshire House is at the corner of Beacon Street and Brimmer Street, where I lived a block away at 50 Brimmer. It could not have been more convenient and I went there often.

The actual bar was, and still is, much smaller than the set in the TV show. The flight of stairs down from the sidewalk and the green awning over the steps leading up to the building's main entrance are still exactly as shown on TV. It was a complete accident that a man from NBC sent to check out possible locations stumbled across the place. Once the TV show started, business took off like a shot. Even after "Cheers" went off the air, Tom was still selling millions of dollars of beer mugs and tee shirts. Tom went on to be Chairman of the Boston Convention and Visitors Bureau and President of the National Restaurant Association. Bet you can guess the name of Tom's large powerboat. It is "Cheers," painted in gold leaf on the stern of his yacht in script identical to the show.

ANOTHER BOATING NAME

Back in 1972, a small group of male sailboat racers on Cape Cod held a a very small and informal annual race from Hyannis across the sound to Nantucket Island on Memorial Day weekend. It began to attract boats from near and far, reaching the point at which it required newspaper coverage, and that is where the problem began.

Local newspapers were hesitant to report the race results because the name of the regatta was too easily recognized. There is still some question as to the derivation of the word, whether it stemmed from the fog off of Nantucket or the better known story about the people in desperate straits in the early days out west who were anxiously awaiting being saved by an Indian tribe named the Fugawi. The question was "Where the Fugawi?" I trust there is not one reader that doesn't understand what you re sawing if you just pronounce the sentence "Where the fug are we?"

Even Senator Ted Kenndy loved to race in the event every year and I bet he knew the true derivation. It is sad that when you search on Fugawi you get so many, all inferior, variations of the story

BIRTHDAYS AND ANNIVERSARIES

Remembering people's birthdays and wedding anniversaries is fun and, in a surprising number of instances, highly beneficial to the person whose day you remember.

I did lead an unusual life, at least partially the result of staying a bachelor until 32 hours short of reaching age 52. I had the usual roommates and friends in college and for several years after graduation. In addition, I ran ski houses for 18 in Vermont and adjacent summer houses (5 guys in one, 6 girls in the other), overlooking the harbor in Marblehead, Massachusetts. As a result, I ended up as an usher in 39 weddings.

Over the years I received many "thank yous" from men who were saved because they had forgotten it was their own anniversary. They were able to buy a gift and avoid being shot, divorced or at the very least, made to sleep on the sofa. On two occasions, both the husband and the wife had forgotten that it was their anniversary. That is *extremely* hard to believe….but true. I have left out the names to protect the guilty.

THE THEFT OF A TREE

There is a more far-fetched story about stealing, but this one also is true. Pat and I were asleep in our home at 430 Quinobequin Road in Waban, Massachusetts, when our Scotty, Bitsy, begin to bark for no identifiable reason at one o'clock in the morning.

The next day, when I was in our driveway headed to work, I discovered the cause of Bitsy's barking. Someone had come into our front yard and sawed off at the base a beautiful Blue Spruce tree that I had spent about ten years nursing it to its current size and symmetry. Bitsy had been awakened by the chain saw, but even if we had discovered what was happening, it would have been too late to save the tree. I bet they were able to sell it for a lot to some business. Appraisals were in the three thousand dollar range, but my insurance company claimed this theft was not covered. Sad, and extremely, irritating. It is unfortunate, but understandable, that someone would do this.

19 AN AUTOMOBILE RACE

Of Sorts, This One Was Hertz vs. Avis

In the early 1970s, when the airlines were ensnarled in travel agency automation wars, there was little going on in the hotel and car rental industries.

We wanted to do the same thing in the case of car rentals, so I approached both Hertz and Avis regarding our interest in installing their computer terminals in our office. Heritage was widely known in the travel industry as the leader in technology, but the car rental companies did not seem particularly interested because they could see the cost but could not identify any benefit to them, other than making Heritage happy. They would save a little employee time handling our reservations, but not enough to offset the cost of installing and maintaining the computer terminals. Eventually, both Avis and Hertz agreed to install their systems at Heritage. I picked a place where the two terminals would be side by side against a wall. We waited. Crates from each of the car rental companies finally arrived. After a long wait, both companies scheduled installation, both for the same day. The two installers went to work sitting on the floor next to each other. My phone began to ring, first a senior executive from one car rental company and then the other, over and over again throughout the morning. I would have to go get the company's installer to come talk directly with his headquarters. Having delayed for so long, both companies and their technicians were now frantic.

As it turned out Avis won the race, and within two hours we learned why it was important. The CEO of Avis at the time was Colin Marshall, who would go on to become Sir Colin Marshall as a result of his role as Chairman of British Airways. At a press conference that afternoon in New York, Colin announced that Avis was once again the leader in their industry, having been first to install a reservation computer system in a travel agency. He said "Avis was once again a leader in technology." The Hertz system became operational before Avis' press conference, but Colin was still able to make the claim and get the favorable publicity. The people at Hertz were furious, and my last call from their VP Sales that day once again asked me to get their technician on the phone. After what I assume was a pretty good chewing out from headquarters, the Hertz installer exploded with "If you had just left me alone to do my job, I could have finished first." Avis got the media coverage. After several months of waiting to start and a frantic morning, Avis had won the "race" by just 18 minutes.

20 ANOTHER BIG FOOTBALL GAME

This Time It Was Southern Cal vs. Alabama

I was headed to San Francisco to race in the International One-Design sailboat racing World Championships. The trip was planned to include a stop in Los Angeles to meet with Russ Decker, who was, at the time, Chairman of the Board of Woodside. My old home state's team, the University of Alabama, was to play the number one ranked University of Southern California in Memorial Coliseum that Saturday.

Russ was an avid USC fan and apparently had very good connections. He offered to get tickets for me and my date for the trip. I was dating Sunny Hoppe, who was from Dallas, and still lives near there. Until writing this, I had thought her name was "Sunne." We had met in Dallas because she owned a small travel agency there. It is not an exaggeration to say that she was drop dead gorgeous with a vivacious personality. Her figure would have put many of the Playboy centerfolds to shame. Walking into a bar with her would (and frequently did) cause heads to spin.

SUNNY

Sunny had flown to Boston for one of the biggest events of the country's Bi-Centennial, the annual concert by The Boston Pops beside the Charles River on the Fourth of July, 1976. The bicentennial was going to be such a special Fourth of July; a huge crowd was on hand. Reports said the audience was close to a million, many of whom had camped out days earlier to ensure a good spot in the audience. In addition to the hundreds of thousands in the park along the river, there were people filling Storrow Drive and looking down from buildings all around the area. The Cambridge side of the river normally attracts a good crowd and the Charles River is full of boats anchored for the concert.

Sunny and I had been in Marblehead racing my sailboat that afternoon. It was awkward because my good and faithful crew could not stand her foul language, protested that after years of dedicated work, they would quit racing with me if I brought her along again. We didn't finish the race until late, so we were lucky to find a parking place in Boston.

I guess there must have been occasions when Sunny was not provocatively attired, but this was *not* one of them. The sight was sufficient to cause the men near the front of the crowd to part, making way for her to walk through to the front and center directly below the stage in front of the conductor. It was a great place to be for that historic moment. The concert's finale, always Tchaikovsky's powerful 1812 Overture, is performed with the addition of incredibly loud army howitzer's firing and nearby church bells ringing on cue to accompany the orchestra's celebration of Napoleon's army being repulsed by the Russians. Even though future performances will not rival 1976 for many years, the annual Boston's Pops concert on the Fourth of July is an event that should not be missed.

USC

Anyway, Sunny was stunning, and no less so on the afternoon of the USC-Alabama game on October 6, 1977. She had flown from Dallas to meet me for a long week in California. The USC fans were even more exuberant than usual because their team was ranked number one in the nation and they were about to beat the renowned Alabama. When we arrived, we discovered that the seats Russ had given us were front and center in the USC former football players section. Russ must have paid lots of money. The tickets were not just great seats, we were seated beside one of the all-time greats of USC football, two-time All-American end, Marlin McKeever. Marlin lettered for USC three years, 1958 through 1960, was an NFL first round draft choice and went on to play 13 years in the NFL (12 for the LA Rams), receiving numerous awards for outstanding play.

When Sunny and I were seated and Marlin learned that I was from Alabama, he stood up and turned to face his buddies, all former USC football players, and said something like "This is my guest, Thornton Clark and his date. He's going to want to cheer for Alabama, so please don't give him any shit. OK?" Everyone laughed and agreed. The game got underway. They were going to have fun giving us grief because the USC Trojans were going to clobber the Alabama Crimson Tide, which was ranked #8. Marlin was next to me but did a lot of looking at Sunny while talking to me. Memorial Stadium was built many years ago for the Los Angeles Olympics. The stands were full of rabid USC fans, with a small contingent of Alabama fans relegated to the seats behind one corner of the end zone. I appeared to be the only Alabama supporter anywhere else.

THE GAME

To everyone's surprise, Alabama led 7 to 3 in the third quarter and then made a great goal line stand, preventing USC from getting a touchdown on several tries from the five-yard line. The Trojans did kick another field goal, making Alabama's lead just 7 to 6, but then Bama made an interception that led to another touchdown, making it 21 to 6 with just under 13 minutes left in the game. For USC, things were looking mighty bad. On their next possession, USC marched down the field, scoring a touchdown to make it 21 to 12. They went for a two-point conversion and got it, bringing the score to 21-14, leaving them just one touchdown and extra point behind.

It got down to where there were just 39 seconds left in the game. USC managed to score again, leaving Alabama in the lead, but only by one point, 21 to 20. Does USC go for a usually-easy kick for the extra point and a tie or try for the two point conversion and the win. They try for the win. USC's quarterback was tackled and was about to hit the ground with his body horizontal, falling backward, but he managed to throw a desperation pass toward the end zone for the score. His pass was intercepted by Alabama and run back past midfield. As I remember it, the Alabama player could have scored a touchdown, making it 27 to 20 but,, knowing the game was over and his team had won, he just stopped in the middle of the field and started to celebrate.

HOW TO CATCH A STAR

There is a little-known additional story about a great quarterback at the University of Alabama. The Universities renowned coach, Bear Bryant, had coached at Maryland. One day he received a call from his friend who was the new coach at Maryland, who told The Bear he should know about a great young player in Pennsylvania. Maryland, as a much lesser team, did not have a chance of recruiting this guy, so the coach gave Bear Bryant, who coached a team strong enough to recruit this guy, the name.

The man Bear Bryant learned about and recruited was Joe Namath.

21 EXTRAS
How To Meet Celebrities

When we were living in Savannah and John Berendt's best-selling novel, "*Midnight in the Garden of Good and Evil"* had just come out, generating a flood of tourists into the beautiful city. Residents had to take visitors around town to see of the many locales that were in "The Book." Most people find it hard to believe, but little old Savannah attracts so many tourists interested in the beautiful homes and the elegant squares that the volume justifies 33 different tour companies. On several of his visits, we got to meet John, who had graduated from Harvard many years after me.

MIDNIGHT IN THE GARDEN OF EVIL
After the book had been around for several years, it was announced that it would be made into a movie. Clint Eastwood was to be the director and advertisements came out in the Savannah newspaper looking for extras. My wife announced that she wanted to try to be hired as an extra, so we got dressed up, stopped in a church parking lot and took the required head-and-shoulders pictures of her on the way downtown. I thought it would be a waste of time, but reluctantly decided I might as well give it a try. There were hundreds of people in the line. Each person submitted their information, confirmed their availability whenever needed, and underwent a brief interview. To our amazement, we were both selected.

You would not be able to spot Pat in the Married Women's Card Club scene of the movie unless you knew the moment to look for her because the scene was rearranged to place the camera where she had been seated and she was relegated to the garden for the entire shoot. The great part was that Clint wanted a picture of the "Club members" on the steps of a great old home known as the "Granite Steps." The color picture was spread over two pages of Newsweek magazine, with Pat's blonde hair easily recognizable at the top of the stairs to the left of Clint Eastwood. You didn't see her in the movie, but we received calls from people who recognized her in Newsweek.

To see me in the movie, you would have to have a DVD and know the exact second to pause it. My face appears large and straight on in the scene at Mercer House when they are carrying the body out, but you simply cannot notice it at normal movie speed.

The interesting part, however, was the way my scene was filmed. The plan had been for the camera to face the front yard of Mercer House, with the back of my head and my left shoulder being up very close on the right, next to John Cusack, who played the lead in the movie. The assistants twice combed the back of my head and brushed my left shoulder. Hair and shoulder where due to be up close in the scene.

Eastwood decided to switch the scene and film it from the other direction. This required taking a lot of equipment apart and moving it from the street into the yard. I got to chat with Eastwood during the twenty minutes it took to rearrange the camera and all the related gear. Lots of people would pay to get to meet and talk with Eastwood and Cusack. Pat and I got paid, not much, but fun. What was funny was the fact that for that year's tax return income from being in the movie was our only "earned income."

I now have more appreciation for the millions of extras in films who follow directions. I failed, badly. If I had looked at the door of Mercer House I would have been close up, facing the camera throughout the duration of the shot. I could not resist the urge to look at the camera. As a result, you only see me if you look at the CD and move frame by frame to the point where my face showed just before it was "photo-shopped" out. If you get a good chance to be an extra, be sure to act correctly.

FORCES OF NATURE

Having done it once, I said "what the hell" and tried again, this time for what turned out to be a poor movie entitled "Forces of Nature." Here, things got even better. Pat likes to kid about my walking close to the camera through the train station, sitting on a bench and reading a newspaper, because my costume was a garish sport shirt, one in which I would never be seen in public. Sitting there turned out to be a very interesting time. The two stars sat down next to me while equipment was being arranged.

Sandra Bullock was attractive, but certainly not beautiful. She looks better in movies than in person, even though she was made up for filming. She sat down next to me on the bench. A minute later, Ben Affleck sat next to her. He and his buddy, Matt Damon, had gone to Harvard, but dropped out after their freshman year. I think anyone would remember the name of the dorm they had lived in. Ben could not remember. When I listed options, he finally confirmed that as a freshman he had been in Wigglesworth, not an easy name to forget.

Sandra's boyfriend at the time, Matthew McConaughey, was there, but I did not know who he was or recognize him. I did not know anything except for what Sandra told me. I was also told that Gwyneth Palthrow was there with Affleck, but I did not recognize her either. This was long before she won her Best Actress Oscar. Because Gwyneth visited girls who lived near us on Skidaway Island, she came to Savannah on several occasions. The sisters she always visited told me that she ratified my impression, telling friends that she had broken up with Affleck because he was "a jerk." Nice to have concurrence in my opinion. Someone else agrees because his wife left him in 2017. Anyway, it was fun getting to talk with this bunch. My pay was only $40 a day but, as mentioned before, many people would pay big money to get to sit and talk with that group.

22 ATTEMPTED THEFT

How Can You Steal A River?

In the mid-1800s, the City of Montgomery, Alabama imposed a tax on all goods passing the city on the Alabama River. This tactic had been practiced in European rivers for centuries. It sounded like a good idea. The problem was that the key person who would be impacted by the new tax, Mr. Peyton Bibb, owned lots of land on the river across and upstream from Montgomery. His goods would have to pass the City. He was *not* happy.

THE RIVER

The Alabama River follows a big loop, resulting in a long peninsula that juts down from Prattville, Alabama. The river flows southeast toward Montgomery and makes a large 370-degree bend to the right, flowing northwest essentially parallel to where it had been flowing southeast 8.8 miles earlier. The narrowest point is just 2,640 feet from where the river was 9 miles upstream. The land on the entire inside of the bend is very low and flat, and a century and a half ago it was owned by Peyton Bibb. When told about the new tax, Mr. Bibb was furious and notified the City that he was not going to pay the tax. The City's response was essentially, "Oh, yes you are." Having heard that, Bibb advised the City that if they did not rescind the tax, he would take the Alabama River away from Montgomery. The City officials just laughed.

All rivers throughout the world seek the shortest route available. When a river floods and discovers a shorter route, it begins to flow via that route, with the current gradually over the centuries eating away at the dirt, digging a deeper channel, eventually leaving behind the old channel which usually remains as a lake in the shape of a big loop known as an "oxbow." If you fly over the Mississippi River near the northern part of Mississippi and southern Tennessee, you can see many dozens of oxbows indicating the river's old course and resulting in a very interesting pattern. What is funny about this is the fact that a river may be the boundary between two states, but when is changes course the boundary line between the states stays the same, meaning there are hundreds of places in the United States where there appears to be a piece of one state on the "wrong" side of a river. A funny example of this is 21.6 miles north of Vicksburg, where Louisiana land is on the east side of the state line, with Mississippi on the west. Look at it on Google Maps.

If a river can eliminate 9 miles of its route and flow more quickly down a steeper path that is just 2,640 feet, it will dig out a new channel quite quickly. Had this happened, it would have left Montgomery high and dry, eliminating its role as a cargo port and as a destination for steamboats plying the route between Montgomery and the Gulf of Mexico.

Bibb found a low area, a slightly greater distance, but lower and easier to dig, closer to Montgomery. He had his slaves begin to dig at what was to be the upstream beginning of the new channel. The river frequently floods the entire peninsula, so once the ditch was dug, the process of the river's switching to its new channel should begin quickly. Bibb was making good progress with the digging.

Rumors about Bibb's progress spread, and Montgomery officials decided they had better take the ferry across the river, ride on horseback to Mr. Bibb's ditch and take a look at what was going on. They were shocked, and rushed home to repeal the tax. The place where the ditch digging was underway remains visible to this day.

Montgomery still has its river.

23 TENNIS, CANOEING AND FINALLY
Another Football Game

There was another man in Boston almost as bad as I was at organizing things. Dick Mount had gone to Dartmouth in the early fifties. After graduation, he belonged to the Longwood Cricket Club. He may have been employed as a salesman for IBM, but his heart was at Longwood.

LONGWOOD

Today, Longwood is a rarely heard word, but for over a hundred years beginning shortly after its founding in 1877, it is was at the center of tennis. Strangely enough, it is named for the home in which Napoleon lived during most of this exile on the remote island of St. Helena in the middle of the Atlantic Ocean. When I say "remote" I really mean it. Napoleon lived in nice large mansion, but St. Helena is1,170 miles west of Angola and 2,200 miles east of Brazil. Very few people go there.

The sport of tennis began with one grass court in 1878 and cricket ceased being played at Longwood in 1933. A student at Harvard and Longwood member named Dwight Davis organized a match against a British team in 1900, and the International Lawn Tennis Challenge became known as The Davis Cup, now the massive elimination involving teams from countries throughout the world.

Another Longwood member was Hazel Wightman, who dominated women's tennis in the early 1900s. She started the Ladies International Tennis Challenge between nations, a cup that became well known as the Wightman Cup.

Longwood was, and is, a great club. Dick Mount was mostly known for being a fanatic at the game of tennis. He lived within easy walking distance of the Club (as had Hazel Wightman). In addition to being an extremely nice person, he was self-deprecating far beyond what people knew. He organized a tournament for members of the Sitzundjibers,in which we were both members, at a now-defunct resort named the Wambeck in upstate New Hampshire. He came up with the idea of a handicap tournament to give everyone a fair chance.

Players were ranked A, B, C and D. Dick was an A, I was a C. If you were playing an opponent one level above yourself, you got to start with a free point, "15 love." In non-tennis terminology, this means one point to nothing, with just 4 points needed to win a game (unless you are tied and it goes on and on). If you were two rankings below, you started with a two point handicap, "30 love." He was the top-ranked player and I was far down in the middle.

Somehow I managed to beat six players and made it to the finals, only to face Dick Mount. He claims the next part of the story is not true, but I know that it was. It was obvious that he did not believe he should win his own tournament, so he threw the match. First, he decided that I would start at plus 30 and he would start at minus thirty, meaning he had to win four points just to pull even and all I had to do was win two points to win each game. The early games revealed that this huge advantage was not enough handicap to result in my winning. The people in the stands must have thought it was as embarrassing as I knew it was. Except for a few minor errors, he could have won almost every point.

To test him, I began to see what would happen once he was on the verge of winning a game. He would invariably commit deliberate "errors" such as a double fault (two missed serves resulting in the loss of a point without my having to hit the ball) in order to ensure that I won the game. He began on easy shots to hit the ball into the net or hit it long or wide of the court when he had to lose a point. This continued throughout the three set match. I was awarded the silver bowl, but certainly did not deserve it.

AND NOW BACK TO FOOTBALL

That whole business about tennis is just to lead up to a football story involving Dick Mount. In those days, before political correctness began to control everything, the Dartmouth football team, a frequent powerhouse in the Ivy League, was known as the Dartmouth Indians. It was in no way derogatory, it was because of the history of New Hampshire and the Indian tribes that had resided there. In the fifties (before the Interstate Highway system), Hanover, New Hampshire was truly off in the woods, with no women (or, at least, decent ones) within easy driving distance. This is why a whorehouse across the Connecticut River in White River Junction, Vermont did a booming business for many years.

Dick had been the head cheerleader for Dartmouth. His official costume involved wearing just pants, with his upper body coated in dark brown greasepaint with a large white "D" on his chest and an Indian headdress. He was quite a sight, especially on a cold day at a football game. One year he organized a group of his college friends and bought a block of about a hundred seats to the Harvard Dartmouth football game. Because after college graduation I happened to have several roommates, all of whom had gone to Dartmouth, Dick invited me to join the group for the game. As Dartmouth was undefeated and expected to clobber Harvard, my seats were placed in the center of the large group so they could lord it over me every time Dartmouth scored and, of course, when they emerged triumphant.

In addition, Dick organized a large group of canoes in which his buddies were to paddle from the Union Boat Club, on the edge of Beacon Hill, the 3.6 miles up the Charles River to Harvard's football stadium. The Dartmouth guys were attired in Indian headdress and I was in a suit with a high and wide-brimmed black "Pilgrim" hat, as would have been the case down in Plymouth when they held the first Thanksgiving. The canoes were filled with couples, so they were not moving very fast. My date and I were in the lead as we paddled up the Boston side of the Charles River, with all of the "Indians" whooping in pursuit of the poor Pilgrims.

CAUSE AND EFFECT

I guess this strange bunch must have attracted a good bit of attention as we paddled upstream. Approaching the Cottage Farm Bridge (sometimes called the "Boston University Bridge), we heard a loud crash on Storrow Drive, cars rear-ending cars ahead of them that had slowed down to see what the hell was going on beside them out in the river.

My poor date had, for some reason, worn a fuzzy white, fake-fur coat. Of course, after a few drinks, Dick gave her a big hug. I did not take her out again, so I do not know if she was ever able to get all that brown grease paint off. It usually gets chilly (Southerners would think of it as cold) in New England in late October, especially as the sun sets. Dick remained topless throughout the game. With our seats in the middle of the big group of Dartmouth grads, we were the central target for what would obviously be the cheering victorious Dartmouth contingent.

You guessed it….Harvard won the game.

24 THREE ALL NIGHT SAILS

Two To Somewhere, One To Nowhere

Sailing all night is fairly common in cruising boats, but not in open racing boats that have no interior features such as beds and johns. When Pat and I were living aboard our 55 foot sloop, we sailed long days and nights back to the United States in May of 1995, crossing the rough Gulf Stream in the middle of the night before making land at Beaufort, North Carolina and had a beautiful evening looking at the lights along the New Jersey shore as we sailed all night from Delaware Bay up the coast to New York. Those trips were deliberate and fun. That is not true of these three stories.

MARBLEHEAD

Ted Baker, a friend in Marblehead, Massachusetts, had a beautiful cruising sailboat, called a King's Cruiser, with a magnificent varnished mahogany hull. One night we sailed out of the harbor and did some drinking. As can happen all too often off the coast of New England, fog set in. This was in the days before Loran and GPS systems that enable people in boats and cars to tell exactly where they are and show the route to get where they want to go. Ted's boat did not have radar, so we could not tell where we were. The coastline in that area is quite rocky and dangerous with several rocks offshore.

Large floating aids to navigation called Bells are caused to ring by the bouncing of the waves and are used to help boaters head toward the sound when the mark can't be seen in fog or darkness. You sail to a mark and identify the mark by the numbers painted on it. You could then match the mark to the chart and see exactly where you are. We heard a bell, sailed to it, and read the identification. Bells in key locations are also lighted, and the identity of a mark is shown on the sailing charts by language such as "five quick flashes," abbreviated for printing on the nautical charts into something such as "5QkFl," which stands for a light that does five quick flashes with a pause before the next sequence.

The mark we found was flashing five times and then going black for several seconds before beginning its flashing again. We searched the chart, looking up and down the coast for anything indicating five quick flashes, which is definitely what this mark was doing. While we did this, we would sail away from the mark steering carefully to a compass course and then do a U-turn 180 degrees and sail back to the mark, reaching it once we got close by listening to its bell. It was, at best, tedious.

The owner of the boat did not want to get closer to shore without being sure of where we were and we simply could not determine where we were. The mark on the chart at the entrance to Marblehead Harbor showed clearly on the chart as displaying 1 quick flash. I was stuck at the helm, sailing away from the mark and then back to the mark. In addition to being tiresome, it was quite boring, but you had to be careful to stay near that mark so you could be sure of finding your way back to it.

At daybreak we discovered the problem, which, of course, was our error. The mark we were at was flashing five times, but the identification on the chart was not the number "1," it was the letter "I" which stood for "Intermittent" Quick Flashes. I believe, to little avail, that 1s and Is should not be used in such fashion. Is the Coast Guard listening?

GLOUCESTER

The Friday evening started out with a simple plan to sail from Marblehead 14 miles or so up the coast to a restaurant on Rocky Neck on the eastern side of Gloucester Harbor. Four couples were in the group, on a sloop-rigged sailboat about 40 feet in length.

We departed Marblehead late one beautiful Friday afternoon in summer and headed for Gloucester. As you might guess, a few drinks were had before and during dinner. The group got to talking about a big party in Ogunquit, Maine they wanted to go to the next night, and someone came up with the brilliant (I use the word quite loosely) idea of sailing to Maine that night instead of going back to Marblehead.

At the time, I did not even know where Ogunquit was, much less how to find it and enter its extremely narrow harbor. I did know I was supposed to skipper my boat in a race at Marblehead the next afternoon, Saturday. This was before the age of cell phones, so I used a pay phone in the restaurant to call the head bartender at the Corinthian Yacht Club in Marblehead who owned a plane, asking him if he would fly up to Maine and pick up three of us and fly us back to an airport near Salem so we could get back to Marblehead by noon that Saturday. I had awakened him, so he had to turn on the lights, find his flight map and determine what airport would be closest to Ogunquit. He selected Sanford Airport, about 20 miles and at most a 30 minute drive northwest of Ogunquit. Because he had to get back to the Club to bartend, he said he would meet us at 10am, the fee would be $25 ($ 8.33 each), and we had to pay if we were late and he had to leave without us. The people who knew where we were headed assured me that we could definitely be there by then, so the deal was struck.

OGUNQUIT

Finally, we loaded up, cast off from the dock and started out of Gloucester Harbor in the dark. Getting out of the harbor was easy, since the channel was clearly identifiable by lighted marks. We rounded the point at the entrance and headed east to round all of the rocky islands that cluster just off the east end of Cape Ann. There are old lighthouses on Thatcher's Island and navigation was easy, even before the days of GPS. My eyes were hurting a bit because I was breaking in new contact lens that, in those days, were all hard lenses and required "breaking in" gradually.

I stayed up at the helm until we were safely around Cape Ann and turned over the helm to a friend, Joe Crosby. Only a few minutes after falling asleep, I was awakened by Joe's date, who said Joe had passed out at the helm and that I had to come back up on deck and sail the boat. This was something less than fun, all night in the pitch-black dark by myself, trying to stay awake and steer safely up the coast, staying close to the coast to avoid the group of rocky islands named "The Isles of Shoals" off of Portsmouth, New Hampshire.

In 2009, an old friend and publishing expert, Charles "Cheeb" Everitt wrote me a letter that included a similar experience he had had sailing with Joe Crosby in a 38' yawl. The boat's owners did not know how to sail. When Joe, below, would not answer Cheeb's calls for help on deck, a young girl came up, threw up and lay down in it. Cheeb had a rough night dealing with the big rollers off of Race Point, before arriving safely (thanks to Cheeb) in Provincetown Harbor. He had spent 8 hours at the helm alone in the dark.

At daybreak, the crew of my boat slowly came up on the deck and began to comb the coast to determine where we were. The boat did not have any sailing charts, so this was worse than driving without a map. We had sailed slowly in light breezes all night, so we still had a surprisingly long distance to go and we were beginning to run short of time.

Unless you know where to look for it, the entrance to Ogunquit is just 270 feet wide and very tricky to spot from the ocean. The view of the harbor's entrance is blocked by a long peninsula that comes down from the northeast, so the gap is barely noticeable. The entrance to the harbor makes an abrupt turn to the right directly behind the rocky peninsula, so it doesn't look like a harbor even when you get fairly close to shore. We were beginning to panic about time, but thought that with some hustling and luck, we could make the ten o'clock rendezvous. Supposedly, a bridge at the western tip of Bermuda is the smallest openable drawbridge in the world, with a gap just barely wide enough for a small boat's mast to pass through. The Ogunquit Bridge is similar.

WOO WOO GINSBURG

How is that for a name? As we came ashore, things suddenly became quite lucky. The guy who was hosting the big Saturday night party was there in a huge convertible with the top down, and one of the people in our group knew him. This was the age of the disk jockey, and Arnie "Woo Woo" Ginsburg was, from 1956 through 1967, Boston's #1 disk jockey, a well-known celebrity. He agreed to drive the three of us to the airport.

We threw our stuff in his car, jumped in and pleaded with him to drive fast, because it was already almost ten o'clock. When we finally got to the small airport after ten, we spotted the plane getting ready for takeoff at the end of the little grass runway. There were no fences or barricades, so Woo Woo drove out onto the field and raced up beside the small four-seater plane while we waved frantically for the pilot to stop. Yes, I have to call him "the pilot" because his name and that of the other two passengers are among those things that are lost from memory. I think his name was Pete, so I will call him that.

Pete stopped, we threw our gear in the baggage compartment behind the seats and climbed aboard. It was about 10:15. When I took my seat in the co-pilot's spot I was handed the flight map to study and find where we could land to buy gas. The examination of the flight map the night before had shown that Sanford had fuel, but the airport was "seasonal" and there was nobody there. We were already in the air in a plane did not have enough fuel to make it back to Massachusetts.

THE FLIGHT

If you live in Sanford and are reading this you will think I am either stupid or insane. The little grass field is now a sizeable airport with several paved runways, the longest being 1.2 miles in length. Sanford Regional Airport now has hangers for many planes and a passenger terminal. Wish that had been the case when we were there.

It did not take very long for me to learn that trying to spot things such as grass runways in the fields and woods of Maine from the air was not easy. I looked and looked without every finding one. We kept flying southwest toward New Hampshire. Finally, Pete said we were almost out of gas and had to declare an emergency and request permission to land at Pease Air Force Base, now the site of Portsmouth's airport, but it was then one of the main bases of the Strategic Air Command, which was responsible for maintaining planes ready for immediate retaliatory nuclear strike if needed on a moment's notice.

There were two large B-47 Stratocruiser Bombers at the end of the runway. Pete spent a lot of time explaining and asking for permission to land in an emergency. The airport control tower kept saying "no." Finally, as we were running out of gas, we landed. Soldiers with guns drawn and pointed at us raced along each side the plane in jeeps as we landed and slowed to taxi where they directed us.

SECURITY

Not usually very impressed by government officials, I was quite impressed that Saturday morning. When we entered a building, we could hear soldiers communicating with other SAC bases, checking to be sure they were not also experiencing any kind of abnormal intrusion. Smart thinking. We were given coffee and donuts while we waited. Luckily, Pete called Pat Mason, who was the Secretary of the Corinthian Yacht Club and had been in the military, had his ID number, and vouched for us to one of the soldiers. Even so, we were kept at gunpoint the entire time we were on the ground.

In addition to quizzing us, the soldiers checked the plane, even to the point of squeezing out some toothpaste and spraying a sample shaving cream from the other male passenger's shaving cream. It may have been a little excessive, but we were impressed. We were, obviously, very appreciative of their having allowed us to land.

They filled the small plane with a full tank of gas and refused to charge us, saying that, by their standards, we required very little gas and that the paperwork required if they were to collect from us would be prohibitive. We were allowed to reboard and take off, much later but a least with enough gas to get home. Running out of gas in an automobile is a nuisance; running out of gas in the air is a whole lot worse.

THE SOVIET UNION

The first time I went to Russia was back when it was part of the Soviet Union. Their security was excessive. I was dressed in a suit and had nothing in the least bit suspicious with me. I had to list all of my money when I entered the country. I was cautioned that this meant everything....from travelers checks to pocket change. Each category was listed and signed. When I returned to the St. Petersburg airport I presented the required bills showing everything I had spent, my hotel, my meals, several vodkas and a few purchases. The amount of money I was taking out of the country had to match what I had brought in minus what the bills showed I had spent. The totals matched exactly.

Despite this, I was taken into a room with just a table and two inspectors (I guess that is what you would call them) and told to strip naked. In the United States you might argue, but here you didn't dare. They went through my clothes and everything in the suitcase. The tested everything such as toothpaste and shaving cream. Let the ACLU experience that and see how much they complain about invasion of privacy in the US.

EAST BOOTHBAY TO MARBLEHEAD

In the mid-seventies, we were working to reinvigorate the International One-Design Class of sailboats. I flew to Norway and negotiated the purchase of the rights to build the boats and the mold in which the fiberglass hulls were made.

The first IOD made in the United States was for an extraordinarily nice older gentleman, Don McKenzie, of the Larchmont Yacht Club in New York. He supplied the funds to purchase the molds. The second boat was for Dr. Jay Lee of Boston. The builder, whose dad, Bjarne Aas, had done the original design in 1935, talked Jay into running up the cost, putting lots of strange things into the boat. Where most IODs had storage shelves, Jay's boat had varnished hardwood cabinets with hinged doors including stained glass depictions of musical subjects such as Jay's violin.

When the boat was ready, several of us agreed to load up all of our tools, drive to East Boothbay, do what is called "fitting out" the boat and then sail with Jay in his new boat from East Boothbay, Maine, to Marblehead Massachusetts, a distance of about 130 miles in the Atlantic Ocean. We drove to East Boothbay early on a Saturday morning, June 12, 1976, thinking we could install all of the equipment on the boat, get underway in mid-afternoon and be clear of the rocks and islands in the Atlantic just south of the harbor.

As it turned out, even with a team of us working, there were so many parts that needed to be installed that it took all day. The sun was setting as we finished the work and got ready to sail south four miles down the Damariscotta River and out into the open ocean. The boat was what is classified as a "day sailor" racing sailboat, which meant it had no navigation system, no radar, no bunks in which to sleep, no galley for preparing food and no lights as are required of boats underway at night. It had a heavy lead keel and an open cockpit.

The area where we worked on the boat in the water was long and narrow between two piers. Expensive boats lined each side of the docks south of the point where Jay Lee's boat was tied up at the far end of one of the piers with its bow facing the concrete wall at the end of the docking area between the piers. There was not enough room for the boat to do a U turn so I stressed the importance of being absolutely sure the line tied to the bow was held as the boat swung away from the pier. We must have the bow into the wind so that the jib could be "backed" to take the boat onto port tack, allowing us to sail out of the docking area. The man on shore could not let go so that the sails would fill with the wind blowing from the right side of the boat, putting us on starboard tack in an area too narrow to turn around safely and which would take us straight into the concrete wall. Unlike a car, you can't stop a boat or back up, you just have to keep moving and turn.

The spare line tied to the boat was fairly short, so my good and faithful crew, Bob Duff, tied two pieces of rope together, tying one end to the boat's bow and holding the other on the dock. When we began to swing away from the dock, still on what would be starboard tack, Bob's knot let go. It was little short of terrifying. Bob had, despite all his years of sailing experience, somehow tied an ineffective bowline knot. Probably the best knot for many things is a bowline, but it is relatively easy to make the knot incorrectly and that is what had happened.

Jay, at the helm of his very expensive brand-new boat started to steer on starboard tack down the middle of the docking area straight toward the concrete bulkhead. He froze. If we continued another fifty feet the water would become so narrow that there was no way the boat could be turned, we would be hitting other boats or ramming the brand-new boat head on into the concrete wall.

I had to push Jay aside, grab the helm, steer as close as possible right up beside the boats on our left so there would be room to tack (this means turn toward the direction from which the wind is blowing so that the wind that was blowing at us over the right side of the boat would be blowing over the left side of the boat), allowing us to head out on port tack toward the harbor. Several of the people on the dock were screaming as they ran down and climbed aboard a large boat on the upwind side of the area to fend off because it did not look as if there would be enough room to tack without hitting that boat. We came within a foot of hitting it, but managed to get onto port tack and head out into the river and south into the Atlantic as darkness settled in for the night.

Jay had brought his girlfriend. I'm not sure that the stories after the trip were entirely accurate, but if she did speak a single sentence, only one person, Hal Nesbitt, wrote that he could remember it. She climbed forward inside the hull, up ahead of the mast and spent all night in that tight little area, only about three feet high at the highest point. Hal later wrote that her one sentence was "I've gotta pee."

Jay had agreed to be responsible for the food and after that day's hard work, the guys were all quite hungry. For some reason we never understood, Jay had brought only canned goods that required cooking. As I recall, the larger cans were corned beef hash. We had no stove. Dinner that night was awful, and the next morning was not much better. As we sailed down the harbor and knew we were obviously sailing south, we discovered to our horror that neither of the two compasses had been "swung," the term for adjusting and calibrating them so that the directions they indicated reflected the direction the boat was traveling. They were not just "off," they were far off and each showed a substantially different compass bearing. We needed to know the direction we were sailing, and didn't.

Sailing from Boothbay, we had planned to sail away from the coast of Maine, passing the coastline of New Hampshire far offshore and cutting around the point of Cape Ann, which juts far out to the east in Massachusetts. We did not want to risk sailing in the pitch black into the rocky coast and we wanted to go the much-shorter direct route. We followed what appeared to be about right for reaching the islands off of Cape Ann, trying to eliminate any risk of hitting the rocks and the submerged concrete breakwater that lurked just beneath the surface at the Cape.

During the black of night, with spinnaker flying on starboard tack, the boat made an unexpected jibe. You can guess who was at the helm. It was not Bob, Hal or me. The boom, barely seen in the dark, swung suddenly and fast from the starboard (right) side of the boat to the port (left) side of the boat, with the boom sweeping fast just above the cockpit as it went from side to side. We were lucky that a sudden and unexpected jibe in the pitch-black dark did not knock a few heads off. It did hit two of us in the back, pushing us into the hull of the boat. For those who were hit, it hurt like hell.

When the sun rose the next morning, we could not see land. Without the benefit of a working compass, we had sailed all night on a course farther to the east out into the Atlantic than we wanted, so it took us most of the day to sail west and reach Cape Ann. The wind was still blowing fairly hard and we were on a "starboard tack, beam reach." Sailing with the wind from this angle to the wind results in the greatest speed but it also meant the boat was heeling to port. Jay, at the helm, misread the course to steer smoothly through the waves. The stern of the boat lurched into the air on a wave, sending those of us who had been sitting properly on the upwind side of the cockpit into the air and landing in the cockpit of the boat.

That should have been no big deal, but I was sitting in the spot closest to the stern of the boat right next to the tiller. When I was flipped into the air, my butt landed on the "rudder post," the point where the long straight tiller by which a boat is steered attaches to the steel shaft that goes through the hull and underwater becomes the leading edge of the rudder. The tiller did not break clean off, but it was broken to the point where it was no longer strong enough to turn the rudder and aim the boat in the needed direction.

Needless to say, my butt hurt something awful, but we had to be more concerned about steering the boat. Luckily, Hal Nesbitt, a very experienced sailor from San Francisco, tied the tiller together well enough that we were able to continue toward Marblehead. The tricky part was steering through the boats in the crowded harbor and making the tight turn into the wind to shoot the mooring. Sailing is supposed to be enjoyable. The connection between the tiller and the rudder was extremely weak and loose, but it held, so we eventually got the boat safely to its mooring.

ONE MEMORABLE DAYLIGHT SAIL

One nice afternoon my loyal crew for many years, Bob Duff, his wife Debbie, and our friend Phil Somersby were aboard my International One Design sailboat, "Tango" for the normal Saturday afternoon race out of Marblehead, this time managed by the Corinthian Yacht Club.

We were doing well, finding ourselves in third place rounding the final leeward mark and beginning the beat to the Race Committee boat marking the finish line. Suddenly, a squall came through, blasting us extremely hard. In this type of boat we had a halyard lock and couldn't take the mainsail down no matter what. Also, we were in an open boat with a very heavy lead keel, so if we filled with too much water we went to the bottom. It began to blow so hard that Debbie went below and brought up four life preservers, which she had us put on before holding hands and reciting The Lord's Prayer. It was quite scary. We made it to the finish line and back into the harbor safely.

The Race Committee reported that the anemometer on their boat had reached about 70 miles per hour, almost hurricane force, and we had had to race through it. One Etchells Class sailboat had filled and sunk with the skipper entangled in the lines. A crewman dove down with a knife and cut him free so he lived. A halyard hook takes strain off the mast in a way I would never have understood were it not for sailing but it means that you cannot lower the sail while there is pressure on it. This was not a relaxing afternoon sail.

EDINBURGH

In 1975, I qualified to race in the International One-Design World Championships that were being held that year in the Firth of Forth, that is the north shore of Edinburgh, Scotland. The superskipper, Bill Widnall, graciously agreed to crew for me, offsetting my lack of skill at sailing downwind. Bill was so hungover during the first race that he barely ever came up on deck to help with anything.

After the racing, we loaded the sailors into two buses and toured Scotland. I had always known about and planned our route to go via St. Andrew's famous first golf course and the Glenlivet Distillery, then usually considered the best. When we got there, the place was closed. It was Sunday, September 7,1975 and their sign read that they were closed on Sundays. Hal Nesbitt and Gar Ward knocked on the door of the distillery and, when someone came to the door, asked if they could let us in because they had the President of the Glenlivet Fan Club of North America in one of the busses. They opened the doors and gave us a great tour, with loads of delicious "samples".

You guessed it; I was the one they had made the false claim about. I received two beautiful books about The Glenlivet autographed by the head of the place. I had to keep a straight face and go along with their scam, but it was great fun for the sailors and very tasty.

25 SITZUNDJIBERS

Strange Name, Great Club

The name was derived from words referencing skiing (sitzmark) and sailing (jibing) separated by "und,' the German for "and." Founded in June of 1955 by my good friend, Don Sohn, the club is still in existence 60 years later, albeit as a sad shadow of its former self.

Today Sitz has deteriorated to the point of being a place for old divorcees to meet other divorcees, with only single members. It had been much more than a social club and membership was comprised of about 400 people, about half single and half married couples. Essentially all were college graduates and many had been at Harvard, MIT, Dartmouth or the top colleges for women throughout the northeast. Largely as a result of Don's background and contacts, Sitz had events involving major public figures and dances and parties in numerous private clubhouses and buildings into which most people would not be allowed.

The club had several parts, one of which was known as the Soldiers Field Dance Committee that hosted formal balls every year at the Crane Estate up in Ipswich, Hall in Salem, and the Harvard Club. Informal dances were held each summer at the Corinthian Yacht Club, at the Cambridge Boat Club and several locations around town. There was a big annual event named "New Faces" every December in Harvard Hall in the Harvard Club of Boston, back before there was a second club downtown. Soldiers Field Forums hosted guest speakers at dinners, usually on the top of the apartment building at 100 Memorial Drive. The two most notable of the speakers were Eleanor Roosevelt and Soviet Ambassador to the United States Mikhail Menshikov, who was ambassador from January, 1958 till January, 1962.

A MARVELOUS SONG

The small event I enjoyed the most was a very small informal garden of a Sitz member's home in Belmont, Massachusetts, a northwestern suburb of Boston. None of us knew in 1963 the man who sang for us and none of us had heard the new song he had just written and which he played the guitar and sang to us that afternoon. My guess is that there were fewer than a dozen of us that got to hear Peter Yarrow sing *"Puff the Magic Dragon" before* the recording of it was released. It was mesmerizing. Little did we know that Peter would become incredibly well known as the leader of the group "Peter, Paul and Mary." I had gotten to sit about five feet in front of him and that cute song still remains embedded in my brain. If you don't remember "Little Jackie Paper" you are too young to be reading this book. What did Jackie Paper bring Puff?

26 GRAND THEFT AUTO

No, This Is Not About The Video Game

In the 1990s, Dr. Ron Finger was the best-known plastic surgeon in Savannah, Georgia. He and his wife, Cheryl, now live on elegant West Jones Street, but at the time of this story they lived in a lovely wooden home overlooking Romerly Marsh, with the Atlantic in the distance. The Finger's home, at 25 Magnolia Crossing, was just down the coast from us in the The Landings on Skidaway Island, southeast of Savannah.

The island had been developed in the early 1970s by Union Camp Corporation, which was taken over in the '90s by International Paper. The private club for residents, named "The Landings," includes six full 18-hole golf courses, 38 tennis courts and two marinas. It was not one of those communities where tourists descended and hotels attracted big conventions…..it was truly for residents only, and most lived there year round.

RON FINGER

Ron collected rare cars, everything from valuable antique racing cars to high-powered current automobiles. His most valuable car was a Ferrari GTO. Ron had a large, well-secured and humidity-controlled garage on the south side of his house, hidden from the street by lots of bushes.

Two men decided to steal the beautiful Ferrari. According to court records, Luther Burris and Don Hartley, could keep an eye on things because one lived across the street from the Fingers. It also meant they could easily enter The Landings through security. As it turned out, the plan had many flaws, not the least of which was advertising the car for sale before they stole it. The ad even showed interested buyers how to reach them.

Anyway, the brilliant team of thieves, needing to know when the Fingers would be out of town, offered a $25,000 bribe to Dr. Finger's secretary to tell them when she knew that the Fingers were going to be out of town. Luther and Don drove through the security gate with a large enclosed truck, which they backed into the Finger's driveway, providing additional cover from view while they broke into the garage. Knowing about the security system, Ron told me that they left the doors untouched and knocked down a sidewall of the garage, on the side that faced east toward the ocean, so they could work completely out of sight. They managed to get the Ferrari out of the garage and into the truck, which drove unimpeded out the gate and off to Florida. Here is where it gets ridiculous.

They had already lined up a buyer, Kirk White, and set up a meeting in Dunedin, Florida. Kirk arrived with a certified check for $2.4 million. The forged "papers" might have been close to looking authentic, but to Mr. White, they were suspect.

Needless to say, when you are about to pay that much for a car, you want to check it out carefully. Kirk asked Luther and Don to start the car. Before he paid, he wanted to be sure that it ran. When they turned the ignition switch, nothing happened, not even that ominous clicking sound of a starter not engaging because the battery was nearly dead. Something was peculiar.

WHAT?

The starter itself was missing, something that the two thieves would have been known if they were the real owners. Luckily, Ron had sent the starter to be worked on by a highly-regarded mechanic, Andy Greene, whose shop was in Garden City, just west of Savannah near the airport. Kirk left with his check.

What do you do when you have stolen such an incredibly valuable car and do not know what to do with it? The brilliant duo drove it to a used car lot where it was pushed up onto one of those raised display stands on which you frequently see cars for sale featured by having them a few feet off the ground. As almost-unbelievable luck would have it, that used car lot was passed by a driver who was quite familiar with great old Ferraris. The car aficionado, knowing enough about Ferraris and their owners, called Ron Finger and asked "Ron, is there any chance you are missing a car?"

The car was retrieved post haste, the brilliant thieves were captured and sentenced to three years in federal prison. Ron had to pay a bit more in personal property taxes to Chatham County.

26 ROBBERY IN BOSTON
In The Best Part Of Town

On October 31, 1982, day I flew to Boston from Belgium on Sabena and had a date that night with someone I had never been out with before. I never went out with her again and can't remember her name. For some reason I also don't remember, she drove her car. It was Halloween, and she was in a hilarious pink-cat costume, all shiny slick material, skin tight, replete with a tail and ears.

DINNER
We had dinner at The Hampshire House (better known for the "Cheers" bar downstairs, on elegant Beacon Street on the "flat" of Beacon Hill overlooking the Boston Public Garden. I had served on Pat Moscaritolo's Logan Airport Advisory Board when he was doing a truly outstanding job of running the airport, so we had joined Pat and his wife for dinner. After dinner, we walked around the corner about a hundred feet to where my date's car was parked on Brimmer Street, at the corner of Beacon Street. When I got in and closed the door, a young man jerked the passenger side door open, squeezed onto the seat and pushed the barrel of his pistol into my stomach.

A good rule is that you should always carry enough money to satisfy a robber. Don't piss him off. I realized, and claimed correctly, that I had no money, not even a dollar. Even pulling out my wallet did not convince him. The rule was certainly timely, but on the one occasion when I really needed to comply with it, I had not. It was probably only a terrifying minute, but it seemed like an eternity. He finally gave up and ran.

We went back into the bar and called the police. It was embarrassing for Pat because he was now head of the Boston Convention and Visitors Bureau. An attempted robbery at gunpoint in such a fashionable part of town was not good publicity. When the police arrived, I was unable to describe the robber. I guess the correct description has to be that is was an "attempted robbery" because the man had not taken anything.

THE POLICE
The policemen were unhappy that I could not give a description of the man…..nothing. They repeated the question, unwilling to believe I could not tell them anything. The entire time it went on I had kept looking down at the finger on the trigger. If the finger squeezed the trigger, a bullet couldn't miss me.

My date told the police three times that she could describe the man, but the cops were not paying any attention to her. I was in a very stuffy grey-pinstripe suit and she was in that bright pink, skintight cat costume. Finally, one of the policemen turned to her and said "OK, cutie, what do you have to say?"

She proceeded to give a thorough description of what I learned had been a young, dark-haired man of middle-eastern extraction. The cop asked where he could reach her and was very embarrassed when “Cutie” gave him a business card that showed she was a professor at Boston University.

HISTORY
Less scary but more expensive were four burglaries. The burglaries are what cost me, including precious family items that are irreplaceable. I didn’t think of installing systems in the apartment I rented on Beacon Hill or in my private office at 131 Tremont St. in Boston. I had thought getting things out of my apartment and putting them in my office would be safer. Not the case. If you have a good security system, be sure to leave it on. Don't skip it just because you are going to be gone a short time. Here is a suggestion.

A RECOMMENDATION
We have an expensive system that includes a cell phone in case a burglar cuts the phone line. If you cannot afford a $35 per month monitored security system, I have a suggestion. In our last three houses we have installed the loudest available sirens, hidden in the HVAC ducts so they can't be seen, and put them on zero time delay. If someone were to open a door or window, they would be blasted immediately by a noise so loud that I believe they would run away and find some other house to attack. If you don’t want to wire the doors, you can use motion detectors just inside the doors and a wireless system; not as good, but better than nothing.

You pay for the sirens once and are done with it. This approach contrasts with the typical single medium-blast sirens on the outside that probably only bother your neighbors when they give off false alarms. Companies on the Internet offer reasonably priced 130 decibel sirens. Four of these in action spread throughout the house are quite painful to ears. You can connect them to a wireless system with control panel, door and window sensors for as little as $100.

Most burglars entering a monitored security system know they probably have twenty minutes before the alarm company calls your area’s 911, the person on duty writes down the information, the 911 person calls the precinct, the precinct dispatches a squad car, the police officer finishes whatever he is doing and drives to your address. Here in Montgomery, I have seen officers following up on a stack of alarm reports, getting to a house across from us 52 minutes after the external siren started blasting. Burglars know they have time to grab some of your most valuable things before they run. I would rather the burglar get surprised and shocked by the painful noise and leave without even coming inside the house, much less taking anything. The police have to respond to too many false alarms.

27 COMMUNION SUNDAY

An Unusual Day in Church

Several kids who were among my best friends growing up in Montgomery, Alabama went to St. John's Episcopal Church, a beautiful church, constructed in 1855 in downtown Montgomery. The building was typical of Episcopal churches of that era, filled with elegant polished brass, illuminated by the sunlight beaming through classic stained-glass windows, including some made by Louis Comfort Tiffany.

YOU CAN SPOT AN "OUT OF TOWNER"

In the early days, parishioners "owned" their pews, and the names of those assigned to sit there were shown on the center aisle end of each pew. The acolytes used to be amused when strangers would come for Sunday services, see an empty pew on the right side of the aisle and take their seats. After a while they would become quite uncomfortable, not realizing that they were in the one original pew that had not been replaced by ones that had contoured seats and backs. This plaque indicated that this had been the pew of what many Southerners called "Our country's first president," Jefferson Davis.

ACOLYTES

One Sunday when my cousin, Bill Marks, and I were "Serving Acolytes," which meant assisting the minister around the altar during communion. Other Acolytes were responsible for counting the congregation and standing beside a row of pews to indicate which people were to walk to the altar rail for communion. The congregation count was relayed on a piece of paper to a Serving Acolyte, who in turn gave the count to the minister so he would know how much bread and wine to consecrate for the communion service.

One problem you always faced was the departure of some members of the congregation before the communion service began, but this was always a small percentage and therefore predictable. One acolyte opened the side door, handed me the slip of paper and I passed it to the Reverend.

One tenet of the Episcopal Church which many people don't know and those who do know probably do not believe is that the red wine and little pieces of leavened bread do not just "represent" the body and blood of Jesus Christ, through a process called Transubstantiation, they actually *become* the body and blood of Christ. You are taught to believe that it is not just symbolic of the body and blood of Jesus, it is really his body and blood. Regardless of what you believe, all of the consecrated bread and wine, must be consumed. At that time, none could be thrown out. Having been advised of the congregation count, the minister must use his experience to judge how much to prepare.

COMMUNION

When the Reverend James Brettman completed the line of communicants, he had lots of wine left over. Not just too much; much too much He stood facing the altar and drank as much as he could, an entire chalice. He refilled the chalice, turned to me where I was kneeling on the left near the altar. Usually, at communion, the chalice of wine is lifted so that a communicant can touch the base of the chalice and take a small sip. The Reverend held the chalice to my mouth and poured.

Today, to avoid the spread of germs, many churches serve the wine in small paper cups. In the fifties, everyone drank from the chalice. He poured until the large chalice was empty. He then went over to Bill on the other side of the altar to my right and repeated the process, but Bill was not able to swallow as much. The Reverend then took another big swig facing the altar before coming back to me. There was not much I could do. Brettman just poured, poured and kept pouring. This happened twice. but I do remember having had too much to drink. He gave up on Bill and just started drinking himself and before coming back to me. It is amusing now to think that I was forced as a teenager, below the legal drinking age, to be made to get drunk by, of all people, my minister.

There is a change in procedure that would preclude this problem from occurring today. A lady from St. Johns explained to me that they can now just store consecrated wine until it is needed again. It's a little like overtime in college football, a rules change that will make the younger generation have no ability to comprehend how games used to end in ties with some frequency.

AT LAST

It was not until this was about to go to press that I accidentally learned the name of the man who caused the problem. It was a very popular man in Montgomery named Tommy Lawson. He had called about something at St. John's and mentioned having been an acolyte. This time I remembered his part in the story. Tommy told me he was dyslexic and had written down something like 271 instead of 127.

Tommy was an actor in New York. The only time I saw him was in his role as the Judge in the trial that was the central event in the great book by Alabama's Harper Lee...."To Kill A Mockingbird."

29 COLLEGE SPORTS
Are They Really "Student Athletes?"

Most of the stories in this book are personal; this one is simply opinion. At Harvard, the football players were primarily students, not the other way around. It is great that most of the nation's colleges have football teams that their students can cheer for and get excited about. It projects the school's names into the sports pages, helping attract many athletes and, to a lesser extent, real students. Some colleges, especially in the Southeastern Conference, can justify paying coachs enormous salaries because an outstanding team can bring in many dollars from tickets, TV fees and, most importantly, alumni donations.

It has, however, reached farcical levels, and the University presidents should confront their generous alumni and return the major sports to some semblance of student participation. The most egregious example was the Georgia basketball team in 2001. Georgia had employed Jim Harrick as the basketball coach and allowed Jim Harrick, Jr. to earn a salary, not just as assistant coach, but also (ostensibly) for teaching students.

The horrendous story received a lot of press at the time, mostly within the State of Georgia, but it bears repeating for those of you who did not see it or simply do not follow sports. The "Final Exam" in Harrick's "college level" class contained 20 multiple-choice questions. This chapter will not bother you with all of them, just the funniest. How many goals are on a basketball court? 1,2,3 or 4? How many halves are in a college basketball game? How many quarters are in a high school basketball game? How many points does a 3-point field goal account for in a Basketball Game? If you go on to become a huge coaching success, to whom will you tribute (sic) the credit? (Note: the choices here were three big name coaches and Jim Harrick, Jr

Now, if you think that is bad, the investigative report showed that Chris Daniels and Rashad Wright were given an "A" for the "course" despite their not attending the class and not even taking the exam. This type of practice does not just have an effect on the athletes, it impacts every other student and has a major negative impact on the image of the school from which the real students have received their degree. The newspapers reported that, upon hearing the allegations, the two Harrick's responded with defiance, saying "They can't prove anything." What a sad joke and what a terrible commentary on college "student" athletes. The truly stupid development occurred in 2014 when there is talk about college athletes will be allowed to unionize. How ridiculous is that?

And it gets worse. In 2019 it appears increasingly-that colleges will begin paying student athletes salaries. I guess that makes sense because, except at some elite colleges, the athletes are just athletes.

30 BAD TIMING

A Ski Movie

Back in the sixties, ski movies were a big draw, attracting many skiers and helping to promote travel to some of the world's most beautiful and exciting ski areas. Three of us had just started a travel agency and the original plan was to market to skiers. One of the three, Lolly McDonnell (now Lolly Mitchell) had founded and was President of the Chamois Ski Club, named for the toughest ski trail in New England (because so few knew the word, much less how to pronounce it, the trail at Stowe is now "The Goat).

The Chamois Trail at Stowe, Vermont was so steep and narrow that you could barely make turns through the trees. The name was derived from a mountain goat, and this was probably the only animal that would have been at home on such a steep trail. It was terrifying and dangerous and, as a result, widened when the name changed.

Lolly had come to know the man who might still be the biggest name in Canadian skiing, having been an Olympic skier and popularized the sport of reaching inaccessible areas by helicopter, Hans Gmoser, was well known in the skiing community. Hans to agree to fly to Boston in 1965 and narrate his movie about skiing in Canada's Bugaboo Mountains.

I filled out the legal forms for the work permit and signed up to be responsible for bringing Hans into the US. Because the Club did not have much money, I signed the lease for renting John Hancock Hall, a medium-sized auditorium on Berkeley Street in Boston. We designed and printed large color posters and fliers to promote the event, which was to be the biggest annual fundraiser for the ski club. Tickets were sold.

Of course, we also paid for Hans' plane ticket and hotel for the night. The performance was set for Tuesday evening, November 9. All was set and ready for the show. At the time, I was working in what was then State Street Bank's headquarters building at the corner of State and Congress Streets.

The problem started at 5:15, but where I was it was 5:19. I was planning to stay at the bank and work until time to leave for the movie and grab a taxi over to the auditorium to set up for ticket sales and manage the evening. The lights in the bank flickered for a few seconds and went out. Normally, when something like this happens, you sit for a while, expecting the lights to come back on. When the electricity goes out at home, the electric company can usually identify the source of the problem and get things back working in an hour or so. Not the case on the evening of November 9, 1965….a date that quickly became known as The Great Blackout.

Yes, people by the hundreds of thousands got stuck in buildings with no elevators (or worse yet, in an elevator between floors) and in subway cars between stations. The problem was later identified as having begun in Canada, spreading down through Boston and New York, affecting 30 million people in eight states in the Northeast. The remarkable thing is that there was no panic. The feeling of camaraderie among all of the thousands walking the streets was incredible, a full moon helped make the absence of street and traffic lights much less dangerous, and crime fell substantially that night. The streets became a great big party.

Everyone may have been in a joyous mood, but it was very difficult to accept the situation, given the money that had been paid and the increasing awareness that the problem was not going to be solved quickly. The Club did not sell any tickets that night, but luckily those loyal skiers who had purchased tickets in advance, for most part, did not demand their money back. Of course, neither Hans nor Hancock Hall was available the next night, so postponing was not an option. It was expensive, but certainly memorable.

One cause of excitement was unccrtainty about what had happened and what was going to happen. There was no radio or television. People in those days did not have cell phones or the Internet. With no power, they would not have been working anyway.

One of the most interesting, and unquestioned, stories nine months later was that hospitals throughout the area were experiencing a massive jump in births. The cause was obvious and caused a lot of laughs, but reports surfaced saying that it made a good story, but was simply not supported by the facts.

GOOD TIMING

It pays to look ahead and see when it is going to be an extra special time to be somewhere. I loved Mt Saint Michel and its incredible tides. The sandy "beach" is so wide and shallow that the incoming tide supposedly moves faster than a horse can run and people die from going out too far and finding themselves unable to run fast enough to stay ahead of the tide when it reverses and starts to come back in.

Seeing the prediction, I scheduled to take my mother and sister to France and be at Mt. St. Michel on the day of a super high tide in 1961. The little town with its cathedral towering above is normally connected to the mainland by a raised, narrow two-lane causeway and is beautiful at all times. Only rarely does the tide come up so far that it covers the road and surrounds Mt. St. Michel.

31 DRIVING MISS DAISY

Actually, The Passengers Were Other People

Today, people are not really taught how to drive; they are taught how to pass a driver's test. Airline pilots pass an elaborate exam, using sophisticated flight simulators, but have to be checked out in new aircraft with which they are totally unfamiliar. Also, they are taught how to handle emergencies and have instant reflexes as a hazard arises. Drivers pass a simple test at slow speeds, after which they can drive dissimilar vehicles at high speeds on Interstate highways or on icy winding roads.

I was lucky enough to pay for real driver's ed, including driving at speeds of 150mph and correcting for side slides and becoming accustomed to understeer and oversteer. This training was available at two race courses, Lime Rock and Thompson, both in Connecticut. I suspect most drivers don't even know what oversteer or understeer mean. I was used to low sports cars that handled beautifully. Today I am stuck with a top-heavy SUV. The Hyundai Sante Fe's Owners Manual has many warnings highlighted-in-yellow about propensity to rollover.

The main thing that needs to be ingrained in a driver is an immediate reaction is not to hit the brakes when you find yourself on a sheet of ice. This has been altered by anti-lock braking systems which provide much better stopping by putting on the brakes using thousands of very brief application of the brakes no matter how hard you push down on the pedal. Problem is you must know if you are driving a car with or without that system. You also don't slow down, much less stop, when trying to get uphill in mud or on ice. You have to maintain steady pressure on the car's accelerator.

Once on a bridge in Alabama while driving my mother and sister to our cousin's house in Anniston, Alabama for Christmas, I saw a car ahead of me on the bridge slide out of control. They were going slowly, probably 35mph, but sliding sideways, facing 90 degrees to the left of where they were heading. They were going in the right direction down the middle of the bridge, just getting there by sliding sideways. The car blocked both lanes and there was no room to get past them. Knowing not to touch the brakes, I kept going, gaining on them steadily but slowly. The car ahead slid to the end of the bridge just in time for me to skirt past them on the grass on the right. Had I touched the brakes we would have collided. Most drivers would have slammed on the brakes.

For years there has been talk about making elderly drivers take a new test before having their license renewed. Toughening up the requirements for a driver's license would face huge opposition so it may never happen. It badly needs to happen, but it probably will not. I hate to think of how many people today have learned to drive automatic transmission vehicles and have no experience with shift cars. They would be unable to handle a great sports car with any shift, much less the ones with a half dozen tight forward gears and a sensitive clutch.

Hopefully sometime in the near future, simulators will be developed and implemented to make sure a person really can drive a car, nor just steer it. We let people drive these heavy machines at high speeds without having any idea how to cope with a wide variety of emergencies.

That reminded me of another example of something people need to do. Learn to adjust and to use your rear view mirrors, keeping aware of what is behind you and beside you. In a spit second you can hit a car in front of you if you turn and look back over your shoulder to see if there is a vehicle beside you. Most cars on an Interstate drive 70mph. That's 102 ft per second. If the driver ahead of you slams on its brakes, you probably will not be able to stop before hitting it even if you have your eyes on the car when it begins to brake. That half second looking over your shoulder could cost you your life.

It is also absurd to let people drive with a couple of fingers touching the bottom of the steering wheel. A friend of mine drives with the wrist of one hand touching to the top of the steering wheel. Such drivers have no ability to react quickly to an emergency. Both hands need to be on the wheel at or near the 10 o'clock and 2 o'clock positions. At the very least, one hand should be around the steering wheel in the right position. Manufacturers should be required to place airbags far enough away from the rim of the steering wheel that they do not blast your fingers when they are activated. This problem is what causes experts today to recommend gripping the wheel at 9 and 3 o'clock.

Texting while driving is not going to go away completely unless it is stopped by technology, and that merely adds another very dangerous component to the problem. We also continue to have a few people who drive in a blinding downpour without their lights on. Stupid, and unfair to other drivers. Maybe driving in bad weather isn't as important down south, but up in snow and ice country some sort of extra testing should be implemented. A good simulator would enable the authorities to check reactions to sudden, unexpected emergencies. Maybe it will become the practice someday. In England, you flunk your test if you fail to "square" an intersection, meaning you don't curve left across any of the oncoming lane aimed at you. You drive until you can turn only into the lane onto which you are turning. Not sure, but I guess that sentence makes sense.

DRIVING IN EUROPE

The vast majority of Americans never even get to Europe, much less do a lot of driving around there. When my jobs required that I be on the road for long periods of time, mostly in Europe, South America and Southeast Asia, my expense account, in addition to things such as hotels and meals, allowed me to rent a car every weekend.

In the US, we all too frequently get stuck behind cars that drive long distances side by side. Cars sit in the left lane of an Interstate and don't even seem to notice when a dozen cars pull out and pass them on the right. I call it "Driving While Oblivious. Driving with earplugs in listening to loud music has exacerbated the problem. You can see why ambulances and fire trucks have to drive so slowly because they cannot tell if someone ahead of them hears their siren and sees their brightly blinking lights.

Even experienced US drivers in Europe put themselves at serious risk of death sitting in the left lanes of Autobahns or Autostradas. Because too many of them are guilty of DWO (Driving While Oblivous), they don't notice when a car far behind them starts flashing their bright headlights. Most Americans don't even maintain awareness of cars close behind them or beside them, much less one a quarter of a mile behind. Many of the major highways in Europe have what by American standards would be considered extremely long on ramps that allow cars to get up to substantial speed before merging into the right lane of a highway. These "ramps" can be a third of a mile in length, contrasted with a few hundred feet in the US. On the best European highways, you can get going 80 before you merge left into the traffic already in the lane you are entering.

A US driver in Germany or Italy who is DWO and sitting in the left lane is probably unaware the there is a car a quarter mile behind them in the left hand lane going 120 miles per hour. You simply should not stay very long in the left lane and you certainly don't change left into a lane without checking carefully what is coming at you from far behind. It is not known as the passing lane for no good reason. That gap between a slowpoke and a car coming fast from behind will close very fast, and the DWO driver must begin to move over in time for the driver behind to be confident that the vehicle ahead will have moved over well before they converge.

I have been driving 120mph and had a car pass even faster.

DRIVING IN SNOW

Living for 39 years in Boston, I am amused by the impact of an inch of snow in Montgomery. On January 29, 2014, Montgomery had about a half inch, maybe an inch, of snow. It was a big storm, driven down from Canada with single digit temperatures, stretching all the way across the deep South. To those of us who had lived up north it seemed ridiculous. It seemed as if every county in the state of Alabama closed all of its roads. The Mayor, Todd Strange, was right; drivers simply do not know how to drive in snow, or worse, on ice. I tried to cheer up friends by telling them how easy they had it compared to my driving experiences in New England.

On the very steep residential streets of Beacon Hill, where there were less than a dozen homes with private parking garages, you had to get up and shovel your car out of a parallel parking place. When trying to remove a foot of frozen snow, you had to be very careful not to scrape your car. What would really hurt was having the snow plow drive by when you had almost finished and bury your car again. It wasn't just having to get the snow off your car: you had to dig a path so you could get your car out into the street. You only had to face major digging out about a half-dozen times a year. The latest that we saw a foot of snow was May 7 one year. Across from John Kerry's home on Louisberg Square at the other end of the small Louisburg Square we watched a car slide very slowly downhill on solid ice for what must have been at least 30 seconds before gently ramming into the side of my date's car.

Driving home from skiing in Waterville Valley, New Hampshire on the evening of February 8, 1969, we were caught in a big snowstorm on Interstate I-93 one night in New Hampshire. Lolly McDonald and I had to spend the night in my little two-seater Jaguar XKE when the Interstate became clogged and traffic stopped. We got in our sleeping bags and started the engine every hour or so to warm up. Police estimated about 11,000 spent the night in their cars on that stretch. State troopers on snowmobiles the next morning came through checking on all the cars and delivering medical supplies to those in need. It was an eerie night. It was several hours later that morning before traffic started moving again.

JFK's INAUGURATION

When we drove from Boston to Washington the night before Kennedy's Inauguration, cars that did not know how to handle the 8 inches of snow clogged the road. We managed to dodge cars and people walking in the highway in the blinding snow, making it through to DC and then to my uncle's house near DuPont Circle, but that meant never coming to a complete stop while weaving through obstacles. Most cars that stopped could not get going again. They had to call out the Army to clear the D. C. streets all night so that the inaugural parade could take place.

That was a great experience because the dad of my date, Sarah Lingham, got us seats up close and center in front of all the dignitaries. We were just halfway between the TV booth up in the air behind us and the podium from which Kennedy gave his inspiring speech. I got a great picture of all the VIPs together around the new president.

The only time I saw all the roads closed in Boston was when Governor Dukakis ordered everyone to stay off the streets and highways in Massachusetts for four full days to give the Army time to clear the 4 feet of snow that the wind had blown into 8-12 foot drifts. I had to have a skeleton staff live in the office for all that time because we had to be open 24 hours a day, 7 days a week, with the peak hours between 3am and 9am to handle reservations for customers in Europe.

WHAT A CAR!

In 1965 I was making too much money and wanted to have something better than my MG. I came very close to buying a used Mercedes "Gullwing" 300SL. The name derived from the fact that, instead of being hinged on the front, the doors were hinged in the middle of the roof. The doors folded up instead of the common opening out.

When open they resembled a gull's wings. Even after 70 years, the 300SL retains its iconic status and well-restored ones can sell for close to a million dollars. I might have picked that car had it not been ten years old and dark brown, a color in which cars should never have been made. It was, and continues to be, one of the greatest models of mass production car ever built.

Instead, I picked a brand new spectacular Jaguar XKE, black with red leather interior for the same price....$4,500. The 1965 was a two seater. A few years later they ruined the look by trying to cram two small children's seats behind, making the roofline higher.

The early XKEs are still rated as one of the very best designs ever, and as a result one resides in the Museum of Modern Art. It was so low to the ground that you felt as if you were climbing down into the seats, which were level with the frame on the side of the car. It was unfortunately known for having "popsicle clearance," meaning (jokingly) that the underside of the car could clear a popsicle stick lying on the road *provided* the stick was lying flat on the ground.

SENSE OF SPEED IS RELATIVE

One day I was driving back to Boston, having spent the weekend in New York with Betsy Burns, another employee of State Street Bank. Today I drive the required 9 miles an hour over the posted speed limit. At least in major open stretches on Interstates the speed limit in many places is now 70mph. When drivers are driving at the posted speed limit and complain that cars are speeding past them, it usually means they are driving the posted speed limit, not the enforced and generally-observed speed limit.

On a deserted six lane highway in southwestern Connecticut that day I decided to begin pushing slowly down on the accelerator. The XKE was very smooth, even at high speed. In that car, you may have seen the landscape going by, but you did not have the feeling of driving fast. Gradually increasing the speed, the higher speed became pretty unnoticeable. Having held it at 115mph for a few miles I let Betsy get used to the speed at which we were passing the scenery, I asked her to look out the windows as I gently slowed down. Finally, I asked her to look carefully at the landscape and guess how fast we were going. After careful consideration, she guessed 10mph. I had slowed to 55, the speed limit in Connecticut at the time, but the speed limit felt like 10mph (at least to her). After writing that, I later decided that the statement was incorrect. 55 felt like 10 to both of us.

MINIMUM SPEED LIMITS

Minimum speed limits are rarely enforced, but should be. Maximums have been 40mph on most highways, dating back to the days when speed limits were 55mph. Now speed limits on Interstates are at the very least in the 60mph range, meaning that most traffic is moving at 69mph. In many places the posted speed limit is now 70, meaning that the traffic is going to be moving at about 80mph. When a person is camped out in a middle or even left lane going 55 or 60mph, cars are changing lanes to pass on the right. The minimum on Interstates should be bumped to not more than 10mph below the posted speed limit.

CONNECTICUT

Shortly after that, in October of 1967, I had to drive from Marblehead, Massachusetts to New York City to look at buying a racing sailboat. I had asked a very experienced boating friend, Pieter Mimno, to accompany me and advise regarding the 30-year-old wooden sailboat I was considering. We had an appointment with the man who was to show us his boat at The World's Fair Marina near La Guardia and we were running late. Somewhere south of Hartford there was very little traffic on a divided highway with a wide treed median, so I started going faster and faster. In the mid-sixties, Connecticut's 55mph speed limit was the slowest in the country. Driving in the left lane of the divided highway as we reached the crest of a hill, I spotted a radar camera on the ground a few feet from the highway.

Before hand-held radar "guns," and ones installed on the dashboards of police cars, the early radars were small boxes painted light green that sat on small tripods about a foot above the ground. Also, unlike today, these cameras were connected by a cable to a speedometer read out instrument in the police car. An instant after seeing the camera, I glanced up to the left and saw the state police car hidden in the trees on a slight hill. Today you frequently see several police cars down the highway on the right side with a group of officers on pullover and ticket duty. I did not know what to expect, but I knew I was caught and was in big trouble. I had inched it up to 135mph, which was smooth in my new Jaguar XKE and I had taken lots of highly worthwhile lessons in controlling cars at high speeds.

I moaned to Pieter and started to slow down to change lanes, moving right preparatory to being stopped. There is more to the story, but the initial portion was one of unbelievable luck. There was just one police car on pullover duty parked in the breakdown lane and its only officer was twenty feet or so behind his car writing out a ticket to, believe it or not, a little old lady in a Volkswagen! It wasn't just that it was a little old lady; in those days Volkswagens had small engines and would not go very fast. It is possible she could have been going 65. I knew they were not going to let me get away with that speed. The men in the radar car must have been screaming over the radio to the officer up ahead to pull me over. I probably should have taken the next exit, but we had to get to New York so I slowed to exactly 55mph and waited.

THEY CAUGHT ME

It wasn't long before I saw the flashing blue lights coming fast from far behind. When the trooper got within a quarter mile or so and saw my car, the flashing lights were turned off and he came right up behind me. I was very careful to continue holding it on exactly 55mph. I knew that was legal and knew he had no grounds for stopping me. He obviously also knew the law and must have recognized that I did, too.

When I say right up behind me it was literally about a foot behind my rear bumper, if that. He was so close that I am to this day amazed he did not touch my car. I had told Pieter not to turn around; just to keep talking. Pieter did watch the police car in my right rearview mirror. The guy sat there for what seemed an eternity, but it was probably not more than 30 seconds. Speeding tickets are not given to vehicles, they are given to a driver. The police in most jurisdictions are required to keep the vehicle in sight from the time the speed is noted until the car is stopped. The police would have to prove that you had not changed drivers while out of sight. It had been ten minutes or so since I had gone through radar, so we easily could have changed drivers. The officer would not be able to claim I was definitely the driver at the time we went through radar.

In that extremely low Jaguar, the cop car completely blocked the view through my rear window. His car was huge and mine was extremely low. He obviously knew there was no way that I didn't know he was there. I often wonder what would have happened had I touched the brakes and he had hit me because of following much too close. You talk about tailgating; this was the most extreme tailgating imaginable other than drafting on a NASCAR racetrack. I just kept looking straight ahead, talking with Pieter and holding it on exactly 55mph.

Anyway, he finally let off a little bit and then pulled up beside me. This was even worse. He nestled over next to me. Pieter could obviously see the huge right fender looming up almost touching the left side of my car. I kept Pieter looking straight ahead and kept talking with him and facing straight ahead with both hands on the steering wheel and my eyes on the speedometer. If there was any doubt that I had failed to see him in my rear view mirror, there was no remote possibility that I could continue driving, keeping facing straight ahead without seeing that fender ahead of me, much higher than my front fender and just a little to the left. I don't know how he could judge how close he was. That Jaguar had big rounded sides. Most automobiles have doors the sides of which are essentially vertical; the Jaguar's doors curved way out from the windows and then way back in. He must have been about an inch away from touching the door beside me.

The officer sat there, probably staring at me, for another 20 or 30 seconds. He must have been really furious. I drove straight as an arrow at exactly 55mph so he had no grounds for pulling me over. Finally, to my great relief, he gunned it and pulled ahead fast until out of sight. Even though it made us late, I hung onto 55 the rest of the way through Connecticut.

RELATED

A great story, *maybe* true but doubtful, went around in 2017 about Highway Patrol officers in Kingsville, Texas. The hand-held radar detector suddenly read "300 miles per hour." It was a jet flying low out of the nearby Naval Air Station. The Corpus Christi Patrol Captain fired off a complaint to the Base Commander, whose response contained great comments. He said the police might be interested to know that the jets computer had detected the hostile radar equipment and automatically locked onto the device, sent a jamming signal, and the plane's sophisticated system had prepared to launch a missile at the target. The pilot recognized the situation and overrode the launch before it was activated. Lucky Patrol officers.

SPEED TRAPS

In the 1950s and 60s, Ludowici, Georgia was the most notorious speed trap in the country. In reality, it was more of a red-light trick than a trap, but this was the title given it. Most remaining speed traps are based upon sudden and inadequately marked drops in the speed limit. Ludowici allegedly added trickery to the procedure. The story was that the police had installed a remote control on the traffic light in the middle of town. Locals knew to use a different intersection so the police could get all of the fines from strangers, frequently "Yankees" driving north to New York or south into Florida. Even today, Southerners like taking money from the damn Yankees.

Wikipedia states that the remote control was in a barbershop that looked out at the street. When a car going fast was spotted, the operator would flip the switch at the last second, almost instantly turning the light from green to red, with only a millisecond devoted to yellow. Time Magazine even wrote an article about Ludowici's traffic trap in 1970 and AAA heard so many complaints that they labeled Ludowici a trap and cautioned drivers about it. Supposedly, they paid for a billboard alerting drivers to the problem ahead.

In the news in February of 2014 was a speed trap in Hampton, Florida, a town that is facing dissolution by the state because of gross mismanagement. Hampton is a strange little town southwest of Jacksonville. The town is essentially a one square mile area, but the city limits were extended on a narrow section of Navarre Ave all the way to State Road 200. It got to be so notorious that a billboard was erected warning drivers of what was ahead. The highway's speed limit dropped abruptly for only a couple of hundred feet and the town brought in hundreds of thousands of dollars from that miniscule stretch of highway. The population of Hampton in the last census was just 477 people, but an astonishing 17 of those were police. The AAA in later years erected billboards cautioning people on Florida Route 310 about speed traps ahead in Waldo and Lawtey. These miniscule towns were getting about three quarters of their income from traffic tickets, all from out-of-towners. Have you ever heard of a city with police being 16 % of the population? This type of enforcement should be banned.

Bryan County, Georgia, just west of Savannah is able to earn lots of income from "speeders" on Interstate 16. Because I-16 just goes through the northeastern corner of the county, it gets loads of out-of-town drivers and almost no locals. Coming south from Atlanta you drive for a very long time in a seventy mph stretch that drops suddenly and without anywhere near adequate warning for a brief stretch. With no exits in Bryan County there is no safety reason for the slower stretch other than to get income from the County.

Yes, I got stopped there and it was very expensive. There was also a construction zone, but I knew there was no construction going on. The orange barrels were pulled out near the highway when they were doing some work and pulled away when no construction was going on. Also, it was 9pm on the Sunday night of Christmas weekend. Contiguous states, Florida and Alabama, have signs that read "fines doubled when workers present." Georgia doubles the fine no matter what and my fine was over $300.

Here we come to the interesting point. Two local lawyers told me that the County Commission had instructed the judge to practice strict enforcement….no leniency and that the unstated purpose was to increase income gained from "out-of-towners." What was really sad and, to my mind very irritating, was the fact that the vast majority of the people sitting in that courtroom that morning were soldiers in uniform from Fort Stewart, which occupies about half of the county. Taking money from them was grossly objectionable.

The lawyers were nice enough to tell me a way to get through it without having it cost me lots of money in insurance premiums. Don't know if it was true, but the advice worked. When I neared the end of my testimony, I included a comment about the unfairness of the heavy fine and the increased insurance cost. When finished, the judge asked me if I would agree to pay the fine in full if he agreed not to report it to my insurance company. I would rather have had the fine reduced, but it was safer not to fight it so I accepted the judge's offer. The Bryan County lawyers had told me that the law required the County to pay part of fines to the State, but if they did not report it the County got to keep all of the fine. The judge had a financial incentive not to report the ticket.

WAZE AND MEANS

No, this is not about the U.S. Congressional Committee; it is about something that I have found few people know about and certainly should for two reasons. Why should anybody that has a smart phone (and I know few who don't) buy an expensive GPS system for their car when there is a much better system available for free.

Waze is basically a sophisticated GPS system, but it has several distinct advantages, one that could save you lots of money. Waze plots your route and the lady inside tells you where to turn. Guess you all know that when a study was made of names given to the lady that talks to you from a GPS one name was by far the most common. It probably stems from the often-heard phrase "Recalculating." At least Pat's more recent GPS doesn't say this. In a nationwide study of names given to the lady who talks to you from the GPS, the name most often chosen for is "Bitch" as in "Shut Up Bitch."

Anyway, the lady in Waze talks a lot like the lady in the common Garmin and Magellan GPS systems. The huge difference is the addition of current traffic, accident and, most importantly, police activity ahead. There is a page on your smart phone on which people ahead of you can easily tap an icon that alerts you to what is ahead. You are not required to do so, but it is very nice to send the messages to cars behind you about what to expect. When you tap the button for breakdown in the right lane the system uses your location at that moment to tell the cars behind you how many miles or feet ahead of them the problem exists.

One day when Pat and I were driving from Miami to Key Largo the alert appeared that there was a police car ahead. It didn't just say police, it said "police car (hidden) ahead." A few minutes later we saw the highway patrol hidden behind a concrete barrier using radar to catch cars coming onto the bridge toward us. Virginia bans radar detectors in cars, has enormous fines for exceeding the speed limit, and can detect if you have radar because the can pick up the transmission of the signal from your unit. They can't detect Waze. I was appalled when Garmin wanted to charge me $85 just to update the maps in my GPS. I wouldn't want to be a Garmin stockholder when enough people discover Waze and learn that they can get a much better system for free.

MY FUNNIEST DRIVING MOMENT

Having parked my big Mercedes on a very slight but icy hill in Marblehead, Massachusetts, I put it in park, got out and started to walk away. Luckily, I noticed my car start to slide, ever so slowly. It would have gained momentum, slid down a steep hill and crossed Atlantic Avenue, possibly hitting a car. A hold with one hand was enough to stop it long enough for me to grab the door handle, get back in and drive it safely down the hill.

EUROPE HAS BECOME UNFRIENDLY TO TOURISTS

There was an excellent article in *USAToday* by Chris Elliott, warning about driving in restricted areas in Europe. They do put up signs in the local language, but not in English. The fines are steep and rental car company's maps do not show the area into which you cannot drive without getting a huge fine. Once I let all the passengers out to visit the Leaning Tower of Pisa, driving around and around the blocks until they showed up at the pick-up spot. I got a big ticket for every time I rode around the block. In Siena, we got caught in a lane with no exit other than straight ahead into the camera that photographs your license plate so that a bill can be sent. They can charge your credit card used for the car rental. The cars behind us would not let us back up. It was extremely expensive.

32 FLYING HIGH

The 1982 Darwin Awards

Here is one that is not from personal experience but is just too funny to leave out. Many people each year anxiously await the announcement of the year's winner of the Darwin Award, the person who has done the most to improve the gene pool of the world by dying stupidly, thereby removing himself from the gene pool. There are usually at least a half-dozen finalists, ranked in order of stupidity, but only one is deemed to be the one most deserving of the award

A California man, Larry Walters, always wanted to fly. He attempted to join the Air Force, but could not pass the eye test. Discouraged, but still wanting to live his dream, Larry bought 45 huge weather balloons, each of which could hold 33 cubic feet. 1485 cubic feet is a lot of helium. He tied his lawn chair to the bumper of his car, filled his balloons and, tied them to his lawn chair. They were in two clusters, one at the top connected to another cluster that was tied to a rope to his lawn chair bellow. There is a frequent thread running through many of the stupid acts over the years, it is involving beer. Larry loaded lots of Miller Lite onto his chair.

At first, he tied to his craft to the bumper of his car and rose about thirty feet. Larry enjoyed the view and thought it would be fun to go even higher. He also took a pellet rifle he planned to use to shoot out a few balloons and cause his chair to lower back down to the ground. Needless to say, he did not understand helium and wind. When his friends cut the tether, Larry's chair shot into the air, climbing to an incredible 16,000 feet. From there, he did not dare shoot out balloons, so he just drifted for 14 hours, eventually into the primary landing approach path for huge jets coming into the LAX airport. Two airplanes went by. I can't imagine what pilots must have thought. It was certainly dangerous to Larry and to the plane, but it was certainly also amusing. The first pilot and co-pilot must have been very reluctant to make a call to the tower. The TWA pilot prefaced his report with the fact that he would be laughed at but his story was true. Obviously, the Air Traffic Control man at LAX was incredulous, so it took some talking to get him to believe what the pilots had seen. The story was confirmed shortly thereafter by a Delta Airlines pilot. Finally, Larry got up the nerve to begin shooting out balloons and returned to earth, unfortunately landing on and becoming entangled in powerlines in Long Beach. He was arrested by the LAPD, the power to the neighborhood stayed out for more than 20 minutes, and the FAA fined him $1,500. A website lets you listen to the pilots' conversations with ATC.

By the way, Larry got honorable mention because he failed to die from his stunt, making him ineligible for the big prize.

33 THREE BIG MISTAKES

All On Just One Trip To Europe

MUNICH

One of my most enjoyable, and fattening, responsibilities was deciding in which country and then in which city State Street Bank should locate its first office outside the United States. When the bank opened in Munich, a team of representatives meeting there in late September of 1969 were staying in one hotel. My boss at the time unfortunately happened to be named Mike Clark.

After the meeting, I was scheduled to meet with a prospective client in Madrid, but there were going to be a weekend between the end of the first series of meetings and the one in Spain. I invited the girl I was dating, D (name abbreviated to protect the happily married), to fly from Boston to Mallorca for a few days, then to the meeting in Madrid and, when she decided to take the trip, we added on stops in Lisbon and the Azores because Pan Am in those days had a stop, at no extra charge, on one of the islands of the Azores, far out in the Atlantic on their route from Lisbon back to Boston.

MALLORCA

The problems started when my date, D, who had arrived in Palmas de Mallorca, the largest city in the Balearic Islands in the western portion of the Mediterranean Sea, sent me a telegram on October 1 notifying me that she was switching hotels. The hotel in Munich simply marked the incoming message "For Mr. Clark" and put it in Mr. Clark's mail slot. Only problem was the slot they put it in was that of my boss, Mike Clark. Yes, it had my first name on it, but they had not paid attention. D had changed hotels because I had used the Fielding's Guide and booked the best in Palma. It turned out to be an excellent but very, stuffy old hotel, downtown, far from the beaches. D wanted to lounge on the beach in her bikini while awaiting my arrival.

When I arrived, I could not believe the deal she had gotten from the Hotel El Cid, the first big hotel as you reached the beach on the road from downtown Palmas. It was fantastic. Later I learned why. Familiar with the hotel industry, I assumed that the hotel was overbooked, had no single rooms and had to give her the huge top-floor suite at the end of the wing that extended toward the beach for the single-room price. It had windows all around and an excellent view down the beach and over the Mediterranean. It was clearly the best place in the entire hotel. Although the décor was quite unattractive, there were a ridiculous number of beds and bedrooms we didn't need. I do not remember the price, but it was ridiculously low, about $80, about what you would have expected for a single room on a lower floor without any view. Something was fishy, but I did not know what.

After dinner, we came back to the room and went to take a shower. D got in the shower first. When I joined her, I heard strange noises from above. It was something that sounded like giggling or squealing coming from above. When I glanced up, I saw at least a dozen eyes peering down through a large open vent above the shower. You could hear the guys as they ran away on the roof. With an incredible body, it was obvious why they had wanted D. in that room and were willing to offer it at such a low price to be sure she took it. The person at the front desk took one look and decided she should be in that suite. The guys had probably been watching D. during the nights before I arrived. All of the rooms on the top floor had the same open-air vents over the showers in their bathrooms, so the guys on the hotel staff must have done lots of sightseeing of previous guests. I suspect the staff had someone assigned to spot us heading for the elevator and notified all of the gang to report to the roof. Looking at the hotel by satellite photo, it appears to have the same vents today, but they now appear to be behind many solar panels.

MADRID

The visit in Madrid was most enjoyable, and the client signed up. As foreign visitors, they took us out for the evening that, in Spain meant dinner at about 11pm. They served lots of drinks before dinner and more at a nightclub after dinner. It was apparent that all of the Spanish men were much more interested looking at D. than they were in entertaining me. The unusual part of the evening was being hosted by the company's celebrity public relations man, someone who, as an American, I had never heard of before that evening.

The guy's name was Jaime Ostos and was, at the time, Spain's leading bullfighter. That is like being the star quarterback of the NFL and the top pitcher in MLB in the US combined. He gave us a bunch of autographed pictures, but I later found fairly soon after that the best pictures in a long article with many full-page pictures of Jaime in Sports Illustrated. Being hosted around town by him was great fun and being with him made it an extremely enjoyable night (or better to say, night and early morning) on the town.

THE AZORES

Next stop, the Azores, a group of relatively small Portuguese Islands located far out in the Atlantic Ocean, roughly one thousand miles off the coast of Portugal, about a third of the way from Portugal to New York. They are beautiful, lush, extinct volcanoes.

Our Pan Am flight landed. Our travel agent, Wanda (one of the best travel agents in Boston), had booked us into a hotel right on the water near the middle of town. We claimed our luggage and walked out to the taxis. Unlike many foreign places where most people, especially those in jobs related to travel, speak English, the people here did not, probably because almost all of the travelers are Portuguese. Very few non-Portuguese from Europe make it to the Azores, and essentially none from the U.S.

I tried pronouncing the hotel name slowly and clearly, but the taxi driver shook his head "no." There was no explanation, just "no." That was hard for us to understand because the hotel should be the best hotel on the island. It should not have been hard to pronounce. The next thing to do was print the hotel name on a piece of paper, hoping that someone could read it, know where to take us and be willing to take us. We unloaded our luggage from the first taxi and went to another taxi. Once inside, we said the hotel name and then showed the paper to the driver. Once again, the driver shook his head "No," opened the taxi door for us and proceeded to unload our stuff. This was becoming a bit irritating. The island was not that big, about ten miles long. We were booked into what I thought was the best hotel. Why would the drivers refuse to take us?

The answer we eventually learned was quite simple. The major airport used by Pan Am was on the western edge of Santa Maria Island and our hotel was about 60 miles away, across the ocean on Sao Miguel Island. It was a larger, more beautiful and more populous island, but it wasn't the island we were on. Our hotel was in the largest city on Sao Miguel, Ponta Delgada. Luckily, there was a flight scheduled to go there in just an hour. I purchased tickets, got the last two seats and took the flight. Quite surprised the travel agent had not caught this, but it happens.

The Azores are remarkably beautiful islands. Because the islands are of volcanic origin, the fine sand on the beaches is all pitch black. If you are accustomed to thinking in terms of the whitest sand, this may sound "dirty," but the stark contrast between the black sand and the white of the waves breaking on the beaches is quite beautiful. The Azores do have a major disadvantage, they are not islands to travel to for warmth, beaches and swimming when you are trying to avoid cold winter weather. The Azores are at about the same latitude as Delaware.

At the time of our trip, there were almost no tourists and the prices were quite reasonable. I have now been to several islands in the Azores, and I recommend Sao Miguel as by far the most enjoyable. The second time I went to the Azores the airline stopped on Terceira, which was not that interesting. Sao Miguel has beautiful scenery, interesting little towns, very hospitable people, unusual beaches and lush golf courses. We were lucky to be there on religious festival day in Furnas when the parishioners covered the main street with designs created by using thousands of brightly colored flowers.

On our flight from Sao Miguel a few days later, the plane was filled by locals, most of whom were natives who had never before been on an airplane. In addition to the terror of flying, they were leaving their homes for the first time. There was lots of screaming and many in tears, headed to Santa Maria for flights to Portugal and ours to the U.S. It had been quite a trip.

CAUTION

The design of the El Cid Hotel was not a unique mistake. The same design mistakes exist in the United States. Near the center of Fernandina, Florida, there is a motel with equipment maintenance halls running down the middle of each building, with sleeping rooms on either side. The halls provide access to all of the equipment: pipes, heating and cooling ducts, electrical connections, etc. The halls are also part of the ventilation system, so there are vents at about eye level in all of the bathrooms.

The louvered vents are of the type that have metal flanges set at an angle to deflect the air flow. When I discovered how they were being used, I notified the hotel. I should have called the police or hired a lawyer to sue them. A hall door had been left unlocked and slightly ajar so, when I walked past, I noticed a man looking through a vent. There were dozens of options in each hallway, so he could move from vent to vent checking to see which bathrooms were in use and had the best "scenery."

We used to go to that motel once a year in the spring for the fabulous antique automobile show, "The Concours d'Elegance" on the golf course of the Ritz Carlton Amelia Island. The Ritz was incredibly expensive, requiring a three-night minimum stay during the car show. Our Landings Car Club got a good group rate each year for one night at that motel during the car show.

The next time there, I found that the motel had at least reversed the angle of the vents, switching them so that the view through the louvers no longer looked into where they could see anybody in the bathroom. This must have meant they had listened, recognized the problem and attempted to correct it.

34 AIRLINE RESERVATION SYSTEMS

A Course entitled "How to Beat Your Competitors, 101"

This chapter is largely about American Airlines and how it won out against its more powerful competitors many years ago. It requires some background info re how I became involved.

As you have read, in 1965 two friends and I decided to start a travel agency. We never would have believed Heritage Travel would grow to become the seventh largest agency in the US with offices coast to coast.

Our partner, who became the principal owner of Heritage Travel in Cambridge, Massachusetts, is a true genius. He did not just have an MBA from the Harvard Business School; Don Sohn had a doctorate (DBA) from there and had taught at MIT's Sloan School of Business before we started Heritage. In those days, travel agencies handled vacations and personal travel. Businesses simply would not use a travel agency, and the airlines incorporated sneaky little tricks to prevent this from happening. Heritage, due to Don's genius and his business acumen, was the first agency to computerize and the first to specialize in business travel in the United States.

Don was the genius behind much of what happened over the next decade in the travel agency business and, to a lesser but still important role, the airline industry. Powerful businessmen like Ruppert Murdock and Carl Icahn flew to Boston to sit down with us and get advice. I may have been the other person in the meetings but it was clearly Don's ideas that they sought.

Don was the first to recognize the potential, figure out how business travel could be handled profitably, served effectively and begin to handle business travel. The first two major corporate clients of Heritage Travel were United Brands and the Gillette Corporation, both of which were headquartered in Boston. Among what became a long string of firsts, Don saw the potential of computerization and talked several airlines into allowing Heritage Travel to have in its offices the reservation computer terminals of their airlines, giving the agency a big advantage in handling business travel. Instead of talking with a traveler or secretary, taking notes, hanging up, calling the airlines and then calling the traveler back, our reservations agents could type the information into their computer, tell the traveler that the flight was confirmed, or continue the conversation reviewing other flight options. It may be simple by today's standards, but it was revolutionary at the time.

Years later, when the American Society of Travel Agents woke up and saw the need for automation, they joined with some of the major airlines in forming JICRS, the Joint Industry Computer Reservation System project. Max Hopper, the computer genius of American Airlines became the senior representative of the airline industry on the project and Don Sohn was appointed by the ASTA to serve as head of the travel agency side of the project. As later stated by Max Hopper, Don made massive contributions to the design of airline systems, especially as they would be used in travel agencies. Some of his ideas were incorporated into American's system for their own use.

Among his many ideas, Don's primary request of American Airlines was that they create a system whereby a travel agency's employees could enter lots of information regarding frequent travelers into American's reservation system so our agents would not have to waste time entering that information in their computer every time a reservation was requested. More on that later.

WOODSIDE

This chapter probably should have come before several you have already read. Representing Heritage in the group on Saturday, July 21, 1973 in Woodside, California when Don Travel (then New York's top commercial travel company), the Haley Corporation (by far the largest in San Francisco) and Cahill-Edmund Travel (at Phoenix's airport), got together at Don Sohn's urging and decided to form what became known as The Woodside Group of Travel Agencies. Woodside eventually included hundreds of offices throughout Europe, Asia, South America plus Australia and New Zealand. After running Woodside from Heritage Travel, the decision was made to proceed at a location in downtown Boston. Woodside had grown to the point where we needed to have an independent identity, rather than being so obviously linked to Heritage. I headed up the office, at first assisted only by my secretary, Betty Giallanella.

As the team of agencies grew throughout the country, we attempted to get computer systems for all of them, regardless of their location. At the time, the only US airlines that had automated a few travel agencies were American, United, TWA and, to a much lesser extent, Allegheny (which was known as Agony Airlines and later became USAir which, until it was taken over by American, was supposed to stand for "Unfortunately Still Allegheny In Reality).

I flew alone to Miami to meet with sales, operations officers and computer gurus at Eastern and then up to Atlanta to meet with Delta. The meeting in Miami was with relatively low-ranking officers; there was little interest, I got nowhere, and remember nothing about the meeting. Eastern was far behind their competition, had little money with which to work and had to attempt to deal with a horrendous union. There is more on this subject in the comments on Carl Icahn having come to see us for advice regarding Eastern and TWA.

My meeting in Atlanta with Delta went much better but was also unsuccessful. The meeting with Delta was, however, much more memorable and Atlanta at a later date would assume a great role that very few know about. There were a number of Delta's senior sales, agency relations, information technology, and management representatives in the meeting. The joke in those days was that Eastern considered Delta its only direct competitor and Delta felt the same way about Eastern. It may have been considered a joke but, in reality, it was the way the two carriers operated at the time.

After politely discussing the potential future in providing automation to travel agencies and how the expansion of reservation computer systems and computerized ticketing and accounting would benefit the airlines, Delta asked their standard question. Was Eastern doing this? I had to answer "no." At the time, thousands of people were having to sort through all airline tickets, trying to read all of the millions of handwritten tickets, and dividing up the monies due from the carrier on which the ticket was issued among the other airlines that were involved in the itinerary. My presentation to Delta focused on computerization of ticket issuance, which Heritage was already doing, and the advantages that would accrue for being able to have computers read much of what was now being handled on paper by the airline industry.

The long-range benefit of computerized ticketing would lead to equipment reading the tickets at airline gates, keeping track of passengers and knowing those who had "no showed." Computers at airline gates would make it much faster checking in passengers and being able to judge how many seats would be available for standbys. We kept talking but that "no" pretty much terminated the negotiation. Delta would learn to regret that when American's SABRE system controlled most of the bookings of agencies throughout the United States and Delta was left in an awkward competitive position. Through their reservation systems, the airline that provided the systems to large travel agencies could study all of the bookings that were being made on their competitors. The most obvious advantage was being able to identify routes that should be added. The area of automation became a battleground for the airlines and, today, virtually every travel agency in the world has an airline reservation system.

Heritage had grown to the point of having a number of systems. Thanks to our volume, our contributions to the design of American's SABRE System and our constant work with American's Max Hopper, we had dozens of their reservation computers at Heritage. There also were two from TWA, one from United and one old-fashioned and extremely-inefficient and slow keyboard with no monitor display from Allegheny. We took on the effort of trying to get systems for the Woodside agencies in the Southeast.

Delta had said no, but with nowhere near the finality that Eastern had. There was, however, one comment at the end of the meeting with Delta that stuck firmly in my memory. It will be embarrassing to Delta to hear how badly they failed to understand where the airline world was headed with computer automation. The senior man in my meeting with Delta was their excellent Vice President Sales, Joe Cooper, who had become a friend while we were attending ATC meetings in Washington, D.C. We were both from Alabama. Having listened to my presentation, Joe and their agency sales manager, Harry Dunham, stepped into the hall to talk. Harry's comment, supported by Joe (and this is an exact quote) was "Thornton, Delta may someday accept your recommendation and put our reservation computers in travel agencies, but I can guarantee that your ideas about airlines' having computer terminals at all the gates in airports will never happen at Delta."

Today, Delta has one of the most advanced systems in airline terminals, doing a great job of electronically reading tickets at their gates and displaying on large screens in order the names of those who are standing by in case seats ended up being available on a flight. This goes far beyond just having a computer terminal at every gate.

So, what happened next?

ATLANTA

The key meeting that determined the strength of airlines during the next decade took place in the Western International's huge circular-tower hotel in downtown Atlanta, at the time the tallest hotel in the United States. The high-quality hotel chain later shortened its name to Westin. I had invited four airlines to make presentations to the owners of the Woodside agencies throughout the country. Believing that they would be the best, I scheduled American last on the program. United's senior management had been led to believe they were the biggest and best airline in the U.S so they should go it alone. Several of their officers had convinced United's senior management that they could win the competition to automate travel agencies. Therefore, United told me they were not interested and refused to send anyone to the meeting.

TRANS WORLD AIRLINES

TWA was first to speak at 10 in the morning. They sent three people, Don Casey, their head of sales (who went on to be President of TWA), Roger Chase, their highly-respected head of agency sales, and Mary Gilliam from their Pittsburgh office. Looks can be deceptive, but Roger (who introduced Casey), and Mary both looked as if they were embarrassed to be there. As it turns out, they should have been embarrassed.

As best I can remember, Casey essentially said these words: "We do not have a presentation because we, uh, are not yet sure what we, uh, are going to do about automating agencies and, uh, maybe the best way to start would be to ask if any of you have questions. The man who owned Commerce Travel in Pittsburgh and had the closest relationship with TWA was in shock. It was one of the worst presentations ever made, possibly the worst I ever heard. TWA's brief comments were not even a presentation. After very little discussion, we said goodbye to the TWA team and, shortly thereafter, American arrived. This single meeting illustrated how inept TWA had become. It was no surprise when TWA ended up in bankruptcy twice. More on this in the section about Carl Icahnn's visits to Heritage Travel seeking advice about airlines.

AMERICAN AIRLINES

Bob Crandall, by this time President of American, was the most dynamic CEO I had ever met, and that includes big names in lots of industries, from Donald Trump, Bill Marriott and Richard Branson to Rupert Murdock. Bob gave an extremely forceful opening statement, reporting that American's Board had just that week approved a multi-million dollar expenditure to enhance American's computer system to suit travel agency needs and that their senior management was in full support of the plan. He thanked Heritage Travel for contributing a lot to the design of SABRE. He then introduced Max Hopper, American's head of computer operations, who went into great detail, supported by an excellent slide presentation (all of which had been filmed at Heritage Travel), about what American was going to do to make their system the most effective for large commercial travel agencies and, eventually, all types of agency specialization. There was lots of exciting news. The audience sat in awe.

Several agencies that had, up until that moment, believed they would be signing up with some other carrier, ere the first of what was to be a long line of agencies signing up for American's SABRE. It precipitated a landslide. Any of those present that day whose agencies were not already automated chose American. The computer features that American was offering and the quality of their presentation were not just the best, they were the best by far. Nobody was even close, and years later United seriously regretted their decision to go it alone.

Later, when he heard about my frustration with Eastern and Delta and my need to have Woodside, represented by agencies in the South America, the Southeastern United States and other areas of the U.S. not served by American, Max Hopper called me and committed American to placing SABRE in any agency I selected to represent Woodside anywhere, even in cities where American did not fly.

By refusing to compete, Eastern and Delta had provided American with a substantial opening in the Southeast, the area that both had considered their private territory. American's domination of the U.S. market continued for years and helped allow American for a long time to be the only US airline to avoid bankruptcy. Unfortunately, that outstanding record finally ended, primarily because of inability to get rid of excessively-expensive work rules and salaries forced upon them by the various unions.

FREQUENT FLYER PROGRAMS

American's Tom Plaskett is often cited as the inventor of the frequent flyer program, probably hated by many airlines today but loved by frequent business travelers who get to take their families on personal trips using their miles. Tom's idea was made possible by the genius of Heritage Travel's Don Sohn.

When the development of airline automation for use in travel agencies was in its early stages, Heritage Travel was the only agency using airline reservation systems at every agent's workstation to book the actual airline reservations, but we had to access hotel information via a microfiche display and keep travelers' information on Rolodex. It was awkward, time consuming and highly inefficient.

Working with American's Max Hopper to develop the enhancements American's SABRE System would need to be most effective for travel agencies, it was Don Sohn who urged Max to include the data on an agency's frequent flyers stored and accessible in American's data base. Max used to fly from Dallas up to Cambridge to meet with us on Monday evenings. This addition to the American computer system, was what led to American's being able to use traveler data, making frequent flyer programs possible.

American took all the pictures for their Sabre marketing brochure in the Heritage Travel headquarters in Cambridge, just across the river from Boston.

GREAT HELP FROM AMERICAN

At Woodside's headquarters, Max Hopper had his team install a SABRE terminal so I could communicate easily with all of Woodside's agencies. This was installed without the normal charge, while knowing that it would not be used to book any reservations. When we did end up being the central reservations control office for Woodside agencies throughout the US and Europe, we ended up with several dozen Sabre sets, plus the reservation systems of all the major airlines of Europe, the systems of the largest hotel chains and all major U.S. car rental companies.

The most remarkable benefit we received from American had to do with accessing Woodside's SABRE from another travel agency. Today, an agency would have to submit all sorts of agreements, have them notarized and wait weeks for the joint access to be approved and put in place.

In the early days of Woodside, when I was traveling around the country trying to talk agencies into joining the Woodside team, it was extremely valuable to be able to sit in their office and access Woodside's computer system, especially our hotel program that American had allowed me to install in SABRE. Our system showed all of the negotiated hotel rates and provided an easy system for passing that portion of an airline reservation to Woodside Central in Boston where we booked the hotels. American had built a special room dedicated to Woodside agencies in their huge computer center hidden underground at the Tulsa airport. They placed in that room modems' offices of each of the Woodside agencies and assigned a special team to work with me.

All I had to do was call our phone number at American's computer center and have them immediately link the agency in which I was sitting into Woodside's network. I could operate the prospective agency's SABRE set just as if they were already on our team. It was one of those times when having my very deep and easily recognizable voice was a benefit. American's staff would answer the phone, recognize my voice and hook in the agency I was visiting and then turn off the connection when I called and told them I was finished. It was an incredible benefit. I didn't even have to tell them my pseudo-code, which was A4W. Agencies were identified by a three digit code, just like all the airports.

ILLEGAL HACKING… or was it?

Several years later, I was able to help American, compensating for all the special help they had given me over the years. Somehow, Max Hopper learned that I was able to access any American flight and look at everyone's reservations and all of their passenger manifests. This included being able to look at any reservation made by American itself or by any travel agency on their SABRE system. Sadly, that capability was used on one occasion when an American plane crashed.

Before the flight was removed from SABRE, I could look in the computer and print out the names of everyone who had died in the crash. I could immediately notify our travel agencies if one of their customers had been killed. During the years we had this capability we did not misuse it in any way to look at reservations of our competitors. Our expertise with the SABRE system came into play when Pan Am 103 crashed and that strange sequence of events is in the chapter you have read about liability.

Later, Max said he did not believe it and, to be sure it was impossible, put some of his most expert programmers onto trying to figure out how it could be done. He was confident that his team had more than adequate security for SABRE. Only once they were sure that there was no way into American's highly protected system did Max call and almost plead with me to tell him how it was done. The conversation did not start that way. His initial comment was that it couldn't be done given the huge amount they had invested in security.

Only after that did he ask for proof that I could get into their computer. He said he would name a flight number and date, daring me to list the people who had reservations on that flight. I put down the phone, printed out the list and began to read it to him. He was in shock. Obviously, Woodside owed American big time for all the help they had been to us, especially to me, so I had to tell him, bringing an end to our special capability. I don't understand how hackers today get into so many companies' highly protected databases. What I was doing was not something I would define as hacking. American had just left a big door wide open and they even had been telling travel agencies how to open that door. They simply overlooked the fact that the door was even there, much less wide open.

For training, you had the new agency employee "Sign In" to SABRE as a level "7," which was their training mode. Spending all that time beefing up their security, American had simply overlooked the fact that training mode worked on American's real database, able to access any and all of their flights and, as a result, the passenger lists for any flight. Needless to say, that door was closed quite quickly.

FIRST CLASS FOREVER

When Don Sohn retired, I gave a big dinner party at my home in Waban, Massachusetts. He had flown many miles in first class on American. He obviously had great allegiance to American and, in return, they gave him unlimited free first-class travel.

American had given me and my bride first class to Geneva and return from Zurich for our honeymoon. I thought it would be amusing for Don to have his own American first-class seat forever, so American's President, Bob Crandall, had his cargo people crate and ship a first class seat to my house so we could wrap it and present it to Don. It was hilarious.

Actually, there were two seats, because that is the way they were constructed.

For the thousands who use American's computer system it is strange to note that, for some reason, SABRE stands for Semi-Automated Business Research Environment.

35 PURCHASING

The U.S. Government Is The World's Worst Buyer,.....By Far!!!!

Governments at all levels have regulations to control purchasing and hiring practices. Corporate executives can hire anyone that they spot as being good and they can fire someone for incompetence or an unforgivable mistake. Governments have to develop absurdly-detailed job applications and can't fire poor employees because they are protected by a union and/or by civil service regulations.

Competitive bidding, required on almost all government purchases, whether US, state or local, can get you in bad trouble. The focus is entirely on price with little or no value given to business reputation. More than was the case in any corporate request for proposals to provide travel service, the government's Requests For Proposals (RFPs) were full of detailed, but frequently meaningless questions. They could not evaluate service, they just had to go by a long list of specifications.

Heritage Travel, as it expanded nationwide from its corporate client base in Boston, began to specialize in serving the special requirements of universities throughout the country and the U.S. Government in Washington. We had a proven record with several large Cabinet level departments of the government. Our largest offices in Washington were in the Department of Agriculture and the Post Office. Our on-site employees in these offices had special training to fit the rules and regulations of each customer. Heritage had a great reputation for service to business travelers, and we had an excellent rating from Post Office and Agriculture. When an agency serving the government suddenly went out of business, we got the call.

Viking Travel, based in Dallas, had made a serious mistake. In a city essentially controlled by American Airlines, Mark Rich, the owner of Viking, saw an opportunity to earn higher commissions by changing from American's SABRE reservations system to Delta's Datus II. At the time, in addition to their being by far the largest carrier out of DFW Airport, American had by far the best computer reservations system. Viking needed the money and Delta needed a better foothold when they were trying to establish their presence in the key Dallas market. The deal was struck.

The joke went around that when Viking needed special assistance for a VIP to fly on American, the agents at American's sales office would say "Viking? We never heard of you." Viking's losses piled up and they went under.

Viking had been awarded the contract to serve three small portions of the US government's travel, a bid package that included the IRS, FEMA and a third that I can't remember. Viking went under in midweek and we received a frantic call on Thursday morning from Alan Shaefer, the purchasing manager at the Government Services Administration in Washington. He asked if we could take on the three federal departments that had been served by Viking. Heritage had no programs to interface our accounting and control systems with Delta because, as you read earlier, Delta had been very late getting into the agency automation business. We were heavily oriented toward American's reservations computer system and would need to install AA's system and transfer all the traveler information into SABRE.

The huge problem was that the call came on a Thursday morning and we had to commit immediately to being fully operational the following Monday morning, somewhat of a challenge with just one business day between contact and required startup. I'll take that back; it was a *huge* challenge. This meant we would have to construct and equip a new office (including lots of wiring for computer installation), provide experienced staff, load into the computers all of the frequent traveler information for all of the three departments' travelers and get ready to begin service in one business day plus the weekend. It was going to be challenging and expensive, but Heritage agreed to take on the challenge. There was no RFP or bid; Alan knew we were the only ones who could do it.

American managed to get the computer equipment flown from Dallas to Washington Friday and installed over the weekend. You obviously could not hire and train people in one business day, so we pulled employees at various levels of supervision and reservations from other Heritage offices around the country, flew them immediately into Washington with only hours' notice, paid for meals and hotel rooms, conducted client familiarization sessions over the weekend and had service up and running at 9am on that Monday morning. It was a massive and expensive effort and it was completely successful. The service level was immediately rated as a big improvement over what the departments had been receiving from Viking. Everything was going superbly.

For several weeks we had to pay for hotels and meals for the staff (obviously in addition to their salaries) while new staff members were hired, put on payroll and trained, especially about our complex accounting systems. It was going to take us a long time to earn enough on these accounts to offset the hefty startup costs.

UNBELEIVABLE

After about six months or so, we were surprised (maybe a better word would be "shocked") to receive a notice that this segment of the government's travel was being put out for bid. Not only were we doing a superlative job, we were a long way from recouping all of the extra costs incurred in jumping into the relationship to bail out the government for having originally selected an agency unqualified for the responsibility.

We assumed this was just standard policy and we would be chosen to continue serving the accounts.

The GSA's response was that they had no choice; they were required to go out for bid at a certain frequency. We didn't like this, but we understood. Alan Shaefer advised that we had taken over the final portion of the GSA's contract with Viking and the remaining time on that contract was up. They were required *by law* to go out for bid. Our reaction, given the highly successful bail out and excellent service thereafter, continued to be that we obviously would be selected for the term of the new contract.

Then came the really infuriating kicker. This portion of the government's business was categorized as a "small business set aside." Heritage Travel was much too large and would not even be eligible to bid. Alan said he had pleaded with the government's Small Business Administration people, but to no avail. Was that fair? Hell no!!!!!!

Going with an agency too small to handle the accounts had gotten them in trouble in the first place. Given my extremely exasperating experiences years later trying to get action out of the IRS, this portion of the business was infuriating. As an example, I had a problem which dragged on for eight years, beginning in 1999. The funniest part of all the evidence is a letter from the IRS in the late summer of 2006 apologizing for not having responded promptly (4 years late) and assuring me that I would hear from them within the next forty-five days. Two and a half years later, at least part of the problem was resolved and I received a check for $6,898.51 in January of 2009. The IRS was inexcusably inept at solving my problem, costing me over $12,000 in interest. The net outcome was that they would apologize for their mistake but would not give me any compensation unless I could prove malfeasance. Incompetence and years of delay were not acceptable reasons to pay. Needless to say, proving malfeasance was impossible. I just had to give up Jumping through hoops to help the IRS came back to haunt me.

EVEN WORSE

Anyone terrified by Obamacare will get a laugh out of how the government selected the credit card system to be used by all travelers on US government business. The must have idiots in charge of purchasing. The public thinks that requiring open bidding and acceptance of the lowest bid protects us from fraud and waste. Take a look at how they picked a credit card company several decades ago.

Visa and Mastercard today are each accepted by about 36 million places worldwide. Even in 2014, American Express was accepted by only 16 million places worldwide. Our brilliant government picked Diners Club, which is still fairly strong in about five countries, mostly in Europe, but rarely ever seen in the US. Many people have never even heard of it. Diners told me they thought the government's usage requirement for their huge number of employees would enable them to sign up many restaurants and hotels in the US. It did not happen. It was a worthless selection by our brilliant government. They couldn't get cost control because very few hotels and restaurants could be charged to their Diners Club system. Unfortunately, a friend at American Express, Frank King (a Harvard classmate), bore the responsibility for their loss of this huge account, but he helped get it back for Amex when the Diners contract expired.

Now, here is the new problem. Amex caters to wealthier cardholders with high credit ratings and, because of their much higher percentage fees to businesses, many millions of smaller businesses will not accept Amex. The choice can easily drive government travelers to more expensive places. The intelligent choice should have been either Visa or Mastercard.

MAYBE THE WORST

One of Barack's greatest ideas was his Clunker Program in 2009. To save gasoline, it would be desirable to get all of the old low-mileage vehicles off the road. You could get a credit from the Federal Government, as much as $4,500, to trade in your gas guzzler toward a new high-mpg vehicle sounds great. My beautiful, comfortable and huge Mercedes 420 SEL had just 276,000 miles on it, but Pat believed the maintenance costs were getting too high and we should take advantage of this opportunity.

The key was the difference between the mileage your clunker was getting and the mpg of the new car you were buying. The government's analysis indicated that my Mercedes got just15 mpg and the new Hyundai Sante Fe I was buying got 23….well above the mpg difference required to get the $4,500 gift from the government.

Only problem was that my old "clunker" was getting 20 mpg. That was 20 mpg period, not just highway driving at a steady 55 with no stopping. The Hyundai really gets only 19 mpg. That's the average. It is usually 20 on the highway, but frequently lower because when the speed limit is 70 I drive 79. Anyway, the government gave me taxpayer's money to buy a new car that got poorer mileage than my supposedly-gas-guzzling old clunker. We miss her, or at least I do.

ONE MORE EXAMPLE

You may remember that we once had a president named Bill Clinton. It was possible, in my opinion likely, that we would have another President with that last name fairly soon (if she didn't get indicted). Boy, are we lucky that I was wrong. Of the many areas into which Hillary Clinton poked her nose, one was travel, a subject with which I was very familiar.

The White House and the press corps, who frequently travel with a large contingent of government employees, is a very complicated and extremely delicate account. It required a great deal of knowledge, specialized systems and a lot of experience.

The White House's travel was being handled very well by business travel experts, some of the most experienced travel agents in the world. Fabricating what later proved to be false evidence, Hillary fired the department manager and staff. Was she authorized?

Hillary immediately brought in an agency that was owned by an old friend in, you guessed it, Little Rock, Arkansas. I bet this result was the true cause of the firing. The new company had an OK reputation, but nothing remotely close to what would be needed for this account. I guess you can't blame the government, it was just Hillary's acting as purchasing agent, needless to say, failing to comply with all of the normal contract negotiation rules of the General Services Administration. I suspect that most critics of what became known as "Travelgate" did not know all the facts behind the story.

It was Hillary at her worst.

35 GET ADVICE FROM THE EXPERTS
Buying My First House

It was great fun as a bachelor, living on Beacon Hill in the midst of things in downtown Boston. At both State Street Bank and later at Woodside, my commute was a short six-minute walk from Beacon Hill across the historic old Boston Common. The last apartment I had, at 7 Mt. Vernon Place, overlooked the lawn of the State House and the skyline of Boston, plus it had a private parking place right out front, a great rarity on Beacon Hill. It was a six-minute walk to work at Woodside and I could look into the office from my apartment. When my apartment building came up for sale, the Unitarian Church had offices on either side and there was no chance I could outbid them for the building in the middle. It was time to look for something to buy. I needed more space, a garage and a tax deduction.

I loved the water, especially the Charles River, and found an affordable house on the river a mile down the street from the office of the girl I was seeing at the time. Having never purchased a house, I did not know much about mortgages. Talking with several banks and filling out applications, I completed one for the Boston Five Cents Savings Bank, a strange old historic name, but at the time the largest mortgage lender in Greater Boston. Their application included a spot where you were to list anyone you knew at the bank. Because I had lived on the floor above him at 45 Pinckney Street for a couple of years, I listed Bob Spiller, who happened to be the President of the Bank. The day after submitting the application, I received a call from Bob. His first question asked if I were getting married. When heard the answer was "no," he asked in a disapproving tone, what in the world was I doing buying a house at this time.

It was February 25, 1981, and interest rates had reached an astronomical level as a result of stupid action by then President Jimmy Carter, and, to quote Bob,"could not possibly stay that high." He went on to say that it was definitely not the time to be taking out a mortgage. I should wait. He said his bank would have to charge me something outlandish, probably 10 ½ or maybe even 11%. He urged me to wait a while because interest rates had to come way down and do it soon. He ended his lecture by reminding me that he was calling as a friend but also that he was president of the largest bank in the Boston mortgage field. I should listen to an expert. For years, Bob was always embarrassed to see me at parties. Soon after his "expert" advice, interest rates under Carter had skyrocketed into the high teens. I think I remember their having gotten as high as 20%. I was delighted I had gone ahead and obtained a mortgage from the Needham Cooperative Bank for 10½%. That was in the good old days. The brand-new house at 430 Quinobequin Road had cost me $100,000 and sold ten years later for $300,000. Now, June, 2019, the Zillow real estate website says it is worth $1.2 million, illustrating the strength of some housing markets, especially Boston.

37 *ELEVATORS*

Why In The World Have A Chapter On This Subject?

Can you imagine climbing many flights of stairs today had the elevator not been invented? Skyscrapers would not exist if elevators had not been invented. Many people have been stuck in an elevator. It's no big deal. You press the red button and someone comes and fixes it.

These two stories are different, quite different. The first, the old one from the forties, is about something you can still see today.

GERMANY

My sister, Carolyn, went to work as a civil service secretary with the occupation forces that occupied Germany right after the end of World War II. She worked in Frankfurt. I still have several of her extremely-long, typed, single-spaced letters home, some of which ran for more than a dozen pages.

Carolyn said most of her work was boring, but her description of the elevators in the I.G. Farben building was hilarious. The building with its unusual elevators still stands to this day, although the company itself was dissolved by the Allies as a result of its close relationship and extremely-valuable work with Hitler in his horrendous war effort.

The young women who worked in the Farben Building had to go to other floors of the building during their workday. For a long time, most climbed up and down the stairs because of their fear of the elevators.

In some skyscrapers today, elevators have one "car" that is constructed with two passenger levels, so that people can be getting on or off at two floors at the same time. This enhances the effectiveness of the elevator, reducing the number of stops as well as reducing the number of elevator shafts needed for the building. The Farben elevators are a little bit like chair lifts at ski areas, where you have to rush out and be seated as the "chair" comes at you from behind and then jump off when you reach the top. The chair never stops.

Most elevators today are suspended from cables, with a powerful winch to pull them up and control them when going down. Relatively simple measurement systems comprised of long steel straps signal the motors when to slow the elevator to a stop at each floor and signal the doors to open on the car and in the lobby to which the doors open. This is not the case in the notorious Farben Building.

To save money, the Farben elevators operate in a manner similar to gondolas at large ski resorts, with the raising of one car being aided by the weight of the other car that is going down. At least the gondola cars stop at each end of their journey. Not the case with Farben.

They saved money on shafts, cars, power requirements for the winches and systems for stopping and opening doors. Once when the towering Westin hotel was under construction in Atlanta, on the top floor I went slowly on my hands and knees up close to the elevator shaft and looked down. At the time, there were no doors. It was terrifying.

Rarely, if ever today, do you see the doors from the lobby to an elevator shaft stick in the open position and have no car there in the elevator shaft. That is not the terrifying part of the story. The cars, themselves, do not stop. They do move slowly, and you have to time your jump to get out or to jump onto a moving car. I guess you get used to it, but can you imagine that system satisfying OSHA and building codes in the United States?

NEW YORK

In the late fifties, as a student at Harvard, I was dating a girl named Elyn Dean, who was from New Jersey and was attending Radcliffe College (since incorporated into Harvard). My parents were making their annual visit to New York and, as they did every year, were staying at the Waldorf-Astoria in The Towers.

There was an old saying and practice that is, sadly, no longer in use. The saying was "I'll meet you under the clock at the Biltmore." Especially in the late afternoon, you would see lots of young people (and some old folks, too) hanging around the steps near the clock to meet friends. The clock was brass suspended in the middle of an elegant brass arch that curved over the path through the hotel. The clock was famous as a rendezvous point. The Biltmore, at 55 E 43rd St., across from Grand Central Station was a very convenient mid-town location with two towers, each having 26 floors and a total of 1,000 rooms. The building was gutted and the steel skeleton used for the Bank of America Plaza Building, where the clock now resides.

The Biltmore had been designed and constructed as part of the Grand Central complex and opened the same day as Grand Central Station. In addition to its location and attractive lobby, the Biltmore in 1957 offered students a great rate. The rate applied to ridiculously small rooms, but who cared? For $8 a night, even back then, it was a great deal, even if the cheap rooms were up high at the top of the hotel. If you shared a room, it got the cost per person down to an incredible $4 per night. Today, in 2019, that $8 rate would be about $72, still incredibly low by today's standards. It was a most memorable night because Dad treated us to tickets to My Fair Lady on Friday, January 30, 1958. Because Dad had bad eyesight, he used Equity Ticket to buy what I later learned were defined as "scalper" prices to get fourth row center seats at almost every show every year. It was a fun evening. Even with my parents present, Elyn and I had lots to drink. The next morning was somewhat less fun with bad hangovers. We had agreed to meet Mom and Dad for breakfast Saturday, January 31, 1958 at the Waldorf, so we piled into the Biltmore's elevator at 8am on the top floor of the hotel. Why in the world would you remember the time you got into an elevator 57 years ago?

The small "student rate" rooms were on the top floor of the hotel, 26 stories up. Our elevator went down normally for a while and then began to shudder and then fall, ending up in the sub-basement. Years later we heard that elevators were supposed to have a brake that stops a fall should one occur. If there was a system, it didn't work.

When the fall began and the lights in our car went out, we knew we had been going down for a while but had no way of knowing how high up we still were. The feeling was bad enough, without the screaming of the seven passengers.

When the car finally bounced to a stop at the bottom, it stopped with the upper-middle of the elevator car lined up with a floor of the building, so that the only way out was to climb up through the opening, hoping that the car did not go down a few more feet while someone was half in and half out of the car. In the dark, we had felt around for a phone. It was not operative.

In addition to ending up in the subbasement, there was an unexpected cause of great fear. The lights had gone out when the car started to fall and, for what seemed like minutes after reaching the subbasement , all the heavy steel cables came raining down from 26 stories above us onto the roof of the car, sounding like thunder directly over our heads. I guess there is a heavy metal arch over an elevator car, so we were protected from the cascade of metal, but the shaking and the noise had everyone terrified.

Anyway, Elyn and I did get out without injury, but we were clearly ready for an early morning Bloody Mary.

FOOTNOTE

Elevator accidents are relatively rare. I was surprised to read that a big coincidence occurred in December of 2011, when a woman was killed by an elevator in Manhattan in a building that also was very close to Grand Central Station.

38 THE HEIMLICH MANEUVER

Be Sure Somebody Knows How To Do It.

In midJanuary, 1980, Woodside hosted a training meeting for all of the Woodside agency managers from around the US and Europe. Two days of meetings were planned, ending with a tour and dinner at the JFK Library overlooking Boston Harbor just south of the city. Because the JFK management thought this would be a good opportunity to show the library to travel agents, Woodside was allowed to use the Museum Pavilion for dinner for a modest fee (not the usual $4,300). They wanted our group to know about the place.

There was a problem. The Pavilion has a great view because two huge glass walls overlooking Boston Harbor are 115 feet high. Our dinner was on an extremely-cold night, January 12, 1980, in the dead of winter, and the place was far from adequately heated. The heat rises to the top of the huge area and the floor where we were was extremely cold. I had on a heavy three-piece wool suit, but still kept my heavy overcoat on during dinner.

We were seated at round tables of eight. About halfway through the dinner, I realized I had something lodged in my throat, but assumed I could swallow it or cough it up. Such was not the case. A man across the table from me asked if I was OK, and I nodded my head "yes." Moments later I realized this was not the case, shaking my head "no" before passing out cold as I slid out of my chair and under the table.

This was in the very early days of the Heimlich Technique and few knew how to perform it properly. I don't know anything about what happened while I was unconscious, but the girl who had been sitting next to me said she ran across the dining area to another employee from Seattle who she knew was trained to perform the Heimlich and rushed her back to me. Apparently, I was too heavy for her to lift, and once lifted off the floor by some guys, my heavy clothes prevented her from giving me the quick jerks of the stomach that are necessary. Later I discovered that both the overcoat and the suit jacket had been ripped off without pausing to worry about the buttons.

When I did regain consciousness, I was lying on the cold stone floor, looking up at a circle of concerned faces staring down at me. Through the circle of people, I looked straight up at the enormous American flag that hangs down from the ceiling of that room. It was quite an experience.

When order was restored and everyone took their seats, I was the only one at my table able to eat dessert, so several gave me theirs. Apparently, I had begun to turn blue and they were still in shock. I had missed the whole ordeal, at least I didn't remember it.

The funny part of the evening was the fact that I was to be the after-dinner speaker. My speech was immediately rewritten to start with the famous joke question "Other than that, Mrs. Lincoln, how did you enjoy the play?"

Prior to that, before anyone had heard of the Heimlich Technique, a girl who lived around the corner from me on Beacon Hill had lost her dad, Dr. Whitelaw, when he choked at the family dinner table. Since then, I have been through two incidents where the Heimlich technique had to be utilized. One was performed in a restaurant by a nurse who recognized what was happening and saved the lady whose husband had nonchalantly said "She's OK, don't worry about her."

There are two things everyone should know. First, ask the person you see choking to say a word. If they can't speak, they almost certainly need the Heimlich applied. The process can include a lot of description, but basically you just stand behind the person, put your arms around them, use one hand to hold the other wrist tightly, and jerk as hard as you can upward into their abdomen.

This deadly problem is faced too often for people not to know how to recognize it and how to do the proper thing to solve it…and do it fast. I'm mighty glad there was one person there that night who knew what to do and how to do it.

39 FOREIGN LANGUAGES
The French Won't Like This One

Back about the beginning of the last century, a simplified language was introduced to assist in talks between people of different nationalities. In the second half of the twentieth century, there was a big movement to support the development of the new language for use worldwide. It was largely based on Spanish, but is a simplified blend of existing major languages in order to be politically correct. The name was Esperanto, and, luckily, despite getting thousands of students, it never caught on.

What is working throughout the world is English. The French, in particular, don't like to hear that, but it is true. When I was working all over the world, having to meet and talk business with people from many dozens of countries, I found that in every instance except one the people in business were fluent in English. I'm not talking about just being able to speak English, in many instances they spoke more proper English than a ridiculous number of Americans today.

Of all of the companies with which I was involved throughout the world, the only place where the managers chose not to speak in English was Sao Paulo, the largest city and by far the largest city for business in Brazil. After dealing with them for a year or so it became apparent that they understood English, they just considered it safer to speak Portuguese and have it translated. In a less formal social environment, they would freely speak English.

Most guidebooks urge Americans, who are notoriously weak in foreign languages, to learn and use a few basic words, obviously simple things such as "Yes," "No," How much?"and "Thank you." That probably is desirable and relatively risk free. Counting in the language of your host country is useful, whether shopping or taking a taxi, but you have to be careful as well as being sure of the exchange rate. One who shall remain nameless once got it wrong and mistakenly gave a female restroom attendant in Venice about ten dollars, for which the lady was most appreciative.

To give you an idea of how trying to do too much with a language can get you in trouble, my best example was a speech in Germany when I went there with a group representing the National Investment Company Service Association to meet with the German equivalent of the US Federal Reserve Bank. It was, in German, called the Bundesaufsichsamt fuer das Kreditweisen. I had practiced a lot in order to be able to say at least a few opening words in German to the very distinguished "Governors" of this powerful German financial regulatory authority.

At the time, I worked for State Street Bank in Boston, where I was involved in opening the bank's first foreign branch, which was to be in Munich. At that point in time, the US Securities and Exchange Commission was doing an excellent job of regulating the mutual fund industry and most foreign countries were far behind on regulation.

The worst examples were the open-end real estate investment trusts. Closed end real estate funds, still common in the 21st century, have a fixed number of shares and trade at prices governed by willing buyers and sellers, frequently at prices below the market value of the properties owned by the fund.

Anyway, with much of the money coming into US Mutual Funds coming from Central Europe, Germany in particular, our team was there to discuss investment regulation with a German regulatory authority, the Bundesaufsichtamt fuer das Kreditwesen which, until 2002, was similar to the US Federal Reserve Board.

My opening words of introduction (in German, or at least what I *thought* was German) in Berlin March 23, 1970 gave my name and stated that I was representing State Street Bank, Incorporated. In German, the words for "incorporated" are Gesselshaft mit beshrankter Haftung (GmbH), which translates to "business with limited liability." Unfortunately (or maybe fortunately) I made a small but, to the Board, hilarious mistake. I had said "Stadtstrasse Bank, Gesselschaft mit Beshranter Hoffnung," which I thought meant State Street Bank, Incorporated. That one slight mispronunciation of one syllable changed the meaning of what I said from "company with limited liability" to "company with little hope for the future."

The good news was that the Bundesaufsichtsamt's Chairwoman, Frau Bauer, joined in all the laughter and very politely advised that they all spoke English and to proceed without attempting any more German. One letter in one word can make a huge and embarrassing difference to the meaning of a sentence, but at least it got things off to a relaxed start. It is interesting to note that State Street now has $27 trillion of assets under its custodianship, and is the 13th largest bank in the U.S.

In the old days, people speaking "American" used to have trouble with words such as "lift" for elevator, and the saying for "I'll come by and wake you up in the morning" which in the English version of English is said as "I'll come by and knock you up in the morning." Quite a different interpretation in American. A much worse example prevalent among skiers is the American description of the small zippered pack that is carried at the small of your back and tied around the waist by a belt. Calling is a "fanny pack" can raise eyebrows in England because "fanny" is a slang equivalent of what it American would be pussy. This is the type of misunderstanding you obviously want to avoid. I have never seen that example explained in any tourist or business guidebook.

HAND GESTURES

Americans have great trouble understanding foreign practices and the vast majority do not do an adequate job of preparing before arriving in a foreign country. This is especially important in business and government

In the category of foreign mistakes, hand signs are a common source of problems. In Germany, tapping your fingers to your forehead with your palm down is the common way of calling someone a dumb idiot. Done by a young American working for State Street Bank in Munich to a taxi driver, this gesture resulted in the young man's being shot seriously enough to be hospitalized for days.

The common sign for "Fuck You" in American is the upward extended middle finger. In Iran, it's a thumbs up, a fairly common symbol of approval in western countries. This illustrates the need to be very careful.

The funniest one I observed was done by a lady who was Vice President Marketing of Woodside, Judy Harrington, who was helping me prepare for a speech in Rio de Janeiro. The meeting was going to be in a fairly-large auditorium, so we were checking out the lectern height, the lighting, the microphone position and the amplification. Judy was communicating between the stage and the control man far away up in the projection booth behind all the seats. Judy signaled for up and down by gesturing with her arm with the palm of her hand up or down. When everything was just right, she gave the standard American "OK" sign by holding up her thumb and index finger in a circle. The only problem was that that gesture was the equivalent. In Portuguese of "giving the finger" to that man. He was furious and came running down into the auditorium and to us on stage.

One humorous example was on my first trip to Korea. Two gentlemen from Cathay Pacific Airlines, Mr. H. Chang and Mr. G Hwang, invited me to lunch at a very nice private club, the Han Nam Club, on top of the peak that overlooks Seoul. They didn't know me from Adam, but had been told by their headquarters to take me to lunch and to answer my questions. The food was excellent and I ate it all. They conversed a little in Korean, called our waiter and talked with him. Of course, this was in Korean, so I did not understand a single word. After a few minutes, the waiter arrived with more food for everyone. It, too, was delicious and I ate it. They called the waiter again and exchanged a few words, after which the waiter returned with even more food.

Only when I returned to the Hyatt that evening did I read the local guidebook which would have cautioned me to leave some food on my plate because, if you did otherwise, you were indicating that you had not had enough to eat and wanted more.

So much for trying to be nice and indicating that I thought the food was delicious.

EVEN HIGH OFFICIALS CAN MAKE MISTAKES

One of the funniest examples Pat and I have seen of how a little word can make an amusing difference is found in the William Jefferson Clinton Library in Little Rock, Arkansas. Among the thousands of things on display is a letter dated July 21, 1994 from Yitzhak Rabin, Prime Minister of Israel, to President Clinton. The sentence starts with "I am delighted to present you with this volume depleting the Biblical Landscape." Even when something is written and carefully edited, it is very easy to overlook "depleting" when it obviously should have been "depicting." If it's important, get a good translator.

THE FRENCH VS THE WORLD

As recently as my lifetime, many French were still resentful of having to conduct business in English, and some insisted upon having us pay for a simultaneous translator. Translators were not cheap, plus you had to rent a microphone and earphones for them. You knew damn well, and it was quite obvious, that the people in the meetings understood English. I think they just wanted to be difficult and illustrate their independence. It did provide an interesting advantage. They could listen, and understand, your English, so waiting for the translation into French gave them time to formulate their response.

The Gregorian Calendar was a huge improvement for everyone, but it was not accepted by the French for years. With the adoption of the "modern" calendar, New Years Day was switched from April 1 to January 1. Only the French refused to accept the change, continuing to celebrate the "new year" on April 1, hence the name of "April Fools Day." Do the French today know that this saying is referring to them?

The French refusal to accept English as the language of business worldwide reminded me of a widely-distributed story, possibly true, about a meeting Secretary of State Colin Powell attended in Europe with a number of representatives of the French Government. When the French complained and asked why the meeting should not be in French instead of English, Secretary Powell's brilliant response was that, had it not been for the English-speaking nations, the French would probably now be speaking German.

The US refuses to accept the metric system. It should be embarrassing to the US that, in addition to the United States, the only other country using feet and inches is Malaysia.

The more amusing one can get unsuspecting people, whether US or "foreign," into trouble. For some reason, in the US we write dates as 2/8/2019, Month, day and year. That just seems "right" doesn't it? Many, probably the vast majority, of Americans do not know that elsewhere the numbers are in increasing periods: day, month and year, so that 2/8/2019 would be accepted by others in the world as August 2, 2019. Especially when the dates are close, such as July 8 (known to Americans as 7/8) and August 7 (known to Americans as 8/7) you can get into expensive mistakes with things such as hotel reservations. As with the metric system, the accepted rules for abbreviating dates should be standardized, but no country wants to be the one who has to change.

ETIQUETTE

Americans usually travel abroad without taking the time to learn the dos and don'ts of the country they will be visiting. This subject was the problem in the story about my first meal in South Korea. In many countries you are being rude if you arrive on time, inconveniencing your host by disrupting them before they are prepared. In some, you are rude if you arrive fashionably late. If you do, you have wasted your host's time.

My wife believes, as do I, that you should never arrive on time, arriving at least a few minutes after the time set in the invitation. In the best-selling book *"Midnight in the Garden of Good and Evil"* the Savannah ladies in the exclusive Married Women's Card Club were expected to arrive in their cars ahead of time, so that they all could open their doors, get out and arrive together at precisely the appointed time, in this case 4pm.

CLOSED CAPTIONING ON TV

When Hillary Clinton was campaigning for President in 2016 there was a discussion on Bret Baier's excellent afternoon program "Special Report" on Fox News. Hillary had issued a condemnation of something. The typist doing the closed captioning made a very amusing mistake (unless, somehow it was intentional). The words on the TV read "Hillary's condom nation." Yes, I have a photo of the screen if you need proof.

Do you think it could have had something to do with her claiming she got screwed in the 2016 election?

40 THINGS FOR FREE

Are Usually Worth What You Paid For Them (Maybe Even Less)

The most interesting consulting story is about a father and son team who sold themselves as consultants to corporations, assisting them in selecting the best travel agency to serve their corporate needs.

In the early days of airline deregulation, some companies did their own thing, and some were big enough to afford the management and the computer systems needed to handle their own employee travel. As the role of the few large travel agencies with huge buying power became more apparent and acceptable, corporate travel managers, or someone pulled from another department to handle the process, frequently hired a consultant or consulting firm to help them through the process of selecting an agency. Because this area of activity was quite new, it was almost always unbudgeted. If there was no money available, the father and son team offered a great alternative…they would do the work for free. I trust you have heard the old adage about something you get for free being worth what you paid for it.

The result was usually much more expensive than the company would have expended for a paid consultant and it all-too-frequently meant the client corporation ended up with a less-than-optimal travel agency. The idea was that the corporation would pay nothing, the consultants would earn their pay from the selected travel agency.

Heritage, the agency I worked for in Boston, was widely acknowledged to be one of the best in the country, and by some as the best. When approached by the father and son because they had been hired by a Boston area company, we refused to sign a contract with them because we recognized the severe problem with their modus operandi. The result was obvious. The consultants could only guide their corporate client to an agency that had agreed to pay them a cut. This usually meant that the client ended up with a poor, or at least not the best, choice of agency to serve them. It meant we were automatically ruled out for consideration by any client company they signed up with this team anywhere in the country. The temptation was to pick the agency that would pay the most to the consultants. That got too many companies into trouble with bad service.

The percentage deal may have been "paid" by the winning agency, but it had to come from somewhere, and it came from two places. The payoff which the selected agency owed to the consultants was an ongoing percentage of commissions generated by the client's travel. Although it never had to show in any department's budget as an expense, it reduced the percentage rebate, legal under the Airline Deregulation Act, that could be paid by the travel agency to the corporate client. By reducing the income to the agency, it reduced the funds the agency had to hire employees and serve the client. The net effect was a lose-lose proposition for the corporation.

A TWIST

The bad twist to this tale occurred when a senior manager at one of the country's largest corporations, GE, called me for advice regarding names he was considering hiring as their travel manager. I had never met the man, but he said he had been told by several people that I would be a knowledgeable and honest source of advice. He talked forever and asked loads of questions, but I did not mind because I thought this relationship would be helpful to my company when it became time to bid on GE's account.

The guy went through a list of prospective employees. One of the ones on his list was the younger partner in the "free" consulting business just written about. I explained to the man at GE the way their consulting business had operated, how the guy under consideration by GE was not respected in the industry and why he should be the only one cut from the list of prospects without further ado. You can guess where this is headed.

GE hired the man, and his boss had the audacity (I preferred the word "stupidity') to tell his new employee what I had said about him in confidence. Of course, it did not just hurt our chances of getting GE's business; it completely eliminated us from consideration.

When I was told the story by my source, one of the country's most powerful travel managers, what he had been told, it hurt, but it felt better when GE got into trouble in this area of activity and I heard from several sources that the termination of the manager's employment was somewhat more than a "resignation."

The next chapter is about a corporation, one of the world's largest, that hired the company that was clearly the most-respected consulting firm, and how even the best can be criticized when their client corporation leads them into an untenable position.

41 CITICORP
As The World's Worst Client

In the early 1990s, one of the world's largest banks, Citicorp, announced that they would be consolidating control of their very large travel budget, were going out to bid and would be using Harold Seligman's "Management Alternatives" as their consultant. The announcement that Management Alternative's senior officer, Harold Seligman, would be representing Citicorp was great news for Heritage Travel because we had a unique respect for each other's skills and reputation, this time making me confident that we had the inside shot at winning the account. Harold was the best in the business.

Even though there were only a handful of agencies qualified to serve Citicorp, their travel manager notified all of the agencies who had small local offices of Citicorp as a client that they would not just be allowed to bid, their bids would be welcome. CitiCorp's decision to consolidate their travel came quite late in the period following airline deregulation when large corporations began using large travel agencies to manage their huge travel volumes, obtaining volume discounts and providing management reports sorted by employee within division. Even though thousands of small agencies had served small local branches of a large corporation for years, they simply could not provide the volume discounts and nationwide service that one of the seven major agencies could. Would you expect a small agency in Podunk that had been handling a few CitiCorp employees to be qualified to open offices across the country to handle thousands?

WASTING OTHER PEOPLE'S MONEY

Citicorp's approach satisfied the unqualified competitors, at least leading them to believe that they were allowed in the contest and would be considered. It took a travel agency a lot of time to study a request for a proposal, develop a plan, estimate the personnel and equipment costs and produce an elaborate customized proposal. The trickiest part was determining the costs and, from that, what percentage you could commit to rebating to the client. Citicorp's travel manager told me that 118 proposals were received. I told her I was surprised that they were really considering that many agencies because only a few were qualified to satisfy the requirements of Citicorp's complex RFP.

The shocking part was when she said she had thrown out about 100 proposals, without even opening them and glancing through them. How would all of those people have felt had they known the way they were treated? They had spent the time and money, only to have their work discarded without so much as opening the envelope to take a look. It gets worse.

Citicorp's unique (and, in my opinion, extremely strange) plan was to have three regional agencies, one for the east coast, one middle, and one west coast agency, plus a dreadfully complicated plan to have an "overall, supervising agency" nationwide. The description of how this was to work made little sense, but the big competitors all had to live with it because Citicorp would be such a large client. The respected consultant would have dreamed up this plan; it had to be the brainchild of CitiCorp's travel manager.

Heritage submitted two proposals, one for the east coast and one for the nationwide oversight role. After a few weeks, the travel manager called and said we had been selected for both roles ...great news. Then something very unusual and untimely occurred. Heritage had a financial agreement with Crimson Travel, giving Crimson's owner, David Paresky, a call option on Heritage's stock. The option was at a low price because Don Sohn, the principal owner of Heritage, had been very concerned about the precarious financial status of his agency and sought the partnership. The following year Crimson's vacation travel suffered and Heritage's profitability skyrocketed to $4,000,000.

David, a truly brilliant and incredibly hardworking entrepreneur (see entire chapter on this subject), had made a deal to buy half of the U.S. portion of Thomas Cook Travel, which at the time was one of the world's foremost travel agencies. Cook had not been doing well in the US and David paid a very good price for his half. He exercised his call option for Heritage Travel on a Friday evening and purchased Thomas Cook on Monday.

The problem was that the other owner was a high profile English newspaper publisher named Robert Maxwell, whose financial problems began to surface shortly thereafter. Then the headlines were about Maxwell's death, frequently reported as a suicide, because nobody could figure out how he died while taking his morning swim off of his huge yacht in the Mediterranean.

A SMALL AND SURPRISING FLY IN THE OINTMENT

Citicorp would not accept my assurances that Thomas Cook would be financially sound despite the involvement of Maxwell, so the plans to have us as the lead agency nationwide were scrubbed and Maritz Travel out of St. Louis was given this portion of the business. Maritz was excellent and highly respected, it was just sad to lose the top role with Citicorp because of events beyond our control. The travel manager at Citicorp said they were in a rush to begin controlling their travel expenses, so we were (essentially ordered) to hire and train staff immediately so that we would be ready when the implementation date arrived. We had to be ready soon.

Citicorp's Request For Proposals (RFP) had been extensive and explicit. At the time, they owned Diners Club, which was not noticeable in the personal credit card business in the United States but was still a factor in Europe and in some business travel in the US. Citicorp's RFP stated that all of the travel data in their request for proposals were exact because they were obtained from Citicorp's credit card information and Citicorp had for some time required their employees to put all travel expenses on the Diners Club card. Unlike most corporations that were putting their travel out for bid for the first time, Citicorp said they had all of the data that an agency would need to know to present an exact bid.

The handling of hotel and car reservations was essentially a breakeven part of the corporate travel business; you made money from the 10% commission on airline tickets. The RFP gave the dollar volume of airline tickets by location throughout the country. Their largest chunk was obviously their headquarters in New York, which we had been awarded, but the RFP for the eastern region showed a sizeable volume of air travel by their employees in Wilmington, Delaware. We estimated we were going to need twenty-one additional employees to serve Citicorp and began hiring them.

WASTING OUR MONEY, LOTS OF IT

Every week, the call from Citicorp's travel manager would be the same, another excuse. The CEO had not signed off on the plan, so it was going to be delayed a little. Every week there was an excuse. She just needed to be sure we were ready to go. We were, but it was costing us payroll for employees we did not need. She had been telling us for a long time that CitiCorp was in a big rush to begin controlling travel expense and service would be starting very soon. Weeks of delay and excuses dragged into months. Expense to us; no income. It got to be ridiculous, but there was nothing we could do. We had no contract and there was no requirement to pay us any money, we would just begin to earn commissions once travel began to be booked through us. My boss was, to say the least, not happy.

Finally, the big day arrives. There is very little business. That is an understatement, there was almost no business. Weeks passed with little increase. Even though all Citicorp employees were supposedly under strict orders to begin using the travel agency designated for their region, there was not much business even from corporate headquarters in New York.

Also, we discovered that there was, for all practical purposes, no air travel out of the big Delaware office, just train tickets, all back and forth to New York and, occasionally Washington, DC. How could this be? The statistics for Citicorp's airline ticketing were all shown in detail in their RFP and described as being exact, having been developed from their Diners Club data. Citicorp owned the rarely seen Diners Club charge card, she said that it had been required for all travel expenses and they were proud to have their exact numbers in their request for proposals. She continued to claim that it was more accurate than any previous request for proposals in the corporate travel industry. Something had to be wrong.

Paresky had gotten a great clause in his contract with the regarding the financing of his purchase of Thomas Cook. The New York bank that ended up owning Maxwell's share of Cook and did not want to be in the travel agency business. They wanted out and looked to David as the obvious best bet to buy the Maxwell half, offering him a reasonable price so they could get cash and not have to worry about owning half a travel agency. This was even worse than a bank's having made a mortgage secured by a home and ending up owning the home. A home could be sold, especially if a bank was willing to take a loss, but this was definitely not the case when half of a very large travel agency was the asset the bank needed to dump.

David's lawyer who had orchestrated the extremely complex deal, told me David had a "put option" under which he could sell his share back to the bank and they would be legally obligated to buy it. It was bad enough for the bank to have millions tied up in the ownership of half of a travel agency, they did not want it all. As a result, the bank lowered the price they sought for Robert Maxwell's half and David ended up owning all of Thomas Cook North America for an extremely cheap price.

THE CONTRACT

About this time, after several months of serving the Citicorp account, we received a contract described as being "ready for signing"...with no discussion, no editing, no nothing. The problem was that the contract we were expected to sign immediately bore no resemblance to what we had proposed as service. The contract included our obligation to loads of things we definitely would *not* do, most importantly a much higher percentage rebate to CitiCorp than we had proposed. The proposed contract also included a number of cost items that could not be covered if we were providing the things we really had agreed to provide. How could this be?

The normal practice in business was to work out the contract and get it signed before you began to provide service. This had had to be skipped because Citicorp was supposedly in such a rush to get underway and their manager was so inept. The travel manager kept citing Citicorp's urgent intent to begin saving money on their travel. Here we were confronted with an unacceptable contract months after we had begun serving Citicorp's travel, what little there was of it.

When I complained, the travel manager said she had gone through and picked out the best parts of the four proposals and combined them into one "standard" contract. She said she did not want to be dealing with four different arrangements and thought it would be better to have them all the same. This was, to say the least, preposterous The other agencies signed and an owner of the one on the west coast told me just to sign it and not worry about. David Paresky concurred with me in refusing to sign.

As I wrote above, Maritz was clearly one of the very best and most reputable corporate travel agencies in the country, but Citicorp's travel manager reported that she had become unhappy enough about her relationship with them that she called and asked if we would be willing to take over as the national agency, whatever that meant. By this time, we knew that the core of the problem was obviously Citicorp's travel manager, *not* Maritz, and we declined. We now knew to pass up what we had, only a few months ago, sought.

GUARANTEED TO LOSE MONEY

Forget the time involved in handling a reservation and issuing a train ticket, the train tickets out of Delaware were generally around $100, so the ten percent commission was $10, not even enough to cover the cost of Fedexing each ticket to each traveler, much less the personnel and related cost of handling reservations. It was a financial nightmare. We began sending a batch of tickets each day to one person at Citicorp's Delaware office for distribution to the other travelers there. Citicorp's travel manager said that the employees did not want to be bothered with distributing tickets and this was "unacceptable." We were to pay the Fedex delivery cost (at the time about $14 per envelope) to deliver each ticket on which our gross income was 10%, about $10. It was easy to tell how many of those we would have to handle to make a profit. The more the business, the more we lost. It wasn't just that the entire commission exceeded the cost of Fedex, it provided no income to cover the cost of agents and all related expenses.

Citicorp's tickets were charged to their Diners Club cards, so Thomas Cook Travel did get paid, but we never paid a penny of the "rebate" percentage we had offered in our proposal. The Citicorp travel manager said that the dramatic decline in air travel was just the inadvertent result of their tightening their control of travel costs. It simply could not have been cut that far, and we still refused to pay.

Things became acrimonious. One funny conference call took place between David and me in his office and the Citicorp team seated around one of their conference rooms with both sides using speaker phones. There was nothing approaching agreement. The conversation ended, but David had not yet reached the button to hang up our speaker phone when we heard a burst of fiery language coming over the line. David pulled back his hand and we sat there listening to the Citicorp's team's fury. We eventually heard someone exclaim, realizing in horror that they had failed to disconnect the conference call but obviously hoping we had hung up and not heard all of their conversation.

OFF TO COURT

Shortly thereafter, we ended up being sued. Citicorp sought payment of the percentage rebate they thought should be paid, even though it was much more than the amount which we had we had offered in our proposal and we had not signed the contract. The travel trade press loved the idea of a suit and counter suit between a large corporation and one of the country's largest travel agencies. It made front page headlines. Thomas Cook countersued.

We finally reached the time for depositions. Luckily, I had kept excellent notes and dates of every conversation with Citicorp's travel manager. I used flash cards and memorized the dates and contents of the numerous conversations in preparation for my deposition. Our company began incurring substantial legal expenses. The depositions dragged on and on, with no resolution. We were not getting anywhere until their counsel during my followup deposition made what was, without question, the dumbest mistake I had ever heard about in business. Not just dumb, incredibly stupid.

YOU GOTTA BE KIDDING!!!

When I complained about the accuracy, or total lack thereof, in the airline ticketing statistics provided by Citicorp in their RFP, Citicorp's lawyer asked why I had relied upon the numbers they had provided. Hadn't I noticed that the supposedly-exact information we bid on as absolutely-accurate air dollar volume for every Citicorp location in the country was shown in their RFP had nothing to do with air tickets; the air dollar volume claimed was just in the exact same percentages each location's personnel count bore to their overall employee count. This meant that a Citicorp office with twenty percent of their employees would show as accounting for twenty percent of their air travel, even if they never used one single plane ticket. That is close to what we faced.

I was shocked. It explained so much about why things were not working out the way we had been told to expect. Instead of being the best, it was clearly, *by far*, the worst RFP we had ever received. It is a shame that her employer probably never learned how their case died. They should have gotten out of having to pay their lawyer. Obviously, we did not pay Citicorp a cent.

THE LEADING BUSINESS TRAVEL PUBLICATION

This subject is not part of the Citicorp saga, but it has to fit here so that the "Epilogue" as the end of this chapter will make sense.

The managing editors of Business Travel News quietly checked with me fairly often on industry subjects where they needed to be sure they had the facts right before they published something. I was honored and the relationship helped us on several occasions. During the early years of the magazine, their annual listing of the largest US travel agencies showed American Express' airline ticketing volume as "n/a," meaning "not available." I was a big believer in good statistical information on our industry. For Heritage Travel it was good to be able to claim in proposals that we were the seventh largest travel agency in the country. The annual survey would clearly be better if the numbers for American Express were included.

Brain Froelich, VP Sales of American Express' Travel Related Services division, said he did not want to supply their volume numbers to Business Travel News because they knew the figures used by the country's second largest agency, Ask Mr. Foster (name later and wisely changed to Carlson Travel) were such a large exaggeration. Amex agreed to be listed if I would assure them that BTN would somehow use the correct number for Ask Mr. Foster.

At first, I attempted to solve this problem by designing a form which defined how an agency was to compute their air travel volume and added a signature line requiring the senior officer signing to certify that the information was correct. The volume claim was to be for travel handled by the agency's United States offices only and was to include only sales by offices owned by the company. American Express had loads of franchises, known as representative offices, that were not owned by them, and they did not consider it fair for Ask Mr. Foster to continue including air volume of companies they did not own and offices that they did own, Ask Mr. Foster employees even admitted to me that their Canadian volume was included. American Express was absolutely in the right.

The President of Ask Mr. Foster continued to sign, certify and return a grossly exaggerated report. This was interesting. The President of Ask Mr. Foster apologetically told me that their owner, Curt Carlson, required that they never supply a volume figure for their air sales that did not include their Canadian offices and Ask Mr. Foster franchises in the US, even though they were not owned by Ask Mr. Foster.

American Express could have increased their sales figures substantially by adding in all of the agencies in the US that were franchisees, plus their Canadian offices, but BTN's annual survey precluded this. Amex was being honest. A writer for Minnesota business magazine regaled me with his stories about Curt Carlson's exaggeration of sales figures in all of the businesses that he owned, and the writer had published two long articles outlining all of the details of Carlson's exaggerated claims. The magazine article amusingly described in detail many of Curt's false claims. The President of Ask Mr. Foster would not reveal their true volume, but some of his employees did. Several AMF executives, in both the United States and Canada, trusted me enough to call me with their sales volumes, so I was able to confirm that all sources matched and assure BTN that what they would be publishing was accurate.

Once I could assure American Express that BTN would use Ask Mr. Foster's honest sales figure, Brian Froelich each year would give me Amex's correct sales figures, which I would pass along to Business Travel News. By giving the American Express figures to me he could continue to claim that Amex had not given out their figures to Business Travel News. I don't know, but wish I had known, how in the world BTN explained it to

Ask Mr. Foster when a figure substantially less than Foster had certified was used each year in their publication. The two BTN people who were the editors during this period did say that the President of Ask Mr. Foster was very upset, but he must have known the statistics published by BTN were his true numbers. It also must have been amusing having to claim something in the paper was wrong when you knew it was right. Anyway, the point is that I had for several years, involving a number of BTN editors over the years, a most unusual role that was kept secret for three decades.

STUPID AND IRRITATING EPILOGUE

Shortly after the Citicorp fraud was detected but before the suit was resolved, BTN published a big annual article naming Citicorp's employee "Travel Manager of the Year." I was in shock when I read the article, and the editor of BTN at least apologized for not having talked with me sooner, before the selection was made and the announcement published. She had been, by a mile, the worst travel manager I had dealt with in all my years in that field. At least partially as the result of Citicorp's travel manager's having received the big award from Business Travel News, she moved to a new major New York employer at what I was told was a significant raise in pay.

42 ANY COST

Divided By Enough People Becomes Affordable

Over the years as a bachelor, I organized a bunch of houses and events where the cost became feasible when shared by enough people. We had ski houses at various areas in upstate Vermont, two that will be reported here that were on the water in Marblehead, Massachusetts, several in Boston (one covered under the chapter entitled "Porter Anderson" and one on a fashionable street on the "flat" of Beacon Hill in downtown Boston.

BEACON HILL, BOSTON

For this to make sense, you need to know a little bit about the one square mile that comprises the area known as Beacon Hill in Boston, a neighborhood that was designated a National Historic Landmark in 1962. In a long list of famous people who have made Beacon Hill their home over the centuries, probably the two best known today are Teddy Kennedy and John Kerry. Teddy was on the flat of the hill in Charles River Square (near Mass General Hospital) and John and Alexandra Forbes Kerry were on the single most exclusive street, Louisburg Square, which includes a small but elegant park owned by the abutters. The annual average family income reported in 2007 was $4.8 million (but I find that number hard to believe).

The average price of houses was $2.7 million and ones on Louisburg square are in the six to twenty-million-dollar range. The Kerry's live at 19 Louisburg Square at the uphill corner of Pinckney. I am suspicious of the income statistic, because there are lots or renters at much lower levels of income who should bring the average down, but it still is one of the most exclusive residential areas in the country.

I lived at 50 Brimmer St., a classic brick rowhouse, narrow but three stories tall. There are very strict building codes controlling any change you try to make to the buildings in the historic district, including something as simple as painting your front door. You have to file an application for a Certificate of Appropriateness and gain approval from the Beacon Hill Civic Association. The front door of 50 Brimmer did need painting so I had a lady who I had come to know suggest a color for the door. Her selection was significantly different than what had been there, so when I completed the work, the change was quite noticeable.

Shortly thereafter, a formal complaint arrived from the Civic Association stating that the color I had used was not an approved color and must be changed. They were very surprised when I was able to respond that not only had the color been chosen by her but also the actual can of paint had been given to me by the lady who was the President of the Association.

THE BRIMMER HILTON

The zoning in the area was certainly limited to single family occupancy, but the doctor who owned 50 Brimmer Street allowed me to sign the lease, knowing that the two large bedrooms on the second floor and four small bedrooms upstairs would be occupied by six bachelors. It quickly got knicknamed "The Brimmer Hilton." When I listed the names that were to appear in the phone book, I included a Mr. Hilton Brimmer so that when it did appear in the phone book it read as "Brimmer Hilton."

At first, there was a mild but noticeable undercurrent of disapproval by the neighbors. The neighbor on one side was the famous maritime historian, Samuel Eliot Morrison, and two doors behind him lived Boston Mayor Kevin White. Today, a well-known Harvard Professor and Chairman of the Government Department, Sam Huntington (now deceased), owned 52 Brimmer.

This is not the subject of this chapter, but it is amusing to note a strange feature of the design of the houses, probably accepted in order to save money on construction. All of the houses in that block between Lime Street and Chestnut Street were built at the same time and they all share common walls with the abutting houses. They also share brick chimneys. Living next door at 52 Brimmer during our early years was a beautiful and charming girl, Joannie Wells, who sadly died quite young of cancer. Her dad, Fred, was an officer at the First National Bank of Boston.

The downstairs at 50 Brimmer included an entrance foyer, a living room, a large dining room, with a small kitchen in the rear. Bruce Listerman, a former Williams College football player, took the bedroom on the second floor front and I took the largest bedroom with bath on the rear. The group had lots of large parties, including loud music, usually in my room where the music system resided.

I hated to think of how much noise the Wells family put up with next door over those years. It was only late in our occupancy of that building that I learned the chimney of my fireplace only went up a few feet above the fireplace itself before the chimney joined the one from the Wells' bedroom. Sound carried easily from my bedroom through the open connection with the chimney into the Wells' bedroom.

It was fifty years later that I learned of a final part of this story. Above my bedroom in a smaller bedroom was my old friend Bill Moomaw. He was part of our group while studying for his PhD from MIT. His bedroom was just under the sloping roof, so that his dormer window could be reached from someone climbing on the roof. I was surprised to learn from him that the beautiful Joan had been climbing out of her bedroom window, crossing the roof and climbing into his bedroom late at night. She was agile and he was a very lucky man.

The highly regarded Harvard Professor of Government, Sam Huntington, who died in early 2009, was one of the first in recent history to predict a "clash of civilizations" throughout the world, precipitated by religion. He became head of the Government Department.

ADVERTISING THE CHRISTMAS PARTY

The Brimmer Hilton residents hosted many parties, one of which was a large party at the Statler Hilton Hotel on a Friday night, December 6, 1963. As the evening went on we began to draw names from a hat until one name was left. The winning couple, Larry Burckmyer and his wife at the time, Molly, were rushed by limo from the Hilton to the airport where they took the last flight to Puerto Rico for the weekend at the Caribe Hilton in San Juan. The admission charge for the party paid for the prize.

To help spread the name recognition of the Brimmer Hilton before the next big party, I had talked with the aerial advertising company that towed signs around in the skies of eastern Massachusetts. Even sharing the cost, the four guys could not afford the aerial advertising company's normal rate for an hour or two, so I asked what they would have to charge for just two circles above Harvard Stadium during a football game. This may have been way back in the sixties, but $25 was still affordable and we signed up. That was just $6.25 each. Boy, did we get our money's worth. The sign, of which I still have photographs, read "Greetings from the Brimmer Hilton." The long sign was towed by an old propeller-driven bi-plane (that means two wings), at the end of a tether so long that I could not get a picture of the plane and the sign together.

On the day of the game and scheduled flight, there was a very strong wind from the northwest. We began to see the plane approaching from its home base to the east in Revere, Massachusetts. In addition to the weak plane, the long sign must have provided lots of wind resistance. The plane moved very slowly above the home team side of the stadium, picked up speed when it turned downwind over the closed end of the stadium finally reaching the northeast end of the visitors' side of the stadium. It turned northwest directly into the wind to begin its second loop. The game was underway and it was genuinely boring, so the plane and its sign attracted more attention than would normally have been the case. The plane could barely make headway into the wind and appeared to be pushed backward occasionally by strong gusts. It was not long before the plane began to get much more attention than the football game. It may have been flying into the wind, but it appeared to be standing still.

When the plane finally succeeded in making it to the area behind the home team side of the stadium, it turned left and once again was suddenly aided by the tailwind. It was like a rocket racing around that side of the circle back to the visitors' side, where it once again undertook the slow trip against the headwind. The boring game did not evoke much in the way of cheers, but the plane got moans and groans when it was pushed to a stop and cheers when it made headway. For our $25, the got much more exposure than anyone would have dreamed.

MARBLEHEAD, MASSACHUSETTS

This beautiful town lies about 15 miles northeast of Boston, up the coast on the Atlantic Ocean. Founded in 1629, the little town in an historic jewel of protected antique home in the old town. The harbor is surrounded by three major yacht clubs (more if you include the minor ones) and it is full of sailing yachts, smaller racing sailboats and an increasing number of powerboats. Supposedly, at the peak in mid-summer, the boat count exceeds 3,000. Across the Harbor on an island connected to the mainland by a causeway over a sandspit lies Marblehead Neck, covered with stately multi-million-dollar homes overlooking the ocean or the harbor.

Although the town boasts a long list of well-known residents and former residents, the name that always amused me was Elbridge Gerry, Governor of Massachusetts in the early 1800s. His name was mixed with "salamander" by a writer to describe a long and weirdly-shaped district intended to result in political advantage for him. The resulting word, Gerrymander, is still widely used today to describe manipulation of voting district boundaries to increase a political party's constituents in such a way as to weaken the opposition. The district that resulted in the word stretched from north of Boston around outside of what is now Highway 128 and ending with Cape Ann as the creature's beak. Marblehead was the right front foot of the monster…the Gerrymander.

Back in the sixties and seventies, I rented two houses (the word "house" may be a stretch of the term) from a Mr. Shepard, who lived across the street in a stately yellow with white trim home overlooking the harbor. The two "houses" were really cottages, made of wood, with porches overlooking Marblehead Harbor. The Corinthian Yacht Club's tennis courts were two hundred feet behind us and the Club itself was only three hundred feet away. It was a great location.

Despite the magnificent views, especially of sunsets across the Harbor and the tower of Abbot Hall, the rent was only $500 per year per house. I got five guys to share the smaller house and six girls to share the larger house next door. The condition in which the interior of the guys' house was maintained resulted in its being called "The Ashtray." The girls' house was "The Six Pack."

Although the uninsulated and unheated houses could not be inhabited in the winter, the $500 annual rent covered the whole year. When we divided up the cost for each guy, each share came to $125 a year. Now if you think that was a bargain, wait till you read the punch line.

Automobile insurance rates in Massachusetts were predicated upon your residence, the place where you normally kept your car the majority of the year. The theft, accident and vandalism rates in downtown Boston were so bad that, when contrasted with Marblehead, it cost $135 per year less to insure each car with the Corinthian Lane house as our address than it would have cost in Boston. The house did not cost us anything; we each saved $10 a year by renting the house. Good cost/value ratio.

The proximity of the girls and the thinness of the walls did result in one amusing, or maybe the better word is embarrassing, afternoon. The phrase "making love" is probably the most inappropriate in common usage today. The girl was one of those that moaned and squealed quite loudly. She was mortified when, at the end of the "activity," there was a round of applause from others in the house. The two houses did not do much to enhance the property values of better homes nearby. The Shepard family sold them to the Corinthian Yacht Club, which a few years later tore them down to build an alternative entrance into their parking lot. There was some great history about those houses that stood on Corinthian Lane in the old days.

WELLESLEY

After paying for freshman year tuition at Vanderbilt, the girl I was dating in high school (Rollin Walker, now Rollin Shaw) came bouncing into Kate Clark's homeroom Latin Class at Sidney Lanier High School announcing with glee that she had been admitted and was going to Wellesley College.

For some reason, I had a Harvard application at home and decided I might as well apply. The deadline had been the day before, so I had to rush to the downtown Post Office to get it in that afternoon's mail. Upon parking at the PO, I took one last look at the application and discovered that an essay was required on the back of the last page. It had to be filled out. When I searched the glove compartment, all I found was one of those little short golf pencils used on scorecards, the cheap kind that had no eraser. My essay had to be written first draft in pencil. When I made a mistake, I could not even erase it, I just had to mark through and keep writing. I don't know if that helped or not, but I got in. Had I gone to Vanderbilt and returned home I would not have had the great jobs I got and been to all the places I have seen. Thanks Rollin.

Later I learned that all the prep school guys had considered various topics for their essay, drafted outlines and then drafts for review and editing by their guidance counselors, finally having their essays typed carefully on their applications. Some obnoxious friends claimed the admissions people must have wanted more blacks and assumed that was what I was, but back in those days you had to attach a photograph to your application.

A picture was taken when Rollin and I boarded the train at Union Station in Montgomery (yes, the train) for the long ride to Boston. The picture that shows in my Freshman Yearbook illustrates the mistakes a southern kid can make being suddenly interjected into the rich private prep school environment of a major New England college. I had a "flat top" haircut and was wearing a creamy off-white sport coat with a brownish-orange knit tie.

Where is this story headed? You get to Cambridge and you want to go see your girl in Wellesley. Before the Massachusetts Turnpike, it was a long meandering sixteen-ile drive from Harvard to Wellesley. Today, at age 18, you probably would not be allowed to rent a car. Even if you could, that was going to be too costly for me to rent a car each weekend to date at Wellesley. I decided to try renting a large enclosed red truck from Avis, which at thc time had a rental location on Massachusetts Avenue, just five short blocks toward Boston from Harvard Square. Lots of kids faced the same cost problem and were delighted when I put up signs in all of the freshman dormitories announcing round trip to Wellesley for a dollar. They were cautioned that this would mean sitting on the floor in the dark in the back of the truck for the duration of the trip. No problem, the truck sold out.

We left Harvard Yard and, after about 40 minutes, the big red truck pulled up to the main gates of Wellesley. Today that entrance is closed and you have to drive around to one side or the other, but in 1955 those large stone towers and iron gates marked the grand entrance and Wellesley College Police on either side of the entrance controlled the flow of traffic, which was fairly heavy on a Saturday evenings. The policemen stopped us, walked to the door of the truck and stated that commercial vehicles were not allowed. When I explained the cargo, the cops insisted upon going around back and opening the doors. When they shined their flashlights inside, they lit up forty eyes staring back at them. The traffic had backed up behind us, but we were immediately waved through.

The next weekend the red truck, luckily in Harvard crimson, was waved through a gauntlet of police cheering "Here comes the Harvard truck!!!!!"

In those days, there was a great nightclub called the Totem Pole where the Newton Marriott now sits overlooking the Charles River beside Route 16 in the Auburndale portion of Newton. It had excellent entertainment and good dancing at prices affordable by students.

I'm just glad we never had a wreck.

43 PARKING YOUR CAR
Another One About Beacon Hill In Boston

People who live in small to medium-sized cities don't have to think much about parking their car. You just drive in the driveway, push the garage door remote and drive in. It's simple, safe and relatively inexpensive.

As a bachelor during my early years in Boston I rented various apartments, almost all of which did not have any place to park. You had to park on the street, and this meant searching for a parking place. The streets of Beacon Hill now have signs that parking is for those with resident stickers only. That has greatly reduced, but not eliminated the time required to find a spot. In the winter, parking became much worse. People attempting to get their car out of a parallel parking spot in deep snow would have to do a lot of shoveling to extricate their vehicle. Prior to that you had to get all of the snow off the windows and hood, working carefully so as not to scratch the paint. It could be a cold, time-consuming and exhausting process. After a few days, much of the packed snow turned to hard ice, making getting into a parking place a dangerous challenge.

Of course, when you returned from a trip or something as simple as grocery shopping, you would frequently have to make several trips of several blocks each way to get things from your car to your residence. One winter, having broken my foot skiing, I would have to climb on crutches up the steep hill to 45 Pinckney Street, and then climb two flights of stairs to my apartment. No big deal on crutches or carrying lots of stuff, but a real struggle when you are faced with having to do both.

When I was living at 50 Brimmer Street on the edge of Beacon Hill in downtown Boston, there was a large three-story brick garage at 70 Brimmer, directly behind what years later became the bar known as "Cheers." People paid monthly to rent their parking place.

In 1979, the garage decided to become a condominium. At the time, everyone laughed at the idea of paying $6,500 for a place to park your car, on top of which today you have to pay almost $200 a month in condo fees and property tax approaching $1,000 to the City of Boston. On top of that, to be safe, the garage has to be staffed, and it is locked when there is nobody on duty. That means that on weekdays you can only get your car out between 6:30am and midnight. Not everyone laughed. One man had the foresight to see how demand was going to continue to exceed supply which, for all purposes, will not increase on Beacon Hill. There is now a huge underground garage open to the public underneath the Boston Common, but this can be a long walk for most people living on Beacon Hill. This gentleman put down what was considered a ridiculous $65,000 for ten places. He could lease out the ones he did not use personally. He made a bundle.in

44 LUNCH FOR TWO

Another story about American Express

Whether your business is large or small, you will get asked to donate something to a charity. This is frequently for an auction, and buyers can usually get great bargains.

In 1975, a man at American Express was asked to make a donation to a charity auction. The agreed item was lunch for two at any restaurant that accepted the American Express Card. The man at Amex approved the donation, thinking that, despite living in a very expensive city, it would probably not be more than $300 (the equivalent of $1,440 in 2019). The auction was held and the man at American Express was surprised to hear that the winning bid had been about $900. Major note follows. Wikipedia indicates that the winning bid was just $300, but that is incorrect. There was a big article with pictures of the luncheon in People Magazine, and the man at American Express would not have been so shocked and terrified had the bid not been much higher than he had expected the meal would cost. He was shocked to learn the amount of the bid and that the winning bidder was Craig Claiborne, the highly-respected restaurant expert and widely-read food critic for the New York Times.

It became worse when he read what Claiborne had in mind, not just incredible meals but rare and obscenely expensive French wines. Articles began to appear in the Times discussing Claiborne's restaurant and menu options. The articles analyzing all the possible restaurant choices went on for weeks. It got worse and worse. Claiborne ended up selecting Chez Denis, a restaurant outside of Paris, and taking a friend, Franey, for lunch. The bill was over $4,000. Once again, remember that in 2019 dollars we are talking about a lunch tab that would be $9,000 in 2019, quite an expensive lunch for two.

It was a 31 course meal with top French Wines and Claiborne was widely criticized for taking just bites of each dish and wasting so much food when so many people in the world were starving. Of course, in addition to an incredible array of dishes, they selected an assortment of great French wines to accompany the meal. Instead of getting blasted for giving away too much, the man at American Express became a hero, at least at American Express. It was not just the coverage in the New York Times leading up to the lunch, pictures of the lunch and lengthy articles appeared in newspapers and magazines all over the world. People Magazine ran an extremely long article with numerous pictures and pages of detail about the restaurant, the courses selected for the meal and the bottles of great rare wines that accompanied it.

The value of the press coverage exceeded by several hundred times the cost to American Express. Amusingly, Claiborne gave the meal a poor review for design, quality and presentation.

45 THEFT OF CORPORATE SECRETS
An Elaborate Scheme (That Worked)

In the seventies, when Heritage started the Woodside Group of Travel Agencies, we ran the operation out of Heritage Travel. As detailed in a previous chapter, I made many trips around the country trying to identify the very best agencies handling business travel. This story happened one day when I was out of town on one of those research and sales trips.

When I returned to Cambridge, I was told that a lady had arrived at Heritage Travel. She apologized for being out of business cards, but announced that she worked for TRW in California and was interested in Heritage Travel and Woodside to serve her employer. . She said she had been in Boston for a meeting, and when the meeting ended early had squeezed in time to stop by our office before having to head back to the airport.

Because people thought she represented a major prospective client, she was given everything, the details of service programs, Woodside's discounted rate hotel directory, and samples of our management reports and all of the information on the recently-established Woodside organization. She left, saying she would be back in touch soon.

Shortly thereafter, it was mentioned in a conversation with Ceb Benisch, the owner of Don Travel, the largest business travel specialist in New York City, that his agency had experienced the same type of visit by a smooth-talking woman who used the same story. We were immediately aware that the whole story was a fraud. When the warning was sent out, we discovered that one other Woodside agency had experienced the same problem. It should have been interesting to know that, although the woman had claimed to represent a company in L.A, she did not go to the Woodside agency there.

We quickly realized that we had all been duped. Our first calls were to TRW. TRW had no employee by the name we had been given and they were obviously innocent of any involvement, but because someone was traveling around the country obtaining information by claiming to be an employee of TRW, they were most eager to assist in apprehending the culprit.

After a few days of exchanging information, including a physical description of the woman (I will quit using the word "lady" from here on," it was decided that the most likely person was an attractive former employee of American Airlines, having been an early manager in their now widespread chain of Admirals Clubs in airports throughout the world. American was nice enough to overnight a closeup picture of their former employee from her personnel file. We thought we had the culprit dead to rights.

What a disappointment. The picture bore no remote resemblance to the person who had visited the agency offices.

Additional discussion led us to believe that the guilty party was a friend of the owner of one of the largest agencies in Los Angeles, which is why she couldn't go into Woodside's office there. This time we were pretty sure we had figured it out. American helped us by doing something highly questionable but very helpful. They searched their reservation system and alerted us that the suspect was booked on a flight from Los Angeles to Chicago, where a highly-innovative Woodside agency, IVI Travel, was headquartered.

Upon hearing she was headed his way, Larry Incandella, the principle owner of IVI, blurted out that he would never let her in the door. I asked him to think about an option. They should welcome the woman into Larry's office, where she would need to make the false claim that she was a representative of TRW.

A policeman was hired to spend the day at IVI, so he could hide in a closet as soon as she arrived, keeping the door open so he could be a witness to who she was and what she claimed. Larry planned to sue the Los Angeles agency that was attempting to steal IVI's business secrets.

The day went by and she never showed up. We did, however, hear years later what had happened. When Woodside began to be highly visible in the travel trade press, another Boston Agency, Fox Travel, organized a team of the second-best commercial travel agencies throughout the country and named it Hickory, a takeoff on Woodside. Hickory also happened to the street on which Fox's owner, Norm Cotton, lived.

The woman from Los Angeles had flown to Chicago to meet in the offices of a Chicago agency to form a second agency consortium, The owner of the Chicago agency did join the group, but was quite embarrassed by what had transpired and apologized profusely. She said that we had been right about the woman who had been the culprit and that all of the materials she had improperly acquired by misrepresentation were spread out on the conference table at the meeting at which Hickory was formed. The Chicago agency owner said it was made clear, as well as being obvious, how all of the Woodside materials had been acquired. The agencies and TRW probably could have taken the woman to court, but it was decided that it simply was not worth it.

The reason that the culprit could not visit Woodside's Los Angeles office was that she was well known in the LA travel industry and would have been easily recognized. We spent a lot of time, but the secrets were acquired, the culprit got away and a new agency team was formed.

46 THE LAST GREAT DUEL
This Was Really Old Fashioned

Duels were in fashion hundreds of years ago, but they do not occur often anymore. Do they ever? The last one I heard about in the States was in 1954. Most duels in the twentieth century were fought with pistols. In those days, pistols were not very accurate, especially when in the hands of a nervous amateur. The standard rule was that the combatants stood back to back, walked ten paces (probably twenty-five feet) turned and fired. This meant that they shot at each other from about fifty feet apart. Pistols had replaced swords as the weapon of choice. When using swords, you were in very close proximity to your adversary, so there was almost no chance that at least one of the participants would not be killed or injured.

A good friend in grade school, Jim Scott, lived in a great old white house in the country, in Waugh, Alabama, which in the mid fifties was way out in the country east of Montgomery. Today it is just off Interstate 85, essentially a part of the city. Jim's parties were always good fun, and this one in 1954 was no exception. Two guys were engaged in a mock swordfight, using real antique swords with their ends taped over. The tape on Sterling Culpepper's sword fell off in mid thrust. I remember looking in horror as Sterling's sword went into the left forearm of Tommy Lawson. Tommy was rushed to the hospital by Sammy Fisher and Vivian Butler (later Mrs. Jim Scott), stitched up and was fine.

EPILOLOG

Years later (in about 2007), a man behind me waiting in line for the bar at a Christmas party said "Are you the real Thornton Clark?" I turned and obviously did not recognize him after 53 years. He laughed and said he was Tom Lawson. His new wife, standing next to him, and two other friends of his, looked on in astonishment as I grabbed his left hand and pushed his shirt and coat sleeve up to the elbow. There on the underside of his arm was the long scar, still clear as a bell

47 CLASSICS VS. MODERN

The Arts, Music and Architecture

Having to travel so much on my job I got to see the art and architecture of the world and to attend concerts in most of the great halls of the major cities. Some of that is reviewed in this chapter. I am also guilty of being extremely critical. This chapter is clearly a personal complaint. It rambles through music, art and architecture. When writing, I noticed that there were many examples that I thought must be "the worst," so that description is used over and over again. I bet you agree with me on most of these.

CLASSICAL MUSIC

It is a sad but true statistic that audiences for classical music are declining steadily, everywhere, not just in the big cities. Even what became well-known under Boston Conductor, Arthur Fiedler, as "POPS" music is heading into decline, although far less so than classical. With the surge of punk rock and rapper music, what songs will constitute "Pops" in a few decades? The popularity of Pops will continue, but the music played will more and more often have to be popular songs that were written decades ago or themes from movies.

The biggest problem is in the area of classical music, and that is where at least some of the problem is solvable. When I was President of the Savannah Symphony Orchestra, we faced severe problems, some the union, but most were financial. Concerts in Savannah started later than all others in the United States. Almost all orchestra concerts in the United States began at 7:30, a few at 7; Savannah was the only one in the entire country that did not get underway until 8pm. This was fine for those who wanted to come into downtown Savannah for dinner at a good restaurant before a concert, but it meant the mostly-older audience had to stay up quite late.

In addition, a large percentage of the audience and the donors came from Skidaway Island, a twenty-five minute drive from downtown Savannah. If a concert ran until 10, as most did, this meant taking 15 minutes to get to your car and out of a parking lot and arriving home just before 11. It was a constant complaint.

I decided that the best, and safest, way to resolve the question was to draft a simple one-page questionnaire asking people to vote. Because I believed it to be a major area of complaint, I included two questions about people's preferences. Regarding the first, there was a massive preference for traditional classical music. The audience liked what was referred to by musicians deriding the attitude as "the old warhorses." The response to an open-ended request for comment was that they not only did not *like* "modern" classical music, they *hated* it.

The Symphony's Executive Director at the time, George Alexsovich, urged me to quit saying it that way and just say that the survey showed the audience "preferred" the traditional. That is part of the problem. Symphonies do not listen to their audiences and wonder why they are experiencing declines in attendance. The comments on the questionnaires clearly showed that it was not just preference for traditional classical, it was hatred of the modern versions. Note that this did not read "intense dislike:" it was true hatred.

When I was attending concerts of the highly-regarded Boston Symphony Orchestra at the famous old Symphony Hall in Boston, Massachusetts, I happened to be up close in the center for the world premiere of a concert by Elliot Carter. I was dating Barbara Peterson at the time and she had excellent season tickets near the front and center. The concert was strange, at best, and awful in the opinion of most. The fancy word would be "cacophonous." It was like kids in the alley banging on trash cans.

At the end of the symphony, most people seated around us refrained from applauding and there was considerable grumbling about how horrible the experience had been. Some of the strongest complaints were stated quite loudly. The conductor, Seiji Ozawa, turned, faced the audience and announced that they were delighted and honored to have the composer present for the premiere and asked him to stand. Carter was only a few seats to our left, so he must have heard the reaction from the audience around him.

MARKETING 101

For one season, I had the Savannah Symphony play what the Artistic Committee of the Board of Directors deemed to be the best known and loved compositions by the great composers. We had on our board some extraordinarily-knowledgeable experts, who spent many days agonizing over the very best choices. Subscriptions went up and dozens of former subscribers, upon hearing of the planned schedule, decided to renew their season subscriptions. Some "experts" claimed that you certainly could not have an orchestra perform a piece that the musicians had played just two or three years earlier. The musicians wanted to add to their lists of works they had performed, so playing the great well-known themes by Rachmaninoff, Tchaikovsky and Beethoven was not acceptable to the musician's union.

From a financial standpoint, it is interesting to note that much of the best work of Mozart can be performed using relative few musicians, a full traditional symphony typically requires as a minimum 55 to 75 musicians, but a "new" work by Mahler results in the need to pay 90 to 100 musicians, each of whom is paid at least the minimum union scale. That resulted in a work that the audience did not like frequently costing $10,000 more to perform than works the audience would enjoy and, more importantly, pay to hear.

I found that a significant portion of the audience would not bother to stay after intermission if what followed was going to be modern. It is more costly to play music that the audience hated than it is to play a great classic that they loved. What kind of business does that? Ridiculous.

The "experts" all recommend what is known as "bookending," which means placing the modern piece between two more recognizable and appreciated works, forcing the audience to sit through the bad one to get to the good one. Bookending is common practice. My understanding is that, in any business, you are supposed to *give the customer what the customer wants*, not tell him what he wants or force him to take what you want him to have, even when you know it is something that will not be liked. If forcing the audience to listen to something bad is not the objective, then why is bookending necessary?

THE BIGGEST JOKES IN MUSIC

John Milton Cage, a composer who died in 1992, was known for introducing "modern style" classical music. His work was of the most extreme modern variety, even by 21st century standards. In 1952, Cage composed a work, *"Four Minutes and Thirty-three Seconds,"* that was supposed to be taken seriously, even though it is nothing more than a stupid joke played on the audiences that pay to "hear" it and see it performed. The score that the musicians play by just reads "tacit, tacit, tacit," which for musicians translates to "silence, silence and even more silence." Not one single note is played. Is that really "music?" The musicians just sit there in their chairs holding their instruments. Maybe even worse is that people pay to go to a performance. The great Encyclopedia Britannica credits Cage's "inventive compositions and unorthodox ideas profoundly influenced mid-20th-century music."

The next subject is in my chapter on the years I spent as President of a symphony orchestra, but I will repeat it here. If you have not been involved in the operation of an orchestra, you may not know that two types of payments usually have to be made in order to perform a work. The symphony orchestra pays the composer (or, if deceased, the owner of the rights) for the right to play the music and a publisher rents out the copies of the music for each musician and a composite score for the conductor. If your symphony wants to "perform" this ridiculous soundless work, they not only have to pay for the right to perform it, but also pay to rent the "music" which of course consists of nothing but blank pages for every "musician." This is one of the best examples of highly-educated, experienced and "respected" experts telling the audience how great this composition is and how much they must appreciate it.

Another joke about music received lots of publicity in 2012. A woman (referred to as "the artist") sat in an uncomfortable chair in the lobby of New York's Museum of

Modern Art. She came every day and sat all day motionless staring straight ahead, without saying a word. This supposedly set a record for the longest opera "performance" in history…seven hundred hours. You can guess what I think about that.

The great old operas composed by the masters continue to attract a reasonable audience, although the interest is declining precipitously. People complain that many operas are too long, some much too long, but that usually means three or four hours. How would you think about an opera that was 700 hours long? Obviously, it had to be spread over many weeks.

The "experts" must believe themselves when they claim such a stupid display is really a great performance, and their official pronouncements get the public to go along with the joke, thinking it is really art. What a joke. This wasn't the act of a bunch of dunces, but maybe on second thought it was. The selection had to have been made by the "highly-educated" curator and approved by the highly-acclaimed Director of the Museum of Modern Art. They have PhDs so their opinion *must* be respected, especially when in contrast with a plain old ignorant person like me.

Albert Einstein was, believe it or not, a violinist. When he made a bad mistake, the conductor reportedly said "What's the matter, can't you count to four."

At this point I will make a recommendation. Having watched many operas in the great opera houses of the world, I suggest you not miss one, even though it is expensive and rarely performed. Verdi's Aida is much more powerful with the top singers and the huge number of performers when it is performed by New York's Metropolitan Opera House. The "Triumphal March" is magnificent. Go someday if you can, but if you can't, watch it on YouTube.

ARCHITECTURE

First, it may be a profession, but I love architecture (at least good architecture) and consider it to be an art. Many beautiful buildings have been built all over the world. Some cities, and most city governments, have to build at the cheapest cost to save money, so we all-too-often get ugly buildings. A few spend much more to have elaborate buildings designed by highly-rated architectural firms. The designs by Frank Gehry and Salvatore Calatrava are so outstanding that they attract tourists to cities just to see the buildings and bridges. Bilbao is a relatively unattractive, industrial port in on the northern coast of Spain. It was rarely visited by tourists but is now a destination only because of the Gehry's Guggenheim Museum. (not to be confused with the original Guggenheim in New York by Frank Lloyd Wright). More recently, Calatrava designed the magnificent Milwaukee Museum which has huge adjustable wings that resemble a bird in flight. It cost a fortune, but it is so spectacular that the crowds have made it a financial success. The architecture of the museum is much more outstanding than the art.

The most spectacular building (as of 2019) is the incredibly-tall Burj Khalifa in Dubai, one of the United Arab Emirates. It is complex while remaining simple. The clean lines of the cylinders stretch toward the sky, with an increasingly small number of cylinders until the final single cylinder that sits atop the structure. Dubai also has the elegant Cayon Tower, which has plain square floors with one major difference: the building twists, with each floor turned slightly rather than being directly above the floor underneath. That is one of the reasons I love Dubai. The all-new city is filled with attractive high-rise buildings and there is a chapter on this city near the end of the book.

What is remarkable is how truly-ugly buildings are constructed, many of which receive acclaim from "the experts" and are therefore considered outstanding, no matter how ugly they are. When I was living in Cambridge, Massachusetts, Boston University had a big-name architect design a tall building to be sited beside the Charles River, The construction includes numerous colored panels randomly interspersed between the horizontal and vertical lines of concrete that comprise the exterior of the building. It looks even worse as the panels' colors have faded over the years.

During my time there, Harvard had classic elegant architecture. Even when they began to utilize modern architecture, most of the new buildings were clean and beautiful as well as being functional. In 2003, Harvard must have decided to make BU look good by selecting a much worse design by the high-regarded architecture firm, Machado and Silvetti Associates of Boston. As you drive north on Storrow Drive past the entrance to the Massachusetts Turnpike you used to see the tower of Dunster House across the Charles River.

Now you are faced with the One Western Avenue graduate student housing building. It is neither graceful nor attractive. It is just plain old-fashioned ugly. It would be easy to get the impression that the contractor was just drunk and got all the windows in the wrong places. The placement of the windows is staggered so that nothing lines up. The exterior is cheap and plain, focusing the eye on the dreadful window arrangement. How does someone approve that and why in the world does someone design something so unattractive? The building is part of the "Harvard Green Campus Initiative," a commendable plan to build more environmentally friendly buildings. That should not mean they have to be ugly.

Harvard can relax and avoid criticism because so many much more unattractive buildings have been built all over the world. Two atrocious designs come to mind. First is the highly-acclaimed Centre National D'Art et Culture" known as the Pompidou Center or simply “Beaubourg” for the area in which it sits on the eastern side of Paris. Paris has been truly outstanding in protecting the city’s beauty. With the exception of the Montparnasse Tower far to the south side of the city, all skyscrapers have been relegated to the northwest corner of Paris in the Centre National for Industry and Technology. What could easily be the ugliest building in the world gains applause from “the experts” for ridiculous reasons. The Pompidou Center was designed with all of the water pipes, electrical wiring, cooling ducts and elevators on the outside facing the street. Ostensibly, this leaves the interior more open and “clean.” It looks like a Texas oil refinery that has been painted in several colors.

You would have to be looking for it to notice any difference inside the center. When you look out a window you do see the buildings infrastructure or, being on the outside, should it be called “outfrastructure?” It certainly isn’t pretty. The brightly colored metal pipes block what would otherwise be a normal view. The building does have one unique characteristic. As the primarily blue, red and green paint began to weather and the building’s “exterior” had to be repainted, they discovered that having to scrape, sand and repaint all of the hard-to-reach pipes and ducts on the outside of the building made it a costly nightmare to maintain. Somebody should have thought of this in advance.

Another example, ugly but not as ugly as Beaubourg, is the Agbar Tower in Barcelona, Spain. It sits at the Place de les Glories on the north side of town. It really is not all that ugly, it is just so bad that it generates derogatory nicknames. The round 474 foot tower, which opened in 2005, simply looks like a giant penis. From a distance, it appears to be silver, with exterior glass louvers reflecting the sunlight. Up close, there are many colors, and at night it is lighted with vivid blue and red areas. The architect who deserves the “applause” for this monstrosity is Jean Nouvel.

Critiques frequently compare the Agbar to the 591 foot tower which opened in 2004 at 30 St. Mary Axe in London’s financial district. This building, although cylindrical, becomes smaller at its base, is pointed at the top, and has graceful lines curling around the exterior. Its shape appears to be more like a bomb. In any event, 30 St. Mary Axe should not be tarred with the same brush as the obnoxious Agbar Tower.

A building that many consider garish is the colorful Grand Lisboa tower in Macau, named the Lisboa because of the Portuguese influence emanating from their maintaining Macau as a colony for many decades before giving in to China. The tower’s shape, like a Lotus Flower, is most unusual, highlighted by changing lights at night. I think it looks quite elegant and fits well with a city that is comprised of many large colorfully-lighted gambling casinos.

How do the professional critics and other “experts” expect people to take this seriously?

VISUAL ARTS

While at Harvard, one of my favorite art classes covered art of the first half of the twentieth century. This included impressionism, but made it through to the era of absurdity, which was just beginning in the late-1950s. Some of the more modern art is quite beautiful, but most people dislike the junk that is purported to be art these days. The dealers, the museum directors, the esteemed curators (esteemed at least in their eyes) and the gallery owners can all talk in glowing terms about a work that, were it not proclaimed to be art, would not be considered art.

I bet that most American's would be shocked to learn that one of the most talked about works of "art" in 1987 was a 60" x 40" photograph by Andres Serrano of a Christian of a plastic Christian cross, complete with a crucified Jesus, in a glass jar filled with the artist's urine. It was entitled "Immersion, Piss Christ." At least in this case many ridiculed it and demanded its removal. The US Congress got involved because the artist had been paid $15,000 by the taxpayer-funded "National Endowment for the Arts." This meant everybody had paid for it. Sadly, this type of stupidity lends credence to the push to defund the NEA.

Robert Mapplethorpe is highly acclaimed for his photographs, but when they were exhibited at Boston's Institute of Contemporary Art, his most-talked-about series of photographs had to be placed in a special, closed off, area so that only adults could see it. It may have been politically correct and he is certainly an excellent photographer, but is a closeup of a pecker in an asshole really art? It may be politically correct to "uh" and "ah" about what great "art" this is, but it is simply not acceptable to the vast majority of people.

At Louisiana, a famous art museum on the water in Denmark 20 miles north of Copenhagen, hung on the wall as "art" is an old, used urinal, nothing else, just a urinal. Duchamp years earlier had submitted a urinal to an "all works will be accepted show" in New York City, only to have this item rejected. In December, 2014, a British review of hundreds of artists rated Duchamp's porcelain urinal as the world's most influential piece of modern art. How ridiculous is that? All too many modern art museums have piles of rocks on the floor or a rope hanging down from a ceiling as "art." To call the urinal "art" is ridiculous. To have it in a supposedly prestigious museum and rated incredibly high is nothing short of preposterous.

In November of 2012 the media reported on a horse that held a brush in its mouth and painted "art" that sold for $2,500 a painting. How do people, no matter how much money they have to waste, buy this junk?

In October of 2015, a modern art museum in northern Italy reported (and apologized) that one of its "works of art" had mistakenly been thrown out by a cleaning crew working at night. The "art" was a room with a tattered banner and a floor covered with dozens of empty bottles of champagne, confetti and cigarette butts. This "installation" was supposed to have great meaning. The cleaning crew just thought there had been a wild messy party and they had to clean it up. You gotta be kidding!!!

In its June 2007, the elegant *"Arts & Antiques"* Magazine had a small article entitled "*One Man's Trash"* with a sentence that started "Mistaking art for garbage might be a running joke among traditional art connoisseurs, but it can be costly for the perpetrator."

Could this next one be the most ridiculous? The February 8, 2016 issue of Time Magazine included a picture of a painting by Kevin Abosch. Not a painting, just a photo. The subject? A potato. Not anything like an artistic arrangement; just a plain old potato in the center of the photograph. Even the artist called the sale "absurd." Sit down and don't choke. The plain photograph entitled "Potato #345" sold for over $1 million. That is a true story, not "fake news" or a joke. Here again, ridiculous.

These keep coming up in the news and it is very hard to decide which one is the most ridiculous.

Some modern oil paintings have sunk to a similar low. Both the Museum of Modern Art in New York and the High Museum in Atlanta have similar "works of art" that are nothing but blank canvas, all white……that's all. At the High, the painting "White Panel II" painted in 1985 by Ellsworth Kelly, is unique because it isn't just white oil on canvas….at least the large canvas is stretched in a very strange shape, three non-parallel side and one curved side. Wow!!!! At least it is more artistic in its shape than the more common rectangular canvases painted all white. These "white" paintings must be outstanding because I have seen them in the collections of Museums around the world.

To be avant garde, your museum must have one, even though it is, as Bill Shakespeare would have written, Much Ado About Nothing." Ridiculous.

In 2013, the famous auction house, Christies, sold a triptych (three truly weird paintings of Lucian Freud, designed to be displayed side by side) by Francis Bacon for $142.4 million. This unattractive work by a largely unknown artist became what at the time was the most expensive art ever sold at auction. More "value" than the greatest name artists. Absurd!!!!!

Another example surfaced in May of 2014. An English artist, Tracey Emin, produced an "installation" that was nothing more than her terribly messy bed with stuff piled beside it.

Things, such as a vodka bottle, her bra and “unmentionables” (her dirty panties) and condoms were photographed so they could be moved and replaced in their exact positions. It gets worse. The “art” has been sold at auction. Guess what the estimated purchase price was? Once you have guessed, multiply it several times. The answer is two million dollars. How is that for the art “experts” convincing the public that this is not just a worthless piece of junk. It gets even worse, much worse. Christies sold it at auction for $4.35 million!

On November 12, 2013, Christie’s held an auction. One of the featured works was “Apocalypse Now” by Christopher Wood, painted in 1988. It is a prime example of what should not be defined as “art.” The “painting” is about three feet wide and four feet high, has all black letters (that appear to be poorly stenciled) on a white background. It contains nine words arranged exactly as shown below:

SELL THE
HOUSE S
ELL THE C
AR SELL
THE KIDS

I have asked numerous people, not in academia or the art business, to guess how much it sold for at auction. My question was asked in such a way that respondents knew the amount had to be ridiculously high. Even so, most guesses were in the $5,000 to $10,000 range. Those numbers would have been bad enough.

Including the buyer’s premium due Christie’s, the Wood sold for $26,400 dollars. How’s that for ridiculous? There are several jokes about this painting and its sale. It had been offered to New York’s super-famous Museum of Modern Art in 1996 as part of Elaine Dannheisser’s collection, a collection valued at more than $5 million. MOMA took a lot of her collection, but refused to accept “Apocalypse Now.”

MOMA, at least on this occasion, had some common sense. This One Is (As The English Would Say) “Bloody Ridiculous.”

In early 2017, the press reported that an artist was producing paintings without using the usual oil or acrylic paint. She collected and painted using her menstrual blood as paint. Would you want to buy one of those? Not just ridiculous…disgusting.

AN AMUSING MISTAKE

On Februray 12, 2018, portraits of Barack and Michelle Obama were unveiled. These two are the first official President and First Lady portraits by black artists. That’s what they wanted but it really hurt them personally. Barack joked about pleading for less gray hair and smaller ears, but at least it looks like him. The background is what is inappropriate for a Presidential portrait.

You may hate Michelle's far left politics but she is a very attractive woman. Maybe you depict her in a weird and busy dress, but why make her face look ugly? If you didn't know it was supposed to be Michelle you would never guess from looking at it. Again, stupid.

48 DELIVERY
Don't Shoot The Messenger

One of Don Sohn's most creative business ideas resulted from airline deregulation. In order to assist a US corporation in reducing and controlling its travel expense, a travel agency had to be able to deliver airline tickets promptly and reliably at least to the client's employees throughout the United States, so that the travel of every employee could be included in the service and shown on the management reports. Agencies, even the largest, simply could not have offices everywhere.

Don's idea for Heritage Travel was simple and effective, but no competitor ever copied it. Even today, in order to have delivery the next morning, you have to get packages into the hands of Federal Express or UPS by early evening, even in the largest cities. Heritage opened a ticketing office at the Memphis, Tennessee airport, immediately adjacent to the Federal Express Hub where packages arrive each weekday night from throughout the country, are sorted in the middle of the night and transferred to planes going out to all the different cities. We did not have to hand over a package to Fedex until almost midnight each night, so it gave Heritage a massive advantage.

Fedex, itself, is a very interesting story. If you have not seen the transfer hub at Memphis, the tour of their facility in the middle of the night was quite a sight to see. Millions of envelopes and packages have to be unloaded, sorted very fast and reloaded with great speed and with very, very few mistakes. Unfortunately, the tours of the Fedex Hub, even during the daytime, for security reasons are a victim of 9/11/2001. Sad. If the tours are ever allowed in the future, you should try to take one.

Most of the story of the creation of Federal Express has been told over and over again, including a feature on TV years ago. The hub could have been in many central US cities, but Memphis was where the founder of Fedex, Fred Smith, had been born. The first night, Fedex flew just 14 jets, carrying 186 packages. You can imagine how much money they lost on that !!!! Fedex went on to lose $27 million in the first two years and was on the verge of bankruptcy. Fedex now has more than 400,000 employees.

There are two funny parts to the story. Heritage Travel's Don Sohn, having taught at the Harvard Business School, loved to repeat the story about Fred Smith's original development of the idea for reliable overnight delivery service. At the time, Smith was attending a college in New Haven, Connecticut. Smith's professor did not think much of the delivery idea, thought it unworkable, and gave Smith's paper a C. Little did he know. Given his Harvard background, Don liked to finish the story by pausing and then citing the fact that the poor grade was given to Fred Smith by a Yale professor, so what could you expect.

49 SONGS ABOUT FRIENDS

Lyrics That Sound Like Fiction, But Are Factual

"The Peanut Butter Conspiracy," BY JIMMY BUFFETT

Jimmy Buffet and some buddies were driving from Southern Mississippi University in Hattiesburg to a Kappa Sig house party on the Gulf Coast in Pascagoula, Mississippi. Pat, the lady who is now my wife, was in Fred Poteet's new gold 1968 Mustang with the guy she was dating, Frank Cain, one of Jimmy Buffet's roommates at Southern. Pat's maiden name was one she either laughed about or preferred to avoid. It was unusual and hard to evade…..Blitch. She frequently said people pronounced it with a silent L.

They stopped at a Mini-Mart to get lunch. Pat was told to get a loaf of bread and a jar of mayonnaise. Her reaction was to think they must have been going to have mayonnaise sandwiches; nobody had any money back then. When she returned to the car, it seemed as if that nobody else had bought anything. Once all were back in the car and underway, the guys started to pull bologna, ham, and lunchmeats out of their pants…..enough for plenty of sandwiches. Pat had paid and had no idea of what the others had been shoplifting. This little caper was immortalized in Buffet's "Peanut Butter Conspiracy" with the lyrics, "Runnin' up and down the aisles of the Mini-Mart, stickin' food in our jeans."

The refrain starts with "Who's gonna steal the peanut butter, I'll get a can of sardines, Runnin' up and down the aisles of the Mini-Mart Stickin' food in our jeans.and the refrain ends with "We all swore if we ever got rich, we'd pay the Mini-Mart back." Well, Jimmy Buffett certainly got very rich and another roommate, Rick Bennett, must have made a lot of money playing professional football.

Wonder if the Mini Mart ever realized how much they lost and who was the culprit. They might consider sending Jimmy a bill, or maybe posting a "Home of Jimmy Buffet's Peanut Butter Conspiracy" sign right near that big round anti-shop-lifting mirror. I think it would make a very amusing and effective advertising campaign for the Mini-Mart. "Jimmy Buffet shops here." or maybe "shoplifts here."

The night the students all returned to campus after Thanksgiving break that year, 1967, the off-campus house the Jimmy and the guys were living in caught fire and Frank Cain died of carbon monoxide poisoning. It was a life-changing event for all of them. Glenda Baldwin, who was Pat's roommate and Fred's girlfriend, got the call about the fire around midnight, and woke Pat with a shake and the words, "Pat wake up, Frank's dead" Miss Ollie, matron of Jones Hall dormitory, would not let the girls leave between midnight and 7 am, but finally allowed Pat and Glenda to go to the infirmary for the rest of the night. They were pretty shaken.

As soon as the sun was up and the nurses set them free, Pat and Glenda borrowed a car and drove over to the burned-out shell of a house. At the front door, they climbed over the yellow crime scene tape and confronted the white chalk outline of Frank's body, splayed on the floor within six feet of the front door. Walking back to the kitchen, they saw his handprints standing out in stark white of the soot-blackened refrigerator. Obviously, he had made it that far, seen the fire in the carport, and tried to reach the front door. Returning through the living room, Pat saw a 6-inch stack of photos sitting on a speaker, and simply took them.

Late that day, friends and roommates with cars organized another caravan to take everyone down to Panama City for the funeral. After the long, sad drive in the dead of night from Hattiesburg, everyone was visiting at the Cain home the next morning. Outside in the yard, Jimmy walked up to Pat and said he had heard she had the photos. She apologized and said she was upset and just wanted a photo of Frank. Jimmy said he would get one made for her since his Daddy had a good camera shop in Mobile. The next week, Jimmy came by the dorm and Pat gave him the photos.

This all happened suddenly. The roommates had not had time to have their clothes cleaned after the fire. Sitting in the church for Frank's funeral was nauseating from the smell of smoke permeating the clothes of some of the roommates. After days of tears, the wake this bunch of rowdies had for Frank that evening was a fitting fun and music-filled send off, complete with Oysters Rockefeller and Bienville, provided by Keith Johnstone's family, who owned the local McDonalds's franchise. Pat thinks the fire started in the carport where one of the many games the roommates played involved throwing darts at a potato hanging by a string. Most of the darts missed the potato and went into the carport wall. One might have hit an electrical wire. Then again, there was the mysterious and unexplained disappearance of the latest roommate, Byrd's front man and guitarist, Roger McGuinn about the same time.

Jimmy had a band in the late sixties, "The Upstairs Alliance" that played wherever they could: "Hattiesgulch," New Orleans, and all over the Gulf Coast. Walking down a Dallas street a few years later, Pat was surprised to see an album cover in the window with Jimmy Buffett's name on it and recognized his picture. The rest is history. He went on to become one of the very best-known names in popular music. His "*Margaritaville* remains his most popular song, " and there are now bars and a huge new hotel on Pensacola Beach bearing that name.

Buffett also wrote a song about *"Frank and Lola from Pensacola"* that my wife, Pat, continues to think was about her. Once again, it was because she was dating Jimmy's roommate, Frank Cain, and they were both from Pensacola, but there was no way to get a good rhyme out of Pat and Pensacola. Who knows? The main bar in the hotel is called "Frank and Lola's" and Pat wonders if she is Lola. Jimmy's boat captain was named Mallory, the family for which the prestigious Mallory Cup trophy in sailboat racing is named and also the source of the name Mallory Square in Key West, where hundreds gather to celebrate sunsets. I have a cute picture of Pat at the helm of Jimmy Buffet's sailboat. His fans, called "Parrotheads" all over the world, celebrate his unique music genre that melds blues, country, sailing, and reggae into a unique R&B, folk rock Caribbean sound he calls "Reefer" music: Not sure if those are sails or smokes but we love his short stories set to music.

A BIG MISTAKE

After becoming famous as a musician, Jimmy went back to perform at his old alma mater, USM. Hattiesburg is one of those backwater places in the South where a dry (no alcohol) jurisdiction is adjacent to a wet one in the middle of town. The University was dry, but that certainly did not keep the students from drinking. When Buffet walked out on the stage the President of the University, John McCain (really) charged up onto the stage and took Jimmy's can of beer away from him.

It was amusing to note that in his several very-well-written books Buffett never mentioned that he had gone to USM. That act of taking Buffet's beer probably cost the school millions in support and donations over the years. Beginning in the 80s, Buffett has become respected for both his writing and his music. His five books,including *"Tales from Margaritaville,"* an autobiography *"A Pirate Looks at Fifty,"* and raucous, fun fiction, "*Where is Joe Merchant," "A Salty bit of Land*" and *""Swine Not?*" have demonstrated amazing talent and growth as a writer. He made his Mama proud, but he really should pay the Mini-Mart back.

EPILOGE

Buffett seems to have reached détente with USM, thanks probably to the naming of his friend and classmate, Martha Sanders, to the USM Presidency. In April, 2010, Jimmy Buffett responded to the BP Oil Spill, quietly bringing together his love of the Gulf Coast and boating of all kinds, with support for USM's Gulf Coast Research Lab and the donation of a newly developed animal-rescue SWAT (Shallow Water Attention Terminal by Dragonfly Boats) boat for use in the BP oil spill response. To embrace the poetic justice and honor the irony, the boat was christened with Jimmy's own brand of beer, "Landshark." Pat never received the picture and she bets Buffett never paid the Mini-Mart back as promised.

"THE TIJUANA JAIL" BY THE KINGSTON TRIO

One of my best friends for many years in Boston was Lolly McDonnell, now Mrs. James Mitchell, living south of Camden, Maine. She went to Stanford with Dave Guard. Both were Stanford Class of '56. Dave was the founder, composer and lead singer in the Kingston Trio. A bunch of friends did drive to Tijauna and, as the lyrics say: "to have a little fun in Mexico." The entire song is about their being stuck in the Tijuana jail because we "ain't got no friends to go our bail."

The song states that they were shooting dice in an illegal gambling spot, but that is not what really happened that night that landed them in jail. They had been drinking (a lot) in a nightclub in Rosarita Beach, a dozen miles south of Tijuana, on the Saturday night of Thanksgiving weekend. Lolly had gone down to San Diego to visit a good friend and her college roommate, Lee Ann Frazee. When it was time to head back to San Diego, about 1am, Lolly while in the ladies room said she expressed concern about how much they had been drinking. Nobody else was worried, so they took off in the car.

A dark car had been abandoned in the dark highway with no lights. Even if the driver of the car Lolly was in had not been drunk, he still might well have hit the car. Lolly says she was thrown from the middle of the back seat, through the windshield and over the hood, flipped over and landed on the highway on her butt. She laughs that it took a long and embarrassing time for all the gravel she got embedded in her butt to work its way out. Having been drinking all night and having had the incident happen so quickly she does not remember and cannot today reconstruct how she missed going headfirst into the car in front or how she flipped and landed on her butt. She was lucky that she didn't land with her head sliding down the highway. When she regained consciousness, she realized what had happened, but knows only one detail. She remembers the sensation of her stocking ripping, having been caught in the ashtray on the back of the seat in front of her as she went flying past.

Finally, the Mexican police arrived and took them to the Tijuana Jail. They all had bad cuts and bruises, but only when she got back to the States did Lolly learn that she had a broken ankle. While stuck in the jail, no medical assistance was offered.

They were stuck in a grim, quite-filthy jail all night and almost all of the next day. Lee Ann finally reached her dad in San Diego. He drove down with Charles Dail, the Mayor of San Diego, who brought the bail money and got them released from jail at 4 in the afternoon. As Snopes would say about a story: the song was based on fact and but has some added fiction. Upon their return to campus, Dave Guard heard the story and wrote the song. It was mostly fact.

For those of us old enough to remember The Kingston Trio, the titles of their songs still bring back great memories. This was in the days when the lyrics told a story, not just shouted profanity. It is easy to remember that Tom Dooley was told to "hang down your head," that poor Charlie couldn't get "off the MTA," and that the people on the "Sloop John B." were "the captain and me." *Tom Dooley* went all the way to #1 on the charts in 1958, but in 1959 "The Tijuana Jail" only got as high as #12.

EPILOGUE

For all of you who loved The Kingston Trio's songs over the years, you may be surprised to know that Dave Guard was the only one in the group that could read music. Lolly says the others just played along. The name had been The Kingston Quartet until 1957, when it became The Kingston Trio. Dave was "in" the Class of '56, but he did not graduate until a year later. He had gotten drunk one night, fallen out of his dormitory window and broken his back. He had to go home to Hawaii to heal, delaying his graduation, but he always came back to reunions with his friends in the Stanford Class of '56.

The driver of the car Lolly had been in never saw it again. The last time Lolly saw him was at their Stanford 25th reunion. Dave Guard died of cancer in 1991 in New Hampshire. Lolly says that, after the accident, she was embarrassed but had to ask the Stanford University administration for special permission to park her car closer to her classes during the three weeks before Christmas Break. By the time she got back on campus in January she had a walking cast.

LOST AND FOUND

There is one funny short story about Lolly that doesn't fit anywhere else. Back when the America's Cup Races were held every time in Newport, Rhode Island, Bob, Lolly's dad, used to fly out from Kansas City and charter a sailboat to go out in the Atlantic to watch the races. He was a great story teller and used to hold court after the races in a bar ashore.

One day, sailing out to watch the race, Lolly dropped her expensive camera overboard. She knew where it happened. When it came time to file the claim with her insurance company the claim was denied. Why? Because her camera wasn't lost; she knew where it was, on the bottom of the ocean. It took a while but at least the stupid insurance adjuster finally accepted it as a legitimate claim.

A SONG IS ABOUT THE STREET WHERE I LIVED

I never had a song written about me, but there is one about the road I lived on while in high school, Woodley Road. A Montgomery journalist, Wayne Greenhaw, on a spring Sunday morning drove Steve Young far out Woodley Road and on the return Steve began composing the song "Seven Bridges Road" that went on to be a big hit by the "Eagles."

A MONTGOMERY NAME

Most older readers will remember songs by The Captain and Tennille. The only problem was that her name was pronounced Ten'uhl, not Ta Neil'. She graduated from my high school, Lanier, and her dad owned the Frank Tennille furniture store in Montgomery.

ANOTHER "SONG" ABOUT PAT

The British Virgin Islands are a fabulous place to sail, beautiful beaches, lots of fun places and protected waters for smooth sailing. One of our favorite stops was sandy beach on a small harbor on the south side of Jost Van Dyke, in the northwestern corner of the BVIs. The island has a famous bar named "Foxys." It isn't much of anything, but the owner, Foxy, is a well-known character. One day the friends in our sailboat's crew were sitting around a wooden outdoor table when Pat got up to go to the lady's room. She had on a black dress over her swimsuit.

On her way back, she walked past Foxy not realizing that he wore a microphone while he sang and played his guitar, so his words were being amplified for everyone in the area. His lyrics were:

Beware those girls all dressed in black
They like their things to be so exact
And when she walks, she looks so sweet
She makes things stand that don't have feet.

Hope you don't need an explanation

TWO MORE FROM MONTGOMERY

Lots of people in Montgomery know that Hank Williams lived here, but few remember that Nat "King" Cole did also. At a fundraiser in Savannah, Pat and I had a great evening seated next to Nat's charming wife. She was also the mother of a delightful singer, Natalie Cole.

The house in which Nat lived has been restored and moved to a spot on the campus of Alabama State University.

50 A COSTLY MISTAKE
(Almost)

My sister was, I guess the right word would be "unusual." She was born in 1916. Shortly thereafter (as I wrote at the start of the Introduction), my mother had a horrible late-term miscarriage in 1919 and was told by the doctors that she could not have any more normal children. That turned out to be true. Telling this is much more fun when you can take a long pause between those last two sentences.

Anyway, Carolyn was 21 years older than I, and spent much of her life as a venomous alcoholic. Some alcoholics are jovial. Carolyn was not. She would stay drunk for days, spouting profanities at my parents, emphasizing her hatred of them. After Dad died in 1972, she continued to live with my mother, so all of Carolyn's screaming was concentrated on Mom. It was extremely tough to take.

Mom and Dad considered having her committed to Bryce, the insane asylum in north Alabama. They did not understand alcoholism and, in those days, the doctors did nothing to correct them. Carolyn remained at home. We had moved in 1952 from 915 East Fairview Avenue to 2200 Woodley Road on the southeast side of Montgomery. My friends asked why we were moving "so far out in the country." The house Mom and Dad had designed and built was surrounded by open space. Our lot sloped down the hill behind and then up a hill that was all golf course of what was then the Standard Club. Carolyn continued to live there and her room became the perfect example of a Pig Pen.

You had to walk a narrow route through three-foot high stacks of stuff to get from the door to her bed. She had loads of jigsaw puzzles. She did not play with them, and even had three identical examples of the same puzzle still in plastic packaging.

When Mom died, Carolyn moved to a small townhouse on Cloverdale Road at the corner with Felder. I had to retain one the nurses who had looked after Mom, but I was still worried. As it turned out, once Mom was gone, Carolyn sobered up and became quite tolerable, bordering on quite pleasant. She did, however, continue to buy stuff and the two extra bedrooms and an attic upstairs gave her lots of space to fill. She did a good job of that.

As the nineteenth century wound to a close, the media were filled with stories about the many types of disasters that were going to occur at midnight on New Year's Eve, a problem that became known as Y2K. Pat and I had flown from Savannah out to Phoenix to spend Christmas with Pat's family and Carolyn had come with us. Unbeknownst to us, she had quit taking her pills and became quite ill. When admitted to the hospital, the doctors said she needed quadruple bypass surgery. It was right before the dreaded Y2K, when people had been warned this was not the time to be in hospital because so much equipment would not be able to function with the change from 1999 to 2000.

Carolyn died around midnight on New Year's night on the operating room table. One of the doctors apologized and expressed what clearly appeared to be concern that his medical team faced a malpractice suit. I ended up needing the money, am pretty sure we could have won, but disapproved of this type of legal action.

It became time to clean out the house Carolyn had been renting. We knew there was lots of junk, but had no idea how bad things were. The most amusing story was about cookbooks. Carolyn literally never cooked a "meal." She could mix up cereal and occasionally cook an egg and bacon, but that was truly about as far as she went. She did make coffee, but that is not what I would call cooking.

In the dining room there was a collection of pretty-good cookbooks.....no big deal because they all had been inherited from our mother. There were about fifty hardcover cookbooks in the small bookcase in the dining room. We put them all in the car to drive to our home, which at the time was in Savannah.

Finishing the first floor, we began to tackle the piles of cardboard boxes upstairs. To ease the clean out, we backed a trailer up to the front door, so we could throw stuff into it from the window above, saving a lot of time climbing stairs.

I began to open boxes of cookbooks. We had learned not just to throw things out because an antique silver goblet had been discovered in the dirty clothes and a valid stock certificate between the pages of a magazine. We did the work fast, but we had to at least leaf through everything en route to the trash. The cookbook count was so ridiculous that I started counting them before throwing them out the window. Compared with the thick bound cookbooks that had been in the dining room, these were generally less expensive, mostly in the $6 per book range (in 1990's prices).

For years we have amused people with this story, asking them to guess how many cookbooks there were. Think about it and figure out your guess before reading to the end of this. Even when told that the story would not be told were the number of cookbooks not so ridiculous, guessers have never come close.

The count of cookbooks (remember, this is for someone who did not cook, much less use a recipe) ended up being just over 3,000.

But this is not the subject of this chapter. While I was racing through the many boxes of magazines and cookbooks, Pat had continued working on more important stuff downstairs. She uncovered a pretty-forlorn old doll. Had I seen it first that sucker would have gone into the trash without a moment's hesitation. The doll even had a round burn in the front of the material, either from a cigarette or an ash from the fireplace. Pat wanted to keep it, and did.

THE ANTIQUES ROAD SHOW

A year or so later, we learned that the Antiques Road Show was coming to Savannah. We also gave a ride to the show for my semi-cousin, General Wilton Persons, Jr. who had been Judge Advocate General of the US Army. I say "semi" because he was not really my cousin, but he always introduced me as his cousin. He was my first cousin's, Juliette Doster's, other first cousin. As a result of his dad's having been Chief of Staff in the White House for Eisenhower (after Sherman Adams' resignation) Will had the only selfportrait by Ike. Ike's friend during the war, Winston Churchill, had been known for his remarkably good watercolor paintings. Ike's self portrait was an excellent oil.

Pat took the little forlorn doll and, as I'm sure you have guessed by now, made it onto the show. As it turns out, the doll was called an "Alabama Indestructible Doll" and had belonged to my mother in 1899, when she was four years old. The woman who made the dolls in Roanoke, Alabama had repaired broken dolls and thought it would be better for children to play with dolls that were less fragile.

The doll I would have thrown into the trash by me ended up being estimated in the $2,000 to $3,000 range. Some show for sale on the internet for as much as $11,000. Pat's interview on Antiques Road Show has aired several times over the years, but it was originally Episode 811 on April 5, 2004. You can see the doll and the show by clicking on the PBS website at

www.pbs.org/wgbh/roadshow/archive/200301A21.html Enjoy

Watching the show on TV does not really tell you how the Antiques Road Show operates. Those thousands of people who show up and try to get on the show don't all come from the city in which that week's show is filmed. Many drive from all over the country, some coming many hundreds of miles hoping to get on the show. Only a handful make it onto the TV show, and that day two of the people in my car made it. This time Pat was easily recognized, so when her show aired, she got phone calls from friends all over the country.

When you see those large and frequently very-valuable pieces of furniture on the show, don't think that people lug those down for consideration. The process is not well publicized, so most people do not know this is an option. You submit what you have, it is considered, and if selected somebody comes by your home and takes a look. If approved, the show sends a truck and movers to carry your piece to and from the place where the show is to be recorded.

People stand in one extremely long line. When you finally get to the first desk, you are sorted into a number of lines depending upon what type of item you have and then begin your wait again. At least this time it is much shorter.

The Antiques Road Show was great fun, in addition to being informative. If the Antiques Road Show is coming your way, find something to take and go give it a try.

IKE

General Persons was very unhappy with the estimate given the Eisenhower self portrait by Coleen Fesko, a painting specialist with Skinner in Boston (now in business for herself and still appearing frequently on the Road Show). Her opinion was that the painting was not by a famous artist. She valued it at just $35,000. I suspected it would be worth more than that someday. Ikc was certainly a famous person.

The interesting fact is that very few who go to the Antiques Road Show and stand in line forever and have their stuff appraised actually end up being shown on TV. I had my wife, Pat, and cousin Wilton in the car that day and they both got on the show. Out of the thousands that day, two of my passengers were selected.

Years later, after Wilton Persons death, I was asked by his family to get involved in finding the best way of dealing with the Eisenhower painting. It couldn't be cut into pieces so part could be given to each of Wilton's kids. The question was how best to sell it. I talked to a half dozen auction houses and got good advice from my first cousin on my dad's side, Phillip Jelley (Senior Vice President, Sothebys) and the painting ended up with my first cousin on my mother's side, Juliette Persons Doster, buying it to keep it in the family. It now belongs to Juliette's daughter, Griffin Fry, in Atlanta.

51 SEX ABUSE
What Should You Do? What Can You Do?

This story needs to be told so people will understand the difficulty of dealing with the subject when something occurs that that most uninvolved people will think should be reported. For me, it is a painful story, but I think it needs to be told. This subject began to heat up in November of 2017 as this book was nearing completion. There are now many complaints about improper action by elected government officials, religious leaders, Boy Scout leaders and powerful business executives. The subject of this chapter is extremely painful because it involves two friends, one of whom was a most generous friend.

The horrific revelations in 2011 about Jerry Sandusky, a former assistant football coach at Penn State, took all of the headlines away from where the problem has historically been hidden from public view. The Freeh Report disclosed that many school officials had known about the horrendous problem for years and had participated in the cover-up. These included Joe Paterno and the University's President.

We read in newspapers and see on TV on a regular basis about ministers, Governors, Senators, Congressmen, Attorneys General, and yes, even several Presidents of the United States, who have been caught in "improper" sexual situations. Oh, I forgot, Bill Clinton clearly pointed and said to all of America "I did not have sexual relations with that woman."

Why are the vast majority of the men exposed in the press our elected officials? Is it because they are the only ones misbehaving? The obvious answer is "no." The reason you read about men in business so infrequently is that they are not observed so closely by the media. This was true in the case of Herman Cain, whose problems did not surface until he became a candidate for President of the US. The complaint against Clarence Thomas in the Senate's vote to approve his nomination for the Supreme Court was from just one woman, so he could claim it was her word against his. The case of Fox News' Roger Ailes was different because there were complaints from numerous women. His sexual harassment actions remained secret until he was sued by a former employee. Categories of employment such as actors, sports stars and rock singers appear free to sleep with thousands of fans, but that hardly ever appears in the media because it is usually consensual.

The principal person in this story is a man who was highly respected in the Episcopal Church, sang in the choir and ran the youth group at Montgomery's St. John's Church: Fred E. Marquette, Jr. He certainly looked effeminate, but in the early 1950s that was not understood and certainly was a subject not broached by families with their kids.

LAKE JORDAN

Fred Marquette was the nicest, most generous, person the kids knew. I certainly valued his friendship, something that makes it extremely painful to write this chapter. In addition to leading the youth group, he invited all of the young boys up to his cabin at Lake Jordan, 11 miles north of Montgomery, essentially every weekend of the summer. He had an antique, beautifully varnished, mahogany speedboat, a 19 foot long Chris Craft Riviera that was kept inside a building up the hill near his cabin. There was a railroad track that ran from the storage building down into the water, making it easy to haul the boat up the steep hill into the storage building, where it was safe from the water and, more importantly for the varnish, out of the sun.

The boys loved it. This was during the early days of waterskiing, and that was what the boat was used for almost all day on every day of the summer weekends. I had started water skiing back when there was no place to buy skis: I had to build my own from a split 2X4 using long screen door springs and inner-tube rubber to hold my feet. Water skis are usually about 5 or 6 inches wide; these were 3½ inches.

The guys all hung around all day in bathing suits, almost never wearing shoes or shirts. In those days you did not know to worry about the long-term effects of sunburn, and everyone became "safely" tanned every summer anyway. It was fifty-five years later that I began getting melanomas. Fred got to have relatively attractive boys around all weekend. Does this sound like Jerry Sandusky?

A real house, much larger and built of concrete block, was constructed years later, up the hill and very close to the road, which was later renamed "Ski Club Road." Fred organized the highly-rated ski club that competed all around the Southeast. The cabin that was the only building (other than the boathouse) in the early fifties was truly a cabin. Most would call it a shack. It had a screen porch upstairs, rickety wooden walls with no insulation (from heat, cold or sound) and was extremely small. The interior walls didn't even have particle board or plaster. The 2x4s showed on the inside of all the walls. The kitchen, for what it was, and the eating area (the word "dining" here would be very inappropriate) were downstairs. Everyone slept upstairs, almost never inside where Fred slept. I always slept with most of my friends out on the screen porch.

THE MONTGOMERY ADVERTISER

Years later the Montgomery Advertiser ran Fred's picture under the headline "Sex abuse victims often repress memories, expert says." Two men had spoken out after many years, accusing Fred, then age 82, of abusing them twenty years earlier when they were between 13 and 15. It must very embarrassing and took great courage to come out and file a public complaint, even after all those years.

The newspaper article, dated June 21, 2002, quoted Lt. Huey Thornton, the Montgomery Police spokesman, as saying Marquette faced two criminal charges of second-degree sodomy. Unlike the 2011 case at Syracuse University, Alabama will still prosecute in such cases without having lost the right due to expiration of the statutes of limitations.

A Professor and Chairman of the Department of Criminal Justice and Sociology at Alabama State University, Jerry Burns, was quoted in the Advertiser article as saying "For the victims, sodomy affects their self-image, and some victims may not be able to enjoy normal relationships with members of the opposite sex." The newspaper reported that the acts in this case had occurred at Fred's home in the city and, of course, at his place on Lake Jordan. The existence of the ski club enabled Fred to be surrounded by young boys all summer for several decades. The article went on to say that, when the police questioned him, Fred had confessed.

THE BOY SCOUTS

According to the article, in addition to his role at the church, Fred had been a scoutmaster for more than 30 years, but had, for some undisclosed reason, been asked to resign. When the story unfolded, the Advertiser quoted Bill Morgan, Boy Scout executive for Central Alabama, as saying Fred had been "asked to step down about seven years ago." Why would an organization ask for a man who had devoted so much time to their program be asked to resign? I trust the answer is obvious. It is sickening today that the number of adults in scouting that have had to be removed totals more than 7,000.

Here I have a problem. The scout leader, when asked why Fred's resignation had been requested, was quoted in the paper as saying "It is a confidential matter." What do you infer from that situation and that statement? Unfortunately, to me, it clearly indicates that something similar had occurred and been discovered seven years earlier. There is enormous legal risk in speaking out and many people feel it unjust to make the problem public, condemning the perpetrator to the title of "sex offender" for the rest of his life. In my opinion, the problem had occurred, been discovered and had been hushed up. It is hard to imagine any other circumstance or explanation. I do not pretend to have any suggestion of a way to solve this problem other than to involve the police and judges.

How many young boys do you think were raped in the 40 years between the time I first observed this behavior and the date he was finally arrested. The problem would have been stopped seven years earlier had the Boy Scouts not failed to take any action. That is not protecting young boys.

Now we come to my involvement, and the reason I can, more than most, understand the bind that young kids find themselves in when encountering this type of situation, even when the victim is someone else. One Saturday night late in Fred's cabin back in the early 1950s, I was awakened by a noise coming through the wall next to the cot on which I was sleeping on the screened porch. The bouncing of the bed, the slapping sounds and the moans and groans made it quite apparent to me what was happening only a few feet away on the other side of the thin wall. People have asked if I had seen this. No, but it simply could not have been anything else.

THE BIG QUESTION

What could I do? I had no clue. In the dark, I looked around the bunks on the porch to see which friends were still in their beds and at least was relieved to see two of my closest friends, one a cousin, were there. By the process of elimination, I knew who the "victim" was that evening, and the future in this case was evidence that Professor Burns was correct. The boy was very smart and had an outstanding education, but ended up a total mess for the rest of his life. I do not think anyone else to this day knows who the boy was and, no, I am not going to disclose it now. Any attempt to report my observation would have been a disaster. No, I am not kidding. That is almost certainly the way my parents would have handled it. I would have been the one in trouble for even broaching the subject and unjustly accusing Fred. I still, after all these many years, have a vibrant memory of that awful night.

In the Penn State situation I am pained to hear in many discussions in the media about how people feel that the person who does not report to the police directly and immediately is guilty. I'm not sure that the word "witness" applies to what you hear but don't see, but I appeared to have been the only one on the screen porch aware of what transpired on the other side of the wall that night. This was clearly because my bed was the one touching the wall through which the sounds emanated. The bed on the other side was against the wall, so that the sounds also included the bed's bumping against the wall beside me.

I was absolutely certain of what was happening. The kid who was the victim was certainly too embarrassed to file a complaint, following the exact pattern that the experts identify as the barrier to prosecution. In addition, who would have believed the victim? He could not have known, and does not know to this day, that I was aware of what transpired. This meant that, even if my parents had listened and taken appropriate steps, the kid would almost certainly have been mortified and even he probably would have denied that anything untoward took place. This would have nullified anything I reported, embarrassing me and accomplishing nothing. When I had dinner with the victim about 60 years later he pointedly asked about Fred and followed the question with a statement that he had obviously had no problem with Fred himself.

This was 40 years later that Fred's actions surfaced and led to criminal court, so there is no way of telling how many young boys met similar fates during all that time. The two who did finally come forward must have been very brave. Fred, born April 25, 1920, is now 98 years old and, according to the State's website, was released December 7, 2009 from Alabama's prison for the Aged and Infirm in Hamilton, Alabama, northwest of Birmingham, close to Tupelo, Mississippi.

I suspect that people reading this will think I should have just gone to my parents or to the police. You've got to be kidding. Would they have believed the little kid who "thinks" he heard something or would they have been more likely to believe the man who was a leader in the church? It was a horribly awkward situation. My dad would have just listened. That may be incorrect. He would probably have "heard" but not "listened." He would just have wanted to avoid the subject and keep clear of any ramifications. My mother would have been the biggest problem. I certainly will never know, but I suspect she would have called Fred on the phone and told him I had told her some dreadful story. The question would have been rhetorical. She would not have asked; she would have appeared to ask by saying "That story certainly isn't true, right?"

Despite all those commentaries on TV, I think the critics simply cannot comprehend what an awkward bind a witness is in, especially if involves a young boy. It certainly is nowhere close to the embarrassment that precludes the victim's saying anything.

It gives me a good understanding of how the young Penn State assistant coach who told his boss, the highly-esteemed Joe Paterno, and the Penn State Athletic Director, must have felt. He did not dare do anything more to report the crime if his bosses would not support him, much less act on their own. It would have been impossible to prove the claim and comply with the law that someone is innocent until proven guilty. The assistant would have been "hung out to dry" for making such a preposterous claim against such a highly respected senior coach. Once again: what can you do? As awkward as it was, I certainly believed I did not have any options for action.

I kept going to the lake house on weekends, along with many of my friends, but knew to be careful.

Fred, despite his age, was first sentenced to 15 years in state prison for sex offenders in northwestern Alabama. You can imagine what an awful place that must be. It was much later that he was transferred to the prison for the elderly and sick before being released.

52 SEX EDUCATION
Or The Lack Thereof

Some schools have "sex education" classes. In many super-conservative states, parents are irate if any school tries to provide even the most basic of the useless biological information about sex. To ultra conservative members of the religious far right and to believers in most of the religions throughout the world, sex "education" was a subject that "should be left up to the parents." Since this is the case, it means that kids are not even receiving the most rudimentary information on this vitally important subject because the parents will not do it.

What little was taught was no better than the old joke about "The birds and the bees." In some instances, as was the case during the 50s, the classes for boys were provided by the YMCA. The problem is these classes were, and to a large extent still are, a biology class at best, *not* sex education. There was nothing close to mentioning very important bodily parts.

Students take English, in those few remaining good public schools study complex science, math and history. Much of this "education" they will never put to practical use. I studied six years of Latin. Parents will never allow schools to provide any information about how to have sex well, much less really teach how to be outstanding at it. For many, it will be the most important subject in their lives and, for all too many, the cause of the huge number of divorces throughout the world, especially in the United States.

One of the biggest causes of divorce is the failure to have sex with a variety of partners so that both men and women would recognize the difference between good sex and bad sex. We also read very sad stories of women caught in a violent relationship with their husbands. I don't know; do some women really prefer "rough sex?" I hear it is common, but I find it extremely hard to believe. An abusive husband is a dreadful problem.

Couples frequently split when they find a better sexual partner. It just happens too often after they are already married. This chapter obviously will offer no solutions to this huge problem but it will make a suggestion for improving the situation. It will just provide some background regarding why kids need to learn by some method other than trial and error.

HISTORY

Sports stars, movie stars and guys in rock bands must have sex many many times. There are numerous stories about rock band superstars screwing several "groupies" after each performance. That could mean hundreds in a single year. Very rich and very powerful men have many opportunities. You have special categories, such as Hugh Hefner, who must have been worn out when he died. Everyone has read about a Tiger Woods, an Eliot Spitzer or a Gary Hart.

We have had loads of US Presidents who slept around. Most people do not remember that the revered four-term President, Franklin Delano Roosevelt, had his "girlfriend" with him much of the time. Eleanor was just left at home. The most amusing was the famous professional basketball star, Wilt Chamberlain, who repeatedly claimed he had had sex with 20,000 women. Even I find that a little hard to believe, but it is certainly within the realm of possibility. Over 30 years, that would be just under two a day. In his position, that was certainly possible. I have heard of male rock stars being followed by young "groupies" looking to give themselves to a superstar, so the star could have sex with a half dozen in one night.

It clearly happens by the tens of millions throughout the world. Still, there are people who literally can't even talk about sex, probably can't even think about it. President Jimmy Carter apologized, thinking he had sinned and cheated on his wife just because he looked at a Playboy magazine. To me, that is abnormal.

In the sixties, seventies and eighties, it was great being a single male. The old question that guys asked guys about their dates many years ago was "Did you get to first base?" I don't think there was ever any exact delineation of where the lines were drawn, but first base was probably holding hands, second base was kissing, third base was feeling around and a home run was getting laid. At least the last is definitely correct. In the 1960s, getting laid became about the same as a good night kiss after a first date had been a few decades earlier. Even if you were not dating, people would meet someone at a party and later just go to bed together. Years after I had settled down and gotten married, people began to be referred to as "friends with benefits." There were loads of those around in the sixties, seventies and eighties.....probably still today. I bet lots of parents don't even know what that saying means.

INDIRECT CENSORSHIP

Having lived for forty years in New England, it was amusing to return to the ultra-religious Deep South and discover that several major grocery store chains and other stores will not even show, much less sell, the typical men's magazines. I'm not just talking about the bad, clearly pornographic and gross ones like *Hustler*; I'm talking about plain old *Playboy,* clearly the most conservative of the bunch and one which, despite the disbelief of people who have never read the magazine, has always contained articles by numerous distinguished authors.

Stores in the South would be boycotted if these magazines could be seen, much less purchased. What was really funny was, having noticed women's magazines in the display racks of supermarkets with opaque plastic sheets in front of the covers, asking why this was done. The magazines concealed from shoppers included the most widely read women's magazines, such as *Cosmopolitan*, *Vanity Fair, Vogue* and *Glamour*. When I inquired, the store managers responded that magazine covers went much too far, "exposing too much" of a woman's body. Although the magazines could be sold, the covers should not be seen by passersby. People would be offended. Those people better not go to a beach on the Riviera.

Some adults even express shock when a fairly common word is used. How can those adults ever come close to giving their children any meaningful sex education? They claim the are the ones to teach their kids, but adamantly object if their kids' schools even give the biological lesson. They claim the subject should be left up to the parents. Good luck!!! It just means they will learn the real story from an older friend. Parents just can't face up to having a meaningful discussion with their kids. Mine certainly didn't.

I may not know all about it, but I think most "rapes" involve men's forcing sex on women; not the other way around. Only once, in Bermuda, did a close female friend try to get me to have sex with someone with whom I simply did not want it. Yes, I know that this is hard to believe, but it is true. Chased by the woman and the female friend trying to "help" her catch me, I escaped by running into a bathroom and locking the door. When they did not stop banging on the door, I climbed up on the john and climbed out through the small window. I probably should have just given in or waited them out, because falling into the sharp branches of a bush, when you are naked, is quite painful. Had they caught me and forced sex, would the police have prosecuted them for rape? The officials consider the word "no" to mean what it says when said by a woman. Would the courts say the same if it were a man who had said "no?"

The disgusting problem is men raping women. I had four close friends who were raped. It must have been an incredibly horrible ordeal for these women. Good sex education should include meaningful training for women in some effective ways of inflicting pain sufficient enough to get even a strong rapist to give up and run.

ABSTINENCE

The churches of the United States try to pretend that the widespread practice of sex simply isn't true. The "Religious Right" imposed upon President Bush (George W.) the ruling that US funds could not be used to teach using rubbers. Rubbers used to be just to prevent pregnancy; today they should greatly reduce the spread of Aids. "Abstinence was the *only* acceptable path." Do they really believe that works? Even when the statistics illustrated how ineffective the abstinence-only approach was, the religious right still insisted that abstinence could be the only way. I thought the Catholic Church had finally given up on the infamous "Rhythm Method," notorious for not being foolproof. The church was blind to the statistics.

Today, many churches appear to have reverted back to the antique belief that couples, even married couples, must abstain from sex unless both parties are doing it with the intent to produce a kid. Dumb or stupid; you take your choice. Today, the people who can least afford to raise kids are the ones who have the most kids, many times the number they can afford to raise properly. In the early 2000s the US spent many millions of dollars trying to teach "abstinence only," but had virtually no impact on world overpopulation and the resulting famine or the spread of AIDS by failing to face facts. Religion overruled facts. Your religious beliefs required that you not accept facts when they conflict with your belief. With the return of Republicans in the 2008 and 2016 elections, our Congress even wanted to block any funding for Planned Parenthood and fights about birth control requirements in Obamacare. Having abstinence as an effective tool is simply more than you can hope for and certainly more than you can expect. Sorry church, sex is here to stay.

The belief that a man should never be with but one woman throughout his lifetime is taught as a religious belief in order to promote the concept of family. In the early days of human life on earth, men were just like many other animals….not monogamous. Living in nature, only the hardiest survived, and men tried to get as many women as possible pregnant in order to increase the odds that one of their children would survive in the wild. The more children you had, the better your chances.

The media are full of reports about many of the world's male leaders getting caught in illicit relationships, usually with a co-worker. The list of elected officials and men in powerful office who have been caught is long and will always be long. The urge that has been around for all of man's existence on earth is not going to stop no matter what. Americans usually remember the names of recent politicians that have been caught, but the record for Presidents of the US goes back to Thomas Jefferson, who the DNA evidence now supports, had kids by one of his slaves, Sarah Hemmings.

Sex outside of marriage is certainly much more accepted in Europe than in the United States. Even keeping a mistress is much more common in Europe than in the States today. When a relationship is uncovered in many parts of the world, the subject just passes by. In the case of elected officials in the US, it almost certainly leads to outrage and a forced resignation from public office unless, of course, you are Teddy Kennedy. He was a frequent, well-known carouser, even when married to Joan. I dated a beautiful girl who at the time was also "seeing" Teddy. My use of the word "seeing" in the previous sentence is an misstatement. It didn't mean she looked at him with her eyes. Many US Presidents throughout history have had relationships out of marriage while in office. With 24 hours TV news channels searching for stories, most can't get away with that these days. Bill Clinton is obviously the most famous recent example of this. The standard joke (or is it just a question?) was "If you were married to Hillary, wouldn't you look somewhere else for some good sex?" When traveling on business while still a bachelor, I was usually amused at the number of married guys looking for a piece of ass while far away from home. This didn't mean that they did not love their wives and children; it just meant they had the drive to seek an additional experience. In all too many cases, with both men and women, the need was driven by the absence of good sex at home. Here again, the need for real sex education and trying him or her out before you pick.

DAD

As a young teenager, I used to love to read Dad's *Playboy* magazines. He had been an early subscriber, back in the 50s. He kept a supply of rubbers in his suitcase. I could count them before his trip and upon his return tell how "good" a trip he had had. He loved my mother and was on the Vestry of the ultra-conservative St. John's Episcopal Church, but he still must have loved to screw. He was the poster boy example of someone you would not have expected to be anything other than a faithful husband.

TRAINING

In the old days, rich men were able to take their sons to a good prostitute for their first time. This did not just involve sex, it included training. This was much more common in Europe than in the US and was a great idea…probably the best way for a boy to gain the required education. "On the job training." Up until a couple of decades ago, female prostitutes were arrested and their customers were never even questioned. Now, traps are set by the police to catch "Johns." This practice should be terminated. Dads in the U.S. usually won't risk taking a son to a prostitute for training for fear of getting caught.

ANOTHER BIG SURPRISE

As a result of the Brimmer Hilton party where a couple won the draw for a trip that left that night, the Sitzundjibers began to run an annual party at Logan Airport that culminated in the winners' getting on a flight to Bermuda at the end of the party. This year I wasn't dating anyone and had no date so it presented an unusual problem when my name was the last one in the hat. Several people argued that I could not select a girl.
It was decided that the girls who wanted to go to Bermuda with me had to put their names back in the hat, knowing that the hotel was booked for just one double bed. Seven girls put their names in the hat. A big argument ensued when a friend's wife insisted upon putting her name in the hat. A girl who had failed to bring the required suitcase won. Luckily, she was probably the only one to have a charge account at Trimmingham's on Front Street in Hamilton, Bermuda so we stopped our taxi while she rushed in and purchased lots of clothes.

53 EDUCATION

Or The Lack Thereof

This story is just an example of how amusingly poor education in the United States has become and how kids can be led to believe something just because they are told it by an elder who supposedly knows the facts.

Alabama's capitol building has lot of areas and items of interest. Of course, as you will, read the House of Representatives has special importance to me because of my grandfather's having been elected Speaker of the House in 1894.

Several organizations give tours of the Capitol. Pat worked for the Senate, being available for interesting tours of the various points of interest. In addition to school groups of all ages. The funniest one had to do with a question from a person in a group he was leading through the Capitol. The South has loads of beautiful old homes that survived the Civil War. Because they were built prior to the Civil War, the term normally applied to them is "ante bellum" which, in Latin, simply means before the war.

One day a tour participant asked about the term "ante bellum." Obviously, you can tell where this is headed. The guide went into a long story about how a woman had very good taste in architecture and started a movement to build these stately old homes, almost invariably painted white, many with large two-story columns across the front. As the trend caught on, the style began to be named after her.....Auntie Bellum. She must have been quite a lady.

AN EMBARRASSING DISCOVERY

In October of 2012 our local newspaper, the Montgomery Advertiser, published an expose about widespread cheating in our public schools. No, this was not about students; it was about teachers and their administrators. the stories were not just about teachers. School administrators, desperate to submit even better scores, made additional "improvements," flagrantly and frequently.

It is a truly sad reflection on the status of our society today. On Tuesday, October 1, 2013, Barbara Thompson, Montgomery's Superintendent of Public Schools resigned. I don't remember reading of anyone else that got fired, at a time when dozens should have been fired and had their pensions revoked. At least some should have gone to jail.

543 ANOTHER CASE OF BAD TIMING

The American Express Card "Don't Leave Home Without It"

Most people do not know that if a customer gives you their credit card number, you do not have to ask what kind of card it is. The first digit of all credit cards indicates what kind of card it is because those numbers were assigned in the order in which the card companies were introduced, beginning with 2, which was assigned to Diners Club.

As mentioned in a previous chapter, although the Diners card is still in active use in Europe, you see few Diners Club cards anymore in the US. Diners was sold by Citibank to Discover July 1, 2008. Diners, founded by three men in 1950, was clearly the pioneer. The three owners started with a few New York friends and 27 restaurants, but by the end of the first year Diners had over 20,000 cardholders and was accepted at more than 1,000 restaurants (small by today's standards, but quite a success back in the early fifties).

If a credit card starts with the number 3, it is American Express. The next card was BankAmericard, introduced by (you guessed it) the Bank of America. Their cards all started with 4. In the late sixties the Bank of America implemented a nationwide system of regional primary banks, identified as "A" banks, each of which could expand issuance of cards through other banks in their territory.

I was involved in the introduction of BankAmericard (which years later became Visa) in New England. It is amusing today to think back on my having to explain to people what a credit card was going to be. This background is why any card that starts with a 3 is American Express, if its 4 it's a Visa, a 5 is MasterCard, and the youngest card, Discover, has account numbers that begin with the number 6.

Shortly after the introduction of BankAmericard, about five dozen California banks, panicked by the success of California's largest bank, banned together to issue Mastercharge, and my former boss at State Street Bank in Boston, Garrison A. Southard, Jr., moved to California to become the first president of Mastercharge. Of course, the name of BankAmericard was made more palatable to other banks throughout the country by changing the name to Visa and Mastercharge followed by changing to Mastercard.

On April 10, 1984, for some reason I can't remember, I took Jonathan Linen to lunch, back when American Express was located at 125 Broadway (down near the tip of Manhattan Island), and he was Vice Chairman of American Express. He wanted to go to his favorite restaurant, Fraunces Tavern. This is an attractive old three-story brick building at 54 Pearl Street. The restaurant underwent major reconstruction, but it still claims to be the oldest surviving building in New York, having been built in 1762. A man who had served in the military but went into politics, George Washington, hosted his generals for dinner at Fraunces Tavern, where he delivered his farewell address.

At the end of the meal with Jon, I got out my Visa card to pay the bill. Needless to say, Jon was shocked. I explained that I had been an original Amex cardholder, way back in something like 1959, but had undergone a long drawn out battle during which Amex claimed I owed them $500, ending months later when they finally realized they owed me the $500. Amex paid, but did not send me a new card and I did not argue that point. Jon asked if this had occurred in 1974 and my answer was "yes." He laughed, said they had massive problems at that time, and that he would send me a new card. That's why my card says "Member Since 1984." Don't worry, that part of the story will be relevant in just a few paragraphs.

All of you readers who are men know that getting married means you recognize that you cannot continue doing some things you did as a bachelor. In this case, my wife of a few months, Pat, was right, making me go through boxes of old papers and throw them out. Admittedly, I had lots of boxes filled with lots of stuff that needed to be thrown out.

This was now early1989 and Pat and I were living on the Charles River in the Waban section of Newton, Massachusetts. One night, working on the island in the kitchen, I came across my old original 1959 American Express card. By today's standards it was quite strange, primarily purple with their Centurion logo in an upper corner. I laughed. Pat was surprised to learn that American Express cards had ever been purple. I cut the plastic card in half and added it to the trash.

This was an almost unbelievable stroke of bad timing. Only two days later I was on a USAir flight and picked up their in-flight magazine to read on the plane. The magazine had an article on credit cards as collectibles, going through a long list of cards and their histories and values. At the end of the article there was a picture of the purple American Express card, stating that it was the most valuable collectible. The article said such a card was worth $500, the equivalent of $1,032 today. Why couldn't I, after all those years, have gone through that box just one week later? I always thought Amex should issue me a card that reads "Member Since 1959." It was their fault that it didn't.

THE UNITED STATES

Credit cards battle over what card a large employer should use as its corporate card for their employees. A big employer that needs many thousands of cards means lots of money to a credit card company, and the competition for that business is fierce.

Because, as covered in a previous chapter, the US Government is one of the most inept purchasers of goods and services, they initially looked only at the rebate percentage in the deal and picked Diners Club for all U.S. government employees, totally ignoring the fact that the card was accepted by very few places other than Europe. Many restaurants in the US did not even recognize the name, and you almost never see it on those signs on doors to a business listing cards accepted. Today, the stickers usually read Visa and Mastercard, sometimes Visa, Mastercard and American Express, occasionally Visa, Mastercard, American Express, and Discover…but almost never Diners Club.

For corporations, Diners Club did well for a while by offering "unissued" cards, just account numbers to which a corporation could use to charge, or have their travel agency charge, their airline tickets. These account numbers could not be used for hotels and meals, but many corporations were nervous about having their credit behind cards held by tens of thousands of their employees. The term "unissued" may not be a "word," but it was the one used in the credit card business. The unissued card approach worked like a charm for travel agencies serving big corporate accounts. The agency got its money essentially immediately and the client company got a month to pay and had no risk of having their employee use the card for an improper purchase. The employee simply had no card.

Because of its percentage charge to businesses that accepted the card, Amex continued to be somewhat exclusive, with a higher creditworthiness requirement for cardholders than Visa and MasterCard. This meant that many businesses were reluctant to pay Amex's percentage, typically 3½ % and up, when they could accept Visa or MasterCard, where fees were more in the 2% range. Bigger accounts could easily negotiate lower percentages. There was another factor that usually went unnoticed by corporations. The American Express card tended to be accepted at restaurants that were more expensive than those that accepted just Visa and MasterCard. If a company really wanted all of an employee's charges on the company's corporate American Express card, it meant employees frequently had to dine at more expensive places, certainly an unintended consequence. Even today, many small businesses will accept Visa, MasterCard and Discover, and refuse to accept American Express.

The biggest change came in 2016, when Costco dropped American Express and switched to Visa. The staggering fact was Costco accounted for about 13% of all charges to the American Express card. Think of all the charges for airline tickets, hotels, car rentals meals and many thousands of different products and services; that is a huge amount of money and for Costco to be 13% of that total is truly amazing. Visa has relatively lax credit standards, at least when compared with Amex.

We just hope that the change will not have a negative effect on the quality of Costco's customers and result in a decline in quality of their products.

55 SHOES

Don't Leave Home Without Them Either

Just like the American Express commercial "The American Express Card, don't leave home without it," the same rule should apply to shoes. Because they are heavy and take up lots of space, I frequently traveled with just the shoes I had on. I have found few Americans traveling in Europe who know why you see shoes left outside the doors of hotel rooms at night.

Many upscale European hotels still pick up shoes, clean and polish them before returning them later that night so they are ready to wear when you get up early the next morning. Some old hotels have a strange little drawer enabling you to put your shoes in the drawer in your room and have them accessible when the drawer is pulled out into the hallway. This certainly looks much nicer than having the shoes visible in the hallway.

One night many years ago, while staying in the Tel Aviv Hilton, I put the one pair of shoes I had worn on this long trip out to be shined. My next event was to address a meeting of the worldwide management of InterContinental Hotels at their annual meeting, this year in Singapore. As I am sure you have guessed by now, when I got up my shoes were not there. No problem, the hotel could certainly find them. They couldn't. I did not have time to go shopping, even if the shops had been open that early. It must have looked strange going through the airport in a suit, wearing socks but no shoes. I knew I would have to go through the Singapore Airport and check into my hotel, but thought it would be easy to buy a new pair of shoes before my meeting the next day.

I don't understand how foot sizes could be so different. Asian feet must simply be smaller. Singapore had a major shopping street with many department stores, all selling shoes. Once again, I was walking in my socks (which was not comfortable on the sidewalks). My feet may be large, but not that large….a size 10 1/2 at the time. Nobody had shoes that big. This was back when a good pair of leather dress shoes could be purchased in the States for $100 or less. It wasn't just a problem looking for a good style, there were simply no shoes that large to be had. I was later told that most Europeans and Americans working in Singapore got "home leave" allowing them to fly home at least once a year at their employer's expense, so they could buy shoes in a major western city. Finally, after two hours, I found one pair my size. They were Bally black leather loafers for what was then an outlandish price…$300. That would be just over $1,000 today, a helluva lot more than most people would pay for shoes. I had no choice; I had to buy them. When I got home I put them on my expense account, explaining to Ceb Benisch, then Chairman of the Board of Woodside, why the cost was necessary and justified.

56 DON'T LET ME HEAR YOU COMPLAIN
Two Truly Bad Flights

Lots of people today complain about problems with flights and express great discomfort when a flight is the least bit bumpy. It is a shame these people cannot compare today's problems with the old days, especially when there were only propeller planes that had to fly at much lower altitudes, frequently through storms.

PAN AM TO BOSTON

One of the scariest flights I was ever on was a Pan Am flight in a large jet from Bermuda to Boston. We were at cruising altitude and the stewardesses (yes, I know today you are supposed to say "flight attendants," but this was years ago and these were stewardesses) had just served the lunch. This was back in the days when you were served a tasty hot meal on a tray. I was relaxing with a Bloody Mary on my tray, thinking about how sad it was to be flying home to the cold in New England. All of a sudden, the pilot yells on the loud-speaker system for the cabin crew to hold on fast. Later, we were told we had hit clear air turbulence, but I never understood how the cockpit crew could tell it was about to happen.

The plane simply dropped. It was not a nose first dive; it was simply straight down. It was quite a drop and lasted several seconds. All of the food went up in the air and plastered the ceiling. Once the plane's wings caught air and the fall stopped abruptly, food of every shape and description landed on the passengers. There was meat in thick brown sauce all over the place, pickles and tomatoes in ladies' hair, and spilled drinks all over everyone. After a minute of recovery, people began picking food out of their hair and off their clothes. The cabin crew advised people to sweep all of the garbage into the aisle. It was quite a sight. Once this was completed, the crew spread blankets over the debris, so people could walk on the blankets, not the garbage.

When the plane landed in Boston, all the passengers broke into applause, happy that we had made it to land safely albeit quite dirty. The remarkable ending was discovered only after we had landed and taxied to our gate. In those days, the overhead compartments did not have doors that hinge down and latch closed…..they were just open, like a shelf. My Bloody Mary had floated up in the air and somehow landed upright without spilling in the overhead compartment. It was still more than half full and appeared not to have lost a drop from its flight off my tray the landing in the overhead compartment and stayed upright throughout the decent, landing and breaking to a stop. It was amusing in 2011 to actually see on TV that a woman had sued an airline for post-traumatic stress resulting from a rough plane ride.

BOSTON TO NEW YORK

Shuttle flights, run by two airlines, have operated for decades several times each hour in each direction between New York and Boston. Although the flights typically show as one hour in length, the actual time in the air can be as little as 23 minutes. When working at State Street Bank in Boston in the late sixties, one of my customer responsibilities was the Putnam Group of Mutual Funds. David Huey, the Putnam Vice President with whom the bank usually dealt, needed us at a late morning meeting in New York City. As is still the case today, the normal way to get between Boston and New York was the "Shuttle." The two competing carriers operating Shuttles have over the years included Eastern, Trump and today American and Delta.

When our team of three from the bank got to the airport, flights were being cancelled all over the place and that was true of both shuttles. We could not "no show" at this important client meeting, so we searched and found that Northeast (also now out of business) had a scheduled flight to Newark, New Jersey (close to Manhattan) with, of all things, a stop in Providence, Rhode Island. We debated going back into Boston and taking the train, but that would have taken five hours or so. The three of us managed to get the last seats on the Northeast Airlines flight and boarded the plane, expecting to be late but at least there for the meeting.

The reason so many flights were being cancelled was the extraordinarily high winds at airports to the southwest of Boston. The old propeller plane consumed some time with landing, boarding and taking off from Providence. After we were up in the air for the second time, it was announced from the cockpit that the Newark airport had just closed because of the high winds. LaGuardia had already been closed, which was why the Shuttles were not operating. JFK had closed, also.

From the cockpit, it was announced that we were heading to Philadelphia and, when that airport closed, on to Harrisburg, Pennsylvania. A few minutes later we were told that it, too, had closed. By this time, the cabin of the plane was almost unbearable. Even for someone who had traveled in lots of rough flights, it was awfully rough. Sue Comeau, later a Vice President of State Street, and I were the only people we could see who were not throwing up into air-sickness bags. The stench was much worse than the awful bouncing around. Vomiting is contagious. In conditions conducive to air sickness, the smell multiplies the effect. In this case the bouncing around combined with the stench had an additional factor....fear. It was *really* rough. After a prolonged amount of touring the east coast, the pilot announced that the best bet was Newark, which had a very long runway in a relatively open area. The airport was "closed," but they were going to allow us to land. We had to land somewhere.

On the first pass, the wind kept blowing the plane far off course trying to line up with the runway. The wind would push the plane's tail to the side, preventing our plane from lining up with the runway. The pilot was going to have to make a final adjustment in flight path and alignment with the runway and then, in the moment that the plane was heading in the correct position and alignment, get down onto the runway before it was once again turned sideways. The plane flew down close to ground and then had to abort, climb and circle around again. This happened twice.

I was in a left side window seat and it was very strange being able to see the runway ahead of us. Near earth, the plane would take wild swings from right wing up to right wing down, repeatedly. The third time, the pilot essentially had to drive the plane into the ground, hitting pretty hard, bouncing to the right with the left wing way up in the air and then bouncing to the left. At long last we landed safely. The cabin still stunk like hell, but we were safe and ready to rush into Manhattan. This was one of those cases where the passengers applauded.

We were running late, but we grabbed a cab and reached the meeting place in downtown Manhattan. As you can guess, the meeting had been delayed till mid afternoon because the Putnam people in Boston had been unable to get to New York. We had flown while they took the slow train. Man, did we wish we had missed that flight. When you are unhappy about being on a "rough" flight, remember this one. I've been on an old commercial propeller plane with an engine ablaze. The problems in jets today pale by comparison.

THE DESIGN OF THE BOEING 747

As Boeing was designing the giant 747 airplane, they considered having windows continue from the sides to the front nose of the first class cabin. It was a great opportunity to give passengers the view they would have had riding in a car, looking straight ahead. Until then, all airlines had had windows on the sides, but no seat looking straight ahead (or anything close to that) because that was where the pilot and co-pilot sat. The 747 was the first plane to have the cockpit upstairs. The thinking was that this would be a great addition, providing a fabulous view that had never been seen by passengers.

To be sure the idea would be acceptable to passengers, Boeing conducted studies and determined that the effect would be traumatic, at the very least quite disturbing, to most passengers. I experienced a little bit of that scared feeling once when headed to Beirut on an assignment for the Sheraton Corporation (in a separate chapter). It made me aware of the reasoning about no windows looking ahead. As we were heading east over the Mediterranean a stewardess said the pilot wanted to know if I would like to sit in the cockpit during the landing. I was delighted. This was one of the many perks of flying everywhere as a VIP guest of an airline, something that could not be allowed today.

The unusual shape of the island of Cyprus, with its long narrow sharp-pointed "panhandle" pointing east, was easy to identify as we passed north of it and began to turn south along the coast of Syria toward Beirut's airport. Beirut's airport runs north and south along the coast, about five miles south of the city. The wind that day was blowing strongly from the west. The pilot, Captain Jack Payne, was having difficulty keeping the plane aimed at the runway. The wind gusts kept blowing the tail to the east, making the plane appear to be headed to the right, "crabbing" its way as it descended toward the runway. It was a very strange feeling. I would usually have kept looking at the great view of the city of Beirut on the left but, in this situation, it was very difficult not to focus on what was ahead. The pilot kept having to steer right to get back in line with the runway. As he descended close to land, he had to aim the plane well to the right of his course until the last second when he turned left suddenly to line up with the runway.

This was not in some big storm; it was a fairly common event. For an inexperienced observer, it was quite scary. I had flown many times in the co-pilot's seat of small planes and helicopters, but that was my only time flying in the cockpit of a large commercial jet. It made it easy for me to understand why Boeing had abandoned the idea of a front-facing window. My thanks to Gulf Air's Capt. Payne, Co-Pilot Ken Hart, First Officer Bob Scott and the Navigator, Jerry Colman for talking with me about their responsibilities and letting me experience this unusual time in flight.

SCARIEST AIRPORTS

There may be ones even worse, but the most- scary airport I landed at was on the island of Saba in the Caribbean. Most major airports are at least a mile long, 5,280 feet. The one on Saba is 1,299 feet with the sea at both ends. At least the passenger planes that fly there are small propeller planes that don't have to have such a long runway. Coming from the northeast, the pilot aimed straight at a cliff, turned left at what seemed like the last minute and touched down on the short runway, screeching to a stop just in time. Note: planes landing on Sint Maarten don't scare the passengers, they terrify the people on the beach just under the plane when landing. On St. Barts, it is people in automobiles who are scared because small planes skim just over the roofs of cars stopped at an intersection before descending fast to land. Landing late and going too far got you into the water.

57 THE PAN AM BUILDING
A Dangerous Place

The huge Pan Am Building looming over Park Avenue in the heart of Manhattan was one of the great landmarks of the City. For some reason I have not been able to find, it sat astride Park Avenue just west of Grand Central Station. The big "Pan Am" signs across the wide sides were visible for miles as you drove or walked on Park Avenue. Driving on Park Avenue had to be diverted onto little curvy ramps up through the building.

When it opened March 7, 1963, it was the largest commercial office building in the world. The building is still there, but most alive today will recognize it as the Met Life Building. The huge Met Life sign replaced Pan Am and is the reason New York City passed a law forbidding such signs on the tops of skyscrapers. Boston passed the same ordinance a few years later when my employer, State Street Bank, put their name in big letters across the top of their building on Franklin Street, the building that used to be its head office. The were somehow allowed to keep the signs when they built a new headquarters. I had several experiences with Pan Am, both the building and the airline.

First was going to meetings with Pan Am's senior management. Pam Am had been the first international airline and, for many years, the world's largest and best. It was the "flag carrier" of the United States in the early days of aviation, going back to the involvement of Charles Lindbergh. Pan Am started its worldwide flights back in the days before airports, so the early Pan Am Clippers had to be amphibians, capable of landing on the water, something that was almost always available, whether at islands or near large cities. It's hard to believe, but Pan Am flew before there were airports.

For a wide variety of reasons, Pan Am went into in a serious state of decline, facing union obstruction and increased competition as most countries throughout the world developed their own flag carriers. A good frequent flyer program sustained Pan Am for a few years, but in the end was not enough. There are extensive comments about this later.

HELICOPTER SERVICE

One of the great features of this huge building was the helipad on its roof. Service to John F. Kennedy Airport was a great benefit for executives who worked in the numerous mid-town Manhattan office buildings. Even back in the seventies, rush hour traffic out of Manhattan in the evening was horrendous. Because virtually all international flights from JFK bound for Europe departed in the evening, catching a flight meant wasting hours in rush-hour traffic and, all too frequently, missed flights, an occurrence that led to missed meetings at destinations. Helicopter service was a fabulous alternative, and it was especially beneficial for Pan Am because at JFK the helicopter landed at Pan Am's terminal.

The lounge bar that served as the heliport's terminal on the roof of the Pan Am Building was a very popular spot for businessmen, many of whom knew each other, to wait for their scheduled helicopter flight. No, this isn't a sexist comment; it was fact. Fifty years ago the vast majority of business passengers on international flights were men. The drive of an hour and a half during rush hour was cut to just 7 minutes by air. The difference was truly fantastic. You could work until 5pm instead of having to leave work early to beat the humungous traffic jam. In those days, relatively few international carriers served Boston, so I would fly to La Guardia, do business in New York City and then grab the helicopter out to JFK for my flight, especially if my trip was to South America or Asia. In addition to saving time, it was fun. The view as you lifted off from the Pan Am Building was magnificent. You rose a few feet before suddenly being high in the air.

On my flight May 14, 1977, I was seated in the window seat on the right, up in the front of the very large Sikorsky S-51 helicopter. People walking to get on the helicopter climbed the stairs from the waiting lounge to a small rooftop room and then walked across the helipad to the steps on the right-hand side of the helicopter.

I watched the people boarding, but I very quickly noticed the right front landing gear that was in view just below my window. It attracted my attention because it was, even to a non-engineer, in dreadful condition, badly rusted and shaking violently. Because helicopter engines are left running while people are boarding, there is a lot of vibration. The front right landing gear looked as if it might just shake apart. On takeoff, the helicopters would lift off the rooftop and back up slightly, so that if the engine were to fail on liftoff, the pilot could clearly see the circular helipad in front of him and guide the copter back to a safe landing on top of the building..

The incredible coincidence occurred just two days later and, although shocking, it was not the least bit surprising to me. On May 16, as passengers were walking between the helicopter and the "terminal," that right front landing gear fell apart. The entire helicopter tipped to the right so that the huge twenty–foot-long blades tilted to the right, cutting to pieces four people who were walking toward the plane. Pieces of people and the broken blade rained down onto the streets below, killing one pedestrian.

A landing gear failure in this situation would have killed people boarding no matter where the helicopter was, but in this case the accident resulted in the permanent closure of Pan Am's outstanding heliport. I wish I had said something about that landing gear, but I am certain any such comment from a passenger would have simply been ignored. Supposedly, helicopter N619PA is still in service in Canada.

PAN AM AGAIN

Just two years previously I had had another bad experience with the Pan Am Building. I was living in the second-floor apartment at 7 Mt. Vernon Place very close to the top of Boston's Beacon Hill. On the floor above there were a bunch of single guys, one of whom was Leon Black, the son of Eli Black, then President of United Brands Company.

Leon later became Managing Director of Drexel Burnham Lambert, controlled several billion dollars of investments, and served as a Trustee of Dartmouth College, from which he had graduated in 1973. In the early 70s when I knew him he was a very nice man.

Eli Black's company, United Brands, is now Chiquita Brands and had been The United Fruit Company, the first major corporate client of Heritage Travel. I had a special love of United Fruit because as a kid my parents had taken me on cruises to Cuba and Central American countries on United Fruit ships that carried a small number of passengers from New Orleans and returned to New Orleans with a large cargo of bananas.

On February 3, 1975, Mr. Black said goodbye to his secretary, locked his office door on the forty-fourth floor of the Pan Am Building, used his briefcase to shatter the window and leapt to his death on Park Avenue. It was a very sad time in my apartment building in Boston.

PERSONAL

I got into trouble several times talking about airlines that were in precarious financial or competitive condition. Eastern and TWA were obvious, as was Braniff. I had also given a speech, supposedly confidential, to Woodside's stockholders about Sabena's awkward position. Once travelers could fly directly from the US to South Africa without having to fly east to Belgium and then south on one of Sabena's many routes to cities throughout Africa, Sabena's business was about to decline rapidly.

The one that shocked everyone was Pan Am, largely because of its history, having been at the vanguard of international air travel. As stated earlier in this chapter, Pan Am's amphibious planes were essential in the early days because they flew to many places that did not have airports, or at least not adequate ones.

Bet you didn't know Pan Am started as a service between Key West, Florida and Havana. Flight crews had to be trained in celestial navigation and use dead reckoning. There is a joke about the word "dead" in this usage. Dead reckoning means flying on a compass course for a given number of minutes and then changing to a new course for a given number of minutes in hopes of spotting your destination. When visibility was bad, the Pan Am Clippers would land out to sea and taxi to the destination.

Bet very few remember that for a while, Pan Am's route to Europe was from Norfolk, Virginia, via landings to refuel in Bermuda and the Azores. I remember, possibly incorrectly, that Pan Am's inaugural 747 flight to Europe January 10, 1970 misjudged a turn on the taxiway and got stuck in the mud. The records show that the delay was an engine problem. Was that incorrect? The flight was delayed so long it took off Jan.11.

ANOTHER MISTAKE

My big problem emanated from a speech to the American Chamber of Commerce in Hong Kong, in which I foresaw the demise of Pan Am. My comments made big news in the Hong Kong newspapers the next morning. I may have been right, but I got a lot of criticism for outlining the problems and predicting the outcome. Pan Am was extremely important in Hong Kong and I should have kept my mouth shut. At least the Chamber of Commerce gave me a beautiful jade abacus as a thank you for addressing them that day.

By the way, my prediction ended up being correct.

58 THE RIGHT TO VOTE
Not Poll Tax, Not Voter ID, But It Works

You hear all of the history about how whites in the South kept poor blacks from voting by charging a poll tax. For any of you that don't remember, poll tax was a fee (albeit very small) that had to be paid by everyone in order to register to vote. It may have been charged to everyone equally, but it was obviously intended to reduce the number of blacks voting and this was easily and correctly deemed discrimination.

Approaching the 2012 elections, there was lots of talk about Republican attempts to make voters show a picture ID at check-in for voting. I am required to show proof of my identity and I do think it a reasonable practice. For those very few who have neither a driver's license nor any credit cards, most states seeking to implement Voter ID offer to give anyone who can illustrate residency a government-issued color photo ID without charge. It doesn't prove citizenship, just residency, but it is accepted.

This chapter is about an insurmountable barrier to voting that should be changed. To my knowledge (which is, admittedly, limited) about this subject, I think most local governments select people to whom jury subpoenas are sent from their lists of registered voters. It is your civic duty to serve. Defendants have the right under our law to be tried by a "jury of their peers," language that sounds nice but frequently results in idiots being selected for a jury. I, personally, have observed jurors being "struck" (which means eliminated from consideration) by a defense attorney purely because they appeared intelligent or conservative.

In the states in which I have lived, if you were called for duty, you were required to show up and, if selected, had to serve… period. Yes, there were some grounds for excuse, usually granted to mothers with small children. Businesses were prohibited from penalizing in any way an employee requiring time off to serve on a jury. Jurors' employers have to leave their jobs unfilled even though that person may be absolutely necessary to the business even in those rare cases when a trial drags on for months. The first couple of times I was summoned for jury duty and went, I filled out a questionnaire, answered questions and was rejected. In the 70s and 80s when I was having to travel on business all over the world being called for jury duty became a serious problem. My trips would frequently require travel out of the country for a month or two at a time, sometimes several months and once, for State Street Bank, almost half year in Europe.

I was allowed to file an application to be excused from jury duty, but the document granting that excuse made it clear in very precise language that this excuse was accepted once and could not be used again. I wasn't even in the United States when the notice arrived and I did not read it and could not respond until after the date I had been ordered to show up. I was in trouble, but got out of it by showing my itinerary and passport, still having to listen to the judge's severe reprimand.

The law simply makes it impossible for a person who has to travel extensively on business to remain on the voting lists. That is the law, but it should be unconstitutional. My trips would frequently require planning many months ahead and every quarter they required committing to dates for meetings to which a dozen board members or many dozens of stockholders from throughout the world would have to plan trips and book flights far ahead of time. I had to produce and conduct board meetings and stockholder meetings in places such as Hong Kong, Rio de Janeiro, London, Paris, Stockholm, and Dubai, in addition to regional meetings each year on three continents and many meetings throughout the United States. With a hundred people flying to a meeting at which I had to preside, I simply could not cancel the meeting when I was summoned for jury duty.

This law forced me to request that I be removed from the list of registered voters. As I said, I think that is unfair and should somehow there should be a way of getting around it, maybe agreeing to be available for weeks when I knew I would be at home in the States. In the four states I have lived in this was not an option.

Theoretically retired and living in Savannah, I encountered the same problem when I was registered to vote, thinking there would be no problem, only to find out that there was. Being President of the Savannah Symphony was not a problem, but it became one when I had had to step in and run the place every day for two years. The first time I was called for jury duty in Chatham County I had an excuse that was accepted. It did, however, include the common caveat that the excuse was granted on the condition that I had to serve the next time I was called. That happened quite quickly.

I simply had to make a business trip for the Symphony, this time to Colorado, and the trip to Crested Butte had to be while their music festival was underway. I flew there to hire the Director of their annual music festival. It was a trip that had to be on a certain date and, of course, that conflicted with the jury summons that I had received. I went down to the appropriate county office, keeping my fingers crossed. I could not believe my luck.

The lady in charge of juror summonses knew me. She was a season ticket subscriber to the Savannah Symphony, understood and accepted my excuse (even though the law said she couldn't) and I made the important trip and hired a new executive director. I think she may have done me another favor because I was never called for juror duty again in Georgia.

Anyway, it may be a barrier to voting that does not affect many people, but somehow it should be eliminated or amended. Years of not being able to vote was unfair.

59 ONE MORE (This Time I Promise It's The Last) FOOTBALL STORY *It's Not Really About Football:It's About Ted Kennedy*

It was decades later that I discovered the man I had seen score a touchdown for Harvard in the annual football rivalry with evil Yale was the man who became the famous Senator from Massachusetts, Edward Moore "Ted" Kennedy. When he died in 2009, he received a massive number of accolades for his years in the US Senate. He had been truly outstanding, *if* you are an ultra-left liberal. His ability to achieve compromise between the Democratic left and the Republican right was remarkable, but the times in his life that I was most familiar with were not admirable; they were despicable.

There are a number of facts about Kennedy, most of which are ignored by the adoring liberal press and therefore by the people. A long list of key facts about the night of July 19, 1969 at Chappaquiddick were truly damning, and should have resulted in Kennedy's going to jail. It was not an "incident at Chappaquiddick," it was almost certainly an attempt at an affair with young girl, followed by abandoning the girl to die by drowning, followed by a long list of attempts to cover up his involvement, and finally by an elaborate scheme to avoid being caught and convicted for his actions. The cover up of his involvement in a death was clearly much worse than the attempted but unsuccessful cover up of a botched burglary that became known as Watergate and forced Richard Nixon to resign in disgrace and resulted in prison sentences for several of his senior officials.

I know I had attended college with Teddy one year, 1955-56. He was from the great Kennedy family and was a quite good football player, but he was already known for having been thrown out of Harvard for cheating on a test a few years earlier, which is why he was still there in 1956. Despite his great mind and magnificent delivery of many speeches during his later career, he could not at the time face a Spanish language exam, and talked a friend, who was a better student into taking the exam for him. This was the first of many situations from which he could not have extricated himself had he not been a Kennedy, a family almost worshipped in Massachusetts. After being thrown out, he was allowed back in after one year.

In football, he was a large but remarkably quick offensive end. The pass that I saw him catch for a score was Harvard's only touchdown in an embarrassing end-of-season loss to Yale, 21-7. Most people don't know that he was good enough to receive a call from an NFL team inquiring about his interest in playing pro football. What a difference that would have made had he been interested in that option and followed that career instead of politics. Teddy went on to graduate from Harvard in 1956, after which he took a non-paying job as an Assistant District Attorney in Boston.

Shortly after I met him at my college graduation in 1959, John F. Kennedy was elected President in 1962 and, to save his Senate seat until Teddy was 30 (the minimum age for the US Senate) JFK got the friend who had been his old college roommate at Harvard, Ben Smith (a very nice man and a friend of mine who was an excellent Etchells Class sailboat racer from Annisquam, Massachusetts, technically a neighborhood within the City of Gloucester) appointed to fill the vacant Senate seat for a couple of years. Even though Ben lived way up in the northwest corner of Gloucester, he raced out of the Corinthian Yacht Club in Marblehead.

John F. Kennedy claimed his request for the appointment of Ben Smith by the Governor was to preserve party unity, but anybody with any sense knew it was to fill the remaining years of JFK's six year term by a person he could count on *not* to seek reelection, thereby leaving the door wide open for Teddy once he met the minimum age required. With no relevant experience whatsoever, Teddy ran in the Democratic primary election against State Attorney General Ed McCormack, who happened to be the nephew of the powerful Speaker of the US House of Representatives, John McCormack. Ed McCormack had an excellent retort for Teddy, but it backfired. The press, already enamored with the Kennedys, made McCormack appear to be a bully.

McCormack's famous line was "Teddy, if your name was Edward Moore instead of Edward Moore Kennedy, your candidacy would be a joke." That statement was true, but ignored by the Massachusetts voters…Teddy *was* a Kennedy. Teddy went on to defeat the Republican candidate, George Cabot Lodge, easily in the general election…Lodge being a lesser but still egregious example of family's name being more important than experience. He was the son of Henry Cabot Lodge, who had been a Senator.

Even when it was happening, the press did not make much of some key facts in the "Chappaquiddick Incident." The language in the press usually read that Kennedy missed a turn and "accidentally" turned onto Dike Road, which led to the little wooden bridge over Poucha Pond, where Mary Jo Kopechne drowned in the back seat. That is a gross misstatement of the events and it clearly led people not familiar with the island to think the great Teddy had just accidentally missed a turn. He certainly would not have intentionally made the sharp turn away from where he was supposedly headed. It gets worse.

First, Teddy did not have a valid driver's license, his license having been suspended. Secondly, and more interesting, is that fact that Teddy had his chauffeur with him at the party on Chappaquiddick that night. Why, after what was described as "a night of heavy drinking" would he take the car keys from his chauffeur if he was really intending to drive back to catch the ferry to Edgartown instead of taking Mary Jo Kopechne to a dark secluded lane for some hanky panky?

Now, here is where it really gets interesting. In his testimony at the inquest, Deputy Sheriff Christopher Look testified about the events following his departure from a party at the Edgartown Yacht Club. He stated under oath that he had the yacht club's launch take his across the very narrow entrance to Edgartown Harbor (essentially at the point at which the ferry runs) and got in his Sherriff's car which was parked near the western edge of Chappaquiddick Island sometime between 12:30 and 12:45am.

There were lots of suggestions that maybe Teddy was not driving that night and that it was really Mary Jo. Deputy Sheriff Look swore under oath that he had seen a car stopped on a very small dark dirt road, the private "Cemetery Road" off of the main paved route from the infamous party to the "Chappy" ferry. Look, assuming the occupants of the car were lost, left his lights on, got out of his sheriff's car and approached the parked car to offer assistance. Shortly after seeing the headlights pulled up from behind, the driver of the car backed fast out of the secluded dirt road.

Look testified that he was about 30 feet away from the car when it started in reverse, and that he was able to get a glimpse of the license tag and the occupants. The parts of the license that registered in his memory were that it started with an L and had two Rs, facts that matched Teddy's Oldsmobile. Secondly, the occupants were a man, *who was driving*, and a woman *in the passenger's seat*. This was not some rumor, it was the testimony of a law enforcement officer. Mary Jo was clearly not just asleep in the back seat, so that Teddy swam out of the car without knowing Mary Jo was even in the car (as so many Tedofiles tried to claim was what must have happened). Some people try to protect Teddy from blame by this ridiculous argument, one that is clearly refuted by the sworn testimony of Sheriff Look.

Finally, from Sheriff Look's testimony, the car sped away and made the very sharp right angle turn from the paved road onto another unpaved road, the Dike Road that led to the infamous bridge. there was absolutely no way he just "missed a turn" and went down Dike Road by mistake as was another excuse by the Tedophiles. The turn onto Dike Road was not just "a fork or turn in the road;" it was a ninety- degree right turn at a place where the main road, paved, leading to the ferry curved left. Again. you simply could not have made this type of turn by mistake.

There is no way of knowing if Teddy really did dive repeatedly into the water (as he claimed) to see if he could extricate Mary Jo. This claim, by Teddy, obviously overturns the theory that he did not know she was even in the car. Why would he have made the sharp turn off of the main road onto a little dirt road if he had not had hanky panky on his mind?

What is known is the fact that he walked a very long way that night without contacting anyone, something he could have done quite easily, probably while Mary Jo was still alive and could have been saved. Was it an attempt to save his reputation? That will never be known, but in my opinion (and that of many others) it is almost certainly true. His reputation was more important than her life. He had probably, as was true many times in his later life, had much too much to drink, and did not want to be caught with a DUI with a suspended drivers license, much less one where the result was death of an innocent young girl.

There was a pay phone near the mainland end of the bridge, where the car was in the water, but that could have been overlooked in the dark. What could not have been overlooked was the house just 472 feet away on the south side of Dike Road, a house in which the lady who lived there testified she left her front door light on all night. This house is close to and clearly visible from Dike Road, the road Teddy would have to have taken leaving the wreck. Forget all the other excuses; Teddy could not have overlooked this house and should have run there for assistance.

Instead of going to that house and calling for help, he walked past the house and continued for just over three miles back to the place where you cross to Edgartown. Here the story varies. I have never really been clear on whether he went back to the party or went directly to the point from which the ferry operates. The evidence indicates he walked to the ferry crossing. Regardless of which option is correct and which you believe, it was a long walk in the dark and it illustrated his familiarity with the roads on the island. Take a look in your computer at a satellite picture of Martha's Vineyard and you can see Chappaquiddick Island on the right, the bridge on Dike Road on the far right and the narrow gap where the ferry operates between Chappaquiddick and Edgartown across the water to the northwest.

Teddy admitted that he swam across to Edgartown and went to his hotel. What was an obvious attempt at cover-up was sneaking into the hotel and climbing upstairs to dry off and change clothes before descending the stairs to make an appearance in the hotel's small lobby area as if he had never been wet. Was he able to make a phone call for help, or at least to report the accident? He did, according to the records, make phone calls to his lawyer and to political cronies that night, but no call to the Duke's County Sheriff until *after* the wreck was discovered in the water the next morning. Is that excusable? I think it was criminal.

Here you get into a lot of damning facts about the inquest and the rapid removal of the body from the State of Massachusetts, without the legally-required autopsy, but that is just additional fuel for the flames. What had transpired previously was ample evidence that the Chappaquidick "Incident" and a cover-up that cost a life, something that Watergate did not.

MARY JO

Another rarely mentioned fact is that in 1962, prior to going north and getting involved in politics, Mary Jo Kopechne had taught school in my hometown, Montgomery, Alabama at Loretta Catholic High School near St. Peter's cathedral in downtown Montgomery. She was very popular with the friends she made during her time in Montgomery. Two of her closest friends were old friends of mine, Jo McGowin and Ed Jones, who had taught with her.

Jo wrote me that Mary Jo "was a sweet prude" and was also "naïve and probably didn't realize how drunk Teddy was."

Even today, I love the haunting old song by Bobbie Gentry, *"The Ode To Billy Joe."* Someone should write an *"Ode to Mary Jo."* Did you know that June 3, 2018 will be the 50th anniversary of the day Billy Joe McAllister jumped off the Tallahatchee Bridge?

EPILOGUE

On a personal note, when the daughter of two of my best friends in Boston got married, Teddy was invited and came to the wedding. Today, the parents think it was disgusting and far beneath his dignity, but can still laugh at how drunk Teddy was at the reception. Not quite what should be expected of a famous U.S. Senator.

Teddy will be remembered as "The Lion of the Senate," but nothing can change my memory of him as a lousy person who should have gone to jail at the very least for the death of Mary Jo and the subsequent cover up. My comment on this subject is that "Teddy was obviously innocent, just as innocent at O.J. Simpson."

60 ROW, ROW, ROW YOUR BOAT
Gently Down The Stream (but in this case....Up)

Having grown up tall but scrawny and suffering from asthma years before they had inhalers and cures, I was never an athlete. I had done a lot of power boating, canoeing, played tennis and golf and been an early waterskier, but never what you would consider normal rough or tough boyhood sports.

ROWING

Arriving at Harvard, I saw signs for the Harvard Crew. Until moving to Massachusetts, I had never been in a sailboat and never even seen a rowing shell of any kind. What was interesting was that the sign offered "Lightweight" crew, also known as 150s. This meant that the average weight had to be less than 154 and the maximum, at the time (as best I can recall), for any one person was 159.

The coach, a Harvard Divinity School graduate student, was Harold Ogden Joseph Brown, who became a good friend. He was known as Joe Brown. Joe died in 2007 at the age of 74, having been an evangelical theologian known for his early involvement and activism as a crusader against abortion. He had become a Professor at Trinity Evangelical Divinity School, after earning four degrees from Harvard and studying on a Fulbright Fellowship.

Harvard has two large rowing boathouses on the Charles River, Weld, located on the Cambridge side of the Charles, available to all students and one, Newell, on the Boston side of the river for the various crews representing the college against other colleges. For beginners, they had a large, heavy, wide and flat-bottomed boat named the "*Leviathon*." Unlike the actual racing shells which were very long, narrow, tippy and light, this boat was very heavy and stable, with rowers on either side and a walkway for the coach down the middle. Joe could walk up and down, observing how the beginner rowers were progressing. I apparently have a very good internal clock, and quite early on was designated to be stroke while in the *Leviathan* and eventually ended up as the stroke of the Freshman Lightweight eight-man crew.

The primary racing shells among colleges is are eights, meaning you have eight men facing astern and a coxswain in the stern facing forward to see where the boat is going, call out the strokes per minute desired, and steer the boat via handles that connect by ropes to the long, shallow rudder on the stern. Today, some shells place the coxswain in the bow. You want the eight to be as strong as possible and the cox to be as small as possible. Our cox, Mario Bryan, was a remarkably small man from the Virgin Islands. You wanted to carry as little weight in the boat as possible, and he certainly contributed to that, plus being a very good steerer. I think he weighed less than a hundred pounds.

Each of the eight oarsmen pulls on one long heavy oar, four on the left and four on the right. Observing a race, you may not notice that all of the oarsmen are on sliding seats. When your hands go as far as you can reach forward and the blade of the oar is extended to its limit behind you (going backwards, remember) the seat slides forward so that your legs are bent at the knee and your butt rolls on the slide almost to your ankles. The primary force enabling you to pull the oar through the water is generated by your legs. The last oarsman at the stern (the "stroke") has to judge the time, and those behind him keep pace by watching the back of the neck of the man in front of them and the tempo of the blades they can see in the water in front of them. I never got to see another oar.

RACING
Races start with a very high beat of very short strokes to get the boat moving. The tricky thing was that everyone else got to go by the oar in front of them while I had to be able to judge how fast to row when given a number. The number was always strokes per minute. The coxswain, who sat facing me, pounded the two wooden handles by which he steered the shell on the sides of the boat to tell everybody that the stokes per minute were about to change. He would yell so be would be heard by the man far away in the bow and I would have to change speed to the new correct count on the next stroke. For some reason I don't understand, I was able to think I was at a number of strokes per minute and then be able to increase or decrease to the required count.

The length of the blades path through the water varies at the start of a race. It's like shifting gears. To get you going from a dead standstill, the length of strokes goes from quarters to a few half strokes and finally to full strokes once you overcome inertia and the stroke count drops down from the mid-forties, high-thirties and mid-thirties to more like 32 or sometimes as low as 30 strokes per minute for the body of a long race. Those initial strokes with those long blades at a rate of a stroke every one and a half seconds is damn tough. Races were usually "The Henley Distance," the length of the historic course in England, 1 5/16 miles. The record times for this distance are just under 7 minutes, so that long shell is averaging about 16.5 feet per second Depending upon where you were in relation to the boats you were racing against, you would sprint as you approached the finish, reaching as much as 40 or so full strokes per minute, which was extremely difficult and exhausting after already covering so much distance.

For a kid from Alabama, it was an interesting learning experience. The weather was OK during football season, except for the fact that you rowed no matter what the weather. Your hands became very tough, and, when it was cold, like claws gripping the two-and-a-half-inch diameter oar handle. Unlike a rowboat with one hand on each oar, both hands are on the same, long oar. The other big difference was lifting the oar out of the water at the end of each stroke, turning it a quarter turn toward you so that it was flat to the water and, while traveling against the wind, as thin as possible before turning back up to vertical and dropping into the water for the next stroke. It is more complex than you would imagine watching a race.

During each stroke, you have to use one wrist, usually your "outside" wrist, to twist the angle of the blade in and out of the water. As I guess is true of many sports, there are nuances that a typical spectator would completely miss. My team that season did well, but certainly not very well. I always thought Princeton had an advantage because of their warmer climate, enabling them to spend more time practicing on the water.

Coach Brown was stern, but fairly tolerant. What he did not like was any display of laziness in a practice session, which usually lasted a couple of hours each afternoon. Races where held upstream in the part of the Charles River between the elegant Longfellow Bridge and the ugly Cottage Farm Bridge, sometimes known as the BU (Boston University) Bridge. The Charles River is now remarkably clean, but in those days it was filthy. If the crew was not working as hard as the coach expected of us, he would announce that we were rowing far upstream to Watertown, where the Galen Street Bridge is about four miles upstream from the Newell Boathouse. It was always a long haul after an hour of practice. This was dreaded as it meant eight miles of rowing after about 7 miles of practice. What everyone knew on hot afternoons was that we would have to row into the horrible stench and the blood in the water from a slaughterhouse that used to operate on the south side of the Charles River at Watertown. In those days, they were allowed to flush all the blood into the water. It was truly awful, but a good incentive for hard work to avoid the trip.

There were a few moments that made the rare trips upstream amusing. Unless the cox is pounding his handles on the side of the shell to get your attention, shells move quite quietly through the water and glide almost silently for a remarkable distance once the rowing stops. On several occasions in this secluded stretch we encountered couples doing things they should not have been doing, thinking that the thick bushes shielded them from the view of cars passing on the major roads that ran along both sides of the river. One time a man was so furious at our interruption that he grabbed rocks and threw them at us when we came back by heading home.

A MINOR BUT MEMORABLE RACE

We did have one minor race against Dartmouth that made major front-page picture of me and my crew in the Boston Globe. Races normally went upstream starting near the beautiful Longfellow Bridge, passing under the long Massachusetts Avenue Bridge at about the midpoint of the race. Because the wind that afternoon was much stronger than usual, the coaches decided to run the race in the opposite direction this one time. Things were OK racing until we passed eastbound under the bridge. I could see the waves breaking over the enclosed stern of our boat a few feet in front of me behind the coxswain. This was no serious concern until they began to splash into the hull of the boat. The water inside the boat made rowing tougher. Riding lower in the water also made it extremely difficult to get the oars out of the water and back to the start position of each stroke. The blades were very difficult to control since they were catching in the crests of the waves on each return and being blasted by the wind. We were trying to do one of those very long strokes of each oar every two seconds.

The waves became more steep and the boats were all taking on water. Our feet, held in position in the boat by shoelaces, were barely above water. As the boat sank lower in the water, it became very difficult impossible to push the oar handles away from you so that the blades would return to the start position for the next stroke without catching in the waves. In those days the Metropolitan District Police used large dark-blue powerboats with inboard engines driving propellers located underneath their hulls. Two of those boats came charging into the area. It would have been much less dangerous if they had stayed away, because they would not be able to see heads of swimmers in the waves.

After finishing and winning the race, I talked with the coxswain and decided my boat should head to the other side of the river to take out. We managed to make it slowly along the side of Longfellow Bridge over to a private boathouse at the Union Boat Club on the Boston side of the river. We could not have made it back to our boat house and, at the time, this was the only place to take out. The Boat Club had a long low dock onto which we were able to disembark and lift the hull gently on one side to drain the water so we could take the shell out of the water. The wooden hull was very thin wood and fragile so we had to get most of the water out before we could dare try to lift it. The Boston police insisted upon taking the entire crew to nearby Mass. General Hospital to be checked out. Not sure why, but the police said it was necessary. Harvard was very unhappy about the damage to the other boats, which were all made of beautifully polished, thin, classic-looking wood. A DNF (did not finish the race) and serious damage are something you do not normally expect in a crew race.

THE TANK

When winter arrived and the Charles River was covered by ice, we moved to practice indoors. Newell Boathouse had a huge "tank," with water on two sides and a fixed simulated rowing "shell" down the middle with an area on each side so you could walk to your seat. The place where you sat was stable and the water beside you was kept moving rapidly past by huge pumps. It was a lot of water to move because you had to have room on both sides for the oars. Everyone was eager for the ice to melt so you could get out on the river in the spring, but the tank enabled you to stay in shape and practice the pull of the oar through the moving water and feather it for the trip back for the next stroke. he boathouse had weights and strength-building equipment, plus spring-loaded mechanical oars, but they were nowhere near as effective as practicing in the tank with real water and real oars.

On that fateful afternoon, my crew was the first scheduled in the tank. We took our seats, strapped our feet in and waited for the huge engines to begin pumping the water past us. As the water began to flow, bubbles rose and kept rising higher and higher above the surface of the water. It was fairly obvious that somebody had snuck in and poured a large quantity of detergent into the tank. Our rowing added to the huge pumps stirring the water into soap suds. The suds kept rising until we could not see the walkway we had to use to exit the tank.

The tanks were shut down and the water drained. The next day, when they tried to start the pumps again, there was still enough detergent clinging to the surfaces of the tank, the pipes back to the pumps and the pumps themselves that the rowing had to be cancelled again and all of the tank's equipment and surfaces had to be scrubbed clean. Days of practice were lost at a crucial time when we were unable to go out on the frozen river. It probably still holds the record as the world's largest washing machine.

They never learned who had done it, but the culprit, a classmate, admitted to me many years later that he had done it as a required club initiation rite. The guilty party was Charlie Devens, a popular and highly respected student, a descendant of the man after whom Massachusetts' large Army base, Fort Devens, is named, just northwest of Boston. I think he said it was a 5 gallon jug of Joy that he had put in the tanks. It did not bring "joy" to all of the Harvard crews who missed days of practice at a very important time.

AN ATHELETE'S DIET

There was one funny result from my weighing less than 150 pounds after a race. I was 6"1", but weighed only 147. At the end of a race in Princeton, I weighed just 139. Sadly, I am now 6 feet and weigh 198. Because the tiny coxswain from Jamaica and I were the two people nearest the stern of the boat, the stern was a little too high in the water, so the rudder barely had an adequate effect on the direction of the boat since so much of it was out of the water. Joe, our coach, put me on a special "diet" in an attempt to fatten me up.

In those days, the old historic bar near Harvard Square was Cronins, a great big barn of a place with about three aisles accessing dozens of booths, each of which I think held six people. I was not a beer drinker, but it was the chosen beverage for attempting to put more weight on me. Upperclassmen were given special meals at the Varsity Club. I bet I was the only student who had Harvard pay for my beer.

61 LIBERTY BANK

This Bank Gave New Meaning To The Word "Safe"

One of my best friends in Boston did not believe in investing money. This sounded old fashioned for many years, but in 2008 he began to look quite wise.

His practice in the seventies and eighties was to buy rare antique watches, gold coins and bearer bonds. To be safe, he kept it all in a large safe deposit at a bank in downtown Boston. Safe deposit boxes play a role, but this story will alert you to two things NOT to do.

First, know that when you sign up to rent a safe deposit box, you sign a clear and rock-solid waiver of liability on the bank's part. There is an obvious reason for this: They have no way of knowing what you put in your box. If something is missing from your box, you have nobody to turn to unless you have listed the valuables and obtained a "Scheduled" insurance policy to cover them. Almost everyone considers their safe deposit box to be just what the name says it is...safe. Sometimes that is not the case.

Liberty Bank was a small little bank in a two-story brick "store front" type building on School Street in Boston, just a few doors down from Old City Hall and just a few doors up the street from the Old Corner Bookstore. The bank backed up to one of Boston's most active parking garages, filled each weekday with the cars of people at work. The entrance was on Washington St. just northeast of School Street. The thieves in uniforms duped bank employees into thinking they were there to check on some systems, and they were allowed access to everything. They easily cut the wires to the bank's alarm system without being detected.

They picked a three-day weekend when the bank would be closed for a long time and the parking garage would be relatively quiet. They drove a large panel truck into the garage and backed it up into a parking space they had identified as the rear wall of the bank. The two back doors of the truck were opened and the back of the truck was up against the wall, so nobody could see what they were doing to the wall from inside the truck. When they succeeded in smashing through the wall and entered the bank, they had lots of time to drill out the locks of dozens of "safe" deposit boxes. Unfortunately, my friend's box was one of the boxes they accessed. Sadly, since all of the things were obviously "safe," he had not purchased any insurance.

There is a moral to this story. First, if you are going to use a safety deposit box, rent one in one of those large bank buildings that typically put their vaults underground inside specially designed protective construction or use a bank that is visible to the public on all sides and is in a frequently traveled area. .

62 POOR RICHARD'S ALMANAC
No, This Is Not Benjamin Franklin's Famous Work,

Richard Fink is an extraordinarily-nice, incredibly-generous friend, now living in Framingham, Massachusetts, a suburb due west of Boston. He was noted for his charitable efforts, leading an excellent jazz band that played at hundreds of fundraisers, usually for Shriners Burn Centers and Children's Hospitals.

Richard was the trumpet player, the leader of the band and still active at both. One story involves the heart of the problem our county, more than any other, faces with a plethora of lawyers and illustrates how people can earn a living without doing any work.

SCHOOL STREET CAMERA

For many years, School Street was the best camera store in Boston. Richard provided knowledgeable advice, top-quality photographic processing, and friendly service, in a very convenient location in the middle of the financial district of downtown Boston. School Street Camera may be a strange name for a business on Washington Street, but is had moved a short distance from a location on School Street.

School Street is a downhill one-way street past the Parker House Hotel and Boston's Old City Hall to where it ended at a traffic light on Washington Street, which was one-way to the left. School Street Camera was located on the opposite side of Washington Street, 20 feet to the left of the T intersection. One night, very late (about 1am), a young woman sped down School Street at very high speed, could not make the turn, and blasted through the heavy steel grate of the type that storeowners pull down and lock to the sidewalk to keep people from breaking the storefront's glass and stealing merchandize.

The police report revealed that the driver and her passenger had had a bit too much to drink (I think it must have been quite a bit too much) smashed through the grate, knocked out the brick bottom of the store's front wall along the sidewalk and the glass windows and display cases above (along with all of the expensive cameras) entered the store and knocked out the even-more-valuable-display case inside. Richard had just invested a lot of money in a state-of-the-art Kodak film processing and printing machine. It was installed in the floor below, but the crash above sent debris down into the innards of the delicate machinery. This was before digital photography.

This would be a story of a tough break, but not be much of a story if it were just drunk driving and insured damage. One absurd result provides evidence of the ridiculous state of our legal system in the United States.

The woman who had been the driver got a lawyer to take her case, claiming Richard should be liable for her injuries because School Street Camera's burglar prevention grate was too strong, causing damage to her, her passenger and her car. Would you believe it? It cost him legal fees but, at least, Richard won the case. Maybe this chapter should have been earlier under "Liability, *Try To Pin It On Somebody....Anybody.*"

PANHANDLING AS AN ART FORM

Panhandling does not sound like an attractive way of earning a living but, done properly, it can be easy and quite rewarding.

Washington Street, where School Street Camera was located, is a very busy pedestrian street, filled with people at most hours of the day and evening and quite crowded on weekdays. The spot where this story took place was on the route of Boston's Freedom Trail, so it attracted a lot of tourists who would pass there only once. A plainly dressed but attractive young girl picked out a spot on Washington Street, opposite the historic Old Corner Bookstore and immediately beside School Street Camera. She would sit down on the sidewalk, lean a hand-lettered poster board sign against the wall and place a bucket beside her into which people could make donations to her cause.

She had developed an elaborate story, capable of getting people to think her need was real and that their contributions would make a difference in solving her problem. She just sat there like a zombie, letting the words on the poster explain her plight. On the poster, she had written that she was not on drugs, but had been dumped by her boyfriend and just needed to raise enough money to get a plane ticket home to her family in California. She managed to keep a forlorn and quite innocent look on her face. In the many times I walked past, I never observed her speak a single word.

Having watched her on many occasions, Richard estimated that she averaged at least a dollar a minute, maybe two, so $60 or more an hour....not bad pay back in the 1980s (or even now, for that matter). On the few occasions I stood with Richard and watched her, she was taking in as much as a dollar every 30 seconds. Not bad. She came back almost every day, but did not bother if the weather was bad. She could make enough in a few hours to satisfy her, so she began to come there less frequently. It must have been enjoyable on a pretty day to sit there and watch the money come rolling in.

Richard paid to have her followed and learned that she lived in a fancy condo she owned in Marblehead, a high-priced town on the ocean north of Boston, She drove a nice Volvo. A widely known Boston newspaper writer published a column about her, but it did not impact her ability to earn a good living.

If it worked in Boston, it would work most places. Anybody want to give it a try?

63 THE TRAUMATIC DUO,
Larry and Richard Incandela

BACKGROUND

This chapter is about a terrifying business experience, much worse than were my stories of emergency landings in planes or a robber with a gun stuck in my stomach. This series of events involved several years of fear, literally fear for my life, or at least serious injury, as a result of a company I had selected to represent Woodside in the Chicago area. The sections of this chapter reveal some ridiculous business shenanigans and the four biggest business mistakes I made in my entire life.

Larry Incandela and his son, Richard, were a serious problem for me and for the company for a number of reasons, as you will read in the following sections. Picking Larry's company, IVI Travel, to be a part of the Woodside Group of Travel Agencies was a serious mistake, but I don't think it could have been avoided. We had top agencies in almost all of the major US cities, but not Chicago. I had to solve that problem. At the time, IVI was by far the biggest and best commercial travel agency in Chicago and went on to become one of the largest and highest-profile travel agencies in the country.

Woodside attempted to sign up as owners of our company the very best travel agencies specializing in business travel in their cities, and this usually meant the largest in each U.S. city. Later, this was in most major countries. Begun in 1973, the Woodside team began as a team of five US travel agencies. As a co-founder and later President, my primary job in the early days was researching potential participant companies (relying heavily on airline references, followed by in-depth personal inspections), leading to my report seeking approval of each agency by Woodside's Board of Directors. With this one exception, my choices were the most respectable travel agencies handling business travel in their cities.

By the mid1970s, Woodside had excellent representatives in most of the major cities throughout the country, the major exceptions being Chicago, Dallas and Minneapolis, three of the most important business centers. Representation in those cities was a necessity if Woodside was to claim, much less succeed, at handling a large corporation's travel in all the major business centers of the country.

IVI was a highly-innovative travel agency serving the Chicago area. IVI was clearly the biggest and best in Chicago and Chicago was one of the very largest business centers in the entire US, so there could be no other choice. IVI was closely allied with American Airlines and were highly instrumental in American's successful invasion into the heart of United Airlines' home territory. By installing American Airlines' SABRE computer reservations system, IVI directed more travelers to American's flights than would normally have been the case and enabled American to track usage by passengers on their competitor's flights and adjust their destinations and flights to and from Chicago to maximize effectiveness.

Woodside needed representation in Chicago so, despite my reluctance, I went with IVI. They were clearly the best in the city. My concern was about the head of the firm, Larry Incandela. He was jovial and a creative businessman and his company had quickly become the most successful in handling business travel in the greater Chicago area, but he was very rough. IVI operated a limo service, and this enabled him to schedule "black cars" to and from O'Hare Airport coordinated with people's flights, and it also meant IVI could claim 24 hour travel service, 7 days a week using the people who were there to handle limos.

He may have been a poor fit with the other agency owners, but he was the only game in town and arguably, the most innovative travel agency owner in the country (other than Heritage Travel). The first story is about Larry's son, Richard, who took over IVI after his dad's death.

A MEETING IN ENGLAND

The head of Woodside's operation in England, the Managing Director of Hogg Robinson' travel subsidiary, wanted to host a meeting of Woodside's Board of Directors in England, May 12-15, 1983. As a site, he selected Leeds Castle, built in 1119, 374 years before Columbus' discovery of the Western Hemisphere. The large castle sits on an island surrounded by a moat 4 miles south of Maidstone in the Kent region of England.

Our meetings were to be in the castle's large dining room, but we had the run of the castle in the evenings. Each person was assigned to a suite, most of which were huge elegant rooms having massive four-poster beds with elaborate canopies over the beds and antique draperies and finery on each side. It was quite something. The suites were named after kings and queens who had slept in them, so the saying they were "Fit for a King" was highly appropriate.

The castle is open to tourists and is now open for rental by the public, but in those days it was quite unusual, in addition to being extremely expensive. Tourists visiting the castle had to remain on routes through the castle, staying behind velvet ropes, off of the carpets and out of reach of the furniture in each room. Once the tourists were gone each afternoon, we could make ourselves at home, and one of the most enjoyable evenings was spent, after a great dinner and a few drinks (maybe many) singing while gathered around a beautiful antique piano played by one of our group. It was a fabulous three days, except for one thing.

THE GUEST BOOK

Leeds Castle justly takes great pride in a guestbook that has been signed by important visitors for centuries. Even though it was a treasured item, we were to be allowed to sign it. As you looked through the pages, history was revealed in the names of people who had stayed at the castle. Winston Churchill had held a secret meeting there with General Montgomery near the end of World War II. He was not royalty so he signed on a single line in the book. Meetings between the leaders of Israel and Egypt had been held at Leeds Castle preparatory to the famous Camp David summit meeting in Maryland. Tradition dictated that the royal family was always to have their signatures on a single page, shared with no one else. It was quite impressive to see the signatures of all the kings and queens who had visited Leeds Castle. The pages were quite large. They didn't sign on a line. They signed in huge letters diagonally so as to take up the whole page.

Almost everyone felt privileged to sign on a line of the guestbook. Richard Incandela had the audacity to sign in huge letters diagonally across an entire page, signing it "Richard I." The entire group was incredibly embarrassed and the Englishman who had hosted us, Brian Perry, had a very tough time apologizing on behalf of his company, Hogg Robinson, and the rest of his guests. Brian had me send another letter of apology, but the head of the castle was still furious. I often wondered how the Castle dealt with that page.

A SHOCKING AND VERY DISAPPOINTING EVENT

As Woodside gained great prominence in the field of business travel, we continued to look for agencies in smaller cities. In some cases, we were missing representatives in large business centers. There was no great choice in Dallas, but there was a good one, Hill World Travel, owned by Lyda Hill and recommended to us by American Airlines. Once Hill World was accepted, the Incandelas complained that they were planning to open in Dallas, claimed that IVI would have been a much stronger representative in that key market, and urged the Board to approve a plan under which a current member agency could "reserve" a city, thereby allowing expansion that would aid the existing member. The tone changed from being able to claim that we had the premier agency in every city.

At least the Board realized that the company needed agencies to contribute to Woodside's income as well as to provide a wider range of service to client companies that operated throughout the United States. A plan was devised whereby a current Woodside agency (everybody knew the only one was going to be IVI) could reserve the rights to a city if they would begin paying a substantial monthly fee and commit to opening within a reasonable period of time.

IVI began to pay for several cities and ended up paying for many. A key business center where our failure to have a representative was Minneapolis. Members of the Board urged me to find an agency in Minneapolis quickly so IVI would not add it to its list of "reserved cities." There were two excellent business travel specialists in Minneapolis, Corporate Travel and John Noble's Northwestern Business Travel. Corporate Travel, for complicated reasons, ended up being Woodside's representative.

Every time an agency was to be invited to join Woodside, I had to conduct and present a detailed study of a city and the information regarding a prospective member agency, including what I could discern from their financial statements, and its list of their largest corporate clients to Woodside's Board of Directors. Rich Incandela had just been elected to the Board, so I had to be careful, even though what I was doing had been endorsed by every other member of the Board.

Prior to the Board meeting by conference call at which the question of adding an agency in Minneapolis was to be addressed, I talked with every single member of the Board except Incandela, stressing my concern at even broaching this subject, much less my fear of having to report to the Board and recommend Corporate Travel as the agency for Minneapolis. Knowing Rich was going to be furious, I pleaded with every single member of the Board and every one of them promised to express strongly their support of my recommendation once the subject came up on the agenda for the meeting and to acknowledge that they had instructed me to take this course of action.

When I made my report by conference call to the Board, there was not one single comment. Not a sound. Every single one of them was afraid to go up again Rich. Did they fear Incandela as so many others did? I don't think the board members would have intended to put me roasting on the fire, but that was clearly what they did. In terror, I reminded them of their agreement and the fact that I would not have dared propose the agency in Minneapolis had they not each and every one said they recognized the severity of the problem and promised to speak up. When there was no comment from a single person, I panicked and reminded them again of their commitment. Still, no one said a word. It was dead silence. I pleaded again. They still did not speak. Rich Incandela did not say a word, but you could easily sense the fire coming through the phone line. Even after my desperate pleas, there was total silence. The vote to admit Corporate Travel proceeded, everyone but Rich voted "yes," the vote went through and the conference call ended.

It was not more than about ten seconds before my phone rang. Rich was livid and at his most violent, threatening me with one of his and his dad's favorites, throwing me overboard wearing concrete shoes into the Chicago River. It was terrifying. He was a board member; I may have been president, but I was an employee.

Two years later, at a Board Meeting in Rio de Janeiro, Rich lashed out at me on this subject once again and finally at least one Board Member, Charlie Benisch, calmly told Rich to back off, that I had followed the instruction from him and all the other Board members. It was too little too late, I was hated by the man who would, ever so briefly, be my boss and who later deliberately and single-handedly destroyed my job future.

Those board members' failure to honor their commitment and protect me from Rich's ire was the single most disappointing moment of my entire life. It was devastating, and not one of them, except New York's Ceb Benisch, ever apologized.

NO APOLOGY DUE

The widely-known joke at Woodside was the general agreement that when Rich Incandela got to be Chairman of the Board of Woodside, I would be fired immediately. That proved to be true. At the start of a Board meeting in Stockholm, he was elected Chairman and I was ousted as President. For years I had attempted to prevent IVI Travel from taking advantage of the other member agencies in Woodside. It was a time consuming, scary, and extremely frustrating endeavor.

I had made another mistake. Largely through the help of Max Hopper, the brilliant head of American Airline's SABRE reservation system, and my work creating and managing the numerous different airline hotel and car rental systems in Woodside Central, I had become quite knowledgeable about reservations systems and the dramatic changes that were expected. My board did not understand that and my Executive Vice President would not accept it, claiming that my refusal to endorse Woodside's spending a million dollars on its own system to link all of the other systems was blocking all progress. On his flight to Stockholm, Bill had taken advantage of time with Ceb Benish before the scheduled board meeting the next day in Stockholm to complain about my refusal to accept his ideas.

IVI Travel had become quite powerful. Add to that the fact that many of the Woodside agencies were afraid of the Incandelas. A key problem, primarily for me, was that I.V.I. would not pay their bills on time. Because of reserving cities, there monthly bills were higher than any other company. I would plead with them and various members of Woodside's Board of Directors would plead with them, all to no avail. They never offered an excuse; they just didn't pay. Shouldn't this have raised everyone's suspicions? It did mine. Once it had become so bad that I had to put my own money into the bank account to cover the payroll.

Russ Decker from Los Angeles, who at the time was Chairman of Woodside, told me to investigate IVI's financial problems. In addition to knowing that Woodside was not being paid large amounts on time and hearing from some of IVI's largest customers that they were not receiving rebate payments due them each month, I had heard that IVI had missed the deadline for its weekly payment due the airlines through their central payment mechanism, ATC in Washington, DC. This was a strict no no, something you simply could not do.

One of my best industry sources, Bill McCoy (an employee of ATC, the airline industry's supervisor of travel agencies), made the mistake of calling IVI's Larry Incandela and asking him if he had really missed a payment. Larry in his menacing style threatened to have Bill fired if he did not reveal who was checking on him and then went to the Woodside Board demanding an apology from me. Larry was powerful, Woodside had become overly dependent upon his payments to cover the cost of operating the central reservations office, and his frequent threats of violence against anyone he perceived as being against him, were hard to overcome. Larry had even threatened to open an office just over the Massachusetts state line in New Hampshire so that he could attack Woodside's founder, Don Sohn, who owned most of Heritage Travel in Cambridge, essentially Boston. I was forced to write a letter of abject apology, even though it was obvious that IVI was not paying its bills on time, not just to Woodside, but to many others.

OTHERS WERE FEARFUL

After Rich Incandela finally got to be the Chairman of the Board of Woodside and I had been ousted, there were highly-visible concerns expressed by the smaller agencies on the team. They feared Incandela. The revolt needed to be quelled, and Rich was urged by the Board to invite all of the concerned owners to meet with him in Chicago. This was clearly to address fears and alleviate concern about his power and abrasive and threatening attitude. What Rich needed to do was to at least appear understanding and benefit the organization by committing to fair play. The meeting was sorely needed.

What did he do? The people who attended the meeting came out of it in shock. If they wanted to remain on the team, they had to live with Rich in charge, but their calls to Boston were unanimously expressing shock at the way things were handled by Rich in Chicago. Instead of aiming for peace and quiet, the atmosphere in the meeting was established when the room was filled, the door to the meeting room was closed and a man was stationed at the door with a violin case in his hand, obviously implying that it contained a gun and that his threatening presence was intended to indicate the complainers were locked in the room and would not be allowed to walk out. How was this threat conveyed?

The attendees told me that Rich had hired Richard Kiel, the actor, to stand blocking the door. You almost certainly will not recognize his name, but you may remember the character he played in the James Bond movies. Richard Kiel was the 7'2" tall, 350 pound actor with the dangerous looking face who played James Bond's evil nemesis, "Jaws," in "The Spy Who Loved Me" and "Moonraker." What a great way to allay fear.

STUPIDITY

You many think it strange to admit to stupidity, but this next part of the Incandela saga was truly gross stupidity on my part. Not just very dumb; I was truly stupid. It was attributable to wishful thinking on my part, but you shouldn't fall in love with your job and the company you built to the extent that it blinds you from reality.

Six months earlier, I had received a call at 2am in Singapore from Joe Kordsmeier, the highly-respected Senior Vice President, Sales of Hyatt Hotels, asking if I would consider their offer to be Vice President Sales of the outstanding hotel chain that focused on corporate business years before most other chains did the same. The confrontation with Rich Incandela was still on the horizon, but I was still at Woodside and did not want to give that up. I guess I was always hoping that the Board of Directors would realize how dangerous Rich Incandela could be.

When I was forced out at Woodside's meeting in Stockholm and became Vice Chairman of the Board, I called Joe, asking if the position was still open. To my surprise, it was and he was still hoping to get me. I said that I wanted to pursue the subject of working for Hyatt. A series of trips to Chicago ensued. I met with the head of sales, Joe, the head of Personnel and the Hyatt's President, Pat Foley, for several days on each of several trips. Quite frankly, I don't see how I made much of an impression on the two new people, but I was offered the job. I was not told and did not know at the time that Joe was about to retire. Most of my talks were with Pat Foley because I would be reporting to him as soon as Joe departed.

I went back to my office on Tremont Street in Boston, overlooking the Boston Common with a great view up the hill to the State House. During the next few weeks, I made several trips to Chicago to meet with their real estate agent and look for places to live and to have more meetings with the Hyatt executives, attending dinners that included their wives. It wasn't just love of Boston, it was dislike of Chicago and, quite frankly, fear of the proximity to the Incandelas. The price of homes in the Boston area went through the roof years later, but at this point prices in Boston were still ridiculously low and what I was shown in Chicago was far beyond what I could afford, even with a big increase in salary.

After a few weeks, I set up two meetings in Chicago, the first with Rich Incandela, to determine where things stood, followed by a meeting with the three senior officers of Hyatt to let them know my decision.

As you might expect, I was lied to by Rich Incandela, and that lie had a hugely negative effect on the rest of my life. He assured me that Woodside was not looking at hiring a President to replace me. I should have known better. It simply did not make sense, but it was what I wanted to hear, and I suspect he knew that. Woodside was "my baby" and I did not want to lose my baby and certainly not leave her defenseless against what I knew would be problems with Rich Incandela.

Having accepted the commitment that Rich was not looking to hire a President, I took a cab to my meeting with Hyatt. If only I had waited another day or two to say "no." When I returned to Boston and relayed to the Woodside officers what Rich had said, there was an immediate, shocking response. They laughed. Didn't I know that the company was about to hire a man I could not stand, John Huggins, to be the new President? I had burned the bridge one day too soon and left myself in a totally untenable position.

CHEATING THE GOVERNMENT

As a result of all the story before this, I went back to my previous job at Heritage Travel. Heritage was exceedingly reputable and highly rated for service nationally. Martin Marietta Corporation, in Bethesda, Maryland, called us and us only about our taking over their business immediately from, as you might guess, I.V.I. Travel. Martin Marietta is a major US government contractor and, as a result, has lots of "cost plus" contracts. Having reviewed proposals, Martin Marietta had selected IVI Travel, which was widely known as the biggest rebater, meaning the biggest financial kickback for Martin Marietta.

The government's cause of complaint surfaced when it became known that Martin Marietta had created, as suggested by IVI, a scheme for concealing the rebates IVI paid to Martin Marietta, so the reduction in cost would not have be revealed to and therefore, shared with, the government. They had created a jointly-owned company that could be used to funnel the improper payments to Martin Marietta. The government paid the higher price and the deal with IVI was concealed. I was very surprised when I read in the newspaper that Martin Marietta had reached settlement with the United States in the summer of 2008.

Back at Heritage, my first involvement started when Martin Marietta called asking if Heritage would take over their account immediately. It was great to have such a good reputation. We had an excellent reputation in the District of Columbia market. We were, obviously, delighted and proceeded to plan. We did not have to compete, we were chosen on the basis of reputation. Our dreams were interrupted when the subject of a contract came up and the purchasing manager at Martin Marietta announced that they would be requiring an absolute guarantee that we could have the office operational on a certain date, so they could set a firm date for terminating IVI. We had established a new branch office for the IRS almost overnight, so several weeks should be no problem. There was a problem.

Martin Marietta's contract was going to require that the agency pay a large penalty ($25,000 per day) if *for any reason* the office was not operational on the required day. I thought that would be acceptable, assuming that they would certainly allow a standard legal exemption in the case of "Acts of God." If everything at Martin Marietta was OK on opening day, we could be confident that the office would be operational. If a fire destroyed their headquarters, it would be beyond our control.

To my amazement, Martin Marietta would not allow any exclusion from the penalty, even if the delay were clearly Martin Marietta's fault. How unreasonable can a company be? Don Sohn just felt there was no way Heritage could take that risk. Anyway, the Incandelas were out, even though we had to decline the opportunity to take their place.

THE SALE OF IVI

In January of 1986, I received a call from Rodney McLauchlan of Bankers Trust in New York (acquired in 1998 by Deutsche Bank) saying he had heard I would be the best advisor on a subject of great importance to his bank. He asked me to provide consulting services at a meeting to be held in Des Plains, near Chicago, at the headquarters of Wheels, Inc. My consulting rate, $2,000 a day ($4,700 a day in today's dollars), was no problem for the bank.

On January 29, Rodney was there along with three officers of Wheels, Inc., Zollie Frank (Chairman), his son Jimmy (president of the company) and Richard Friedman (Executive Vice President). Bankers Trust was also represented by Marjorie Greenspan. To my surprise, the subject was their possible acquisition of a one-half interest in IVI Travel. I spent the day answering questions, providing details of how the commercial travel agency industry operated. Wheels decided to proceed with the purchase.

Price Waterhouse was brought in to audit IVI and Coopers & Lybrand to provide the "Due Diligence." It was apparent, at least to me, that the Incandelas had concealed millions of dollars in current liabilities (many seriously overdue) and, to my astonishment, both the "expert" Price Waterhouse and the Coopers & Lybrand auditors had failed to uncover it. They were preparing to sign off on their audits. When asked, I told them where to look and how to look. For starters, they called some of the customers who had called me about IVI's failing to pay them. The accounting firm had to talk with the travel managers of I.V.I. major clients.

When the audit was completed, I was advised by Manufacturers that the hidden liabilities were so large that the amount that Wheels had agreed to pay for 50% of the company should result in their owning 80%. The Incandelas were to continue managing the business, but the revelations should have alerted the Franks to the risk of dealing with them. The Incandelas had concealed a huge amount of liability. Jimmy Frank told me that Incandela had refused to sell 80% and insisted that it had to be 100% or nothing.

The deal went through and Richard Friedman was moved from Wheels to serve as President of IVI. Only once the deal was done did I learn what had precipitated the sale.

When the sale had gone through, Rodney McLauchlan disclosed to me that Bankers Trust and Northern Trust had been giving IVI one last chance to raise capital before shutting IVI down and turning the company over to the banks'"workout" teams to sell off any assets and dissolve the business. My work with Wheels resulted in their paying millions for IVI, putting millions of dollars in the Incandela's pockets. Had the deal not gone through they would have lost it all. Also, Bankers Trust and Northern Trust would have lost tens of millions in unrecoverable loans.

If I had only known I could have steered the discussion in a different direction. The assets of a travel agency would have been an extremely small percentage of the huge loans due if it had ended in a workout. I always wondered what would have happened if I had not told the accounting firms where to find the concealed liabilities. Is it a prosecutable fraud to conceal major liabilities, something that had to have been done knowingly? The answer appears to be "yes." Would Wheels have sued? Would the Incandelas have gotten away with it and would Wheels have had a claim against Price Waterhouse?

I just wish I had insisted upon a percentage deal with Price Waterhouse that, instead of my earning a few thousand dollars in consulting fees, had required them to give me a percentage of what the millions they would have been liable for had their audit failed to uncover the dreadful situation. The sale had also saved many millions for Bankers Trust and Northern Trust, and would have resulted in the Incandelas losing all of their money. Given the incredible amount of pain the Incandelas had caused me over the years, I just wish the sale had fallen through and they had lost all the money. To have been the one who saved their money for them was an ironic twist at best.

Later, when I presented Wheels with a bill for my time advising them during the takeover of IVI, they flew to Boston to talk with me and very nicely paid me double my bill.

EPILOGUE

It is called "Just Desserts." Rich Incandela invested money in a private "club" near Chicago. Apparently, he could not resist making a "little extra" money from the club's members, whose monthly bills were charged to credit card accounts each member had designated. The false charges grew until members began to notice that there were frequent and sizeable “charges” for drinks and dinners on their bills, even though they had not been at the club on the dates reported. Rich was convicted and served a few years in prison. He emerged with plenty of money and Judy Harrington, who had been the Marketing VP of Woodside, left her nice husband in Auburndale, Massachusetts for Rich.

If only the sale to Wheels had fallen through and IVI been taken over by the two banks and shut down, with the Incandela’s losing everything. My fault.

A good friend told me that Rich had come to a Travel Trust International meeting in Dallas wearing jeans, a T shirt and a cowboy hat, looking to find a buyer for I.V.I. but having no takers. David Paresky, a member of TTI. confirmed that story.

64 PROPER ATTIRE

How You Look Can Make All The Difference

SPAIN

Having flown to Barcelona on business and completed my work there on January 12, 1982, I checked out of the Ritz and had all morning free before my flight at 2pm, so I asked the Concierge if he would get me a taxi with an English speaking driver to show me the city and then drop me at the airport. It was my first visit in Barcelona and I wanted to see some of the city before I had to fly out.

It may have been an exaggeration, but the concierge claimed there was no such thing as an English-speaking cab driver and that he would get me a limo with an English-speaking driver/tour guide. It was more expensive than a taxi would have been but not that much more, plus I appeared to have no alternative, I accepted.

The driver took me to several of the most important sites, including that fantastic Sagrada Familia cathedral designed by Spain's famous architect, Antoni Gaudi. Construction of the cathedral had gotten underway in 1882, but the work is ongoing, scheduled for completion in 2026 (if they are lucky, and construction does not fall behind schedule). Even though it is still far from finished, the construction site attracts more than two million tourists each year. In addition to the unusual architecture of the cathedral, there are many buildings throughout Barcelona displaying the elegant design style of Gaudi.

We were still in the tour plan when we began to pass through crowds lining the streets and noticed that we were in a line of black limos inching slowly up the street. My driver advised that the line must be for the gala VIP celebration of the opening of the Picasso Museum and that, arriving in the limo in my dark gray pinstripe suit, I could probably get in. When we finally reached the entrance, a man in uniform opened my door and guards waved me through the entrance, which was surrounded by security. I was welcomed over and over again as I was waved into the celebration only because of the way I looked.

Barcelona's Picasso Museum occupies five medieval palaces connected to form the museum. I must admit that, despite having studied Picasso in college and owning one of his works, the art itself in the museum was not that interesting, certainly not up to the Picasso collection of oil paintings standard in some of the great museums of the world.

I had agreed upon a time at which the driver was to meet me and continue my tour before heading to the airport. It worked like a charm. It can pay to look as if you are much more important than you are, and it certainly resulted in a nice afternoon getting to inspect the new museum with all the bigwigs of Spain. Barcelona is a very interesting city to visit. They operate a very effective tour bus system with A and B routes, the loops of which come together on La Rambla, the main street, so you can change easily from one to the other.

THAILAND

Boats have always been a special interest of mine, whether sailing in one, cruising the world in one, looking at beautiful old boats or seeing elegant shipmodels in musuems.

I was on business, this time in Bangkok, but my being there at that time was not a coincidence. I had read two years earlier that there was going to be a parade of the royal barges and numerous accompanying military ceremonial barges down the Chao Phraya River celebrating the anniversary of Thailand's Royal Family on April 5, 1982. Thailand's king, King Bhumibol, had been born near Harvard University at Cambridge's Mt. Auburn Hospital in 1927. He was crowned in 1946, and in 2009 was the longest reigning monarch in the world.

Many other countries in the Far East had to be covered on that trip, but I was able to schedule myself to be in Bangkok on the day of the celebration of the ruling family. The boats involved are all quite long; the King's golden and elegant barge is 138 feet long, rowed by large teams of oarsmen seated on either side of the boat. A man at the stern controlled the giant rudder and another gave instructions and provided the beat so that the oarsmen could stay in sync. The four most elegant barges have seats with canopies for the royal family, and the boats have elegant carvings all glistening with gold leaf.

I had no idea where I was when looking for a place to watch the parade. Stumbling across some sort of official reception, I decided to give it a try. Once again, my conservative suit paid off. Without showing any identification, I was whisked through security into a large reception with ample food and drink for the VIP guests. When the barges appeared to the right upstream from the party, I joined the other (mostly Thai) guests on the walkway along the riverbank to watch the royal procession.

After the royal barges had passed, I walked out on a dock to get a closer view of the other boats, and got a real close view when one of the lesser barges hit the pier while trying to tie up.

Once again, the only thing that got me in was my suit. Can you imagine getting through security today at someplace like the White House or Elysee Palace without your credentials and invitation's being thoroughly checked?

65 AMUSING MOMENTS IN THE AIR

Two Flights, One Too Long

GULF AIR

In the early days when the United Arab Emirates were just gaining prominence, Abu Dhabi was the most interesting of the emirates and the airline based there was Gulf Air, later headquartered in Bahrain. Gulf Air was not very big, but did an excellent job, primarily on the routes bringing Europeans and Americans to the gulf region.

Having been given a free first-class ticket by Gulf Air, heading on behalf of Woodside to meet with airline executives in Abu Dhabi, I was seated in first class in the middle of a group of people whose final destination was Africa for big game hunting. My wife had lived most of her adult years in Dallas and I love most Texans. To this day, Texans are among the most fun friends we have. The people around me were obnoxious Texans, utilizing every opportunity to display their wealth and talk about it. Not only were they loud and egotistical, they were dressed in what I considered outlandish attire. Cowboy shirts, hats and boots are fine, but ones adorned with jewels were a little bit much. I will take that back: they were over the top.

The Texans regaled the passengers with tales of where they were headed in Africa to shoot all sorts of wild animals. The stories would have been bad enough if they had not been broadcast to their fellow passenger in such loud voices. What was about to happen could not have happened to me at a better time. The plane landed and taxied toward the terminal and slowed to a crawl on the tarmac (or whatever you call the pavement) before reaching the terminal. A voice from the cockpit asked me to identify myself. The pilot said I was to deplane here. The plane stopped and the passenger door opened. There were two long limos waiting at the bottom of the steps. The pilot said, on the aircraft's address system, that the first parked beside the plane would take me to my hotel and I was to hand my baggage claim checks to the driver of the second limo so that he could claim my luggage and bring it to me later.

I was delighted, but in shock. I just wish I could have looked back and seen the faces of those obnoxious Texans. The special treatment could not have happened at a better time. By the way, you may have read about airlines that have for years been ranked as the best in the world. This accolade had usually been bestowed upon Asian airlines: Air New Zealand (for five years), Singapore, Thai or Cathy Pacific. Today, the best by far in my opinion are Emirates, Etihad and Singapore. The "bedrooms" in first class on Etihad are unequaled, essentially very small rooms with fold-down-to-flat "beds" and closable doors. For $20,000 to $30,000 you can get a room with a large queen-size bed. Emirates' airport hub, located remarkably near downtown Dubai, is huge and beautiful. Just like its owner, the government of Dubai, Emirates does everything *truly* first class.

Wish they had existed back when I was flying to Dubai. An amusing coincidence, years later the Dubai National Airline Transportation Agency (DNATA) bought my stock in Woodside.

The most recent survey by airlinerating.com states that they include in their comparison "environmental leadership." Do you think many travelers take that into account at all when selecting a carrier? They put Etihad down in 6th place and Singapore in 3rd. Not one single US airline is in their ranking of the Top 10, and I don't take issue with that.

The foreign carriers do have a huge advantage over those in the U.S. The operate not one single "domestic" flight and most of their international flights are long distance.

KUWAIT AIRLINES

I only got to fly Kuwait Airlines once. It was from London to Kuwait, a longer flight than you might imagine, about 2,900 miles (not much less than that flight over the Atlantic from Boston to London). You may recall from Gulf War I that Kuwait, a very small country, is at the northwestern corner of the Persian Gulf, immediately south of Iraq. Traveling on a free ticket, I found myself seated in first class on a 747 with just one other passenger, a Brit, in that entire section. After takeoff, we struck up a conversation and I eventually moved and sat in the aisle seat next to his seat beside the right window. This was one of those unusual 747s where in a seat close to the front you had an eerie feeling from looking slightly ahead rather than just out to the side. As written earlier, 747s were constructed with the nose closed in to avoid the very eerie and sometimes, on landing, scary sensation of looking straight ahead.

The man said he had to fly to Kuwait fairly often and always hated it because, although the food was fine, you could not get a glass of wine, much less a stronger drink, to go with it. What happened then was a great surprise.

The stewardess rolled up a large cart covered with different bottles of booze and wine with a silver cooler of ice and beautiful glasses. She said that she was in shock. She did not know who I was, that it normally was absolutely prohibited due to religion, but the drinks had been loaded upon the plane and she had been instructed to bring me whatever I wanted to drink. I was happy, but the thirsty guy beside me was ecstatic. I did have to explain why my job resulted in this kind of treatment and that I was en route to meet with some senior executives of Kuwait Air. A long trip turned out to be truly memorable.

THE LONGEST FLIGHT

Over the years, I have listened to many complaints about long flights and jet lag, some regarding what I would have considered relatively short flights such as TransAtlantic. This business trip I took was truly exhausting, even for me, a fitting ending after two good stories. For those of you who complain about long flights, this story should make you feel better.

My trip originated in Boston with a 6,600 mile flight to Tokyo for a day of meetings. When I finished my meetings in Japan sometime in the afternoon, my flight took off from Tokyo. That flight's destination was Perth, Australia, with a stop in Hong Kong on Cathy Pacific. This segment was just 1,797 miles (roughly two thirds of the way across the United States). Hong Kong's airport has now been replaced by a huge new airport, Chek Lap Kok, way out northwest of Kowloon, but until mid-1998, Hong Kong's airport, Kai Tak, stuck out into Hong Kong Harbor, right in the middle of things. It used to be a challenging landing for the pilots and passengers were known to get nervous, too. The airport had only one long runway, it wasn't that long by current standards for large jets and it usually involved approaching from the west, clearing a mountain ridge by just 300 feet before diving down to the start of the runway. You had to touch down close to the start of the runway because if you overshot you were in the harbor (as one jumbo jet did). When planes skimmed over that cleared ridge, passengers felt as if they were looking in the windows of buildings on both sides. It was hairy.

I don't have a record of what day or year it was, but it was Chinese New Year at about nine o'clock and as we approached the Hong Kong airport we had a great view of all the fireworks being launched from barges in the harbor. After that, on to Perth, way down in the Southern Hemisphere on the southwest coast of Australia. This segment of the flight, by itself (about 3,600 miles), would be considered by most people, pretty long

There was a long wait before my next flight, this one being so bad that I only remember the name of the airline. It was South African Airlines flight 283. The flight flew west from Perth and landed on the island of Mauritius to refuel before going on to near the southern tip of Africa, landing in Johannesburg. Mauritius is a 38-mile-long island far south in the Indian Ocean, east of Madagascar. This flight alone, 5,581 miles, was so long that they helped pass the time by serving five meals and showing four movies. That flight alone is more than double flying New York to Los Angeles.

South Africa is strange in that it has three "capital" cities, one legislative, one judicial and one administrative, none of which is the country's largest city, Johannesburg. I shaved in the plane's restroom and tried to get cleaned up and presentable before getting off the plane and going to the Westin Hotel to give my speech at lunch. Then it was back to the airport to catch British Airways #54 that evening to London. From way down south near the tip of Africa, the flight took off in the evening and refueled at exactly midnight in Nairobi, Kenya, before continuing to London. We landed at Heathrow near London at daybreak the next morning in time for me to get on BA's 277 morning flight to Boston, where I had to speak at a small dinner hosted by the Sheraton Corporation that night.

I don't want to hear anybody complaining about being tired from a "long" flight after they have read this. That series of flights totaled 27,166 miles. I am surprised I was able to stay awake through that dinner. I have flown westbound around the world several times, but that was always with many stops to do business in major cities. By the way, jet lag bothers you much less traveling westbound than it does eastbound.

SHORTEST AIRLINE FLIGHT IN THE WORLD

While talking about countries and airlines in the Persian Gulf, it is appropriate to mention a very unusual fact about one of the smallest countries in the area. Bahrain is a little island on the western edge of the Persian Gulf, just a few miles off the coast of Saudi Arabia.

Bahrain had always been afraid of its huge, powerful and extremely-conservative neighbor, Saudi Arabia. You could see the coastline of your destination, Dharan, Saudi Arabia just 25 miles away as you took off from Bahrain's airport. It may be the only place where you can see your destination as your plane lifts off from your airport of origin. In my days there you had to fly to travel between the two countries (I guess some took a boat).

Until recently, the flight between those two countries was the shortest scheduled route for flights anywhere in the world. The planes essentially just took off and began their approach to land. Flight times in airline guides are normally the gate to gate time. In this case, the time actually in the air was just a few minutes. I only had to fly this route twice. For years, both countries avoided the idea of constructing a bridge to connect the two countries. It would be relatively easy, a short bridge over shallow water. Why not?

The Saudis were nervous about the prospect of their carefully-controlled population having easy access to what they believed to be the relatively-wild living on Bahrain. Conversely, Bahrain was nervous about the prospect of falling under the super-conservative rule of Saudi Arabia. Finally, the King Fahd Causeway, was built, and no serious problems resulted for either country. Recently there have been problems between the Saudis and the minority that controls Bahrain. Given the existence of the bridge, I doubt any airline flies that route today.

A SCARY NIGHT IN THE SKY

My nighttime flight was not all that scary but many passengers were quite apprehensive. The pilot had to reassure them several times. I had to fly to Seoul, Korea on business and had been given a first class ticket by Korean Airlines. My trip had to be arranged far ahead and all my meetings in Korea had been scheduled. As luck would have it, my flight on Korean #007, a 747, was the first plane to take the route from New York to Anchorage and finally Seoul after flights had been suspended a few days earlier because of the Russians' shooting down on September 1, 1983, Korean Airlines Flight 007. It strayed over Russian territory. Many Americans know that Alaska's Aleutian Islands stretch in a long arc west of Alaska but do not know that there is also a long line of Japanese Islands stretching northeast from Japan's Hokkaido Island and that both of these long chains of islands stretch essentially all the way to Russia.

On long international flights the normal practice it to follow a "Great Circle Route" which is the path you see if your use a globe and stretch a string straight from point to point. When shown on a printed page the arc looks curved, and therefore longer. In this instance, that Great Circle Route would take you over the 800-mile-long Kamchatska Peninsula and then over 421-mile-long Sakalin Island, both Russian. Pilots had to deviate and be sure to fly south, staying clear of Russian territory. Korean Airlines Flight 007 had flown over Russian territory, Sakhalin Island, and was shot down by a fighter plane. It would have been obvious to the fighter pilot that it was a passenger plane, but US Russian relations at the height of the Cold War were very tense, and this event made it much worse. Although the plane was Korean, the Russians blamed the US. The passenger plane had already crossed the island and was back over the water when shot down near Moneron, a small Russian Island 32 miles west of Sakhalin. All 269 passengers and crew aboard were killed.

All of the passengers on my flight breathed a sigh of relief when we had passed uneventfully beyond where the tragedy had occurred just a few days earlier. I had gotten a right window seat in first class so I could look at the lights of Sakhalin as we flew by in the dark.

When a passenger plane crashes, its flight number is removed from use and a new number assigned to future flights on that route. For some reason, this one stayed as 007, an interesting number given the James Bond books of the time. I bet very few Americans know that there was a land battle on US territory during World War II. There was just one, on Attu Island in May of 1943, where 580 Americans were killed, just 211 miles east of Russia. Also in the Aleutians, Semisopochnoi Island certainly is thought of as far west, but because it is technically in the Eastern Hemisphere, west of the International Dateline, it is *by far* the *easternmost* part of the US.

AN EXTREMELY IMPORTANT RESULT

Korean Airlines Flight 007 caused a major change in US policy when the Reagan Administration gave the world the right to use something that had been a U.S. secret called DNSS. The Korean Airlines tragedy resulted in the world's being allowed to use our Global Positioning System. GPS provides much more accurate navigation for planes and boats and, although less important, for automobiles and hikers.

66 WHAT A SURPRISE!!!!
Kendall Square, Cambridge

Earlier there have been several mentions of Heritage Travel, started in1965, when two friends, Don Sohn and Lolly McDonald (now Mitchell) and I decided we should get together and start a travel agency, many decisions had to be made. The agency, started with one manager and his secretary, grew to be the seventh largest in the US, with offices throughout the county, but its start was less than auspicious.

One of the first things you have to do is decide what you want to do. The idea of a travel agency emanated from the fact that Lolly had started and was the President of a great ski club, the Chamois Ski Club of Boston. We ran charters every winter to ski in Switzerland, took large groups every year to Aspen that included stops to ski Vail each of Vail's first twelve years in business, and last but not least, groups to ski Australia combined with New Zealand and a trip to Chile and Argentina. Having no idea of ending up specializing in business travel, our subtitle was "The agency for skiers."

The next thing we had to do was pick a name. Lolly was from Kansas City, Missouri, and knew the Mark Hall family. You probably don't know that they are the reason the big greeting card company got named Hallmark. We liked the name, and decided our company could denote similar quality by adopting the name "Hallmark Travel." Our lawyer, Bill King, supposedly checked everything out and proceeded to set us up under that name. We opened a bank account with New England Merchants National Bank and had checks and business cards printed. I still have some of those.

Fairly soon thereafter, I received a phone call from the owner of a small agency in downtown Boston. He called to our attention the fact that his rinky-dink agency in Boston with the awful name of "Jimminy Cricket Travel" had also used the name Hallmark Travel. Although this name had not been recognized by our contacts in the airline and travel agency businesses, all we would have had to do was look in the phone book. There it was, clear as day. Don was across the Atlantic in the Canary Islands, so Lolly and I had to pick a name, and our choice was Heritage Travel.

The next decision was where to locate the office, and this was more complicated. In the early sixties, airlines had city ticket offices and some offices in the suburbs. There were also many travel agencies scattered throughout Greater Boston. In order to receive approval from the airlines (it was called "appointment") to be in business, you had to show a need for your business, and this meant you could not locate near any existing airline or travel agency office. The airlines were successful for many years in prohibiting travel agencies from having offices at airports because there was obviously no "need."

It was difficult to find an unclaimed spot. Don was one of the few who did not just have an MBA, he had a doctorate from the Harvard Business School, and Lolly had graduated from Harvard's B School in their first class to accept women. Don had taught at the B School and the Sloan School of Business of the MIT near Cambridge's Kendall Square.

I had graduated from Harvard College, so somewhere in Cambridge appeared interesting. Agencies were already in business in Harvard Square (the heart of Cambridge) and at the other major squares throughout the city. Don knew Kendall Square well. It was pretty desolate; there was almost nothing there, certainly no major business and virtually no residences, other than MIT offices and dorms, but we had little choice.

The good news was that, it might take years, but Kendall Square was about to become a bustling center of activity. The President of the United States at the time had been, as most of you had heard, another graduate of Harvard named John F. Kennedy. As a reaction to the Soviet Union's shocking success with Sputnik, the first manmade object to circle the earth, Kennedy had announced the creation of the National Aeronautics and Space Administration, with their stated objective being to place a man on the moon fast. Bringing the huge development to Kennedy's home state, NASA was to be headquartered in Cambridge. Because of the heavy involvement of scientists at MIT, NASA headquarters were to be at Kendall Square, which, despite the name, is a triangle.

Hundreds of old buildings were torn down and a large area of Cambridge, several dozen blocks, became barren dirt. Construction on the high-rise office tower that was to be NASA's executive offices at 55 Broadway was underway, just one block from the center of Kendall Square. Heritage was well positioned to handle the massive influx of customers.

THE SHOCKING AND SAD SURPRISE

You sometimes find places or streets or places named after someone who had a major effect on the place. I said in jest, and at that, still not well received, that Kendall Square should be renamed Lee Harvey Oswald Square. His assassination of Kennedy that fateful day in Dallas resulted in Lyndon Johnson's becoming President. He wanted all those NASA jobs in Texas, certainly not in Massachusetts. "NASA Headquarters," sat empty for many years before becoming the Massachusetts Department of Transportation.

Finally, after many more years, the dozens of blocks of barren land were filled with office buildings, including many high-tech companies that wanted to be near MIT. Heritage's location, 245 Main Street, was finally a great place to be.

67 LOGAN AIRPORT
An Exciting (and deadly) Night

Flying back to Boston on Northwest Airlines coming from Great Britain sitting at a right side window in first class, I was talking with some IBM guys flying home from Glasgow.

Because I served for many years on the airport's Advisory Committee, I was quite familiar with the airport. Planes landing from the northeast using runway 22 R (this indicates the direction when approaching from the northeast, in this case 220 degrees from due north) usually touched down on stripes painted on the runway a few hundred yards past the water of the harbor, well before coming abeam of the control tower on the right. Our plane stayed in the air until the point where the control tower was abeam out of the right-hand window. That meant our plane had wasted 4,700 feet of runway…almost a full mile. Needless to say, I expressed surprise at this.

Once we were on the ground, the pilot made the engines blast in reverse but could not slow down enough to make the normal right turn onto the taxiway to head to the terminal. He had given up so much or the runway that he had had much less than normal runway to come to a stop and turn right onto the last exit taxiway. When the pilot reversed the engines it felt as if he had slammed on the brakes, finally coming to a stop very close to the end of the runway.

Shortly thereafter, a World Airways jumbo, in my opinion, must have had the same problem, but it went off the end of the long runway and crashed into Boston harbor. From the end of the runway where the last exit from the runway to the taxiway sat, it is another 1,951 feet to the water of the harbor. The World aircraft broke in two just behind the cockpit, with the nose of the plane falling into the harbor. The break was near the front of the first class compartment, and some seats at the split point went into the harbor. They never found the two men who had been in those seats. We were stuck for a long time after retrieving our luggage, hearing the siren's blasting while they closed the tunnel access to and from the airport into Boston to allow fast passage of ambulances. In those days, the old Sumner Tunnel was the only way downtown.

It was very awkward being interviewed by the National Transportation Safety Board in the months following. I thought something had to have been wrong with the landing system that night, causing planes to stay in the air much too long, leaving too little runway for them to stop. The airport was immediately shut down after this happened about 7:30 that evening. NTSB did not sound the least bit interested in my information.

68 SKIING

Expert Advice From "Friends" (or were they?)

The best way to snow ski well is to start early in life. This is fine if you live in Massachusetts but a bit difficult growing up in Alabama. I started too late, in my late teens in college. Skiing all over the world, including five continents (even Africa), was fun and I could get down a mountain on expert-rated trails, but I never learned to be an expert. I blame the problem on bad advice from good friends who *were* expert skiers.

Going straight is generally easy; it is the turns that are difficult and that difficulty increases dramatically the steeper the terrain and the longer the skis. During the late sixties, the Graduated Length Method came into use. You started on short skis that were easy to control and, as you became more proficient at turning, moved up to longer and longer skis. It was long before that method became known and accepted.

For my 6 foot 1 inch height, starting in the 170 centimeter range would have been the generally accepted length under GLM. That would translate to just 5 feet 7 inches. My friends had told me that you should reach up with your arm and buy skis the length of where you could reach with your fingertips. My first skis were 220 centimeters (7 ft. 3 inches) and, even worse, they were super-stiff Kastle brand that were needed by expert racers seeking the fastest speed. Softer, more flexible and much shorter skis would have been much better for a beginner.

Unfortunately, my version of the GLM that was the reverse of what it should have been. The "friends" had me changing in the wrong direction, moving shorter and shorter until I settled on 185 centimeters (about 6 ft. 2 inches), but this was years after I had done most of my skiing. The other problem was having friends who were expert skiers who wanted to ski the expert trails…here again, skiing with them was *not* the way to learn. They also loved Aspen's Ruthies Run, which had absurdly-steep moguls (mounds of snow created by many skis going around them). The experts used the moguls to help their turns; I just worked my way around them.

A SCARY AFTERNOON

One of the worst things my "friends" did was get me to join them skiing New Hampshire's Mt. Washington. Mt. Washington did not have a ski lift (and still does not), and it gets lots of snow (Tuckerman Ravine supposedly averages about 75 feet a year) and Mt. Washington holds the record for the highest winds ever recorded on earth. To get to the top, you took a small bus up the mountain. When you skied the East Snowfield, you had to ski down and then climb back up to take another run. This was only feasible in the very late spring. I skied there only once, May 16, 1965. A friend posted on YouTube a video of my skiing Mt. Washington's east snowfield shirtless and wearing shorts. The video is still on youtube. Search my name and Tuckermans.

It was fun because I didn't fall into what is remarkably sharp snow. So far it was a fun day, but late in the afternoon Dick Kirk and Tom Brennan laughingly told me they had deliberately waited so long that the only way down was to ski over and down into Tuckerman Ravine. It does get less steep like the sides of a bowl as you ski down, but looking down from the top, the Headwall appears to be a cliff of snow, *not* skiable.

Most ski slopes may look steep but are only about a 35-degree slope. Beginners slopes are more like 15 degrees. Expert, "Black Diamond" trails get up into the mid 40 degrees. The lip of the Headwall at Tuckerman Ravine is about 65 degrees. To me, it looked more like 80 degrees. Remember a vertical wall is 90 degrees. When you get to it and know you have to go over it the feeling is one of total terror.

From the crest of the lip the snow below you is so steep you can't see it directly beneath the lip. Luckily, I learned that the best course for me was to ski south to a point where the lip of the ravine was less steep. After I got the nerve to start I got down about a hundred feet before noticing a man climbing up in front of me. In contrast with walking up a slope, I took a picture of the man with his skis on his back jabbing his hands into the snow in front of him as he kicked the toes of his ski boots into the snow to climb upward a short distance below The Headwall. Hopefully, that indicates how steep steep is.

An annual "Inferno" race was held annually since the thirties. A skier named Toni Matt on April 16, 1939 went over the lip of The Headwall going so fast he did not dare try to turn, schussing the entire trail in 6 minutes and 29 seconds. It took me an hour and a half. In summer skiing the East Snowfield, you have to weave your way down through numerous rocks.

Once you get to the bottom of the ravine, at least to the end of the open area above the tree line, it is still 2.3 miles on a narrow trail to the highway where our cars were parked at Pinkham Notch.

ASPEN

For about fourteen years, I organized Chamois Ski Club flights to Denver for large groups to ski Aspen, Colorado, back when Aspen Mountain was still named "Ajax," before Vail opened. In later years, we would fly to Denver, rent cars, drive over the dreaded Loveland Pass (before the big tunnel was built), ski one day in Vail and then on to Aspen. We skied Vail every year for its first 12 seasons. If I had paid enough attention to mortgages and short-term rentals, I should have bought Vail's Clocktower (which housed one multi-floor apartment) for just $29,000, right in the middle of town.

I organized a picnic every year in a fairly flat area at the start of the Buckhorn Trail. Amusingly, years later I discovered that a friend in whose wedding I had been an usher had attended one of those picnics and had a picture of us to prove it. Harry Shaw was later President of Huffy Bicycle.

SNOWMASS

Running the ski club that brought lots of business to Aspen every year, I was invited to ski Snowmass in a very small group hosted by D.R.C. Brown, the man who had helped get Aspen Ski Corporation started in 1946 and was serving as President. Snowmass didn't open until December of 1977, so in March of 1976, the group had to ride up the mountain in a Tucker Snowcat…there were no lifts yet.

We were served lunch at the top and then started to ski down. With no skiers on the mountain, there was nothing but very deep powder. I had never skied in powder and quickly learned that it was an entirely different skill. You couldn't see your skis down in the snow. Because I was by far the poorest skier, the others left me and I skied alone, something you should never do, especially in deep un-broken powder.

Suddenly, I fell and found myself head down in the snow with my feet still strapped in the skis directly above me. My bindings did not release and I suspect that was a good thing. Had a ski come off and slid down the mountain, I suspect it would have been close to impossible to walk down in snow so deep.

The snow must have been at least seven feet deep because I couldn't reach the ground beneath my head. It was arduous, exhausting, very time consuming and incredibly difficult digging away at the snow until I could get my skis back under me and begin skiing down. If I had not managed to dig out, I would have been left hanging upside down to die. You couldn't see me. They might have discovered I was missing, but under the snow on that huge mountain I doubt they would have found me.

Just like we were taught at summer camp that you should be assigned a buddy with whom to swim, skiers in remote areas should abide by The Buddy System.

MY FUNNIEST SKIING

Once again flying home to Boston from meetings in Germany, the bank's lawyer, Bud Page, and I decided to come home via Morocco, a place most Americans miss. It was marvelous, very interesting, certainly exotic and, way back in the late 60s, very inexpensive. We spent a few days exploring Casablanca on the Atlantic coast, before getting a rental car and driving inland and 141 miles south to Marrakesh.

The hotel we stayed in, the famous Mamounia (now about $500 per night) today is far down the list of hotels that now includes elegant and very expensive ones such as a Four Seasons. The entire city is splendidly exotic.

From there we drove south again, this time only about 50 miles, to Morocco's primitive ski area, Oukaimeden, in the High Atlas Mountains.

It may have basic facilities, but it was quite an experience. The drive up the mountain to the ski area passes through what I would call desert and the ski area itself is only about 150 miles from the vast expanse of desert that stretches across all of northern Africa.

The Moroccan army was training there and it was strange to see men carrying lots of military gear on their backs while skiing and others galloping back and forth at the bottom of the lift on camels. The trails, mostly the open slope of Jebel Attar Mountain, are poorly marked. I recommend Marrakesh, but unless you are an avid skier who wants to be able to say you have skied in Africa, don't bother.

69 AN ANNUAL CRUISE IN CALIFORNIA
The Tinsley Island Regatta

San Francisco has two major annual bachelor outings. The first one, Bohemian Grove, is quite intellectual and attracts leading scholars, senior government officials and top corporate executives from all over the country.

The other, the Tinsley Island Regatta, is for members of the St. Francis Yacht Club, at the time all males, the most prestigious yacht club in the western U.S. Tinsley Island is the "exclusive and elegant" property of the St. Francis Yacht Club, located in the middle of the San Joaquin River, about 65 miles upstream from San Francisco and just a dozen miles northwest of Stockton. The Club is exclusive, but their island was *not* elegant. I was delighted to be invited by Eric Scow as a guest for the famous regatta held September 28-30, 1976. Three of us were in his very small sailboat. The third was Clay Jackson, about whom there is some info at the end of this chapter.

On the final day of the Regatta, all of the beautiful power yachts take a tour of the rivers and canals that exist around Tinsley Island. Guests who arrived on smaller boats are invited on board the beautiful yachts for the annual cruise, which is largely a parade of beautiful power yachts.

First, we came upon a small open boat anchored in one of the rivers. In the boat were a man in the stern with the outboard motor and in the bow stood a fairly decent looking but scantily attired woman, holding up a sign that said she was available for something like $50. Everybody got a good laugh out of that, but I did not know there was more ahead.

The second boat had a less-decent-looking woman more scantily attired advertising her availability for $25. This went on and on as the women became less and less attractive and the asking prices came steadily down. Probably the better way to describe it was that the subsequent women were more and more unattractive. Maybe "gross" would be the best word.

Anyway, the finale was a woman you would have trouble imagining, very fat and very ugly. Her sign read for you to "come and get it," she would pay you. Even at that rate, there would certainly be no takers. My question was where in the world did they find a woman willing to be the one in the final boat? Standing there in any boat naked would have been bad enough.

I do not know if the regatta still gets away with this great interlude. I don't even know if it has survived as an all-male event, but it appears to still be in late September and is now called the "Stag Cruise." This all took place in public waterways near Tinsley Island.

While the parade was underway, a few small boats with families, including young kids, happened to pass the places where the women advertised their wares. They must have had quite a shock.

BOAT NAMES

The boat I was on for the Tinsley Island Regatta was a Tartan 30, a thirty-foot long sailboat that was pretty crowded for the three of us, especially when it was time to sleep. The boat had an unusual name that became well known throughout the world of sailboat racing. The boats name was "ICFIGIN." Eric also had a beautiful racing yacht, also named *"ICFIGIN."*

Years later, Eric's daughter, then a student at University of California, Berkeley, wrote a paper on marketing of tee shirts with the boat's name and logo. In addition to writing the paper, which got her a very good grade, she actually sold the items bearing the ICFIGIN logo along with the word. The word ICFIGIN and the design are trademarked. You can Google the word and see that it has trademark #75717164. The professor for whom she had written the paper and who had given her the good grade, finally could not resist and inquired about the name. Prudes should not read the next paragraph.

It stood for "I Can Feel It Going In Now" and the logo used on the flags and the tee shirts was a black red and yellow flag which, once you knew what the word meant, was obviously a black pecker with red balls against a yellow background. I wonder how many parents saw their kids wearing those T-shirts and never learned the meaning.

CLAY JACKSON

Clay was a lawyer in San Francisco who, as a powerful lobbyist, had spent time in prison for attempting to bribe a congressman. San Francisco's Nana Lee, told me that Clay had worked out in prison, losing lots of weight and getting in good shape. She said he was arguably rated as California's most powerful lobbyist. He was always a big guy, having played football at USC, weighing 270 pounds. Nana said that USC was nicknamed the "University for Spoiled Children." I certainly did not know any of this when I was spending days on the boat with him.

70 ANCESTRY

The Good, The Bad and The Very Bad

A GOOD GRANDFATHER

For my first 66 years, I never paid any attention to my ancestors. I did know that my dad's father, Thomas Harvey Clark, had been Speaker of the House in Alabama in1894. He had been editor of the *Selma Times* shortly after the Civil War and was hired from there as an editor by my hometown newspaper, the Montgomery Advertiser.

I think of him every time we drive downtown because Interstate 85 goes "under his house" which was what is now up in the air on the Lawrence Street overpass.

Upon his retirement, he was presented with a beautiful sterling silver service, probably still out there in the world somewhere. He-was also given an elegantly carved, gold-handled black walking stick, the handle of which was engraved "To THC," I had this on the coffee table in my apartment on top of Beacon Hill in Boston for many years and, foolishly, left it out on display. It was stolen in the 1980s, so if you know where it is, I would love to have it back.

When this story comes up the most frequent comment is that, saying it was in 1894, I must be talking about my great grandfather. No, Thomas Harvey Clark was just my grandfather. He was born in 1857 (lived through the Civil War) and my dad was born August 1, 1890.

There is one funny story about the girl grandfather married, Carrie Marks, one of my grandmothers. In the 1960s a good friend, Jimmy Loeb, was the principal financial supporter of Landmarks, which organized, purchased and moved many old buildings from around the city into the area now known as Old Alabama Town. It is now comprised of a few dozen antique houses on or near Montgomery's North Hull Street. Jimmy told me he had donated the money to pay for the house my grandmother grew up in on Goldthwaite Street to be moved down the steep front yard to the street, left on Goldhwaite and then right onto the steep hill of Bell Street, through downtown and on into Old Alabama Town, where it is rented by Landmarks to the Alabama Nurses Association.

Shortly after the move was underway, the house fell off its rollers as the movers tried to negotiate the turn downhill onto Bell Street and it took a good while to get it lifted back up. The house had blocked the entrance to the motel, possibly the first in Montgomery, causing the loss of business. Not, however, as much as they claimed. The motel sued Landmarks, a non-profit, for $10,000. Jimmy said he laughed at them, saying "They were welcome to sue but the non-profit had no money."

A BAD GRANDFATHER
I also know that my mother's dad, James McLendon, had run off, deserting my Mom, her sister (Juliette Persons) and their mother (Mabel Maude Champion McLendon), leaving them destitute during The Great Depression). In those days, in Alabama, her name was pronounced "May Bell."

It appears that grandfather was charming and a good talker. After leaving his family, he somehow found his way to Kentucky (I was corrected, having thought it was Missouri), where we were told he married the daughter of the state's Governor. His "new" wife and her dad must have been in shock when it was discovered that he had not bothered to get a divorce from his wife, my grandmother. He was tried, convicted of bigamy and put in jail. My aunt and my mother thought this was great, at least well deserved, but inadequate punishment for what he had done to them. Note that I have tried to verify this old family story but have not been able to find any evidence that the part about bigamy ever happened. Three people, all now long dead, did tell me it was true.

This was one of those instances where a family does not want to acknowledge that a close relative even exists. For sixteen years I believed that both of my grandfathers had died many years earlier. The death of my father's father was easily apparent. There was simply no mention, ever, of James McLendon…according to my mother and her sister, he simply did not exist, which I interpreted to mean he had died.

One day when we were living in our new house on Woodley Road the phone rang and I answered it. The man said he was my grandfather and had just called to congratulate his grandson because of an article about me that had just appeared in the local newspaper. I was not sure how to respond and was obviously very surprised to hear that I had a living grandfather. It was little bit like that incarnation of evil in the Harry Potter series, Voldemort, who could never be called by name.

I continued listening when my mother walked into the dining room about forty feet away. When she asked who was on the phone, I turned and said that I was talking with my grandfather. She charged across the living room, screamed that I did not have a grandfather, grabbed the phone from my hand and slammed it down on its cradle. Many years later I learned that he lived in a little yellow house on Highland Avenue at the corner of Polk Street. To my knowledge, I don't think I ever saw him. We never even knew (at least I didn't) when he died.

A VERY BAD GREAT GRANDFATHER (or was he?)
When living in Savannah, I learned that my great, great, great, great, great grandfather, George Mathews, had been Governor of Georgia in the late 18th Century, first in 1787

and then again in 1793-94 He was, strangely, governor twice, having been elected, served his term, not run for re-election, and then ran and won again. He had also been a general under George Washington, a member of the Virginia House of Burgesses and had represented Georgia in our country's first Congress (March, 1789 to 1791).

I couldn't wait to tell two local lawyers who were experts on the history of Savannah and Georgia. When I told them what I had discovered about my ancestor, the two history buffs, Ty Butler and Walter Hartridge, snickered and then really laughed. They proceeded to tell me that my ancestor had probably been the biggest crook ever elected to public office in the state.

In the late 1700s, the grant by the king that was originally "Georgia" extended all the way from the Atlantic to the Mississippi River. Georgia's northern boundary was from just south of Highlands, North Carolina, all the way to 9 miles south of Memphis, Tennessee. This is why you see that straight line that is still today the northern border of Georgia, Alabama and Mississippi that stretches all the way across the three states. The other line is for the most part the southern borders of Georgia, Alabama and Mississippi. It is the primary reason that beautiful stretch of white sand beaches that are in the Florida Panhandle do not belong to Alabama.

In January,1795 Governor Mathews signed into law the act of the Georgia Legislature that sold Georgia and to their cronies, first 40 million acres, land which would become a major portion of Mississippi. They later sold similar huge amounts of acreage, once again, about 40 million acres, in what became Alabama. These sales occurred on several occasions. Because one of the primary companies purchasing the land was named after the Yazoo River in Mississippi, the sale became known as the *Yazoo Land Fraud.* A significant number of the legislators had accepted stock in the Yazoo Land Company, essentially bribes, to get them to vote for the sale, which was priced at about one cent per acre.

To the public, it was an outrageous transaction. The citizen protests wended their way all the way up to the US Supreme Court, which in 1810 ruled in *Fletcher v. Peck* that the legislators were duly elected and authorized to pass such a bill, and that the Governor was duly elected and therefore empowered to sign it into law. The chapter in Wikipedia reads that *Fletcher v. Peck* "was a landmark United States Supreme Court decision, the first case in which the Supreme Court ruled on the constitutionality of a state law, the decision also helped create a growing precedent for the sanctity of legal contracts, and hinted that Native Americans did not hold title to their own lands." The really-interesting fact is that the suit had involved collusion between the plaintiff and the defendant, seeking to get the highest court to establish firmly their rights to land. Fletcher and Peck were both owners of land in the deal which was threatened by a Georgia law seeking to overturn the sale.

The case established their clear title to the lands. Amusingly, *Fletcher v. Peck* was one of the clues in the great old TV show Jeopardy on March 11, 2016.

A highly-respected Montgomery historian, Mary Ann Neely, told me that the Supreme Court decision, although barely mentioned today, was the second most important early decision made by the US Supreme Court. The first, which everyone studying the development of US law knows about, was *Marbury v. Madison* in 1803, the case that established the boundaries between the executive and the judicial branches of government under the US Constitution. I spent a whole year at Harvard studying the evolution of the US Constitution, primarily illustrated through Supreme Court cases. I studied *Fletcher v. Peck* but, at the time, had no clue that I had any family involvement.

It is interesting that Pickett's History of Alabama, the enormous, highly-detailed early history published in 1851, credits Mathews with opposing the legislation before finally giving in and signing it. Pickett starts a paragraph with the sentence "Governor Mathews was a man of honor and integrity" who had vetoed the first Yazoo bill.

There is also a very small town, Mathews, just east of Montgomery, Alabama. It, too, is a beautiful unspoiled area of large farms. Amusingly, and unknown to many here, its best-known resident was a baseball player for the New York Giants, having hit the home run in the bottom of the tenth inning during the 1954 World Series to win the game. I remember watching Dusty Rhodes hit two game-changing home runs, not knowing he was a kid from down the road near Montgomery.

On the subject of the panhandle of Florida, an area in which at least the western portion looks like it should be part of Alabama, George Mathews was very much involved. In 1811 he was commissioned a Brigadier General by President James Madison and led an expedition to capture "West Florida" from the Spanish.

He went beyond his assignment and began to find interest in "Eastern Florida" from residents wanting to escape Spanish rule. On March 13, 1812, he led a declaration of independence from Spain. His base was the "Island of Ferdinanda," which is known today as Fernandina (a cute little town what was one of our favorite stops when Pat and I were living aboard our boat). Anyway, Mathews' early successes caused Washington to fear the actions might lead to war with Spain, so he was ordered to curtail his activities. George headed to Washington to plead his case, but died August 30, 1812, en route in Augusta, Georgia, where he is buried in an Episcopal Church graveyard. George had a very interesting life. Was he good or was he very bad?

A GOOD MOTHER

Mom was a character. Everybody loved her. She got people to have fun. At parties, she frequently sat down and played the piano, emphasizing tunes that everyone could sing. As noted earlier, she had founded the Montgomery Women's Golf Association and won the city championship several times. She taught Sunday School at St. John's Episcopal Church in Montgomery for years and was the head of the "Pink Ladies," the team of volunteers at what was many years ago the only major hospital in town, St. Margarets.

Mom was great fun and a highly-regarded hostess, having many parties in the home we moved into on Woodley Road when I was 15 years old

Earlier, there was a chapter about a party for golfers by the organization my mother had founded, the Montgomery Women's Golf Association. There were, however, three stories that were rarely, if every mentioned, one sad, one a mixture of amusing and sad and finally a scary one about conning the elderly.

A BAD SISTER

My sister, Carolyn, was a beautiful girl. She had not done well in schools, but she was quite smart and, when sober, pretty logical. In the mid-1940s she had gotten to be almost thirty years old. She had been courted (how is that for an obsolete word?) by a very rich, good looking and intelligent lawyer, Inge Hill. The family scrapbooks contain pictures of Inge with Carolyn on our family's annual visits to Bacons By The Sea in the charming liitle Gulf Coast town of Mary Ester (a tiny area right beside Ft. Walton).. I never knew why that did not work out, but I always wished that it had.

Year later, Carolyn finally had a boyfriend and liked him well enough that she agreed to marry him. His last name may have been Divine, but he definitely was not. Plans were made, desired gifts were registered at the leading stores, and everything was planned for the out-of-town wedding. Many engraved silver gifts from Kleins were received and stacked in our home.

For several days Carolyn argued with my mother, stating that she had changed her mind and did not want to go through with it. Mom would not consider this option. "It was too late to cancel." Everything was set and engraved gifts had been received from most of my Mom and Dad's friends. As the big day approached, Carolyn was pleading to get out of the deal. It was frequent enough and loud enough that, despite my very young age, I was quite aware or the family feud. Carolyn should have just said "I don't" instead of "I do," but that was much more difficult in those days than it would be today and she was facing a very strong mother. Carolyn went ahead and got married.

For all practical purposes, the marriage lasted only a couple of weeks. Joe Divine, her husband, was in the military in World War II and went away on duty after two weeks. He simply disappeared. I did not ever see him again and I don't remember my sister's ever hearing from him or seeing him. To most of my mother's friends, the word "divorce" had a clear connotation of disgrace. I don't think my mother ever realized what she had done. Even when Carolyn reached her fifties, my mother could not understand why Carolyn had so many problems. She had become a violent, vitriolic, hate-filled alcoholic. On too many occasions, Mom would ask me what she should do to bring my sister up "right." It was simply too late. The hostility, mostly against my mother, and alcoholism continued for another forty years.

We went through the ceremonial cutting out of his picture wherever Joe Divine had been included in a family scene. Luckily, except for the wedding, there were few of those. Of course, all the pictures of the ceremony and reception were thrown out. The only sad reminders are silver goblets and a few other silver items engraved with a "D" which Pat and I still have.

THE TOWN'S BEST DOCTOR, BUT MAYBE NOT *THAT* GOOD

My cousin, Jane Mathews, married and became an excellent doctor. As Dr. Jane Day, she was by far the most successful and popular internist in Montgomery. In those days, this type of practice was generally referred to as a "family doctor."

Jane was tough; she never minced words. I suspect that some considered it dreadful "bedside manners," but it was effective. When a tough approach to a patient was needed, Jane was really tough. She also had to move quickly if the numbers I was told are correct. Supposedly she had about 10,000 patients. She worked hard all day and made house calls in the evening, during the day if there was a serious illness. She would frequently show up at our house to see how we were doing after she had finished her house calls in the evening. This would usually mean that she showed up about 8pm. Talk about a hard worker. I thought Jane was great and that could be said by almost everyone in town. Jane was a true legend. Mom was lucky to have her as a close friend.

My aunt, Juliette Persons, had a retirement home on a bayou in Shalimar, Florida, just off of Choctawhatchee Bay. The one-story house was very nice.

After "Uncle Bill" Persons died, Mom and Dad were visiting Juliette at her home on the west side of Poquito Bayou in Shalimar. The house was very close to the end of the bayou and Bill and Juliette had always been furious at the boats pulling water skiers in the smooth waters of the narrow bayou turned around in front of the house, damaging the dock and land. Since Mom and Juliette were fixing lunch, Dad mixed his usual gin martini and, since he wasn't feeling well, went to the bedroom. Mom and Juliette kept working on lunch. When they came out carrying lunch they found Dad dead, at least Juliette knew he was.

Jane was a great doctor. Mom was extremely stubborn and had enormous faith in Jane's abilities; a little too much. Mom refused to accept the idea that her husband of more than 55 years was dead. Her idea was to put Dad in the car, drive to Montgomery and take him to Dr. Day. Aunt Juliette said Mom's words were "Jane will know what to do." Juliette's daughter, also Juliette (known as J II, there are now a J III and a J IV), related the story as told by her mother. Juliette I had to argue long and hard with my mother to get her to abandon her plan and notify the authorities.

Needless to say, it would have been highly illegal to transfer a dead body across county lines, much less a state line, no matter how noble the intent. Finally, Aunt Juliette prevailed. The local coroner did his job, and Dad was transported home legally. I hate to think of what would have happened had Mom carried out her plan. It might have been awful, but still amusing, what would have been Dr. Day's reaction had Mom pulled up in the parking lot behind her office with Dad in the car.

My mother had a contagious personality. She had many friends and, even though I am obviously biased, I can't remember her ever having had an enemy. She was, to say the least, charming. I have to admit that I was closer to her than to my dad. I wish I could have grown up to me more like my mother.

A CLOSE CALL

During her later years, my mother used a CPA, Carl Robinette, to do her taxes. He was fairly young but had several years of experience, a small but nice office on South Perry Street and good references when she first hired him. When her mind became weak he tried to take advantage of her, attempting to convince her that if she sold all of her real estate and stock investments she could have a lot more income. Had I not accidentally learned of the accountant's scam it would have been disastrous.

Carl wanted her to "invest" all of her money in his race horses. It came too close to happening. With her mind suffering from old age, she had decided to accept his recommendation. Luckily, she happened to mention it to me just in time. Shortly thereafter Carl had to declare bankruptcy and went out of business. Served him right….to say the least.

A POPULAR UNCLE

Two funny stories involved my uncle, Major General John W. Persons (for those of you who do not know, this is the second level of rank as a general, above Brigadier General).

The use of the first name was required by the Air Force, but everybody knew him as "Bill." He was a character, worthy of an entire book.

Bill had wanted to join the military at the outbreak of World War I. but was too young and needed a college degree. His solution was to enlist in Canada. Bill's brother, Bert, told him he could get his degree from Auburn in three years, but Bill wanted to fight the Germans and was determined not to wait that long. He didn't want to wait at all. Bill "borrowed" his older brother's papers and had a forger copy them using his name.

Bill was accepted into the Canadian Royal Flying Corps, serving from March 1917 to January, 1919. He had a quite distinguished carrier, including flying the famous route "over the Hump" for General Chennault. Another interesting coincidence: Chennault had commanded the Fourteenth Air Force and was years later succeeded by Uncle Bill.

General Chennault

Don't know where else to put it so I will interject a funny story about Chennault. The history books show that he believed that his pilots performed better in the air if they could enjoy sex when on the ground. He did not want them going to dangerous brothels in Asia so he established military whore houses where the women were inspected by doctors frequently for venereal disease. When General Chennault's boss learned about this unusual solution, it was stopped fast.

Amusingly, in the December 22/29, 2017 of The Week magazine, a story reported that a women, Captain Sally Williamson, in the Australian Army had proposed to have sex workers "service" troops in combat zones to ease their loneliness. Her plan was shot down. Déjà vu, from the distant past.

Bert Persons

Bill's brother Bert, officially General Wilton B. Persons, had worked under a guy in the military who later went into politics, Dwight David Eisenhower. Most old people (like me) today remember the saga of Sherman Adams, who served as what is now called Chief of Staff, for Eisenhower in the White House. Adams had been caught accepting a Vicuna coat from Bernard Goldfine and forced to resign for this "terrible offense." Eisenhower replaced him with Wilton Persons.

Luckily, in those days there was no 24-hour-a-day cable TV news so the forgery never surfaced. General Wilton B. Persons' son, Major General Wilton B. Persons, a West Point Graduate, later served at Judge Advocate General of the Army. At least he was known as Wilton. When Bert went off with Eisenhower, Wilton stayed here in Montgomery with Gordon Persons, later Governor of Alabama, so he could graduate from the school he had been attending in Montgomery and wanted to graduate.

US Military Service
Bill did many things during his years of service, the most important being Commander of the Fourteenth Air Force, stationed at Randolph Field in Texas. In this position he supervised the training of 72,000 Air Force Reservists and Air National Guardsmen from 22 states. Among his many decorations, he was awarded the Legion of Merit.

For a while, Bill was here in Montgomery based at Maxwell Field, on the west side of the city. Very few people who live here know that a field out there was where some early pilots named Orville and Wilbur Wright established the world's first commercial flight training school. Today, Maxwell is the home of the renowned Air War College. People exploring the historic graves where my parents are buried in Oakwood Cemetery are usually surprised to come across areas of graves with metal crosses for the many English and French pilots who died in training at Maxwell.

I have a gravesite with my parents that is nice because my mother installed a marble retaining wall and it has a beautiful large tree. The big advantage is that, being at the top of the hill, it has a great view of the City and the Alabama River. If I am going to be there for a long time, at least I will be in a place where I can enjoy the view. The problem was the large buses that go by headed to the grave of our most famous country singer, Hank Williams. At least, they now take a different route.

A Day in South Dakota
Bill was involved in many interesting events, but one of the most amusing was how he, for some reason, was flying a plane containing 42 US Congressmen over the Black Hills of South Dakota to go pheasant hunting. The plane developed mechanical difficulties, the engines failed, and the plane was on the verge of crashing. Needless to say, the important passengers did not have parachutes. Facing several problems, Bill managed to land the plane safely.

The congressmen as a group led the vote to honor Bill with the Distinguished Flying Cross and it passed easily. Uncle Bill refused to accept the DFC on the grounds that he had just been doing his job. He asked what would have happened to him if he had crashed. His name would certainly have been more well-known had the 42 Congressmen been killed.

Birds vs. Squirrels
As mentioned a few paragraphs ago, when retired, Bill and his wife, Juliette, built a house in Shalimar on the west shore of the narrow Poquito Bayou. Yes, I know, it had a different name then; not to be used these days. Companies make lots of money selling

many kinds of "squirrel proof" birdfeeders. From my experience, most are ineffective. The best fed creatures at our bird feeders were not the birds.

Bill had a solution about which I suspect many readers will disapprove. His birdfeeder was suspended below a wire between a tree and a kitchen window on the rear of his home in Shalimar. The feeder had a wooden, tented roof design with two thin metal rails on either side on which the birds could stand while reaching in and getting the seed. Squirrels learned how to climb out the wire, drop down onto the roof of the birdhouse, climb down to one of the rails and steal the food.

Bill took a normal household extension cord, ran it out to the birdfeeder and attached the ends of the wire to the pair of rails that served as the "perch." The cord was brought to the house and run through a kitchen window so that Bill could watch for intruders and plug the wire into a 110-volt outlet once a squirrel reached the perch. This would, today, certainly infuriate the ASPCA people, but it was quite effective. It did not kill the squirrels, but it sure scared the hell out of them. Those that had been guilty of attempted theft soon learned not to come back. Bill loved his role.

My parents raised chickens in the back yard of our home at 915 E, Fairview Avenue during World War II. I did not mind bringing in the eggs but I had trouble eating a chicken (essentially a pet) after having had to wring its neck. I hated that assignment but could not get out of it.

When the war ended, our chickens were given a rare treat, rare at least for chickens. Bill wanted our chickens for his yard when he was commanding Tyndall Field (now Tyndall Air Force Base) southeast of Panama City, Florida. He flew up to Montgomery where the chickens were put on board his bomber at Maxwell Field and flown to Florida. It was probably in coach class. Maybe it should have been called "Coop class."

DAD

Dad was an extraordinarily nice gentleman, an honest business man, a business leader and a loving, albeit tough, father. He was a cotton broker, buying bales of cotton from gins and then selling them to mills around the southeast. In addition to working in his office learning how to grade cotton, I rode in the car with him on his drives around to the various places from which he made purchases or to which he made sales. This was an important part of my early education.

Many years later I read an article by a child psychologist who took the position that it was very bad to do what my dad did for me. While riding in the car with him, I had to conjugate verbs, but most of the time the conversation was about math. In the early stages it was adding in my head, first two and later three and four numbers at a time. A lot of time was spent on multiplication tables going far beyond 12x12 (which is where most education stopped). Sometimes it was computing square roots. It didn't just consume time on those long hours of driving; it was good early brain exercise.

In the office, he made me learn how to type without looking at the keyboard. This skill was put to good use typing papers in college. When home computers arrived on the scene, this was much more useful than I would have thought. He had not allowed me to limit my learning to just the letters. With a piece of cardboard covering my view of the keyboard, I learned all of the symbols and, more importantly, the numbers. I also learned to enter numbers in a desk calculator without looking.

Today, I am puzzled by the level of horrendous and dangerous misbehavior tolerated in public schools today and this obviously flows from the lack of proper parenting at home. The subject of controversy is the role and effectiveness of corporal punishment. I probably was quite well behaved compared with most kids so I rarely needed painful punishment, but it did happen. Dad never used a paddle or anything that could risk injury if applied hard enough to hurt, but I did occasionally deserve what I guess would be described as "a switching."

I learned to behave at all times to avoid being sent into the backyard to break a branch off our peach tree, strip it of leaves and small offshoots and bring it in for Dad to use. If the branch was too small, I had to go back and get a better one, come back in to face the music and drop my pants in preparation for its application on my bare butt. A hard switching certainly stung, but I would not consider it dangerous. It worked.

I did comment earlier about the "equipment" Dad took when he was going away on business by himself for several days. Other than that, he was always very nice to my mother. As I guess is true of many husbands, he was not enthusiastic when she would want to spend money on the house, but he almost always let her have her way.

When offered water to drink today, if the situation is appropriate, I tell people that my Dad always disapproved of drinking "that stuff" straight. He thought water should always have a little bourbon or maybe scotch in it. On Sundays, after church at St. John's, we always went to a restaurant on Montgomery Street named the Elite. Any person from a place other than Montgomery would pronounce it "uh-LEET'." Here it was the EEE'-light. Any service of booze on Sundays was illegal, so Dad's "coffee" mug always arrived with no coffee, just bourbon.

Years later I learned that an Alabama Governor John Paterson also liked his "coffee" this way. When an Alcoholic Beverage Control inspector discovered this violation at the Elite, he went bouncing into Governor Paterson's office to announce the great discovery he had made. Paterson had to tell Ed Azar, his ABC Board head, to shut up and back off. The practice, to the delight of many in Montgomery, continued.

Business

Dan had been President of Montgomery's Downtown Business Association and worked very hard at promoting downtown. He would be absolutely amazed at how much of downtown has been beautifully and effectively improved in recent years, with loads of new businesses and, even to my amazement, apartments for lots of people.

Dad was furious when Montgomery got its first suburban mall. It was far out Norman Bridge Road and named "Normandale Mall." In 1954, it was one of the earliest suburban malls in the entire country.

Dad had always liked owning a new car every year, despite the high cost of that first year's depreciation. He bought a new Ford every year and our family drove four Fords. When Ford became the first dealership to move its business out to the suburbs, Dad ordered the family to sell their Fords. From that moment on, we all had Chevrolets.

71 A GREAT WIFE
It Paid To Wait; I Got Very Lucky

It paid to spend many years looking. I made it as a bachelor all the way to 34 hours shy of my 52nd birthday. Had I married any of the ones with whom I had come close, I would probably have been divorced and broke from paying alimony to several. I was lucky enough to find a fabulous choice. I do not recommend waiting till age 52, but my experience leads me to believe kids should not rush into marriage as quickly as they do today. And, yes, they should get married, *especially* before having kids.

FRITO LAY
Most people in the US, probably almost all, know about Frito Lay's products, including specific ones such as potato chips and Doritos. What very few know is that, although owned by Pepsico, Frito Lay generated much more profit for the parent company than does its signature product, Pepsi Cola. As I recall, the difference was about double.

Pat did loads of important work for Frito Lay in their engineering department. One of the most important was going incognito to meet with officials in cities in which Frito Lay was considering building a plant. She had to determine a city's ability to handle large amounts of waste water that would result from the company's production lines. The intent to build had to be kept secret until a location was selected and the land was acquired. During that period, she wrote the water guidelines that were accepted by the State of Arizona. Pat, having been in engineering for years, was made travel manager when airline deregulation made cost negotiation with airlines attractive for companies.

In my job handling corporate travel, I met many corporate travel managers from throughout the country. Many were not qualified to negotiate with huge airlines. Pat was outstanding. She worked in Frito Lay's beautiful headquarters in Plano, Texas.

THE SYMPOSIUM
One night when Heritage Travel was producing its annual symposium on business travel in New York City we held a reception for out-of-town guests in Don Sohn's large suite at the Sheraton New York. Most of the guests had arrived by the time I got there, so I had to wend my way around the room stopping to great guests along the way.

As I neared the end of the route, I was introduced to a lady who managed travel for the Frito Lay part of Pepsico. I was a major customer drinking too much Diet Pepsi and loved Doritos. I was once awarded a gold Cross pen and pencil set as a result of one of their bottler's telling the story that, until I came along, he had never heard of any individual's having a hundred cases at a time delivered by 18 wheeler to the customer's home. I drank a lot of Diet Pepsi.

The lady was from Dallas and had been speaking with one of my salesmen in our Dallas office. The two salesmen had gotten Heritage Travel the Bell Helicopter and J.C. Penney accounts. One salesman, Steve Spaulding, had called on Frito Lay, but whenever the lady called him with a question regarding our symposium he repeatedly (according to her) said "I don't know, you'll have to call Thornton Clark." She came to believe that this Mr. Clark did not train his salesmen well.

When I reached out to shake hands and said I was Thornton Clark, the lady (you may guess by now she was Pat, later my wife) shook hands but the look of disdain on her face showed so badly that her first word might as well have been "Damn." She claims it was just "Oh, no," but my evaluation is accurate. I knew I liked her from the moment I met her, but this feeling was definitely *not* reciprocated. At the time, I had no clue re why she reacted so negatively. I was the person who would be speaking at and moderating the symposium her company had sent her to New York to attend.

U.S. OPEN TENNIS

I had to stand, give a talk and moderate the symposium for six hours the day after the reception. I had been invited by Avis to the U.S. Open Tennis Championships for years and was planning on going that evening. I asked Pat to come with me, but she said she had been invited by Avis and was already going with some of her co-workers from Pepsico headquarters north of New York City. Avis said I should ride in the limo they were sending for the Pepsi people.

Pat's Pepsi friends called and cancelled, so I lucked into riding with her in the limo with just the two of us. Years later she started telling people that she felt safe because my having made it to 50 years old meant I obviously had to be gay. This changed when somehow the conversation disclosed that I had just broken up with a long-standing girlfriend four weeks earlier. The subject of my just having sold my racing sailboat and having purchased a cruising sailboat was mentioned and she was interested in this, having enjoyed sailing Hobie Cats on lakes in Texas.

Before the evening of tennis which, on Thursday nights, was always was the men's quarter finals, Avis hosted a reception before guests went to the stadium. I kept trying to get Pat to sit with me. She thought she had poor seats but that mine were even worse. Because they were so high up in the stadium, she called them "nose-bleed seats.

What I knew would happen was a standard Avis practice of sending out very poor seats to you in the mail in case you did not make the trip. They would always come around and ask me for "my ticket" before giving me my excellent ticket. Pat did not believe me and insisted over and over again that she was not going to sit with me.

When Pat finally saw that I had been changed from lousy seats to excellent courtside box seats near the net she began to sound like she might change her mind. She decided on insisting upon one condition: I had to promise to take her sailing. Neither of us could have dreamed that this would lead to as much sailing as we did together in New England, Europe, Asia, and a year and a half of the east coast of the United States from Canada to Key West and a winter in the Bahamas. Anyway, she did end up sitting with me.

Pat comments that she watched some great tennis but does not even remember who played that night. Thirty years later, *to the day*, Avis' CEO at the time, Joe Vittoria, wrote me that the players we watched that night were Lendl and John McEnroe. Joe also commented that Avis served Pepsi at the reception and made a point of bringing Pepsis to Pepsico President, Wayne Calloway, because at the time the US Open sold only Coca Cola. During the reception, Pat had introduced me to Calloway, but I had no clue who he was while we were talking. As we were leaving she asked me what did I think of her having introduced me to him. Only then did I learn with whom I had been speaking.

Pat remembers a story about Luciana Vittoria, wife of Joe, who had had at the last minute to sew several little red-lettered "Avis" patches onto the left sleeves of Ivan Lendl's tennis shirts. Avis was delighted that she put that logo on the shirt because the next morning the New York Times ran a large front-page picture of Lendl's serving with his left sleeve bearing the Avis name front and center in the picture. As I recall, Joe said Avis had paid $5,000 to Lendl to wear that patch and luck made it well worth it.

SEATS

In addition to giving us seats in a court-side box, Avis did something almost unbelievable. Pat sat on my left and on my right a beautiful young bartender set up a full bar next to me while she sat in the next seat, ready to serve. She didn't wait for a glass to be empty, she was constantly refilling for both of us. It was quite a night. When the matches finally ended it was lucky that we had an Avis limo in which to ride back into Manhattan. We went to the Stage Deli on 7th Avenue for gigantic sandwiches. The only disappointing moment was her refusal to allow even a simple good night kiss.

The next day I went back to Boston, but Pat stayed and, as the guest of Avis, played in the pro-am matches. This included a pass to the women's locker room, where she saw an interesting array of famous tennis players.

BACK IN DALLAS

On Monday morning I started calling Texas. Pat's secretary became adept at making up excuses. Pat was "in a meeting" or Pat was "out of the office." It went on like this for a week and it became increasingly obvious that the excuses were untrue. I was extremely disappointed. Pat never returned a call, and it was painfully obvious that she was going to great lengths to avoid even talking with me. I simply could not understand it.

I had had a wonderful evening and had thought she enjoyed it, too. How could she not even accept a phone call? I found this hard to believe, but she later acknowledged that she thought I was just calling to work on getting the Frito Lay travel account.

Finally I said what must have been the magic words: "Tell her it is about sailing." That worked. She immediately answered the phone and agreed to fly to Boston for the annual turnaround of Old Ironsides.

The USS CONSTITUTION

In those days the USS Constitution, maintained as the oldest ship in the US Navy (by over 200 years), was pulled away from its dock, paraded around the harbor pulled gently by tugboats and put back with its opposite side to the dock so that the sun would weather one side and then the other.

My sailboat was in a slip on the north side of Commercial Wharf in downtown Boston. We pulled out early, moved south a few hundred yards and anchored at what I believed was a safe distance. The Constitution had been positioned near Logan Airport on the opposite shore of the harbor. As many hundreds of boats approached from the south, the Coast Guard made them anchor much farther away from where the Constitution was placed. We were the closest boat by several hundred yards.

The weather could have been worse, but it certainly wasn't good. Sitting in a sailboat in the rain is not the most attractive way to watch fireworks. We drank and waited for darkness when the fireworks from a barge near the Constitution would begin. We very quickly learned that, with the wind blowing from the east, fireworks shells began landing on the deck of our boat. No meaningful danger, but an interesting sidelight.

EDUCATION

Many people in the US have a college degree. A relatively small number go on to get a graduate degree. Pat earned a Masters Degree in Natural Science (mostly Geology and Water) at Oklahoma and went on to get another Masters at SMU in Dallas, this time an MBA. During her early years she taught Biology all over the country: Florida, West Virginia, Oklahoma and California.

Today, it makes things complicated during football season because there is usually at least one of "her" teams playing at any time. She still cheers for Oklahoma and for the Dallas Cowboys.

EXPERIENCE

Pat's background included engineering work for the Williams Companies, a major factor in the pipeline business. The negotiations with cities and counties throughout the country regarding Frito Lay's prospective sites for plants was tricky, requiring fast thought in addition to lots of knowledge. Through imaginative steps, she succeeded in gaining large savings on air travel for Frito Lay employees. It was a good job, but she wanted to live near the water, and the opportunity to explore that possibility arrived.

Her dreadful experience being interviewed by General Electric is contained in the chapter based upon the premise that something you get for nothing may be worthless, maybe even worse than that. Pat flew to New York to be interviewed by General Electric at their headquarters in Bridgeport, Connecticut. She doesn't just remember it as a very poor interview, it was by far the worst ever.

The guy grilled her for thirteen hours, leading her to be sure that this was not a job she wanted. GE had had problems with their corporate travel for a long time, making it very important to the company, resulting in the hiring process even including Pat's meeting with Jack Welch, the highly-respected head of GE. The job of travel manager for a huge corporation was extremely delicate.

Reluctantly, as long as she was in the area, she accepted my recommendation that she interview at Time, Inc. Their headquarters were in the center of Manhattan and she felt strongly that she did not want to live in that huge city. Most people don't know how many major magazines are published by Time, in addition to their eponymous magazine, Time. When I was kid there was Time, Life and Fortune. The newer names include Sports Illustrated, Money, and People. The guy in charge at Time, Inc., Tom Larkin, interviewed Pat and quickly offered her the job. She declined.

Weeks later Pat wanted to visit me again in Boston, so she asked Larkin for a free ticket from Time to have a follow up interview because it would allow her to visit me. Larkin told Pat that he had interviewed 52 but she was still the one they wanted. He offered her the job, but she did not accept it, telling him that he could not afford her. After the interview, she flew to Boston, from which we headed to Key West for New Year's.

Key West is a great, fun small city, and I had a friend from Boston who was an outstanding artist, Bob Kennedy, who had a home in Key West and several studios there. He showed us around all the bars and restaurants for several days. I don't know how Tom Larkin found out that Pat was in the Holiday Inn in Key West, but he chased her down, reaching us at 10:22pm as we were about to head out for New Year's Eve. He offered to double what she had been making in Dallas. Today she describes this as an offer she could not refuse. She said "Yes."

TIME, INC.
Time is an incredible company, for a while located overlooking Columbus Circle and Central Park in one of the most beautiful office buildings in Manhattan. Many books have been written about Time, but I will tell just four amusing stories.

Every company that I worked for did not allow alcoholic beverages in their offices. Most of my employers approved of your having a glass of wine at a business lunch. This was especially true when working in Europe. In many cases it helped and, despite what the IRS disallows as a business expense, talking over a long lunch can be a very effective way to get a new customer or to keep an existing one.

I had never heard of a company that allowed alcohol in their offices. Time had a most unusual policy in this regard. Employees at the manager level or higher were entitled to a bar in their office, with the booze inventory maintained in a cabinet by a Time employee in charge of booze. At the end of the day, word would spread that someone was having a "Pour" in their office. You were invited to go there and pour yourself a drink.

Pat's department had a highly experienced staff to handle company travelers, with kid glove treatment for the VIPs. The most experienced, Ralph Spielman, was assigned to handle the photographers and all of the models that were to be in the next year's Sports Illustrated Swimsuit Edition. Sports Illustrated had been criticized early on for focusing in one issue on something other than sport, but that annual edition always sells like hotcakes, especially where the sexy cover is visible on newsstands. One year when Pat was there, the top model was Elle McPherson. Ralph got her to autograph a large poster of her. According to autograph theory, it reduced the value by her having written "To Thornton" above her signature, but I think she increased the value by doing something else. Instead of signing in a common place, the lower-right-hand corner of the picture, Elle autographed her left tit.

AFTER WORK
Most of the managers had to work late on almost all evenings. About eight, they would frequently agree to meet at one of New York's best-known bars. Pat very quickly learned the secret. You certainly did not drink something like scotch or vodka. You drank wine, but diluted as wine spritzers. If you don't know what that means, they put ice and water in the wine to dilute its strength.

On many occasions, Roe, Pat's boss' boss, would arrive late, usually about 9pm. It wasn't just that she would pick up the tab for the drinks, she would then take a bunch of them out to dinner, usually at one of New York's top and extremely-expensive restaurants. I very quickly learned that I should not try calling Pat until very late in the evening and we finally ended up agreeing that she would call me when she got home from "work," frequently around midnight.

Her apartment was on the twenty-first floor of a very large apartment building, the Barkley, overlooking the East River. Her view included seven bridges and she could look out and see planes landing and taking off at La Guardia Airport. In the distance, you could just pick out where Long Island Sound widened. It was a great view, but the cost of that apartment was the single biggest factor in making Manhattan such an expensive place to live. It wasn't just the rent. When we were living in Boston and Savannah we never took a taxi. In Manhattan you need a taxi quite often, frequently several times a day. Unlike cities where it can be tough to spot a cab, in mid-town Manhattan the main streets carry a veritable sea of yellow taxis.

THE COST OF LIVING

This is the prime reason that statistics re cost of living by Chambers of Commerce can be so misleading. The cost of living in a far-from-good building in a marginal neighborhood can be several times, not just double what it is in most other U.S. cities. She was paying about five times as much as what a similarly-sized apartment would have been in Boston.

When I left college and went to work for the Irving Trust Company, headquartered at One Wall Street, I learned this lesson very quickly. When Dad had taken the family on the annual trip to New York they had always stayed in the Waldorf Towers and had gone to a Broadway show almost every night, followed by dinner. Dad had very poor vision and hearing, so he always bought seats about the fourth-row dead center. It was great, and I had gotten used to it. The chapter about this experience is labeled: Elevators.

When I got a date to go to the theater, I would call David, dad's contact at Equity Ticket, which was west of Broadway on about 43rd Street. The price on the tickets was high, but not that bad, so I took dates to the theater several times in my first month in New York.

Boy, was I in for a shock. My tickets were being charged to dad's account. When he received the first month's bill it brought an abrupt halt to my theater experience. I didn't realize that Equity was a scalper and that the tickets were not just more than their face value, they were many times as expensive. Way back in 1959 the first month's bill was $900, the equivalent of $9,600 today.

I had chosen my job for several reasons, not the least of which was that Irving Trust had offered the highest starting salary. Today you will laugh, but way back then it was $5,280 a year. Even then you could not live anything approaching comfortably in New

York City for that. I rented in Brooklyn Heights for most of the time, moving later to East 82nd Street way over near 2nd Avenue..

BOSTON

When we got married and lived in the Waban portion of Newton, in the suburbs west of Boston, Pat got a job as travel manager for Bain & Co, a company that was well known in business circles but essentially unknown to anyone else until Mitt Romney ran for President. I used to joke that, from a husband's perspective, Pat's office was, for husband's, in the world's most dangerous location. From her office, she could walk a few feet, take the elevator and be in Neiman Marcus, nicknamed "Needless Markup."

Living today in Montgomery, it takes us about a seven-minute drive to get from our garage to the middle of downtown, where she worked for the Senate in the State Capitol building. I would guess that for those who live quite far out to the east, it probably still takes only twenty minutes. Living just south of Wellesley in Dover, Massachusetts, our commute was rarely less than forty-minutes, frequently almost an hour.

It is sad to hear anti-Mormon comments today. As I had experienced in the case of Bill Marriott, Mitt was one of the nicest, most honest and congenial persons you could do business with or work for. Pat and I campaigned for Mitt in 1994 when he ran for Senator against Ted Kennedy. The Kennedy name was still worshiped in Massachusetts. Mitt did OK, better than expected, but was still nowhere close to winning.

DOVER

About 15 years before I met Pat I was canoeing one day down the Charles River, beautiful little river that winds its way through many of Boston's nicest suburbs. I always carried a street map and, when I spotted a beautiful piece of land in Dover from my canoe, I marked it down on my map. A few years later I was exploring on Yorkshire Road in Dover and noticed a second-rate, hand-lettered "For Sale" sign nailed to a tree. There was no mention of its being waterfront property. By most standards, the lot was large, over 2 acres and it had 280 feet of frontage along the beautiful river.

One of the things you couldn't tell from the street was that it didn't just look out at a long beautiful stretch of river, 117 feet wide at this point. The hill looked across the river at an Audubon Preserve all along the opposite side of the river. From our large windows on the back of the house you could look up and downstream at a third of a mile of the river and not see a single other house. We enjoyed seeing canoes go by in the summer, ice skaters in the winter and great blue herons all the time. What was really amusing was a discovery made when looking at a USGS topographic map of the area. Directly across the river there was a very large rock outcropping, large enough to be identified by the government's cartographers as "Clark's Rock."

The lot I had purchased sat there for years until I met Pat. We worked with an excellent architect, John Becker, to design a spectacular home. It was strange in that we wanted traditional Georgian look on the front with double hung windows, brick and a traditional roof with tall brick chimneys at each end, while the back that looked at the river was modern with huge single-pane windows looking out at the view of the garden below and the river beyond. It was a little ridiculous because we built about 7,000 square feet. From the river, some people passing in boats thought it was a four-story condominium. One boater called out complaining to our neighbor, saying he thought condos were not allowed in Dover. We installed the wires and pipes and built a full width standard staircase to enable us to finish off the fourth floor if we ever wanted to do so. That has been done by the current owners. with a spectacular view from the large picture window on the fourth floor.

SAILING

What was sad was that the company I had worked for was sold to American Express. Since my specialty had been taking large corporate accounts away from American Express, I knew I would not last long. I lost my job. It was nice being the first person to be let go. Shortly after that they started letting many go. Luckily, we were able to sell the Dover house for more than our cost. My only job offers were in New York and not wanting to do either, we decided to be "homeless" and just go sailing.

We sold our 43 ft. ketch (that means a sailboat with two masts, the shorter one aft, but ahead of the steering wheel) and bought a extremely well-designed layout in a 55ft. boat, *Eagle*, with just one mast (called a sloop). With easily handled roller furling for the jib and electric roller furling that, at the touch of a button, could pull the mainsail completely into the mast, I could sail the boat by myself. Pat's and I sailed 15,000 miles together, in the Caribbean, Thailand, the British Virgin Islands and the Dalmation Coast of Croatia. In *Eagle,* we spent an entire winter in the Bahamas, but mostly explored the east coast of the United States between Canada and Key West. In the IntraCoastal Waterway, we would typically stay somewhere a few days and then travel 60 miles or so when we were ready to move. On some days sailing in the Atlantic, we covered 250 miles per day.

THINK TWICE, MAYBE THRICE

I didn't think twice, I must have thought a half-dozen times about getting married. I wouldn't recommend to any young person that they wait as long as I did to get married for the first time. Many of the girls I dated a lot over the years would have been good choices, but I suspect I would have been dead broke paying alimony to several of them. After a lot of searching, as the lyrics to the song say, you really will know "when the right one comes along."

I love good food. One of the oldest sayings is that a young man searches for a bride who can cook as well as his mother had. I found one who not only loves to cook complex meals, she does it much better than my mother did. It isn't just great food, her preferences (with the exception of her *not* liking anchovies on pizza and my hating her favorite soggy green boiled peanuts) exactly match mine. When we give a dinner party, she works extremely hard for at least two days preparing. Even standard dinners for just the two of us are truly "dinners," not just suppers. It is also important that our tastes in many areas are quite similar. This extends far beyond food to style, home design and decorating, art, sports, music and politics. Just as in the case of cooking, you all too frequently hear about couples who don't get along because the husband wants to watch football on TV all the time. Pat loves both college and pro football and is absolutely addicted to tennis tournaments. Guys (and girls), if you rush into marriage at an early age your chances of picking the wrong partner and ending up in divorce go way up. Girls having kids as unmarried teenagers are just begging for big trouble throughout their lives. I guess you can't outlaw it, but parents need to be tough in telling their kids that certain paths in life are insane. Drugs are obviously a problem but, in this case, it seems like millions of adults are making the same mistake.

SIDE NOTE

Some people will remember that the Concorde essentially just flew the Atlantic, with British Airways flying the New York-London route and Air France between New York and Paris. Even for so many years in the travel business, I was not aware until my wife told me that Braniff had flown the Concorde between Europe and Dallas. Because she was the Manager of Travel for Frito Lay in Dallas, she was taken as a guest on Braniff's last flight of their Concorde. Airlines were forbidden to exceed the speed of sound over the United States, having to wait until flights were out over the ocean where the sonic boom created when the speed of sound was exceeded would not blast everyone on land below. Pat said that they were all told that rule, but that the pilot that day had gotten up close to Mach 1 (the speed of sound) and then goosed it briefly up faster than sound while over land en route to D.C.

IRAN

There are many, but I think one of the most amusing moments for Pat was at the swimming pool on the top deck of the R5 (a cruise ship sold when Renaissance went bankrupt and renamed "Nautica" as part of the Oceanic Line) as we went close to Iran passing through the 32.5 mile Strait of Hormuz. We had come down the Red Sea, visited Djibouti, sailed east in the Gulf of Aden, stopped in Salalah, Oman (not worth it), visited Muscat, Oman (well worth it) and were heading north into the infamous Straits of Hormuz where our first stop was to be Qatar in the southwest corner of the Arabian Gulf.

The Strait of Hormuz is the "choke point" at the entrance to the Arabian (some still call it Persian) Gulf. From Muscat, we headed east and then north through the Strait of Hormuz, through which a huge percentage of the world's oil has to pass when tankers leave the ports in Iraq, Kuwait, Iran, Bahrain, Saudi Arabia, Qatar and the United Arab Emirates for ports throughout the world. To minimize the risks to huge cargo ships, the navigation charts have channels for northbound ships on the right and southbound ships on the left. Since ships entering the Gulf have to stay to the right of 16.3 miles, staying west of the Iranian 12 mile from shore zone can cause many problems, making it easy for Iran to claim a ship has strayed into "their" territory.

The Strait at its narrowest point is just 32.6 miles wide. This may sound like a lot, but it is congested when you consider the huge number of large tankers passing through the Strait. From the swimming pool, we looked up when a military plane passed us just above our port side headed in the opposite direction. From the markings, we could see that it was an Iranian military plane that had flown out from Iran. They passed quickly by our port side, turned and came up low and quite close on our starboard side, just high enough for those Iranians to have a view of all the women in bathing suits, something they don't see much of in Iran these days.

Since they were now travelling with the ship, they had more time to slow down and enjoy the view. The plane did, gradually move ahead. The plane immediately did a U-turn, came down our port side and took up their viewing position from starboard again. Pat's great idea was to get all of the women to drop the tops of their swimsuits. She expected this would shock the Iranians and hopefully cause them to crash. Unfortunately, nobody accepted her plan and the plane eventually took off back toward the Iranian Coast.

QATAR

Our first stop in the Arabian Gulf was Qatar. The harbor at the capital, Doha, is now a magnificent port with marinas and parks with many tall skyscrapers. Qatar had been the only country around the Arabian Gulf that I had not visited before. When we were there it was mostly sand and small dirty buildings, much less developed than Dubai had looked like when I first visited there on business in about 1977. In December of 2,000 there was little to see in Qatar. The only things we remember were visiting a raptor store and a camel auction. We could have purchased a camel at auction for just $100. We mused that our association bylaws at The Landings covered lots of things but did not even mention, much less rule out, having a camel. I do think we might have had some problems taking a camel on the ship. In Doha, the excitement began when we got back on the ship and the crew prepared to cast off and head for the port I had told everyone they would love…Dubai (on which there is a separate chapter at the end of the book). After sitting at the dock for a long time, the captain came on the ship's intercom and announced that we had a problem. The government had announced that the harbor was closed because of the Islamic religious holiday, Ramadan. We were forbidden to leave until daylight the next day. I knew this meant we might have to skip Dubai, a place I loved and was looking forward to showing Pat. We had already had to skip Sana'a and Aden in Yemen, because the Islamic terrorists had just bombed the USS Cole in the harbor at Aden.

The captain then announced that we were going to violate Qatar's rules and leave the harbor without permission. We looked down from the starboard side as the ship's crew ran down the gangplank onto the dock and raced to where the ship's lines were tied to the dock. They cast off, ran back to the gangplank and jumped aboard. One advantage of a new ship is that it had bow thrusters and stern thrusters. These are essentially propellers mounted through the hull that can be used to blast sideways in either direction, so we just moved sideways away from the dock until we were far enough out to turn to port and gun the engines so we could make our escape from the harbor.

STRAITS AND CANALS

You usually hear of the Strait of Hormuz, but rarely ever hear of another, equally important, Strait that is just 18 miles wide, the Bab al-Mandab Strait that is the southern entrance to the Red Sea between Yemen and Djibouti. We had just gone through there a week or so earlier. It is only about half as wide as the famous Strait of Hormuz between Iran and Oman. Looking at maps, people can have little concept of size and distance. Connecting the Red Sea to the Mediterranean by building the Suez Canal eliminated the long voyage around Africa's Cape of Good Hope when traveling from Europe to the Far East. The Suez Canal may be an uninteresting canal to look at or pass through, but it cuts the voyage that had been 13,300 miles from Athens to Bombay (yes, I know it should now be called "Mumbai") from 13,200 miles to just 4,200 miles. The Red Sea, that doesn't look all that big on maps of the world, is 1,382 miles long, a little bit longer than the coast of the United States from Boston to Key West. The Suez had a massive impact on trade, giving you an idea of why the construction of the Suez Canal was such an important accomplishment, but it is not something to see.

It is interesting to note that the Exodus Route, essentially always said to have crossed the Red Sea, did not involve God's "parting the Red Sea" because the Jews fleeing Egypt did not cross the Red Sea. The Jews crossed the Strait of Tiran, only about 8 miles wide. The Exodus was from the eastern shore of the Sinai Peninsula, where the Gulf of Aqaba joins the Red Sea. Crossing the Red Sea from Egypt would have been a hundred miles.

CONCLUSION

Anyway, the net result is I could not have made a better choice for a wife. We have had a huge number of delightful experiences together. Pat was an absolutely-fabulous partner with whom to share my life. As I said; I was very lucky.

72 YOU CAN'T COME HOME

Yes, You Can, But It Is Awkward

ALABAMA

No matter where you have lived, I suspect most people have feelings about the place they were born and where they grew up. You don't see many Nazi organizations in Germany, but the Confederacy is still a part of life in the South. Too often in the newspaper you read of someone's belief that the Civil War was precipitated by taxes imposed by the north. Many whites today simply don't accept the fact that the central problem the South had *was* slavery.

Too many Northerners (my dad called them Yankees) know very little about the South. When I was a kid, the largest exports were cotton and peanuts. Most people are surprised to hear that Alabama's largest export these days is automobiles. What a change. The "foreign" car manufacturers here are booming, largely because of less-expensive labor and the Right To Work law that has so far kept out the unions.

The Confederacy is still thought of as Southern Pride, for most not carrying any connotation of slavery. It is hard to explain but easy to understand how many cannot accept that.

CIVIL RIGHTS

Yes, it was bad for many years, but my opinion is that the South is more integrated than the north. We live on a nice street surrounded by black families, one next door, one behind us, and one across the street (this one having three of the nicest kids we have seen anywhere). It is awkward reliving the history of several hundred years, but that is all in the past for most people.

The percentage of blacks in Montgomery is about 54%. Where Pat and I lived in Dover, Massachusetts it was less than one half of one percent black.

There is still a fear of blacks, especially gangs of teenagers, but that in the north it is a legitimate reaction to the police statistics. It is not prejudice that causes most of the mug shots of arrested thugs to be black. Nationwide, blacks may be just 14% of the population, but they commit a much larger percentage of the crimes.

Whites vote for qualified blacks; blacks clearly vote for unqualified blacks when the option is a highly qualified white. This is not a Southern problem, it is a national problem, evidenced by disasters such as Detroit, Baltimore, Chicago and at least from a financial mismanagement viewpoint, Jefferson County (Birmingham) here in Alabama.

I fear that the entire country is digging a hole for itself with public education. When I got to college, I discovered most of the kids had been given excellent educations at extremely-expensive prep schools and most of those institutions had at the time almost entirely white students. The whites in the South will eventually regret having spent so little on public education and come up with tougher laws to ensure that kids go to schools and have the proper incentives to get an education.

RELIGION

Religion in Montgomery is pervasive, in stark contrast with New England. As I have said, Montgomery is the Buckle at the center of the Bible Belt. It is amusing that Wikipedia under Bible Belt lists a number of options such as Dallas for several seminaries, Lynchburg for the largest Evangelical Christian University, Nashville for its 700 churches, Tulsa for Oral Roberts and Charlotte for Billy Graham.

Wikipedia had just written about Vermont's having 34% of its population "non-religious" and Alabama's having just 6%. Montgomery, at the heart of the "Heart of Dixie" is far more religious than the enumerated options.

In all those years living in New York, Boston and Europe, I don't remember having heard grace given once, other than on special days such as Christmas and Thanksgiving. In Alabama grace is said at the start of most meetings and even by people in fast food joints like McDonalds. One friend goes on and on so long that it seems more like a sermon.

SCHOOLS

The public schools in Montgomery are not bad, they are horrendous. Part of this appears to be traceable to the teachers union, the AEA, but I think the primary cause is the parents, followed closely by the community's attitude. There is one truly outstanding public school, LAMP, but it is a magnet school, attracting the cream of the crop of those who don't go to the private grade and high schools.

COST OF LIVING

Residents of Montgomery simply cannot believe how much lower their property taxes are than elsewhere in the country. Admittedly it was a beautiful home in Dover, Massachusetts but the taxes on the house we built are about $24,000 a year. The taxes on the small house we owned for ten years just south of Savannah were about $7,000 annually (not really, but this was the total cost when you added in fees for services normally covered by property taxes, such as fire department and trash pickup).

In Montgomery, our taxes recently went up to $960 per year, and that is for a house that is 38% larger than our house had been in Savannah. It also includes trash pickup twice a week and yard debris once a week. People may have heard that our taxes are low, but be totally unaware of how huge the difference is. Montgomery and Savannah are in neighboring states at very close to the same latitude and our taxes there were seven times as much in Savannah as they are here.

There is a high sales tax, 10%, and this is derided as regressive, as is taxing groceries. The property tax should be much higher, but you won't see many candidates winning elections by campaigning on a plan to raise people's property taxes.

I believe quite strongly that everybody should bear some burden of the taxes. It is absurd how high the percentage of citizens who pay no income tax has become. Democrats may rail against the "regressive" tax, but I think it is fair. Is it really "fair" that 50% pay no income tax?

With the exception of products sold nationwide at established prices, many things are much-less costly here. When you are retired, a much lower cost of living is a big benefit. It is also a prime reason that government should not try to enact a minimum wage that is exactly the same in every place. Living in New York City is many times as expensive as Alabama.

SPORTS

TV reduces the impact of being unable to see all of my old favorite teams live. It is probably better to watch the New England Patriots and Boston Red Sox on TV rather than live, especially once you get into the NFL playoffs when games are frequently played in extremely cold and sometimes snowy weather.

Baseball is a different story. Fenway Park isn't just clothed in history, it is a great place to watch the Red Sox. For many years I had the opportunity to sit in a close-to-home-plate box seat or a luxury box overlooking the infield. Montgomery has a charming new "retro" baseball park, but it is difficult to get excited about watching the "Biscuits," a team on which I cannot name a single player. Seeing the Celtics or the Bruins live in Boston Garden was much more fun than watching on TV.

Where Alabama is incredible is college football. The Southeastern Conference has won almost all of the recent national championships, and Auburn (the closest university to our home) and Alabama (the most famous) have won a majority of the most recent games. The state is fanatical about its football.

The tailgating before major games reaches heights unattained by other conferences. A huge number of cars and pickup trucks bear bumper stickers for one of the two teams and an amusing number fly window-mounted flags above their cars.

Even residents who did not go to Auburn or Alabama are expected to "declare" their support and we have several friends in that category who are avid fans of one or the other. We appear to be successful in cheering for both teams except when they are playing each other. It is sad to observe that so many fans of one school hope the other school will lose even when playing against an opponent from some other state. Some actually claim to hate the other school.

MARDI GRAS

Elsewhere you will read comparisons of Mardi Gras and the Carnivals in Venice and Rio, my two favorites. In Montgomery, the black-tie balls begin in September and run steadily through to the finale, the white tie Phantom Hosts Ball, on the Sunday before Lent.

Dad had been one of the original members of Phantom Hosts. When I was invited for the first time after returning to Montgomery, I expected to see some in white tie (as stated on the invitations), many in tuxes and maybe even a few in dark blue suits. What a surprise. Hundreds of guys in white tie and tails with not a single one in a tux. You didn't see that in Boston.

HISTORY AND POINTS OF INTEREST

The number of beautiful and interesting things to see in Boston is staggering. Hundreds are really significant, such as the site of the Boston Massacre where the first colonist was killed by the British in the American Revolution.

There is the site of the first public school, the first subway, the first World Series game and golf's first Ryder Cup. The harbor is full of ships and many hundreds of pleasure boats. There are hundreds of outstanding restaurants. Greater Boston has several of the world's leading universities, hospitals, and libraries.

Given my background in travel, one of the most illustrative contrasts is Boston's Logan Airport. In Montgomery we have Delta and American, actually small regional airlines *representing* these two. In addition to 14 domestic airlines (several of which, like Delta and American, fly worldwide) that serve Boston, at Logan you have Aer Lingus, Aeromexico, Air Berlin, Air Canada, Air France, Alaska, Alitalia, British Airways, Cathay Pacific, Copa, El Al, Emirates, Etihad, Eurowings, Hainan, Iberia, Icelandair, Japan, Lufthansa, Norwegian, Qatar, SATA/Azores, Scandanavian, Swissair, TAP Portuguese, and Virgin Atlantic. Quite a list: 26 foreign carriers.

You can fly non-stop, or at least on one airline, to many places throughout the world. The route I wish had existed when I was having to fly on business is non-stop Boston all the way across Europe and some of the Middle East on the great Etihad or Emirates Airlines.

STRANGE FACT
Most people, even those who live here, don't know that the County and the City are, by strange coincidence, named after different people.

The City of Montgomery is named for a general who fought in the American Revolution, Major General Richard Montgomery. The County is named for Major Lemuel Putnam Montgomery, who was killed in the Creek War at the Battle of Horseshoe Bend in 1814.

ENTERTAINMENT
In Boston, we could frequently see concerts by the biggest stars. There were magnificent classical music performances in Boston's Symphony Hall. The coasts, north and south of Boston, provide beautiful sailing. The top skiing resorts of New Hampshire and Vermont are a few-hours drive away.

New York City and its incredible variety of things to do is just a short flight away, and going out to Logan to catch a Shuttle is like hailing a taxi…no reservations.

COMMENT
I did come home. It is great having so many childhood friends around but difficult to leave a major city and move back to a small one. Montgomery is quiet and pleasant. There are traffic jams, but no big ones, certainly nothing approaching the massive backups I have faced in New York and Boston.

Yes, it may get very hot in the summer, but we have something that helps a lot. It's called air conditioning. When I was growing up there was no air conditioning in the house and none in cars. You may be hot outside during July and August, but that is nothing compared to the dangerous snow, ice and sub-zero temperatures in New England.

When you have lots of old friends, Montgomery is a most enjoyable place to live.

73 MY CAREER AS A FORGER
For The 13th Largest Bank in the US

In the late sixties, ownership of a stock was evidenced by an elaborately engraved stock certificate. One of the funniest examples was stock in the Playboy Corporation. So many people had purchased one share of stock in order to have the Bunny on the stock certificate that the cost of printing and mailing all the required quarterly and annual reports was far out of proportion, forcing Playboy to try to buy back all of those single shares.

Banks have various levels of signature requirements on different types of documents. Some required the signature of an officer of the bank, others required multiple signatures if the amount involved was very large. When stock certificates had to be issued and in the case of a custodian bank for mutual funds, held by the bank, each certificate could not exceed one hundred shares and every one had to be signed by two officers of the bank. People dreaded being called for "signature duty." If the computerized system had not come along and eliminated the requirement of engraved certificates for every 100 shares of a corporation, the bank today would have to have hundreds of full time employees just sitting there all day doing nothing but signing stock certificates….and, remember, the signers had to be officers of the bank.

Once, in the late sixties, State Street Bank found itself with a document that was so important that it could only be signed by the bank's President, it was urgent that it be signed, and H. Frederick Hagemann, Jr., the bank's Chairman of the Board, President and CEO, was out of town and would be for several days. The document simply could not wait. It had to be signed that day and it had to be signed by the big boss. I don't remember how it came about, but I was summoned to the executive offices to forge Hagemann's signature.

His was an awful signature, one of these ones that had every letter legible and most of the numerous letters involved lots of strange wiggling around. This was one of those deals where I could study his signature and practice, but the final had to be done once on the actual document and that first try had to be right. It had already been signed by the other party to the deal. It was scary, but my attempt was close enough. I was not allowed to see the title of contents of the contract, just the page at the end for the signature.

Over the years, I have heard of people who got into trouble forging signatures to legal documents. This document was extremely important and there must have been a lot of money involved. I wonder what would have happened if the forgery had been discovered and the deal cancelled or was declared illegal. I suspect that Hagemann had to be told when he returned, but his senior officers may have preferred just to keep it secret.

I guess I should have worried about what would have happened if my action had been discovered. Knowing what I know today about how some people operate, I would not be surprised if all the senior officers who knew what had happened would have denied their involvement. I don't know how they could have explained my having been the person who signed the document. I was probably safe on that because they would have to have requested my action, provided me with the document that had to be signed and then delivered it once it was "duly executed." I almost wondered how they found someone to notarize that they had witnessed Mr. Hagemann signing the document in their presence.

Hagemann was a brilliant and highly-respected expert in the field of banking. In 2009, it is interesting to note that Mr. Hagemann, a very conservative gentleman and banker, way back in 1965, had expressed concern about the risk because "banks are more highly loaned than at any time since the 20s." What would he have thought in 2008?

EXPENSE ACCOUNTS

The bank gave me the responsibility for selecting in what country and then in what city State Street should open its first foreign office. I had to travel throughout Europe a lot. The choice was quickly narrowed down to Belgium, England, France, Germany, Italy and Switzerland. This was reduced to England and Germany. Returning after a couple of months on the road, I had a $12,000 expense reimbursement form, filled out in great detail. Fifty-three years later, in today's dollars, the amount would be more like $85,000. That might raise some eyebrows!!!!

The bank's chief financial officer never liked me and this time he thought he had caught me good. On the list of expenditures to be reimbursed was $300 for a bottle of wine. That was in the late 1960s, so the equivalent of a couple of thousand dollars today.

I was called from 50 State Street to the CFO's large and elegant office in 225 Franklin Street, where I was met by another officer and the lady who reviewed expense accounts joined the meeting. The conversation, if that is what you could call it, began with a question about whether I really thought the bank was going to reimburse me for such an outrageous expense. My foolishness was obviously not going to be reimbursed. They must have studied the restaurant bill very carefully to find the charge for wine that would have been on the bill in Deutchmarks.

I drew out my response for a while by telling them that during the business luncheon with two top executives of one of Germany's largest banks, I had mentioned an article in the previous-week's *Time* magazine about a special type of German wine called Trockenbeerenauslese. These wines were incredibly sweet and expensive because the vineyard risked leaving some grapes on the vines until a light frost, which made the grapes wrinkle up and increase their sugar content. The grapes had to be individually picked by hand and, if they were ruined by a severe freeze, would be worthless. I went on to mention that I really disliked sweet wines, but this was a big topic in Germany that week and that was why it was ordered.

This still, obviously, was no excuse for my having ordered the wine. I knew it would not pacify them, but I used the background to drag it out and let them dig their hole deeper and deeper. The CFO was uncontrollably mad at me.

In fishing, it is called "setting the hook." Having waited a long time, I was delighted to tell them that, if I were not going to be reimbursed for my expense, they needed to take up the subject with George Rockwell, President of the bank, who had been the one who insisted that we have that wine. That shut them up "real fast and real good."

The other side, actually the reverse, of the subject of expense reimbursement was a trip to Pittsburgh to call on a bank customer assigned to me, Federated Investors. Their officers' favorite place to go for lunch was up on the crest of one of those steep ridges that look down across the Monongahela River at the city.

You could drive a long way over a bridge, around to the end of the ridge and up to the restaurant, but it was relatively easy to get there on foot by walking from their office across a bridge and up via an unusual steep cog railway called "The Incline." That expense report had loads of expensive things on it, but I got called on a 25 cent item, "the Incline," which was listed under "Transportation." The financial people just wanted to know what in the world an incline was. It illustrated how carefully they reviewed expense accounts, at least mine.

GREAT WINES

While on the subject of outstanding wines, I will deviate into two more wine stories.

In 1982 the final awards banquet of the International One-Design Class World Championships was held at Jordan Pond House just north of Northeast Harbor, Maine. As President of the Class I was there and the dinner happened to be on August 8, my birthday. The dinner was hosted by Peggy Rockefeller, who had the famous C. Douglas Dillon at her table.

Dillon had been Ambassador to France in 1953 and Secretary of the Treasury from 1961-1965. He had held numerous important positions ranging from President of New York's Metropolitan Museum of Art to President of the Harvard Board of Overseers. He also was known as the owner of the excellent Chateau Haut-Brion vineyard in France, my favorite Bordeaux in those days and a chateau rated near the absolute top of the great

French wines. Maybe I should have saved it but I went ahead and drank the bottle of Haut Brion that he gave me that night as a birthday present. It is one of the four top-rated wines of France. I had earlier been buying Haut-Brion by the case, for $48, just $4 a bottle. That year would now fetch in the thousands.

The other one that resulted from getting to dine on expense accounts and having to travel throughout the world all the time was when I was dining alone one evening at La Tour d'Argent in Paris. Having met me on previous visits, the owner, Claude Terrail, sat down with me for dinner and ordered one of the very best wines, Chateau Petrus. Luckily it was free because I would have not gotten away with having that one on my expense account for a meal by myself.

The third wine story, also Chateau Haut-Brion, is in the chapter about Bill Koch.

"I WANT MY MONEY"

At State Street Bank, my largest responsibility was the relationship with Fidelity Funds. My employer, unbelievably successful now, was already outstanding back in the mid1960s, especially in the field of service to the mutual fund industry. State Street was responsible as Custodian Bank for as much of the fund industry as their next four banking competitors in the world *combined.* The bank is now truly huge in this field, with trillions of dollars under custodianship.

When mutual funds or, for that matter, stocks involving stock certificates, were sold, you had typically attached a "stock power" on which the signature had to be guaranteed by a "national (this meant US chartered) bank" or a member firm of The New York Stock Exchange. This was sometimes a bother but generally very easy to handle in the United States and not much more difficult in most other parts of the world.

The guarantee of the signature protected the bank or other recipient of the shares and, in the case of mutual funds, protected the issuer of proceeds from the sale of shares. Stocks were generally purchased through brokerage houses, but mutual funds began to be sold by people who did not work for a brokerage house and they were increasingly in parts of the world where there were no US banks. During this period (before Nixon changed the deal and the dollar rapidly slid in value) most of the money coming into the mutual fund industry was from Germany, Switzerland, Italy and the Middle East.

The bank's mutual fund accounting department dealt with many complex issues every day, requiring large departments to handle all of the paperwork. One day a unique problem surfaced. A sheik in Saudi Arabia wanted to sell his Fidelity mutual fund shares, so his request had been mailed to the bank. The material delivered to the bank was just that….a written request, giving the correct account number, signature and other relevant information. There was, of course, no "signature guarantee."

One of our top-rated employees, Paul Archibald had, as he was wont to do, mailed a response and put the pending documentation in his desk drawer. Weeks passed and another request arrived by mail, this time somewhat more forcefully demanding payment, but still not providing the required signature guarantee. This requirement was standard procedure in the investment industry, not just a bank rule. Part of the bank's contract with its fund customers required that it receive all proper documentation before acting.

Paul wrote and mailed another letter. As I recall, by the time the issue was brought to my attention, the problem had dragged on for a couple of months. State Street received a fairly-terse (that's an understatement) telegram from the man in the Middle East demanding his money. He still did not supply the required documentation, but this time I urged Chester Hamilton, the Treasurer of Fidelity Funds to approve the transaction.

The risk in doing that appeared to be much less than would have been the case had we, once again, refused to send the man his money. My decision was to pay without the required documentation. The telegram I had received from the Arab investor read "I have taken Fidelity's representative into custody and, unless my money is wired to my bank without further delay, his right hand will be cut off at the wrist." I trust you can understand why we complied with that "request."

A VERY SMALL MISTAKE

On July 5, 1967 we had a very awkward meeting with Chester Hamilton. State Street's Custodianship Department had made a "rounding error" in pricing one of Fidelity's mutual funds. We had rounded up a penny when it was a fraction of a cent, but should have been down. Pricing billions of dollars for many mutual funds had to be done frequently and fast. You would not believe the amount of trouble you could get into with the Securities and Exchange Commission by a fraction of a cent error.

GERMAN LAW

On January 11, 1971, Barrons published a large article about banks and mutual funds trying to do business in Europe, primarily West Germany. The article by Neil McInnes was devastating. As mentioned in the preceding story, a very large portion of the money coming into the US mutual fund industry was from central Europe, primarily from Germany on behalf of investors in Germany, Switzerland and Italy.

State Street had just opened the location I had selected in Munich to expand our service to the mutual fund industry. The Barron's article over and over again led you to believe that most European countries were looking to bar their citizens from investing in the

United States via mutual funds. I was the point man for State Street's bank in Germany at the time and I was the only person quoted in the devastating article, and it was the same, awful, out-of-context quote over and over again. The writer never tried to call, much less talk with me, but I must admit that the quote he used was something I had said. My primary problem was that, taken out of context, it made me and my employer look really stupid. Unfortunately, it was very embarrassing to State Street Bank, resulting in the bank's calling an emergency meeting of the Board of Directors to address this subject. The article had made the bank look inept or stupid and, of course, terrified our largest clients, the country's leading mutual funds.

Before proceeding to open the bank in Germany, State Street's lead lawyer in Boston, Bud Page, had spent an inordinate amount of time working with a German lawyer, Jurgen Killius, to be sure we complied with all regulations. The Barron's article did correctly, as I had stated before the German equivalent of the Federal Reserve Board, cite the troublesome paragraph in German banking law as 'obscure." It was quite well hidden and went unnoticed in all the legal research. The problem was not in the law everyone examined, it was in law on a separate subject, only referenced by the regulations everyone knew about. The relevant law stated that any foreign bank acting as custodian for a mutual fund must provide security "comparable" to that of a German bank.

The truth of the matter was that US law and tight supervision by our Securities and Exchange Commission provided much-better assurance to investors than any European laws, but the German law's hidden clause about "comparable" was being interpreted by their banking authorities as meaning "identical" to German law. It was the fact that our systems and procedures were so superior to anything we found in Europe that made us believe our service was sorely needed and would be highly successful.

The big difference between the US and Germany was that in the US banks did not manage their own mutual funds. US funds were organized by independent companies; banks merely protected investors by serving as independent custodians of each fund's assets. Because of the tough US requirement requiring bank custodianship of all assets that funds could not falsify records and report owning stocks or bonds that they did not really have for investors. In Germany, it was the banks who managed and controlled their own mutual funds, a completely different type of relationship.

The German law required a mutual fund's custodian bank to hold twice as much cash or securities from non-fund clients as from mutual fund customers. State Street's new little Munich subsidiary bank was far from qualifying and under a strict interpretation, even the giant parent bank in the US would not come close to satisfying German law relevant to custodianship as it was being interpreted. As I wrote earlier, in the mutual fund custodianship business, State Street was bigger than their next four competitor banks in the world *combined.* The very large parent bank in Boston had only about 5% as much cash as the German law would require if enforced regarding US bank serving mutual funds that could be sold in Germany. When carried to the extreme, an interpretation could have been reached that US protection was not comparable and the all US funds would have to cease selling in Germany or switch to a different bank. It got worse.

Several European countries, most notably Switzerland, were reported in the Barrons article as having begun drafting similar language for their applicable laws. The mutual fund industry did have a serious ethical problem because of the wild operation of what were known as "overseas" funds, the most notorious of which was Bernie Cornfeld's Investors Overseas Services. These rapidly-growing funds were usually based in small countries, frequently tiny offshore islands, that provided no regulatory oversight. These countries liked having the large amounts of cash in their banks and did not care what happened to any foreign investors. State Street had, when asked, wisely refused to serve IOS. I could see the debacle that lay ahead for most offshore mutual funds and we could not risk being tied to it in any way.

To give you an idea of how bad it was, I talked with a new "open-ended" fund investing in real estate. One obligation of a custodian bank was to perform an evaluation of every fund's asset value twice a day so that investments in and investor sales of mutual fund shares were always executed at an accurate current value. At least today it is once a day.

The offshore real estate fund's plan was little short of terrifying. Because the real estate mutual funds claimed real estate was going up at about 18% every year, operators just expected their custodian banks to increase the value of their fund by .0493% every day. There was no way you could appraise every building once a year, much less every day, and how were you to establish value? The offshore mutual funds claimed adding a little bit every day was the only way it could be done. The obvious result would be that the "value" of their investments would go up every day and there was *no* mechanism for the value to come down. Wouldn't that have been interesting in 2009? Obviously, I had sense enough to turn this type of prospective customer down, but note that one I had rejected did find a small offshore bank that was willing to do it to get the business. Such practices were a concern in the rest of the world, but not in the US. We operated under tough, well-designed rules.

People used to kid me that I had selected Munich because of its beauty as a city, its proximity to great skiing in Lech, Austria (just 188 miles away, where I did go on winter weekends), and the summer sailing on Lake Starnberger See just a dozen miles south of the city. The primary reason for selecting Munich was entirely business. Much of the flow of money from Europeans into US mutual funds was coming through Bavaria, the southern region of Germany, with Munich as its capital. Once the bank was open, we quickly discovered this was not the result of German money; there was a lot of money coming from Switzerland and Italy and Munich, in Bavaria (the southernmost part of Germany) was the closest city to reach.

We had Italian cars arrive at the bank with trunks packed with suitcases full of cash....all old dirty bills that were difficult and very time consuming to count. From one of the doctors who had gotten his Italian Lire out of his country I learned that everyone knew an easy way to evade the border guards leaving Italy. Unlike the little narrow two-lane highway passes that you must go through to get from Italy into Switzerland, there is one fairly large city that straddles the border, Chiasso, Switzerland. It sits just 2 miles west of the famous Villa D'Este on Lake Como and a 276 mile, five hour, drive north to Munich. There are several streets in Chiasso that people know they can take to get from Italy into Switzerland without having to go through Customs inspections.

DON'T ARGUE WITH THE TREASURY DEPARTMENT

In the late 1960s, State Street Bank purchased a supply of imitation gold bars to give to major customers. They looked like gold and must have been made of lead to be so heavy. They were covered with something that looked much better than gold leaf. The caption on the reverse read that they were 22kt gold plate. They were inscribed with what looked like official stamps. In the lower left was a seal that read "Assay Office, New York, NY." In the upper-left corner it read "FINE 999.8." That would be mighty pure gold. As if each "bar" had been weighed, across the center at the bottom it read "OZs. 19.591." At today's prices those 19 ounces of gold would be about $25,000, hard to believe for that little four-inch-long bar.

On the back of the bar was a six line long stick-on disclaimer (that could have easily been peeled off), explaining that it was a reproduction of what the Treasury stores at Fort Knox, that it was plated in 22 kt gold and that "If it were of solid gold the value would be approximately $687.95." That doesn't sound "approximate" to me, but it does illustrate the increase in the value of gold in fifty years and a concurrent decline in the value of the dollar vs. gold. The Treasury Department claimed (probably correctly, that these gold bricks looked much too close to the real thing and ordered the bank to destroy all that they had and all that had been passed out. I kept mine. Wish it was as real as it looks, but it serves fine as a paperweight.

74 FRIENDS

You should, but probably don't, know their names

WILLIAM MOOMAW

Bill moved to Montgomery after World War II and attended Sidney Lanier High School with me. He joined a small club that I ran after the school banned fraternities. The Poet Hi-Y was under the auspices of the YMCA, but it was as close to being a fraternity as you could get. Bill Chandler, for many years the Executive Director of the Y, allowed us to pick the guys we wanted for members and it resulted in many of our best friends all belonging to the club of 24 guys. Eighteen are still alive and get together for reunions.

Bill was good looking, tall, had a great personality and was very intelligent.

Bill was admitted to Williams College in the northwestern corner of Massachusetts. For those who have not heard of it, Williams is frequently ranked as the best small liberal arts college in the United States. Bill also earned a PhD in Physical Chemistry from the Massachusetts Institute of Technology. Now *that* takes some doing!

During college, Bill would frequently stay with us in Cambridge when he visited "The Big City" and, after college, was one of my many roommates over the years while he was getting his PhD. He went on to become a professor at Williams and subsequently at Tufts University's Fletcher School of Law and Diplomacy near Boston. He has become one of the world's leading environmental experts, consulting for countries throughout the world and helping to shape agreements between nations trying to protect our environment from further degradation.

His name did not surface (as it should have), when he was one of three scientists who drafted the Kyoto Protocols and was a lead author of the report by United Nations Intergovernmental Panel on Climate Change awarded half of the Nobel Peace Prize in 2007. Bill was not just part of the large team whose report shares the Noble Peace Prize for their report, but he had served as the Principle Lead Author for the UNPCC report.

Although a few outspoken opponents still try to discredit the consensus of qualified scientists on the subject of rapid global warming's being caused by man, even some of the skeptics are at last realizing that the whole world faces a horrifying problem and better get to work on solving it soon.

Dr. Moomaw (I must admit that I still have trouble thinking of him as anything other than "Bill") has just retired as the Director of the Center for Environmental and Resource Policy at the Fletcher School. Bill's dad, Colonel Moomaw, had gotten his pilot training from a fairly well-known instructor…Charles Lindberg.

MORRIS DEES

Most of the revered leaders of the Civil Rights Movement are black. Morris is white, but he has made enormous contributions to rights in the United States, risking his life as a result. He grew up on a farm east of Montgomery, in an area called Pike Road, which was way back then considered far out in the country to the east of town. He was quite creative and good at making money. It began early in life. While in college, he somehow obtained the list of classmate's birthdays and the addresses of their parents so he could mail advertisements offering to deliver birthday cakes to the students. The parents loved it, as did the kids, and Morris did a booming business.

Morris later got into the cookbook publishing business. At the end of the 20th Century, when the President of the Savannah Symphony Women's Guild planned to make loads of money by publishing an extremely fancy cookbook, including lots of color photographs of oil paintings of various foods, Morris told me that the only people that really made money off of cookbooks were the publishers. Most ladies' organizations thought that publishing their excellent recipes would make lots of money. This would almost invariably end up in their having to plead with their members to buy cookbooks, and in the case of Savannah, the Symphony Guild was left with a large and expensive inventory.

Morris' first business partner was Millard Fuller, with whom he founded Fuller and Dees Marketing Group, the company that sold cookbooks. In 1978, Millard founded Habitat for Humanity, which has now constructed million of homes for the poor in more than 80 countries throughout the world. They have helped a staggering 22 million build or improve the place they call home.

Morris earned a degree from the University of Alabama Law School and, after selling his business, devoted his life to the legal defense of minorities, primarily helping the blacks who were still being subjected to segregation and discrimination in the South. He has led the battle against hate crimes of all shapes and descriptions. In 1971, Morris co-founded the Southern Poverty Law Center and in 2016 (at age 80)was still there as Chairman and Chief Trial Counsel.

One of his first civil rights cases, Smith v. Young Men's Christian Association, involved the complicated way that the YMCA avoided desegregation in Montgomery. The head of the Y at the time was a friend of mine, Bill Chandler, the man you read about earlier in discussing the Poet Hi-Y. Morris had been a member of the Poet Hi-Y and mentions in his book that Bill Chandler had forced him to resign from the club as a result of using a relatively minor cuss word (Morris thinks it was "damn," not much of a curse by today's standards). We still consider him a member and he came to a reunion of the club in 2017.

As the case against the Y progressed, Morris added Bill Chandler personally as a defendant. Bill had constructed a deal with the Mayor of Montgomery, who closed all of the public swimming pools in the city to avoid having to desegregate them and secretly funded the Y, which would operate pools as a "private" organization, not governed by civil rights law. Years after Morris won the case, he and Bill became good friends.

Morris devised a plan for attacking hate groups like the Ku Klux Klan. All too often, the leaders of hate groups that promoted violence would escape prosecution while their foot soldiers were left to do jail time. Morris devised a strategy to sue the hate groups themselves as well as their leaders in civil suits demanding substantial monetary damages. Cases were won and the overall effect was the bankrupting of the Klan in several of its forms. In his most famous case, Morris won a $7 million judgment against the United Klans of America, on behalf the mother of a Klan lynching victim in Mobile, Alabama. This was the same Klan group responsible for so much of the violence during the civil rights era, including the horrific bombing of the 16th Street Baptist Church in Birmingham that killed four young black girls. The SPLC has been successful in numerous similar cases since then.

The original SPLC headquarters building was firebombed in July of 1983. The Ku Klux Klansmen who had set the blaze were caught and convicted. The sad and staggering fact is that more than thirty people have been jailed for plotting or attempting to assassinate Morris or to blow up the SPLC headquarters.

One night after a high school reunion party in 1980, we sat up in the window of Morris' office overlooking the city of Montgomery. The large picture window might appear to have been vulnerable, but he assured us that the window was tinted to prevent a view from the outside, in addition to being bullet proofed. Morris outlined all of the defenses designed into the construction of the building.

Although the headquarters have been moved across the street to a much larger and more-easily-defended but ugly moderately-high-rise office building, the previous office remains a sightseeing attraction for people wanting to view the elegant little Civil Rights Memorial designed by Maya Lin. The elegant black granite fountain is designed to show the water flowing out of the bowl and over the names of all those who lost their lives in the battle for civil rights for African Americans.

The unbelievably sad news is that, despite fantastic progress in reducing racial tensions and gaining equal rights, there is still much hate group activity throughout the country, not just in the South as you might think.

Even today, when you pull into the driveway of Morris' home, you are met by armed guards who have to be there twenty-four hours a day, seven days a week. He did a magnificent job of renovating and decorating his home, two blocks from where I grew up as a kid. There are several books by or about Morris and an inspiring movie entitled "Line of Fire, the Morris Dees Story."

In late 2008, Pat and I had dinner with the Deeses, delayed because Morris was flying in from a court case in Kentucky and had to be interviewed before dinner for an early morning national TV show which aired the next day. It was sad to hear that there were still threats against Morris' life, and that there had just been a major one that week. At dinner, this brought up another subject which doesn't get any notice, but which needs to be said.

Our country had its first black President. Nothing, however, would be as devastating for our country than to have Obama assassinated. At least we made it past that.There is one worse possibility.

Several of the national security experts have commented that things may be nice for now, but it is not a question of "if," but "when," will terrorists succeed in exploding an atomic bomb in the United States. Our Senators succeed in getting ridiculous amounts of money spent on Homeland Security throughout remote and sparsely-populated states. To get the votes for funding, the money has to be spread over every state, when the focus and most of the money needs to be spent defending the most likely targets, New York City and Washington, D.C.

Given their 2001 success in Manhattan, Washington, DC becomes the most desirable target for the terrorist's next major plan. The Pentagon was damaged, but that plane that our heroes forced to crash in Pennsylvania was almost certainly headed for either the White House or our nation's capitol. The terrorists will try again. It is risky that so many think the war on terrorism has been won. It will get much worse and go on for decades. Homeland Security better guard New York Harbor and the Potomac River, the least likely and therefore likely-to-be chosen routes picked by terrorists.

There will be loads of "lone wolf" attacks killing people in cities throughout the country. These will be sad, but nothing compared to what will result from the next "big one."

If you are a Senator of Representative reading this, be damn sure you allocate several times the normal funding for Homeland Security and the Secret Service so that we are doing everything we can to prevent a catastrophe, not just wait and wring our hands wondering how it happened after something has happened. Keep your fingers crossed.

In the meantime, people need to appreciate how incredible it is that someone continually risks their life to benefit the poor and oppressed. Morris is a remarkable man.

Epilogues

Here there are actually four epilogues. Is that possible? There is one about hunting that I did not remember, but Morris told one evening. They follow below.

Good Will Hunting (No, Just Hunting)

When Morris and I were in high school we frequently went out hunting after school. We would get out, drive home, pick up our shotguns and head our hunting. The best hunting, especially dove, was out in fields east of downtown where we now live in Vaughn Meadows, now full of houses and considered "midtown." Going home was wasting time that could have been spent hunting. Morris says he started putting his shotgun in his car and driving to school. Since they were valuable and he did not want his gun stolen while his car was parked, he said he started bringing his shotgun into Lanier High School and putting the gun in his locker. When I tell this story orally, I always end it with a long pause, followed by..."I don't think they allow that anymore."

Once again, it is truly remarkable and admirable that a man who has done so much for civil rights can raise personally very large amounts of money for a truly worthy cause while accepting only what for his position and role could easily have given him many times what he elected to be paid by the SPLC while risking his life for his work on behalf of others. He may remain unknown to many Americans, but he is truly a hero.

Sad Ending

In early 2019, the nation was shocked to see on TV or read in newspapers and magazines that Morris had been fired by SPLC. I knew that there had been a letter from employees about 24 years ago and had been told that it was a complaint about Morris' behavior. What never, to my knowledge, surfaced in the recent news, was a story that the SPLC President, Richard Cohen (who years ago reviewed what I had written above to be sure I had the facts about Morris correctly) had received a letter on the morning he fired Morris. Supposedly, the letter led Richard to believe he had to take action without delay, firing Morris to avoid a very serious problem A few days later Richard resigned as President. When I wrote urging him to stay at least for a transition period, his emailed response was "That train has left the station."

The contents of that alleged recent letter have not been disclosed as of mid 2019, but may come out because a lady has been hired to do a "forensic" investigation of things at the SPLC. A sad ending to a remarkable career. At least Morris has found and married a very intelligent, young and beautiful new wife.

Still taking on the difficult tasks
Alabama faced a very awkward election in December of 2017 in which voters had to choose a person to replace Jeff Sessions as Senator. The winner of the Republican Primary was a notorious judge, a former Chief Justice of the Alabama Supreme Court. This sounds fine until you learn that he had to be removed from that office, not once but twice.

In both instances, Roy Moore made headlines around the country, in all cases very negative. His stated position is that he puts his religious beliefs above the law. In the first case it involved buying and placing a huge granite stone in the middle of the lobby to the Alabama Supreme Court building displaying the Christian religion's Ten Commandments. When faced by a panel of judges that ordered it removed, he refused. In Alabama, justices are elected and with Alabama ranked as the most religious state in the nation he got re-elected despite having had to be removed from office. It was no surprise when he had to be removed from office again, this time for ordering Probate Judges around the State to defy the laws of the country on homosexuality and same sex marriage. Now the state has stupidly change the law so that judges no long issue marriage licenses to anyone. This reminds me of the City's closing all swimming pools more than a half century ago.

The religious right all supported Moore and he was a Republican in an extremely "red" (Republican) state. When the election was just a few weeks away, four women had come forward saying that Moore had made improper sexual advances years ago. The number quickly doubled. As a result, thousands of former supporters deserted him. Many of my friends were mad at me when I admitted that I had voted for Doug Jones, the Democrat, narrowing the Republican majority in the Senate.

I simply could not vote for Moore. Jones won. Many residents voted against Moore because of his improper actions toward women, not his serious transgressions against the laws of his country. Had Moore been elected it would have been a major embarrassment to Alabama in the eyes of most of the country and the world. Most unfortunately, in 2019, he is again running for the Senate.

Morris was a leader in the fight to get Moore removed from office both times. I am reminded of a bumper sticker from an election in 1964 in Massachusetts involving Edward "Teddy" Moore Kennedy. The signs read "Please No Moore." I should reprint those today.

A most unusual talent
Even his close friends who do not know it, Morris is a remarkably good tap dancer.

PORTER ANDERSON

Porter was one year ahead of me at Lanier and lived on the opposite side of the street from my house on Woodley Road in Montgomery. He was another example of someone who was remarkably intelligent.

Porter went from Montgomery to Emory in Atlanta and then on to the Harvard Medical School in Boston (yes, that is correct, most of the University is in Cambridge). In 1996, he was honored with the Lasker Award for his development of a vaccine that protects against Type B Hemophilius Influenza, the virus that leads to Meningitis. He has also been awarded the very prestigious Pasteur Award.

Emory University's magazine in the spring of 2011, in a very interesting article, credited Porter with saving 668,661 children by devoting twenty years of his life to inventing a vaccine to prevent meningitis. The Center for Disease Control states that about twenty thousand US children contracted Hib-related meningitis annually and that 45% of these were left with permanent damage. CDC goes on to state that such cases, thanks to Porter, have decreased in the United States by 98 percent. The number of lives saved continues to grow and the impact of the vaccine is huge worldwide

It was particularly interesting to me, because I had almost died of meningitis in 1949, before there was any accepted cure. Stuck in the hospital for a month being given shots every forty-five minutes, I was saved only because my uncle who, as a general in the Air Force, was able to get an experimental sulfur drug released from Washington for me. In the introduction to this book, I commented about being born after my mother had been told she could not have any more normal children. Meningitis leads to mental retardation, deafness and even death in children. I guess the first two of those are be true in my case.

In making the Lasker Award presentation to Porter, Nobel Prize winner Dr. Joseph Goldstein stated that "no other vaccine has ever shown such a rapid and dramatic effect in virtually eliminating a fatal disease. It is a truly remarkable achievement in the history of medical science."

Porter made lots of money and, instead of spending it on himself, created a foundation to donate money to a range of non-profit institutions that work in areas he believes are important to the future of our country and the world. His foundation has focused on the rights of women and the need to protect our environment.

Porter had been one of the two guys who traveled by canoe down the Alabama River from Montgomery to Mobile Bay with me back in 1954. It was a very memorable trip and there is a chapter about one event on our trip.

Porter overcame a very serious accident at the corner of Lebron and Fairview Avenue, two hundred feet from my home, when his motorcycle was hit by a car, badly damaging his left leg. The leading internist in Montgomery at the time was my doctor and cousin, Dr. Jane Day.

Jane insisted that it was too dangerous to try saving the leg and it should be amputated without delay. Porter vehemently opposed this, worked hard on rehabilitation and walks so well today that you would not notice that he had ever had such an injury.

There was a long article in the Seattle Times in 2017 about large financial support for Porter's vaccine provided by the Bill and Melinda Gates Foundation. Porter had gone back to Boston and worked to develop a less expensive version of his vaccine (about five cents a dose) so it could be made available to kids in third world countries. At this point, it appears the number of lives saved from meningitis, in poor countries, is more than two million.

Porter is a very quiet, extremely nice, but modest person who has sought no publicity for his contribution to the world. In January, 2018, he was honored with an award from the Queen of Thailand. I wish I could get the Montgomery newspaper to write about the tremendous contributions to the world by a kid who grew up in Montgomery.

Related Story

Way back on April 15 of 1912, just over a century before this is being written, the Titanic sank in the Atlantic and 1,511 people perished. One bit of information that is rarely mentioned is the huge fare discrepancy on the ship. First Class was $4,353, the equivalent of $109,000 today (and tickets were in demand even at that price). Third class was just $30. People complain about first class flights being so much more expensive than coach, but on the Titanic, first was 145 times as much as third. Most of the stories of that historic night are sad, but one rarely-told story is quite uplifting.

One of the first-class passengers on the *Titanic,* a young man named Richard Norris Williams, was due to become a freshman at Harvard that year. He and his Dad stayed in their cabin until it became obvious they had to climb up on deck. As the *Titanic's* bow aimed deeper and deeper into the ocean and the Williams were together up on the deck, Richard's dad was hit and killed by the huge forward funnel that fell and hit him. The funnel created a large wave that knocked Richard off the deck and drove him toward a small inflatable life raft.

When Richard reached the badly-damaged lifeboat its canvas sides had collapsed so there was really no "boat" into which he could climb. There was barely room for him to hang onto the lifeboat's wreckage. He agreed when one man asked if he could put his arm around Williams' shoulder to make it easier to hold on.

When Williams felt the man's grip slack off he saw the man slip to his grave. Williams managed to hang to the side of the raft for five hours in the sub-freezing water waiting to the rescued. The water wasn't just very cold, it was 28 degrees. Most people in similar situations gave up and gave in to the sea, but Richard was able to hang on until rescued.

When the cruise ship *Carpathia* responded to the Titanic's distress call and was the first ship to arrive at the scene, Williams was one of the ones rescued. The ship's doctor insisted upon amputating Williams' legs, believing that they could not be saved and that they were endangering Williams' life.

Truly Incredible

Williams refused, and with a determined mind and much effort, fully recovered the use of both legs. This alone would be a remarkable story. The amazing story is that Williams did not just recover, he went on to play tennis, and he didn't just *play* tennis. Richard won the US men's championship in 1914 (just two years after the Titanic sank) and again in 1916. He was decorated for bravery in World War I. Richard was awarded France's highest decoration, the Chevalier de la Legion d'Honneur.

Twelve years later, playing tennis in the Olympics, he won the gold medal. Amusingly, that victory was mentioned on TV during the August, 2016, Olympics in Rio, but without mentioning any of the story that make it such an incredible accomplishment.

There is a funny part of Williams' story that night. The father and son sat around in their stateroom for quite a while, his father certain that the Titanic could not sink. After all, the ship had been touted as "unsinkable." When the two Williamses finally decided they better move up on deck they started down a hallway and encountered a steward loudly banging on a door to warn a passenger inside. When the occupant would not open his door, the younger Williams smashed the door open with his shoulder. The passenger would obviously thank him, but the ship's steward threatened Williams, stating that he would report him for damaging the property of the White Star Line. I think there was a little more significant damage to the Titanic that night.

Yet Another Related Story

Most people have never heard that a man, Morgan Robertson, fourteen years *before* the sinking of the *"Titanic"* wrote a novel about the sinking of a cruise ship, the *"Titan,"* that was claimed to be unsinkable but hit an iceberg bound for New York. In addition to the uncanny name similarity, the two ships were remarkably similar in many respects, from length of ship to their both hitting an iceberg on their starboard side at night in the month of April. That is truly an uncanny list of facts.

Among the long list of similarities is that the *Titan* in the book sank 460 miles from Newfoundland and the *Titanic* sank 405 miles from Newfoundland. The shape of the four huge funnels on the "*Titanic"* were essentially identical to the *Titan*'s funnels shown on the dust jacket of the book. Even the unusual design of the stern of each ship was the same. The name similarity is beyond uncanny. The book's title, "Futility" was changed later, after the *"Titanic's"* sinking. It is amazing that this story is not repeated at all, much less often.

Another fact that is barely mentioned is that the "*Titanic's"* route to New York was not from Southampton, on the southern coast of England, to New York. She sailed to pick up passengers almost due south across the English Channel in Cherbourg, France and from there to Queenstown, close to the middle of the southern coast of Ireland. The reason you don't find this big harbor on maps is that the city's name was changed to "Cobh."

And Yet Another, This Time The Last Related Titanic Story

Yes, I know I have too many stories and, yes, this may not be the best place to put it, but it will have to do. A friend with whom I played golf twice a week, Bill Romeiser, had a remarkable history, but never mentioned it. He was a survivor of the Titanic. His father had died that night but he and his mother made it in a lifeboat. It happened to be Lifeboat #6, the boat that had also carried Molly Brown.

There was an enjoyable Broadway musical entitled "*The Unsinkable Molly Brown*,' so named because she had survived the sinking of the *Titanic*. Molly had cut up and given pieces of her heavy coat to be used to wrap and keep babies warm, one of whom was Bill. Wish the family had saved the coat. Bill never mentioned his surviving the *Titanic*, but when he died, my wife was allowed to listen to a recording of his telling the whole story because Bill's wife, Ginny, belonged to P.E.O. with Pat.

Strangely, the Titanic sank almost exactly 2,000 miles from Southamption, where it started its ill-fated inaugural voyage, and sinking almost exactly 1,000 miles from New York City.

SHEILA WIDNALL

Sheila was married to a good friend, Bill Widnall, who in the late 20th century was one of the world's best racing sailors. They were, to say the least, a brilliant couple. Bill, a professor at M.I.T, was on the team tasked with figuring out the navigation required to get the Apollo spaceship from Cape Canaveral to the moon.

I cannot come close to comprehending how you compute the thrust, exact time of life off, speed and trajectory required to get a spaceship from one moving body in space to another circling around it many thousands of miles away. You somehow have to determine the exact moment and amount of power needed to get the huge rocket into the air so that it could circle the spinning earth and leave orbit at the right time to reach the moon as it spun around the earth. Bill was not the head of the team, but I was told by some of the early astronauts that he was credited with contributing most to the solution.

Sheila was at least as smart, if possible, maybe even smarter. She was Institute Professor of Aeronautics and Astronautics at M.I.T, and a senior official at that great University. Sheila served as Associate Provost and Chairman of the Faculty at M.I.T. and was elected President of the American Association for the Advancement of Science. Because of her intelligence and experience she was, among many other things, she was a consultant to Boeing.

Bill and Sheila sailed with us a number of times. Bill, having won the International One-Design World Championship something like nine times, agreed to crew for me when I qualified one year to race in that event in the Firth of Forth, just north of Edinburgh, Scotland. They sailed with Pat and me in the Chesapeake and several times in the Caribbean.

On one such occasion, we had chartered a 50 foot sailboat out of the Dutch part of the island of St. Martin, sailing as part of the Winter Cruise of Marblehead's Eastern Yacht Club. -What made it unusually interesting was the fact that, as we were approaching the date for our trip, Sheila's name was about to go before the U.S. Senate for approval as our country's first ever female Secretary of a branch of the Defense Department. As you might guess from her experience, she was to be Secretary of the Air Force.

One day we were anchored in the midst of a bunch of cruising yachts in the magnificent harbor of St. Bart's. As is the practice, most boats listened to a marine operator who, each morning, broadcasted the names of boats that were being sought by radio. Of course, everyone can listen to the broadcast and hear everyone else's messages. One day the operator announced the name of our boat, stating that she had an urgent message asking Sheila to call the White House. This certainly raised the eyebrows of everyone anchored near enough to see the name of our boat.

A Promotion?

Finally, we get to the funny part. Sheila had quite a reputation, with an incredible record in a highly-complex area of education. Her job at M.I.T. was up there near the top of all professorships in the world. Her mother was obviously quite proud of her daughter. You may not believe the conclusion to this story, but Sheila told it and swore that the punch line was true.

When Sheila called her mother to say that she had been selected to be Secretary of the Air Force, her mother asked "With all of your experience, shouldn't you be able to get a better job than being a secretary?"

Fear of Flying

One more funny. To the Widnalls it was the proper thing to do. When their kids were young, they adhered to a policy of always flying on separate airplanes. This seemed to me to be strange, given their expertise in the field of aeronautics and their extremely high IQs. The number of deaths in automobile accidents is a huge number of times greater than that of air travel. In recent years, the average deaths in airlines has been one in every nine million passengers each year, and a big chunk of these are in foreign airlines with much weaker standards for maintenance and pilot experience. In 2017, deaths by commercial passenger planes in the United State dropped incredibly to zero.

There are thousands of deaths in cars every day. The number is the staggering fact in comparing danger. I have learned to be careful in examining statistics; they can be very misleading. In looking at automobile fatalities in the US it is common to cite the number of deaths per 100 million miles driven. Every year for the past decade automobile deaths per year had exceeded 30,000 in the U.S. alone.

Worldwide between 1966 and 1973 deaths in automobiles exceeded 50,000 annually and between 1999 and 2007 they still exceeded 40,000 every year. Worldwide, deaths from airline flights in 2016 were just 249, and a lot of those were truly second-rate carriers.

I asked Bill and Sheila if they drove in separate automobiles. They did not.

Epilogue

My old friend and business associate in the travel business, Don Sohn, had a fairly common policy, limiting the number of officer-level Heritage Travel employees on a single flight. We had a corporate customer that had lost their senior management in a crash, devastating the company, so we were all painfully aware of the risk.

Don's travel policy for Heritage Travel was most unusual but quite sensible. He believed in protecting the company by limiting the number of senior employees on a flight to just two, but there was an interesting and logical exception. Frequently we had to fly to give sales presentations to a major corporation for which we needed three or four senior officers.

When Don was along, which was often the case, he did not care how many were with him on the flight. His reasoning: If he were killed, he didn't care how many died with him because he would no longer own the company.

THE KOCH BROTHERS

There are four. I only know two…Bill and David. In the early days, Bill said one of the reasons he liked me was that he knew I disliked his twin brother, David. There was a good reason for that and you can read the story later. They are both quite interesting. Bill became a friend before I knew what a Koch was.

BILL KOCH

Bill may be best known for his money and, to a lesser extent, for his wine collection, but I know him as an extraordinarily nice guy and for his having won sailboat racing's biggest prize, the America's Cup, in 1992.

He didn't just put up the tens of millions to finance the design and construction of the boat, named America3; he co-skippered the boat in the races. That "3" is supposed to be up higher to mean "cubed," but I could not figure out how to make my computer put it up where it belongs.

Anyway, Bill spent the money, sailed onboard during the races, co-skippering with Buddy Melges. He frequently took the helm on downwind legs of the course. Pat and I flew to San Diego to watch Bill race for the Cup. Because of the light winds in the Pacific at that point, it wasn't very exciting racing except for the fact that our friend, Bill, won.

Following his victory, Bill gave millions to support the first boat to try for the America's Cup in a boat crewed entirely by women. They didn't win, but they did well and it added a lot of interest to what had always been a man's sport.

Bill had played basketball at M.I.T. and was very smart. Sorry, that's a gross understatement…extremely smart. He did get involved in a legal hassle with his brothers over control of their dad's company, Koch Industries out of Kansas. He lost, but still had many millions.

My funniest story about Bill involves a day in New York City. At the time, I was dating Barbara Petersen. We had read in the New York Times that there had been a huge art auction at one of the top auction houses in Manhattan, I think it was Christies. The next day, when our taxi pulled up to the Shuttle Terminal at LaGuardia for us to fly back to Boston, I hoped out of the cab and went to fetch our suitcases from the trunk.

As I was doing that, a black limo pulled up behind us and out jumped Bill Koch. He saw me, ran up and offered to carry Barbara's suitcase. I had no opportunity to tell her about the person who was carrying her suitcase. We walked together into the terminal and, because there is no assigned seating on Shuttles, ended up sitting with him on the plane. He had been in New York for the big auction the day before, and there was lots of newspaper coverage of the works of art that had been sold.

Bill pulled out the catalog of works, on which he had noted the prices that each work had brought. At the time he was married to Joannie Granlund, a lady who also belonged to the club called the Sitzundjibers in Boston, which I ran for several years for Don Sohn and to which Bill, Joannie and I belonged. Joannie was Bill's first wife.

Looking through the auction catalog, he stopped and commented that he had bought this statue. Barbara became more aware of the person next to whom she was seated when she saw that the price he had paid was just over $2 million. Several pages later he got to another statue with a similar price tag that he said he had purchased and that he was going to be in real trouble with Joannie when he got home because she had made him promise that he would not buy more than one.

During the conversation, Bill learned that Barbara was a mapmaker. Actually she was more than that word might convey; she was an excellent cartographer. Weeks later he called me, got her phone number and asked her to make elegant four color maps that could be given to guests giving directions to his homes. She was delighted and did a lot of design work to make them beautiful rather than just utilitarian. Bill paid $25,000 for the design only to be told by his security manager that it would be too risky to have these maps out in people's hands.

My wife, Pat, and I had dinner at the Harvard Club of Boston with Bill and his third wife, Bridget, just after they had married in 2005. Bridget is a beautiful, charming and talented lady. She had been a Rooney, the family in Pennsylvania that, among many other things, owns the Pittsburgh Steelers of the National Football League. Bridget is charming and a great match with Bill.

I knew he had been married to a second wife, but I knew nothing about her until years later. Having grown up in Montgomery, Alabama and living there now, I was very surprised to hear that his second wife, Angela Browder, was from Montgomery.

Angela had been married to Sonny Gaunt, son of a well-known business man in Montgomery. I never met her, but the people who knew her said that she was unbelievably beautiful. The words used most frequently in people's description of Angela were "drop dead gorgeous." They also said that she was from quite modest means and that Sonny had played "My Fair Lady's" Henry Higgins' role in polishing her into a sophisticated jewel.

A funny side story about Bill has to do with his great wine collection. He spent years and lots of money collecting all of the vintages of several of the greatest names in French wine history and is an acknowledged expert. He had a truly incredible collection, 43,000 bottles, and I knew about that. What I didn't know was that there is a problem with this avocation. It is forgery. Bill says that there have been many instances of this in recent years. In 2013 he had four lawsuits going over wine that was not what it had been claimed to be. His fight to catch forgers was featured on the TV show "Sixty Minutes" in 2017. Friends who love good wines thank him for spending money to stop this scam.

When you are talking about many hundreds of thousands of dollars being spent on rare wines, there is a great temptation to forge. Bill says the forgers go to great lengths to print labels and use old bottles to make the lousy wine bottle with no historic value or great taste look like the real thing.

One lawsuit in particular was amusing. Bill said that his suit would have cost the forger much more had he been able to get his case heard by a jury in the South's Bible Belt. In his defense, the forger had said that putting some wine in a bottle should be OK because "even Jesus turned water into wine."

Despite all of the billions, Bill to this day remains an extraordinarily nice and extremely intelligent gentleman. In 2013, when I was charged with raising funds for a major arts exhibition at the Montgomery Museum of Fine Arts, I was running out of time and failing to reach my target, Bill generously helped with a large donation which I used as the "Best In Show" Award.

One day in early 2016, when Pat and I were having lunch at his incredible Palm Beach home, he asked in what year we had been married. During the lunch it had come out that my favorite wine had been Chateau Haut Brion for a variety of reasons, a subject in a different chapter. It was not just the taste; I had been given a bottle by the owner of the vineyard on my birthday many years ago. Bill asked us in what year we had been married. Pat answered that our wedding was in1989 without knowing that he intended to give us a bottle of wine from that vintage. I loved Haut Brion and had been buying it in the sixties for $48 a case. It is rated as one of the finest wines in France.

Wine

After lunch, Bill asked if we would like a tour of his wine cellar. Needless to say, the answer was "yes." It is a true cellar, located underneath the house, with its own security system and a complex computer program for tracking inventory. It is quite a cellar, the size of several large rooms in most houses, with an arched brick ceiling and many rows of racks to hold the wines. There is none of the $5 per bottle wines Pat and I drink with dinner at home.

The collection is truly incredible, even though it had only 43,000 bottles. When his "Things I Love" collection of art and other things was on exhibit in Boston's Museum of Fine Arts it had been stated that he owned every vintage of the great Chateau Lafite Rothschild. He looked at the computer and walked to the aisle and slot to get the Chateau Haut Brion. When he pulled it out he said "Why don't I give you two?" I wasn't about to argue against that. He ended up giving us a third bottle, this time a very good Montrachet. Of course, you can't carry bottles on a plane, so it did result in our luggage being opened and searched by the TSA. Glad they didn't confiscate the bottles.

The only big problem was trying to decide what to do with it. Should Pat and I just sit at home and enjoy it by ourselves are do you invite close friends for dinner so each can enjoy a glass? When I looked online the last sale of 1989 Chateau Haut Brion was for $18,000 a case in London. We had trouble swallowing it knowing it is about $250 per glass. Later I looked on the Internet and found a long list of bottles of the 1989 vintage and found them in the $2,200 to $3,352 a bottle range. It is sad, but most of what we drink today is Yellowtail Chardonnay at $9.80 per double bottle, Costco's in-house Kirkland brand Cabernet Sauvignon at $8 for a double bottle. It is interesting that the ritzy Whole Foods market amazingly sells "Three Wishes" Cabernet Savignon and a fairly good Chardonnay for just $2.95 a bottle. This could spoil the image of the store.

On May 19, 20 and 21, 2016 Sotheby's sold for Bill at auction 20,000 bottles from his collection, including a number of cases of the 1989 vintage Chateau Haut Brion. The incredible catalog sold to prospective buyers at the auction was 91/2 inches by 11 ½ inches and 1½ inch thick, including pages of great full color photos of the wines and the chateau from which each had come along with great photos of Bill and his home from which the wine had come. Luckily, my first cousin once removed on my Dad's side of the family, Philip Jelley, is Senior Vice President of Sothebys and sent me a copy of the catalogue. Philip had handled the estimating of Bill's wines for the auction.

The art in the Koch home at Palm Beach is not as good as many of the museums I have visited all over the world….it is better. There are many rooms full of original paintings by many of the world's most famous artists. The biggest names in Bill's collection include Cezanne, Miro, Whistler, Renoir, Homer, and Picasso. Because I love maritime art, it was great to see in the collection Montague Dawson, Fitz Hugh Lane and Buttersworth. Bill has many sculptures by Remington (my favorite sculptor) and Botero (whose huge super-fat nude women are my least favorite). For me, the most interesting was his sailing room that contains all of his trophies, beautifully constructed models of all of the boats that have raced for the America's Cup and a full-size replica of the America's Cup made in solid silver by the original jeweler, Garrard of London.

Bill's primary home is one of just two in the area that stretch 1,160 feet from the beach on the Atlantic to the Intracoastal Waterway. The other, just eleven houses down the street is named Mar-a-Lago and belongs to a guy named Trump. These are the only two properties in the area that stretch from the Atlantic to the lake (the reason The Donald's place is named "Mar-a-Largo." It is awkward trying to thank a friend adequately when the tour of his home is one of the most enjoyable memories of my life. It is unusual to find someone in this day and age who has loads of money and also has excellent taste.

One of the most interesting things about visiting Bill's "Bear Ranch" southwest of Aspen, Colorado, is getting to listen to the historians than he has on staff who tell great stories of the Wild West while touring all the exhibits in the seventy-building "town" Bill has assembled. The historians tell stories to guests in the various museums. There were many; I will include just one here.

One of the major but lesser-known names in the Jesse James gang was Cole Younger. He happened to visit a little ole lady who was desperate and in tears, sometime around 1870. She owed $500 on her mortgage and the bank was about to foreclose that day. Cole, the robber but in this case generous person, pulled $500 in cash out of his bag and gave it to the lady. Needless to say, she was ecstatic and most appreciative.

When the banker arrived on horseback later that day to foreclose, he was shocked and delighted when she handed him the $500. That may not sound like much, but it would be the equivalent of $5,984 in today's dollars. He wrote "Paid in Full" on her mortgage, handed it to her and road away on his horse.

Here's where it gets amusing. The James Gang had waited to surprise the banker on his way with the $500. Probably too obviously, they stole the $500. Should the word be "restole?"

In June of 2019 we had a fabulous time at Bear Ranch. When we got to the airport at 5:15 for a 6am flight to Aspen via Dallas, we checked our luggage and went upstairs to the TSA security checkpoint. There was a line backed up more than 40 people and it was moving very slowly. Many missed their flights, including us. We canceled our trip and then changed our minds, finally deciding to take the same flights the next day. Man, are we happy we did?

It was marvelous. Once lady who was in charge of our visit, Mary Glor, was fantastic over and over again, answering questions, helping with things and finally, with her husband, getting up at 5:30 to see us off. She even texted several times to be sure we had gotten home OK.

Bill has collections of many things besides art. His collection of guns is fabulous, expertly arranged to display the development of various types and make of pistols and rifles over the years. It even has a Gatling gun.

On two nights during our stay, shows were brought in to perform in the saloon, complete with bar and stage. On our last night, the country and western singer was Jeneva Rose, who was charming and very talented, having been a finalist on American Idle. Remarkably, she accompanied herself by playing nine different string instruments.

DAVID KOCH

For much of his life, Bill's twin brother, David, has been Executive Vice President of Koch Industries, lived in New York City and is known as one of the "Koch Brothers," infamous to liberals because of their large financial support of conservative politics. David is Bill's twin brother, younger by 18 minutes..

David may have lots of money, in Forbes Magazine reportedly $43 billion, but he has been generous with it. One example is the theater at Manhattan's Lincoln Center that has been renamed to honor David as a result of his $100 million donation. He has given many millions to the performing arts and to support of history in the country. In this category, David made the news on May 2, 2012, by donating $35 million to the Smithsonian for a new building to house dinosaurs on the Mall in Washington, D.C. Most recently, he has donated about $35 million to landscape with gardens and fountains the sidewalks of the entire four blocks of Fifth Avenue in front of Manhattan's Metropolitan Museum.

David, along with his older brother, Charles, bears the brunt of all of the liberal criticism, bordering on hatred, for their support of conservative causes and candidates in US elections. I think David should be applauded for his philanthropy and his support of sensible politics.

Forbes Magazine rates him as the richest man in the State of New York. That takes some doing.

As an example of the current buzz words, "Fake News," a first cousin of mine, a devout liberal, told me she was furious at David for the Koch Brothers' support of Donald Trump. This subject came up as the result of seeing David's name as major financial supporter of Ken Burns' excellent TV depiction of the Vietnam War. Problem is, Republicans were mad at the Kochs because they *refused* to support Trump.

Fifth Avenue
David purchased Jackie Kennedy Onassis' condo at 1040 Fifth Avenue and lived in it for years, but it was too small for his wife and kids. I thought I was quite late waiting until age 52 to get married for the first time, but David beat me by six years, making it to 58.

David's most spectacular houses are his residence is on the beach in The Hamptons, at the eastern end of Shinnecock Bay, and his house on Palm Beach's Ocean Boulevard two miles up the beach from his twin brother, Bill. For many years, David's primary residence was not a house; it is a huge apartment at 740 Park Avenue. Amusingly, it was built by James T. Lee, who happened to have been Jackie Kennedy's grandfather.

Conservative Politics
It is unfortunate to see David and his older brother being blasted by the media, especially TV's MSNBC, for their support of conservative positions in government. I know of no facts, but it is widely reported that the "Koch Brothers" are by far the two largest donors to conservative philosophy in the United States. David isn't just conservative. He had run for Vice President of the United States on the Libertarian Party ticket several decades ago. Daddy had been one of the key founders of the George Birch Society.

A Beach Party
My funny story about David Koch goes back to the 1960's in Boston. As mentioned earlier, my great friend, Don Sohn, had founded and led a social club in Boston called the Sitzundjibers. One night at one of our parties, this time an annual beach party at the Manchester Bath and Tennis Club, David had had much too much to drink. I can say it that way because years later that was his description of the evening. The club's rectangular swimming pool was surrounded on three sides by the clubhouse. There was a raised deck over three sides of the pool, as I recall about nine feet above the walkway around the pool and constructed right out to the edge of the pool with a three foot high railing.

David threw the wife of the manager of the club, fully clothed, from that high, second floor railing about 12 feet above the pool, into the swimming pool. You might think he just pushed the lady into the pool. It was worse than that. For years, that was all I knew about David that night and that was bad enough. Forty or so years later David told the rest of the story providing some other key events that evening that I had not observed.

David said that he had gone into the club's dining room and dried himself off on the draperies, before heading into the kitchen. I know there is a kid's game called Mumblety-peg, in which you try to throw a knife so that it sticks upright in the ground as close as possible to your toes.

I don't know what it is called when you throw a knife so that it sticks in a wall, but that is what David says he did with the super-sharp chef's knives in the kitchen. Needless to say, the club's employees were terrified.

Don and I spent months apologizing to the head of the club and pleading to be allowed back, but we were never successful. Bet nobody at the Manchester Bath and Tennis Club knows that the man who caused such a furor that evening is now the richest man in New York.

Sadly, in July of 2019, David is suffering from the advance stages of Alzheimers and we are told he does not have much time left to live. At this writing, he is being kept and loved by his beautiful wife in their Palm Beach home.

The "First Brother"

Largely unknown, the oldest of the four Koch brothers is Fred, who had dated a friend named Julie Madden, who was a close friend of my very close friend and business partner, Lolly McDonnell. Lolly grew up in Kansas City not far from the Koch family in Wichita. Fred Koch brought Julie to a party at Lolly's home at which Lolly's mother taught Fred how to Charleston. Bet not one of the Koch brothers remembers that story.

More Knives

The subject of chef's knives in the kitchen reminded me of another unusual moment. The Chamois Ski Club in Boston conducted many ski trips, but we also got groups to the beautiful islands of Bermuda every year, usually just after skiing season ended. Over the years we stayed in many different places, but one year we took a bunch of cottages at a beautiful resort named "Ariel Sands" on the Shore Road overlooking the Atlantic.

One morning at breakfast I was sitting with my date when everyone heard screams emanating from the kitchen. We were sitting there hungrily waiting to be served, something that seemed to be taking forever. Our table was closest to the kitchen door so we could hear the screaming begin to include sounds of terror. A minute or so later men covered in blood began running out the door past us. The knives in that kitchen had been used for much more than just throwing them at the wall.

EUGENE FODOR

Eugene was incredibly talented, a good, but difficult, friend. There were two well-known Eugene Fodors living in the US at the same time. Even though the better-known Fodor was the founder of the highly-regarded travel guidebooks and a travel client of Woodside's New York office, the Fodor Pat and I came to know was the violinist.

Eugene was awarded the top prize in the famous Tchaikovsky Competition in Moscow in 1972 and won the Paganini Competition. The Russians did something strange, incredibly disgusting, and certainly unfair, awarding the prize to Eugene but declaring that there were two "winners." At the height of the Cold War, Russians simply could not accept the fact that an American beat their "great" Russian violinist. Everyone there felt that Fodor had won it hands down. Arts all too frequently suffer from politics. Years earlier, Eugene had made his debut as a violin soloist with the Denver Symphony at the age of 10.

Pat and I met Fodor through the Conductor of the Savannah Symphony Orchestra, Philip Greenberg. Philip had known Eugene for years and Philip, as a violinist, had taken Master Classes from Eugene and Itzhak Perlman. Eugene was so impressive when he first played with the Savannah Symphony that we brought him back to Savannah a number of times. His playing was so marvelous and his stage presence so powerful, the audience absolutely loved him. We agree with the comments about Eugene's being irascible. He was certainly egotistical and could be very hard to deal with, but at times he was very charming and frequently willing to play for friends in our home at 21 Chatuachee Crossing in The Landings, on Skidaway Island southeast of Savannah.

We were nervous about his leaving his beloved Guarneri Del Gesu and Stradivarius violins hidden under the big green leather sofa in our house. With a good alarm system, we were not as worried about an $11 million theft as we were about fire. For a long period of time, Philip Greenberg left a box full of very valuable bows underneath our bed, thinking they were safer there than they would have been in his home while he was going through a very nasty divorce from Shannon. I had to testify twice during those battles, the divorce and the custody case, so I know how nasty his wife could be.

Eugene used to lull us to sleep playing one of his violins in our living room late in the evening. A recording is enjoyable; having him play for us was an incredible privilege.

Eugene loved of this great Guarneri Del Gesu violin. Most people, even lovers of classical music, think of a Stradivarius when they think of a very good, extremely expensive, violin. Prior to Eugene, I don't think I had ever even heard of a Guarneri, much less held one or heard one played.. Guarneris were preferred over Stradavarius violins by some of the world's most renowned violinists, including Itzhak Perlman, Jascha Heifetz, Isaac Stern and Yehudi Meuhin

The composer who wrote what is arguably the most beautiful (and difficult to perform) works for the violin was the Italian, Niccolo Paganini. This is why the major violin competition in Genoa, Italy is named after him. Paganini was gambling, bet his Amati violin, and lost. As a result, he accidentally came across a poorly maintained Guarneri. Pagamomo loved it so much that he played it and it alone from that point on.

Guarneris were made by a family of luthiers (that's people who build violins) in Cremona, Italy from about 1641 to 1762. The family member generally considered the best of all was Bartolomeo Giuseppe Guarneri, who produced violins in the early 18th century. Because his violins bore a label that included the Greek acronym for Jesus Christ, this Guraneri's violins included the words Del Gesu.

Eugene was very generous with his time, probably as a result of his friendship with Philip Greenberg. At the turn of the century, the symphony women's guild used to host a series of fundraising parties and dinners in people's home, events known as Parties a la Carte. One of these dinners was at the beautiful home of the symphony's most generous supporter, Bob Jepson. One evening at a $150 per person dinner in their home, Bob and his wife Alice worked in the kitchen and served the guests. Bob said they would not do that again because it did not make enough money for the symphony.

He suggested, and we gladly accepted, Bob's idea that we have a very expensive dinner and make it attractive by having it be exclusive. The price was to be $1,500 and he, personally, called his friends and with remarkable speed sold out all the places at dinner. Instead of people's complaining about the price, I had people calling me, as President of the Symphony, expressing great irritation that they had *not* been invited to the dinner. I had to tell them that each host determined the invitation list. From then on, there was no problem having the dinners be sellouts. We had a variety of big-name musicians, but Eugene was the only one who performed twice, always free of charge.

Why isn't Fodor better known among the great violinists of all time? The problem is traceable to drugs, not just the usual, his wife told us he had been using heroin. This led to his becoming an unreliable guest artist. An orchestra would promote and sell the tickets to a concert only to have him not show up. His drug problem led to his skills being panned in a dreadful article in the New York Times. Philip Greenberg worked hard to get Eugene back on track and to resurrect his career, but the bad reputation made it impossible to get acceptance by the country's major orchestras. Nevertheless, those who heard him play knew how great he was.

Epilogue

There is a funny story about Philip and violins. He is a very reputable and highly regarded dealer in expensive violins, a field in which honesty and trust are extremely important. He has a shop in Manhattan. One day he had to take four violins from his uptown hotel to show a prospective buyer in lower Manhattan. When it came time to head south Philip discovered that a guy named Bill Clinton was en route to speak to the

United Nations General Assembly. Taxis could not travel through the area where all the crosstown streets were blocked. He had to hop on the New York Subway, taking in his arms about four-million-dollars worth of violins, and they were *not* insured.

Epilogue II (Or Maybe It Should Be Epilaugh)
The funniest story about Philip took place at a party in Allborg, Denmark, a city known for its strong drink: Akvavit, or Aquavit. At a party celebrating Philip's having won the Malko Award, the royal guests started to toast, drinking Akvavit. Philip says he declined, saying he did not drink (a fact we certainly knew). Philip did not even drink wine with dinner. The important men at the party said "this is not drinking, it's toasting." They, as usual, first toasted the Queen, Margrethe II, who was the patron of the Malko Competition and really liked Philip because of his double win in her country. Then they toasted the Prince and third, Philip. This went on and on. After about eight toasts Philip says he was drunk.

Someone took a picture of him with the Queen and it appeared on the front page of the newspaper the next day. The picture was of Philip sitting in the Queen's lap with his arm around her shoulder. The headline read "Malko winner gets familiar with the Queen." It is important to note that in Danish the word "familiar" has a meaning far beyond what it usually means in the US.

BOB CRANDALL
For many years, Bob was President and CEO of American Airlines. Of all the people I had to deal with in business, Bob Crandall was the most dynamic and creative business leader. He had a financial background at TWA before he moved to American, giving him a very good handle on financial matters even though he had moved up to be the big boss. Bob became President of American on July 16, 1980.

Bob was also quite informal and down to earth outside the office. My wife, Pat, was very impressed when he showed up with his wife and kids for a cookout on our boat during the Fourth of July fireworks in Marblehead Harbor. Bob rolled up his sleeves and pitched in to help. He did the same for his wife, Jan, when we dined at their home.
My best memory involved Bob at a reception during a quarterly meeting of the owners of the Woodside Group of Travel Agencies. The party included senior executives from all facets of the travel industry and the party was in my suite at the hotel. The hotel had not staffed with enough bartenders to keep up with demand, so lines developed waiting for the bar. Seeing this, Bob took of his suit jacket, rolled up his sleeves and announced that he was going to bartend. He did.

I was somewhat embarrassed, despite the obvious need for his help. When asked later, Bob responded with a comment that was both amusing and revealing. Not only was he eager to pitch in and help, he had an ulterior motive. He told me that, when standing around, he all too frequently got stuck talking for too long to someone with whom he really did not want to talk. There were too many that wanted some special favor from him. By standing behind the bar, he got to talk briefly with lots of people and avoid being stuck with any one.

The funniest story about Bob has to do with penny pinching. Even as a powerful senior officer of a major corporation, Bob personally looked at ways to save money. Back in the days when airlines served real meals, he had cited the money American was saving by deleting one olive from each salad. It was hard to accept that just one olive per salad could make any noticeable difference in cost, but he swears it was true. The story that follows has been told many times, but you may have missed it.

Saving Money

Once upon a time, Bob went with a group of American Airlines' financial executives to visit their large hub in Puerto Rico, where flights from North America connected to flights spreading out to cities throughout South America. One of the line items in the budget that struck Bob's eye was the cost of security. To save money, he asked if the local manager could cut the security guards from every night to just three nights a week. Potential thieves would not know which nights the guards were going to be there.

Bob's plan was implemented and there were no thefts, so on his next inspection trip he suggested using guard dogs at night instead of the expensive people. This saved more money and seemed to work fine, so on his next visit he suggested just having the dogs a few nights each week. Thieves would not know which nights the dogs were going to be there. Security continued to work OK. On his next visit, once again examining costs, he had an even better idea. Make a recording of dogs barking and play the recording each night, saving money by not renting the dogs at all.

Of course, people say this story is apocryphal, but I have been assured on many occasions that it is true. Pat and I were amused about three decades later to see Bob recite this story on a CNBC program entitled "A day inside American Airlines." His leadership is still a key to why in 2009, long after Bob retired, American remained the only major US airline that had not had to fall into bankruptcy. When this was originally written it ended with "Let's hope it stays that way." Unfortunately, they finally had to go.

At lunch with Bob and his wife, Jan on August 18, 2017, he told us he had appeared on CNBC again the day before, this time to blast Donald Trump. We couldn't tell Bob that, despite the personality, we preferred Trump to Hillary. When you look for Bob on YouTube, you can find many of his TV interviews on CNBC.

Wish I Had Been Invited To This Birthday Party

At that lunch Bob told us a funny story involving Donald Trump. Bob had flown to Marrakesh, Morocco as the guest of Malcolm Forbes for a huge birthday party to which many US chief executives were included. While there, Bob got a frantic call from his office in Dallas saying he had to rush home because Donald Trump had just made an offer to buy American Airlines.

Trump's offer on October 5, 1989 had been $7.5 billion. This was $120 per share for 68.7 million shares outstanding and immediately resulted in AMR stock jumping $16.87 to $99.87. Trump already had 3 million shares of American and he had just paid $365 million for the Eastern Airlines Shuttle, making it the Trump Shuttle (story in another chapter). Bob needed to leave immediately, so he asked Malcolm for the use of his jet to get him to Zurich where he could get American's flight back to Dallas. Bob went on to say that a group of Japanese banks had made an offer to buy United Airlines. That fell through and was followed by Trump's retracting his bid for American.

Bob also said that Malcolm had brought Marilyn Monroe to the party. Hate to think how much that cost him.

Conscious Parallelism

This subject is here because a lot of people don't know what those words mean and how they applied to the airline industry. It is appropriate because Bob got into trouble when Howard Putnam, then President of Braniff Airlines (remember the story chapters ago about the expensive breakfast), recorded a phone conversation with Bob and then turned it over to the government.

Airlines are an extremely complex business, totally unlike businesses that can simply put a price on a product. Airlines can charge more per mile on heavily travelled routes or at peak times of travel on any route. Getting together with a competitor in any business to agree upon a price has for many years been illegal because it was considered to be price fixing, conspiring with a competitor and agreeing to stick the public for more than they should have to pay. Airlines could raise the price of tickets and immediately start to lose income. Travel agents, today even individual travelers, can look in a computer and instantly see which carrier has the lowest price on the required route. You can't raise prices and not lose customers unless all of your competitors match your price. That is a prime example of conscious parallelism.

The same equation applies to an airline that tries to get more business by lowering it prices. Now, before you read on, note that there are today a few airlines that get away with this, notably Southwest. When a carrier lowers it prices, all of its competitors normally have to decide what to do. Their officers predict the number of passengers they will lose if they don't lower their price to match the competitor but they also know the amount of income they will lose if they do match the price. It is a bad Catch 22.

Many years ago World Airways, based in London, started attracting loads of passengers with super-cheap fares. British Airways took a hard look at it and decided it simply could not cut their prices that far. Only once World Airways went under did it become known that *they had been losing money on every single ticket they sold.* The loss was reported to be $34 on every ticket. Competition among the airlines is tough, and a major reason so many airlines have gone under. Customers do get the benefit of price competition but airlines are a business in which that leads to bankruptcy.

Bob Crandall's problem at American was an offshoot of this, and one that can get you in trouble if you act in the normal way found in conscious parallelism. American, with its deep pockets and huge fleet could have destroyed Braniff through competing in a way that Braniff simply could not afford. If the big guy does that to protect himself the government accuses him of being a bully. Bureaucrats are notoriously lacking in knowledge about what you have to do to build and protect your business. Had Howard Putnam agreed to raise Braniff's prices, his airline might have survived. I doubt it, but they were digging a big hole for themselves doing things the way they were doing

The government should never have ruled that an airline could not announce a price increase with an effective date later than immediately. Five decades ago, airlines would announce a price increase to be effective for reservations booked beginning in a month or two. This gave them time to see if their competitors would match them. If the competitors stood their ground, the airline could just cancel that price increase before it became effective. This might not have helped customers, would it would have made airline company survival more likely.

Amusingly, when we were having lunch in 2014 at the Singing Beach Club with Bob and Jan, he pulled out a tee shirt that he still had from our wedding 25 years earlier. It had our names and the date plus a beautiful picture of the schooner on which we had our rehearsal dinner and on which we sailed out of the harbor following our wedding reception. Everyone knew we were headed for Europe on our honeymoon, but we had not bothered to tell them the 114 foot schooner on which we were sailing out of Marblehead Harbor was just taking us down the coast and into Boston Harbor to the fireboat dock to go into the terminal, where we flew to Geneva on American.

CHARLES NESSON

That is his name, but I never heard him called anything but Charlie. He was a good friend during college days at Harvard and I was an usher in his first wedding, to Sally. Charlie was brilliant and achieved an incredibly high score on the Harvard Law School

Entrance Exam in his junior year, only to be turned down by the Law School because of poor grades. He worked to get better grades his senior year and was admitted. He was not just admitted, he was incredibly brilliant, ranking first out of more than five hundred students in his class. At the Harvard Law School that takes some doing.

Charlie's most memorable event was as a defense lawyer for Daniel Ellsberg in the 1971 Pentagon Papers case. He had a distinguished career in many areas, including serving as a professor at the Harvard Law School. He had a special, for me embarrassing, impact on the State of Alabama. When Charlie was with the Justice Department, his first case was "White v. Crook," that made race and gender-based jury selection in Alabama unconstitutional. Juries comprised of one race are clearly more inclined to vote in favor of the defendant if he is of the same race. Juries should be mixed.

After Sally and Charlie were divorced, I dated Sally, who was a beautiful and very sweet girl. Sally gave me a beautiful oil painting by her best friend, Priscilla Bowden, who I had dated in college and who had been one of Glamour Magazines "Best Dressed College Girls" in America. Strangely, I had dated three girls that had been featured as Best Dressed in Glamour over the years. Priscilla became a highly-awarded artist, especially in the ritzy communities around Southampton, near the eastern end of Long Island.

One night, after we had had much too much to drink, Charlie decided he was going to get to his dorm by swimming across the Charles from Boston to the Cambridge side. He took off all but his underpants, gave his clothes to me to carry across the Larz Anderson Bridge, and dove headfirst into the Charles River. In the dark, he had not seen all the rocks and came back out bleeding from head to toe.

The embarrassing dinner was at my home at 430 Quinobequin Road beside the Charles River in the Waban section of Newton, Massachusetts. Since I would be hosting such a prominent lawyer, I invited my lawyer, Bud Page and his wife, and planned a great menu. Charlie brought his new wife, whom I had not met until that evening. I bought the best big filet mignons and, as bad luck would have it, prepared a delicious first course that included beef broth, only to find he had become a vegetarian, as was she. They moved the food around but never ate a bite. So much for treating them to a super meal. It was very embarrassing.

THE DEFINITION OF A TRUE FRIEND

Several mothers in Atlanta used to bring their children to play in a park. My first cousin, once removed, from Anniston, Alabama, Griffin Fry, was among them. Several of the ladies had gotten to know each other for years, but still did not know much about the group, other than the fact that their kids were friends and liked to play together in the park. Talking while their kids played, the women used first names and, remarkably, did not bother with last names. Even if they had used last names, the key name in this story would not have been recognized so the cute story would have remained the same.

There was no thought given to who was important or who had lots of money. They were just friends who had kids that were friends. One day, for some reason, they started discussing the Nobel Prizes, and the question came up about why the Nobel Peace Prize is awarded in Oslo, Norway while all other Nobel Prizes are presented in Stockholm, Sweden. Nobody knew the answer.

One young mother named Amy, said she did not know, but would ask her dad. My cousin, Griffin, got a questioning look on her face and asked why Amy' dad would know. Amy replied "Because dad won the Nobel Peace Prize." As you have probably guessed by now, her Dad was President Jimmy Carter, but Griffin had never made the connection. I hope Amy was flattered and realized that Griffin had become a friend, not attracted by any knowledge of Amy's ancestry, but because Amy was such a nice person.

75 NOT FRIENDS

Just People I Knew

Many on the list of people in the book are as a direct result of my living in Boston, my education, my job and traveling so much. The big names frequent the big cities. I probably would never have met a single one of these had I spent my school and working years in Montgomery. In every one of these cases, it was interesting meeting a celebrity, even though it most of these instances it was no more than a meeting. The list would be too long had I included people to whom I just said "hello," such as the Dalai Lama, with whom Pat and I rode in an elevator.

DONALD TRUMP

This guy was far down in the list when I first started writing, but he has increased in importance since them, so I moved him to first. Having known him many years ago, I would never have had any idea, no matter how remote, that he would be elected President of the United States. It was as surprising to me as it was to Hillary. Maybe that is not quite true; I suspect she was in shock.

Producing and moderating annual symposiums in Boston and New York for years, I got The Donald to be one of the speakers on my program in Boston in 1989. As is true of many speakers, his staff sent me a standard introduction to use. It was too long and not very effective. The best word would probably be "boring." I thought more detail about a recent accomplishment would provide a better insight into his ability to get things done and he agreed, accepting my rewrite.

In his introduction, I focused on his renovation of the Wollman Rink, a very large ice skating rink in the southeastern corner of New York's Central Park. New York had, as government bureaucracies all-too-often do, had screwed up the job, spent way too much money and found themselves facing the decision to waste all that money and give up. There was no sign of the finish line. They decided to give up.

Donald stepped in an offered, personally, to get the job done and do it under budget and within the established time frame. There are two important conclusions you can draw from this. First, there are many reasons politicians running bureaucracies worldwide have proven to be extremely inept at what were essentially business management decisions. The second was that Trump, a businessman, was able to do it.

When talking about the large size of Wollman, I had been saying that it was huge, capable of accommodating a thousand skaters at once. Several people scoffed at that number, accepting that it was big, but not *that* big. Before completing this book but wanting to be sure I had the facts correctly, I thought an official number could be identified. I called the Wollman, explained what I needed, and was put through to Dale

Klied, the General Manager of the Wollman Rink. I was quite surprised, pleasantly, when he said I had *underestimated* their capacity….it was in fact 1,500 skaters on the ice at a time. The Wollman is an enjoyable part of living in the big city, used by many of its residents. It is due to The Donald that it still exists.

I was delighted to be given a plastic, credit card-size "positive space" pass on his Trump Shuttle. Amusingly, although I was still single, the card read "Mr. and Mrs. Thornton Clark." Lots of free flights are subject to "availability." If the plane is sold out with paying passengers, this level of pass holder goes not get on.

In those days you did not have to go through elaborate security or show any ID. I could fly with a date to New York for free. It made for some great weekends. We could spend the day prowling the city, have dinner and get to La Guardia for the last flight back to Boston. In addition to that pass' helping me visit Pat often once she moved to New York, she could fly with me to Boston.

Because we both loved boats, Pat and I enjoyed enormously being invited twice aboard The Donald's spectacular 281 foot yacht, the "*Trump Princess*" for cruising around New York Harbor. To give you an idea of the yacht without going into a long list of details, it had five decks, 3 elevators and sleeping accommodations for 52 staff to look after guests. I think it was too much, but there were 296 telephones.

The "Trump Princess" had belonged to a notorious arms dealer named Adnan Kashoggi, who had named the yacht "Nabila" after his daughter. Adnan had allowed the boat to be used in great scenes in the 1983 James Bond movie "Never Say Never Again" in which the boat was named the "Disco Volante," which, in English, means flying saucer.

Donald had purchased the yacht for the bargain price of $23 million, not quite a third of what it had cost to build. In case you didn't know it boats, like hurricanes, are always named for females, never males. The US Navy is an obvious exception, but that is logical. Now that hurricanes are named for men, I suspect someday the boat tradition, too, will die.

In addition to The Donald's combing his famous hair (which Pat remembers watching with amusement), there is one funny story. How would a man with so much money save so little on something that would be very noticeable while not fitting his image. He had taken the time to repaint the helipad, changing the standard black circle with large white "H" on the stern of his yacht to "T." That "T" was not visible to people on the yacht.

Whey you came aboard the *"Trump Princess,"* you entered a circular foyer with the elevator in front of you, with a beautiful, inlaid, marble floor. In the center there was a marble "N" for the yacht's previous name. Why in world would you spend so much money on the yacht and on promoting the Trump name, only to leave the initial?

The Donald's first talk of running for President, in 2011, brought laughs from many people, but I thought he would have eliminated the bull and make many things work better, eliminating the huge amount of waste. I don't care how much you may despise The Donald, he gets things done that need to be done.

Willingness to take The Donald seriously began in 2015. Many people agreed with his positions on delicate subjects, even though his ideas were widely believed to be "politically incorrect." I considered that to be a major positive. Democrats cannot accept, and maybe don't know, that the steady increase of "entitlements" as a percentage of our country's budget will force the country to pay less of their income for highly-important things such as defense. As China becomes more aggressive and keep seizing territory (does this remind you of Adolph Hitler in the thirties?) our entire future depends upon being strong, the reverse of apologizing and giving billions to the largest supporter of terrorism in the world. Some Europeans talk negatively about The Donald and our country, but they need to think about many things.

The US spent billions and lost many thousands of lives saving Europe from Hitler. The Europeans would not have escaped without our huge amount of help. The Marshall Plan, costing us a huge amount of money, enabled the rapid recovery of Europe after World War II, helping them avoid the risk of falling into communism.

The words "fair share" can mean different things depending upon who is saying them, but in some cases the meaning is obvious. Europe has been depending heavily on us for the cost of defending themselves for eighty years. At the inception of the North Atlantic Treaty Organization, the agreement was that every country would pay a percentage of their gross national product. That would be fair. Obviously, the United States would pay the largest number of dollars, but each European country would pay an amount relative to their ability to pay. Such has been far from the case. No President before Trump has spent a minute trying to get the European countries to pay what they owe for their own protection. Most have for years been paying much less and getting away with it.

Do many Americans understand that our commitment to NATO includes our obligation to go to war with Russia if they just march in and take Estonia, a NATO member country? Most Americans have no idea where tiny Estonia is. Russia's economy may be much smaller than ours, but they have been steadily testing our willingness to stand up to their aggression. The "took" the Crimean segment of the Ukraine without any meaningful response from the West. They have seized control of Eastern Ukraine without much in the way of repercussions. Does anyone really believe that, having seen they can get away with it, they will not continue to invade other European countries. Obama did not know the meaning of drawing a red line. When Trump used that phrase and the Syrians used chemical weapons, he had the U.S. retaliate, punishing them for this atrocity. Quit complaining about Trump's being anti-European and hope he wakes you up to the need to have a much stronger defense and that you should start now, not say you will within a few years as Germany and France have said, to make it a more-expensive priority. The Europeans should pay up starting NOW.

THE SHAH OF IRAN

This one will be much shorter than the previous because I only spent one day with him. I had come to St. Moritz in the past with the ski club from Boston, but on this trip I was by myself and happened to be skiing alone in St. Moritz early one morning. The area that I enjoyed the most when staying in San Moritz was the wide and moderately steep Corvatch, a few miles down the road from St. Moritz itself.

Early one morning, I was the first person on the fairly-large gondola, a lift in which you stood holding your skis while the gondola whisked you through the air to the top of the ski run at a pretty fast pace. The gondola was probably capable of holding at least thirty, maybe forty, skiers. Only two others got on, the easily recognizable Mohammed Reza Pahlavi, the Shah of Iran, and his bodyguard. His pictures had not conveyed adequately what a small man the Shah was.

Because we were the only people in the gondola, we said good morning and then began to talk on the ascent to the top of the ski run. When we reached the top, I expected him to ski off into the distance. He was a much better skier than I. I had skied a lot of expert slopes around the world, but in relatively poor form and much slower than the really-expert skiers. The Shah was a true expert but, when asked, I immediately agreed to ski with him and was able to keep up with him only because he was tolerant enough to ski a bit and then stop and wait for me. I suspect he regretted having asked.

At the end of the day he invited me to visit the mansion he was restoring just downhill from the center of St. Moritz. It was still a mess under construction, but it was clear that the large ornate rooms were going to be splendid. The "house" occupied a block to itself and was very attractive both inside and out.

The Shah was "guilty" of modernizing his country, recognizing Israel and secularizing the Iranian government. Since he was overthrown in the late seventies by the Iranian Revolution, we are stuck with a super strict and very dangerous radical Islamic country, controlled by the religious leaders and supportive of terrorists throughout the world, especially in the Middle East.

Unlike too many of the world's dictators, the Shah was a very nice gentleman. He was known for being a stiff, straight-laced ruler but one-on-one with a total stranger he was very friendly and gracious…many times what you would expect from the stern ruler of a large country. Iran had been very backward. He had turned it into a modern, fast-growing country with excellent religious tolerance. His country would be much better off today had he not been driven from power. I had to travel to Tehran just once, and the country had already come under strict Islamic control. In those days Tehran had only one top notch hotel, the InterContinental.

J. ROBERT OPPENHEIMER

This one is hard to classify because I did much more than just meet him. For some strange reason I was selected to be in a very small group of Harvard students to meet with Oppenheimer evenings while he was residing at Harvard.

Oppenheimer was an incredible theoretical physicist, far beyond anything I could come close to understanding, despite having studied physics. That was true of almost all the students, so his focus was on the moral issues faced as a result of the atomic bomb. Oppenheimer is frequently referred to as "one of" the inventors of the atomic bomb, but subsequent evidence indicated to me that he was truly the primary brain leading the huge team of scientists examining how to proceed in developing the bomb. He should be considered "THE father of the atomic bomb

One of the issues that was intermingled with the question of morality was Oppenheimer's long-time involvement with associates who were considered Communists. He had been under tight surveillance for decades and was eventually stripped of his security clearance, a very awkward position for someone who had the brain to develop the bomb that saved hundreds of thousands of American lives, and many Japanese, who would have died had the United States had to invade Japan. He became at the same time a hero and a villain, a most unusual combination. When Roosevelt died, Truman had authorized continuation of the bomb's development and had signed off on its use against Japan, but he had come to despise Oppenheimer because of the scientist's moral concerns about the use of what he had developed.

Oppenheimer's primary problem was the conflict between his ethical concerns and the attitude of the strong anti-communist feelings, especially among elected officials, at the time. The development of the bomb was kept a secret from the vast majority of Americans who were unaware of the enormous development project that consumed three and a half years between the inception of the bomb's development, known as The Manhattan Project, and the explosion of the first bomb July 16, 1945. It worked and a bomb was dropped on Hiroshima just three weeks later. It would have been disastrous if the Manhattan Project had had to be conducted under the relentless prying of today's press. Don't go protesting the existence of the bomb today, be thankful for the lives it saved and hope it never gets in the hands of a "evil" country that will use it. If a very poor and hostile country like Yemen was given an atomic bomb by Iran, it is likely they would use it to wipe Israel off the face of the earth (a threat the Jews have faced for many years).

Most Americans, even today, when complaining about the invention of the atomic bomb and all the Japanese who died in 1945, don't remember that Nazi Germany had initiated work on a nuclear weapon about three years before the U.S. Can you imagine what a difference it would have made in World War II if Germany had built atomic bombs and the US had not? Oppenheimer said we are very lucky and he was right.

It has now been about three quarters of a century since the first use of an atomic bomb and the spread of much more powerful atomic bombs among many highly-untrustworthy nations, especially Iran and North Korea, is terrifying. The dangers Oppenheimer saw coming years ahead and feared are only now becoming a highly-visible threat to the survival of mankind. Against what country will we fire all of our long range ballistic missiles if we were attacked by terrorists and we only have moments to decide whom to destroy if we are about to be annihilated?

My personal opinion is that one of the idiots will get through security and take out a city. In my opinion, Washington, D.C. is the most likely target, unless it is the Fat Brat and his missiles can only reach the west coast from Korea. It would be catastrophic to an extent Americans are not able to comprehend today. I just hope our inept government bureaucracy is smart enough to protect us from major attacks. On this extremely important subject, which party is most likely to focus on our defense and which is more likely to focus on free this and free that for everybody? If you think it is the Democrats, you are very naïve.

Needless to say, it was an incredible experience getting to hear Oppenheimer discuss the moral issues he had faced and how he dealt with them. The students were like reporters interviewing the man at the very epicenter of the atomic bomb and having him answer informally, completely, and in understandable terms about the enormous mental conflicts he faced. After the first session, I rushed to read up on what information was available but sadly most of what could be found in the 1950s, before the Internet, was almost entirely slanted against Oppenheimer.

It was one of the most extraordinary experiences of my life. Oppenheimer could not have been more generous with his time and willing to answer even what must have seemed to him to be very-naïve questions. Physically he may had been quite short and small, but, oh, what a brain. The resulting impression, when combined with his very soft-spoken manner was that he was a very frail person. That could be true, but he was certainly an incredibly strong and brilliant person.

NELSON ROCKEFELLER

Nelson may have been Governor of New York, but he loved his home close to the water in Seal Harbor, Maine. He sailed his "International One Design," the class that I was world president of for ten years. When he was selected to be Vice President (replacing the disgraced Spiro Agnew) under Nixon, the picture Newsweek Magazine chose to use in their first article on this subject was a picture of Nelson sailing his International One Design on the coast of Maine. He was not active in the class, but I got to meet with him once in Manhattan on the subject. As a result, I had one brief but amusing encounter with him a few days later in Rockefeller Center.

The number two man, Stan Zukowski (known as the "Zuke)," at Don Travel in New York was with me, having just entered an elevator, reached the back wall and turned around. As a group of men arrived to get on the elevator, Zuke whispered to me that one of the men was the Governor. Zuke was absolutely flabbergasted when Nelson said "Hello Thornton, how are you." Zuke kept telling the story every time an opportunity presented itself.

The best story about Nelson involved the circumstances in which he died. His wife was named Happy Rockefeller. She was not the woman he was in bed with when he had the heart attack and died. What a way to go. As the saying went, "Happy" was not happy.

T. S. ELIOT

Having studied T.S. Eliot's poetry in college, I was surprised by Andrew Lloyd Weber's Broadway musical *"Cats."* Many of the lyrics were taken verbatim, or close to it, from Eliot's fifteen poems comprising *"Old Possum's Book of Practical Cats*," that had been published in 1939. This is another example of something I would never have expected.

In an intellectual article about T. S. Elliot in the July-August 2015 issue of Harvard Magazine, Adam Kirsch writes at length about "*The Wasteland*" but never even mentions "*Old Possum's Book of Practical Cats."* Yes, "*The Wasteland"* is considered the "great" work of Eliot, but I bet many more people today remember his cat characters and their names in the musical "*Cats*" than any of "*The Wasteland.*" There are many memorable "characters" in the musical that are remembered decades after the long-running Tony-Award-winning musical closed, including Macavity, Mr. Mistoffelees and Old Deuteronomy. Many of the lyrics in the most memorable songs in "*Cats*" are very close to the words in Eliot's poems.

While a student at Harvard, T.S had belonged to a Harvard "final club," the Fox Club. The final clubs were very conservative versions of what at other colleges would be called fraternities. Most were housed in great old antique buildings in the Harvard Square area of Cambridge, Massachusetts. In my days, all were "men only" except on a few nights each year and one of the ones that was men only was even more strict....the Porcellian Club was members only....period. The Fox Club still sits in an antique two story white wooden building facing JFK at Mt. Auburn Street. With Fox's many sources of major donations, it makes no sense for me to give them a little money every time they ask. Fox had a member named Bill Gates of Microsoft fame.

A very small group (I think it was five) of us got to spend an evening drinking, talking and dining at a round table with Mr. Eliot. Given the opportunity, I couldn't believe how few members took advantage of it. At the time, Eliot would have been 70 years old, but he seemed much older. He was a very quiet gentleman and it was a most enjoyable time. I was surprised that, even though he had been a member of the Fox Club many years earlier, he took time to spend an evening with such a small group of undergraduates. He gave me a copy of his "Complete Works Of T.S.Eliot" and autographed it. I'm very happy that he did, and I cherish it today. He used the old-fashioned way of signing, marking thru his printed name and signing his signature below it.

I know it hurts the sale value to have him address it to me, but that added a special note to my memory of the evening. When I did consider selling it, I received and offer from a book dealer in New York for $1,000. Very soon thereafter I was offered $3,000. Beautiful book, great memories.....still have it.

FIDEL CASTRO

When Fidel overthrew the government of Fulgencio Batista, victoriously capturing Havana January 8, 1959, he was hailed as a hero by much of the world. The US had supported Batista, but the effort was inadequate and it was one of those times when the liberals were furious that we were supporting a dictator who was seen as oppressing his countrymen. What a mistake that was.

Shortly after the overthrow of Batista, Fidel and a group of his team decked out in camouflage-style military attire with "jack" boots descended upon Cambridge, Massachusetts, culminating in an overly long, what I would describe as bombastic, speech to a crowd in Harvard Stadium, across the river in Boston. Fidel's group had pranced around the streets of Cambridge near Harvard Square for a few days, without Fidel. He showed up on the afternoon of his speech, during which time I managed to get in a handshake and a few words. Fidel was the hero of the moment, especially in super-far-left Peoples Republic of Cambridge.

I had gotten his attention, resulting in his stopping, by calling out that I bet I was one of the very few Americans in Cambridge who had been to Cuba twice. I was totally in the dark regarding the details of the Cuban Revolution and was taken in by the press that lauded his success. Fidel was almost worshipped by the liberals of the time. He said I was one of the few Americans he had met who had been to Cuba. If you had to pick a single word to describe him in that brief encounter, it would be "haughty." It has now been almost sixty years and in 2017, and Fidel may be dead but the bastard's brother is still having a devastating impact on the Cuban people, much more than Batista ever did.

It is too often the case in the world that the overthrow of a dictator by "the people" results in the emergence of another dictator. Keep your fingers crossed regarding the "Arab Spring," and hope it doesn't deteriorate any deeper into fall or winter than it already has. The continuing turmoil in the Middle East is largely Sunnis vs. Shiites, so let us hope it stays that way. Having spent a good bit of time in many of the Islamic countries of the world, I think most of them will end up being run by Islamic clerics imposing strict Sharia Law and supporting the killing of "infidels," i.e. us. Heaven help the rest of the world, especially their idea of the devil....The United States of America.

RUPERT MURDOCK

My three meetings with Ruppert took place because he purchased a group of travel magazines, published out of New York. These included "Travel Weekly," the primary publication of the travel agency industry in the United States and for which I used to write, and the "Hotel and Travel Index."

The publisher of the various newspapers and books brought Rupert from New York up to Heritage Travel in Cambridge. The objective was to meet with Heritage's genius, Don Sohn, but I was included in the meeting, which consumed most of a day. Here again, this is a man despised by much of the world, especially following the hacking scandal involving his British newspaper. He makes money in many ways, but the main one is still publishing major newspapers. All of the apprehension about his purchase of the Wall Street Journal appears to have been unwarranted. The Journal has, if anything, gotten better under his leadership. It is still my primary source of meaningful information, today much more on politics now that I am no longer in business. It is revealing, but very sad, to read that today the majority of the population gets its "news" from Facebook. Scary.

Rupert knew that having a picture of a sexy girl in a British newspaper helped sales, but he has not done anything like that to the WSJ. Rupert has led the way in using beautiful female anchors on Fox News TV. Rupert must be doing something right because in recent years the Fox News Channel attracts as many viewers as CNN, HLN, and MSNBC *combined.* It is quite something when you can build in a relatively short time span a company that exceeds in audience size the total of its major competitors.

The Publisher of Hotel and Travel Index for many years was Melinda Bush, who now lives in Miami. Because of my role in the travel industry and because she was single and needed a date, I was invited to Rupert's home in Manhattan for dinner, December 14, 1987. Rupert's condo was on the top floor of a building overlooking Central Park on Fifth Avenue at the corner of 88th street. I think it was Two East 88th, but have not been able to verify that). His current place is many times larger, the $57.3 million top four floors of One Madison Avenue.

The hostess that evening was Rupert's wife at the time, Anna (the nice one), not his most recent wife who went after him in a nasty divorce. After dinner the charming one gave me a private and very interesting tour of her garden above their condo. It was comfortable for that time of year. Anna's rooftop garden had many beautiful plants, a marvelous view of Central Park and a 360 degree view of the New York skyline. Even though it was on a busy street, the roof was remarkably quiet and peaceful.

The battle that Rupert found himself embroiled in regarding phone-hacking and bribes for information to feed his tabloids, especially Britain's *"News of the World,"* was a sad interval, close to the end of an incredibly successful career.

His FOX news channel is Pat's and my favorite, at least the "Special Report" show chaired by Bret Baier that frequently included our favorite political expert, a truly brilliant and delightfully caustic commentator and syndicated columnist, Charles Krauthammer. His death was a said day for political journalism.

I love the penultimate page and the two preceding opinion pages of the first section of each day's Wall Street Journal, so we are most appreciative of Rupert.

RICHARD BRANSON

Richard used to come to the States a lot when his highly successful Virgin Atlantic Airlines was growing fast in Transatlantic service. He originally rose to prominence as the owner of Virgin Record Stores in England. He is now Sir Richard Branson, is a multi-billionaire (in US dollars) owns several hundred businesses under the Virgin name and is still probably best known for Virgin Atlantic Airways. He has sponsored and participated in some incredible feats including the first plane to fly all the way around the world without landing or refueling in flight and for establishing numerous records for balloon flight. Richard is also pioneering in the incredible business of designing planes, maybe they should be called spaceships, capable of taking paying passengers into space for a look down at the earth. Richard's story should probably have been a full chapter.

Richard has donated tens of millions to various environmental efforts. He is quite a flamboyant character, always great fun to be with in a bar, where he captivated audiences (especially pretty women) with his very masculine appearance, his great personality and style in everything from small groups to speaking at large conventions. If you think he looks interesting today, you should have known him thirty-five years ago.

When a male President of the National Business Travel Association (formerly the NPTA), was about to be replaced by a female, E. J. Hewitt, Richard was scheduled to deliver a talk to the large convention. At E.J.s request, I urged Richard *not* to use what he told us he was planning to say in his speech to the convention. He planned to say at the end of his brief talk, the phrase "The King is dead, long live the Queen," but of course he said it anyway. The convention loved it, and E.J. did not seem to mind.

Richard's Game

Most people don't know that Richard was the inventor of a great new British game.

One of the funniest Branson stories was about my being flown to London as a guest of Virgin and visiting his home. My wife complained about my trip, especially upon my return after she heard about Richard's unique game for entertaining guests. In editing this paragraph she changed "complained" to "critical" and "envious" but I think my choice of words better described her reaction. Richard and his wife lived in a beautiful home outside of London, with a small but delightful little brook flowing through one side of the large backyard. I don't know if there is an American word for the little flat-bottomed boat he had in the brook, but I think the English call it a "punt." Anyway, it is a fun way of traveling downstream on a beautiful afternoon. I searched, but was unable to determine if he still owns that house.

Richard kept a very large, elegant, white tent in his backyard for entertaining, beside the large grass area where his special game was played. Most people are aware of, even if never involved in, the old card game of Strip Poker. The basic idea is if you lose the hand, you have to take off a piece of clothing. Boys were always assuming they could win and get the girls to take off their clothes. The game was best played after a few drinks; the motive was fairly obvious. In a few cases, my impression was that some girls were happy to lose.

Virgin Atlantic Airways attempted to continue the old (unfortunately illegal in the States) idea of having stewardesses who were both female and beautiful. Today, I still prefer (quietly, of course) to call male flight attendants "male stewardesses." Those great old days are gone; but Richard still maintains a large percentage of attractive females at all levels of his staff. He is quite like Rupert Murdock in publishing and TV, knowing that most men want to look at beautiful women, which is why you see very few really ugly women as TV anchors and weather meteorologists (no matter how expert they may be), and you see lots of beauties on Fox TV, where they complain about having to wear short skirts and sit so that their beautiful legs, always crossed, show well on TV.

In Richard Branson's backyard, the game was a great variation of what Americans almost universally consider an archaic and boring sport….cricket. The very idea of "Strip Cricket" made it exciting, enormously so when you saw the looks of the Virgin Atlantic stewardesses with whom I played Strip Cricket in Richard's backyard. My wife, Pat, said she did not think many, if any, of those stewardesses were virgins, but the way the game progressed you did not even come close to finding out.

For inexperienced Americans, trying to hit a small cricket ball with a bat is even worse than trying to play golf your first time. In golf, at least the ball is sitting still just waiting to be hit. In cricket, the ball is traveling fast and, in contrast with baseball, has to bounce off the ground in front of you before you swing. It is also extremely difficult to pitch the ball accurately. Unable to hit and knock down the wickets with the ball thrown from a distance made it almost impossible that afternoon to get anyone out, so there was little progress in stripping made by either side. It had sounded like such a good idea.

Pacific Southwest Airlines

This is a sad one. Many years ago, long before Virgin Atlantic, there was a small intrastate airline named Pacific Southwest (PSA) that flew frequently between San Francisco and Los Angeles. Lots of Heritage Travel's customers who did business in California flew to one of these cities and flew home to Boston from the other. Los Angeles/San Francisco is a heavily flown route.

One of Heritage's primary claims was saving money for our corporate clients. PSA flights were noticeably less expensive than the much larger national airlines, usually American and United were the carriers flying the triangle from Boston. Because PSA was not part of the airline consortium that handled ticket transactions involving multiple airlines and interstate routes, we had to issue separate tickets for the PSA flights. It involved more work, but it paid off in two ways.

Far off in Boston, Heritage became PSA's largest issuer of tickets outside of the State of California. It is disappointing that no other east coast agency took the trouble to deal with PSA. It may not have been much money, but it illustrated the extra steps we took to save money for our corporate clients.

Forget travelers that didn't like complying with company policy to save their employers a few dollars. Men loved PSA because the airline hired only truly-beautiful young women and had “hotpants” and very-high-heel shoes as uniforms. For those of you too young to remember those great days, hotpants were spectacularly short shorts, making good looking legs even more stunning.

It is hard to remember those days, but airlines were able to get away with hiring only beautiful young women, *no* men. Even Hooters restaurants can no longer hire only women as servers and airlines have to have “male stewardesses,” or whatever.

At that convention where Richard insisted, despite my pleas, on saying “Long live the queen” another person told a remarkably dirty story to the luncheon that was comprised largely of ladies. The speaker was Atlanta’s great comedian, Lewis Grizzard. He said that two guys on the sideline were looking at a dog that had run out to the center of the football stadium, rolled over on his back and started licking himself in “the place.” One man said “I wish I could do that.” His friend responded: “You better not do that; that dog would bite you.” Most of the ladies laughed, some were in shock and a few didn’t get it.

Richard Told One On Himself

Not a joke; just a probably embarrassing story. In the Novermber, 2017, Readers Digest, Richard Branson was quoted as having said “If you’re embarking around the world planning to fly non-stop in a hot air balloon, don’t forget to take the toilet paper. Once, we had to wait for incoming faxes.”

It is interesting to note that in a 2017 survey listing the top ten best airlines in the world, they ranked Virgin Atlantic in 5th place and Virgin Australia in 4th. Quite an accomplishment in a few years.

PAUL McCARTNEY

I got to sit with Paul for about an hour, but he obviously did not want to talk about the Beatles. It is sad that the Concorde has quit flying across the Atlantic between England and the U.S. and France and the U.S. It was quite an experience and, for those who needed to make the best use of their time on business or had the money to spend, cutting the flying time between Europe and the U.S. in half was a major benefit. For me, it also reduced the impact of jet lag, especially westbound. This flight had very few passengers.

The tickets were so expensive that the passenger volume was not enough to be anywhere close to financially viable, but the high cost meant you sat in the plane with lots of rich people. For years both the English and the French governments had subsidized the operation of the Concordes as a matter of national pride. Until the very end, they tried to keep the planes flying, even in the face of higher and higher fuel costs. The Concordes devoured huge quantities of fuel.

The planes themselves were a little bit like being in a small tube. The diameter of the plane's fuselage was much smaller than the jets in service on most airlines, and much much smaller than the huge jets in service on most long flights. The cabins were so small you felt cramped, especially when you stood up.

Even after flying the Concorde several times, it was exciting to watch the Machmeter climb past 1, which indicated we had exceeded the speed of sound.

On one flight from New York to London, I was seated on the left at the window. I had not noticed the couple in the row behind me, but did overhear their conversation. At the time, Paul was married to his first wife, Linda, and she was on the flight with him.

For some reason, Paul must have decided he wanted to talk with someone else for a while, so he asked if he could sit beside me. Although he disclosed that he was a Beatle, he gave no indication of wanting to talk about it. He just wanted to talk about things that were happening in the world. It was quite awkward for me in that I obviously would have loved some personal memories of the life of such a famous singer and, once again, should have asked for his autograph. That was something that just was not done, or, at least, I thought it improper. I still regret not having ended the visit with that request. After about an hour he went back and sat with Linda. The flight only took something like three and a half hours and a good bit of that was climbing after takeoff and descending for landing.

Another amusing thing about the Concorde occurred on afternoon flights from Europe to New York. Because the planes flew so fast, you could see the sun "rising" ahead in the west.

TED TURNER

Ted was enormously successful at a number of things, both in business and in sports. Everyone was skeptical and many laughed at him when he founded CNN. Who in the world would want to watch the news all day? Even the "experts" said it might be an interesting concept, but there would never be close to enough audience to make it financially feasible. What a mistake that was.

I suspect that some people watching the programs on TV today think TNT stands for an explosive. In broadcasting, it stands for Turner Network Television. Ted decided to build a 12 meter yacht, the class of boats that at the time was the type in which all of the races for the "America's Cup" were conducted. Sailing had evolved from wooden construction to fiberglass. Ted's boat came out of the mold pure white, long and as boats go…..sexy. She had long graceful traditional lines, in contrast to the weird, high-tech catamaran racing machines used when racing for the America's Cup today.

As luck would have it, in 1976 I was starting to build a fiberglass sailboat of the International One Design Class. It was just over 33 feet. about half the size of Ted's boat, but quite similar in shape. My new boat came out of the mold in East Boothbay, Maine as pure white fiberglass. Neither boat had a waterline or any paint on the bottom. Also, the two brand-new white hulls ended up next to each other in Ted Hood's Little Harbor Boatyard in Marblehead, Massachusetts. Many commented that the boats looked like mother and daughter.

Ted was there frequently during the installation of all the complex equipment that had to go into the boat. When his boat was ready to sail, he began to be accompanied by his large crew to begin practicing. Ted was noisy, and his crew was equally loud and boisterous. They also made frequent use of profanity. Not just the simple words in fairly common use today; the team was known for being extraordinarily crude and loud.

Restaurants needed customers and large groups could help a lot toward turning a profit (especially if they drank a lot), but several restaurants said they learned to dread the arrival of Ted and his entourage, who would all-too-frequently drive other patrons, especially if young children were involved, out of the restaurant. Unless they were in the category of sailing fans who wanted to listen to all the talk, people seated near Ted and his crew would get up and leave a restaurant, on many occasions without finishing their meal or paying their bill.

Ted may have been a successful businessman and, by winning the America's Cup, an extremely successful yachtsman, but that is still no excuse for having been so loud, crude and rude.

BRIAN JENKINS

Of all the names I say you will almost certainly not recognize, I suspect this one is near the top of the list. You may have seen him being interviewed on TV news about his area of expertise: security, especially terrorism. He was the head terrorism expert at The Rand Corporation, advising corporations around the world regarding how to keep their employees safe when travelling.

Because of my involvement advising so many large corporations regarding their travel policies, I was invited to participate with Brian on a video discussing various aspects of travel safety and security, in my case how corporations should deal with the subject, what they should and should not formalize as corporate travel policy and how to protect their employees when traveling on business to dangerous parts of the world.

The videotape, "Terrorism, The Corporate Concern," was produced by Varied Direction, Inc. of Camden, Maine. It is not worth looking at after all these years, but it was fun getting to know Brian during the recording sessions in New York.

ARNOLD SCHWARZENEGGER

Having breakfast with Arnold was a total surprise. This was when he was known as the world's most recognizable body builder and beginning to star in action movies such as "The Terminator." When I was dating Eileen Prose, she hosted a TV show early every weekday morning, interviewing a wide variety of celebrities. Eileen was very smart and articulate, and had been a runnerup Miss America, winning the talent portion of the competition with her singing. Her job meant she frequently had to prepare by reading a new book most nights and had to get up extremely early and go to work before sunrise to be ready to go when the cameras came on.

I usually recorded her shows to watch them after work on what would now be an antique VHS recorder, but occasionally I would go to the studio to watch the show. I happened to go on a day when her guest was going to be Arnold. We ate the sandwiches he had brought while waiting for his time to go on the air.

This encounter was one that I would barely have remembered had he not gone on from being the "Terminator to being the "Governator" of California. The state badly needed straightening out, but the largely far-left population of that super-liberal state was successful in blocking most of his attempts to correct the many problems. California is so badly mismanaged that it probably will be one of the first states to require bailing out by the US taxpayers (after Illinois). Now he has been caught for fathering a child (now a teenager) by his housekeeper. That was truly stupid and, to my mind, inexplicable. Maybe, if you are stuck with a genuinely ugly wife, you stumble across a stunningly beautiful woman and end up in bed with her. The maid he screwed was downright "two-bagger" ugly and his wife attractive. There may someday be an explanation.

TOM WATSON

Tom was the extremely important and greatly admired head of IBM. He was a true genius in the early days, before people like Microsoft's daddy, Bill Gates, were born.

Tom said he had been a very poor student in school, in addition to getting into trouble with stunts such as putting skunk odor in the ventilation ducts. Can't imagine how he did that. Under his more famous dad, Tom had questioned IBM's focus on punched cards and saw the future in electronic computers. It was his push into this "new" area that made IBM so dominant for many years. Tom was President of IBM from 1952 until 1971, leading the company to incredible success. Under Jimmy Carter, he served as US Ambassador to the Soviet Union during a very difficult period.

One year Pat and I were sailing up the coast of Maine with my good friend Bob Duff and his date, Roz Allen. Her family had a home on Round Pond, so my wife (at that time, my date, Pat), flew from New York into Portland and came by taxi to Round Pond to join us for the cruise. Roz subsequently was nicknamed "Round Pond Rozzie."

When we tied up at the Brown's Coal Wharf Marina on the southern edge of North Haven Island, Roz asked if we would like to visit the famous Tom Watson. Obviously, our first reaction was that she was kidding. She claimed otherwise and said she would walk a hundred feet to the pay phone (they had them in those days before cell phones) and call him. To our amazement, she returned to the boat and said Tom would pick us up in about half an hour. We scrambled to get cleaned up and dressed.

North Haven is an island that has many beautiful homes along the water, especially on the heavily-trafficked-by-boat channel that runs east/west separating North Haven from South Haven. Pat and I had been twice to the spectacular home on Iron Point, which commands a great view of the channel. The Watson home was inland, pretty close to the northeastern corner of the island, on Oak Hill Road.

We were met with surprising hospitality, having expected to be considered intruders into their personal lives. Working as a computer programmer and manager for years, Bob was in heaven getting to talk so long with the hero of the computer industry. I wish I had brought my camera and, more importantly, had the nerve to take a keepsake picture of the two of them sitting on the sofa talking with Tom's arm up behind Bob's back on the small sofa in the living room.

I was more interested in art, especially maritime art, so when Tom's wife, Olive, offered a tour of the house and their barn (which contained most of their collection), Pat and I eagerly accepted. Tom had been an avid and highly-acclaimed sailor, having built 7 sailboats named "Palawan." I never learned the reason for that unusual name. It is the name of the very long and beautiful island that sticks down to the southwest in the Philippines. Tom's love of sailing was reflected in his art collection.

The paintings in the house were great, but I quickly learned that the most interesting works were in the barn. I had a few numbered prints by some of the best-known nautical artists, but the Watsons had many of the original oil paintings. In the house, they were displayed in what I can only call "normal" fashion……a single painting at eye level on a wall.

In the barn, there were so many paintings that they had to be hung three paintings above each other on the high walls. There were works by most of the greatest maritime painters. In addition, the Watsons had an extensive collection of antique scrimshaw, the pictures made by carving on whale's teeth.

Olive was an excellent tour guide, spending time making comments she must have had to make many dozens of times. Tom's love of flying resulted in his having a collection of airplanes and he had built a runway behind the house. The 2,900 foot long runway runs parallel to Pulpit Harbor Rd.

He had generously allowed the runway to be used when needed for medical emergencies on the island. Without this option, getting someone from the island to a boat, to shore, and then to a hospital was a time-consuming ordeal. The existence of the runway undoubtedly saved lives. Sadly, as exists even more today, the fear of liability forced Tom's lawyers to advise him that he had to stop this generous practice. Our welcome to the home, the stories and tour were quite a surprise, making it a delightful day.

GOVERNOR MICHAEL DUKAKIS

When I knew him he was Governor of Massachusetts. The Dukakises lived two blocks away from my apartment at 30 St. Paul St. in Brookline. I would never have guessed that he would become the Democratic Party's nominee for President of the United States. It wasn't just that he was a bad governor, he was supported by a far-left liberal state legislature. To me, it was no surprise that he lost the Presidential election by a huge margin. As I recall, he only won about a half dozen states (one of which, of course, was Massachusetts). The most common description of his loss to George H.W. Bush was "landslide."

I was dating a beautiful young girl, Barbara Petersen, who was sixteen years younger than I. She was an excellent map maker, owning a company in Cambridge called Interarts, which represented an outstanding map company in Sweden. She had been rushing to complete a job for the State of Massachusetts (yes, I know that it is technically "The Commonwealth of Massachusetts, but everyone thinks of it as a state). Her project was a map for the State Highway Department and it absolutely had to be designed, printed and delivered in time for the opening ceremony of their new headquarters out west of Boston, an event which was to be hosted by Dukakis and televised. This was a deadline that she simply could not miss.

I was invited to attend a luncheon to celebrate the opening of the Marriott Copley Place hotel in Boston and the invitation for June 26 included my right to bring a date to the luncheon. I certainly hoped Barbara would come with me; but she repeatedly said she had a major conflict, would try, but probably could not.

When the day arrived, I offered to help Barbara at the printer, loading up the maps in my car to take both her and her maps to the Highway Department event. I was still hoping she would come to the luncheon at noon with me, but at 11am it was looking increasingly doubtful.

Finally, everything fell into place about 11:30, she said yes, and we raced to the luncheon, which was only a few blocks away. We were sent to one of many round tables only to discover that our seats were at the one designated as the head table and the only one with place cards showing who was assigned to each seat. I was honored, but not surprised, that I was seated next to Bill Marriott, but Barbara was in shock to find herself seated next to Governor Dukakis. The four of us were at a table of eight.

When she got to the ceremony where her maps were to be used it was absolutely hilarious when her contacts at the Highway Department, who had purchased the maps, learned from the Governor that he had just had lunch with Barbara. She didn't regret squeezing that lunch into her very busy day.

I was not a fan of Dukakis and I must have said something to piss him off because the Boston Marriot gave me a picture of the two of us standing facing each other and he has a really-nasty look on his face.

GOVERNOR ENDICOTT PEABODY

Peabody was never called "Endicott;" he was "Chub." I met him at the Union Boat Club near the Charles River at the 144 Chestnut Street in the area that is called Beacon Hill but is really better described as "The Flat of The Hill," because the blocks along the Charles River are quite flat. The Club was named because of its involvement in rowing, with an antique boathouse out in the Charles River across Storrow Drive from the clubhouse and all of the homes on Beacon Hill.

I met Chub as a result of his being almost as poor a squash player as me. That is a bit of an exaggeration, he was clearly better than I was. The main building of the Union Boat Club is devoted mostly to squash courts and I would meet him there to play squash on many weekday evenings after work. It was convenient because I lived just 460 feet away at 50 Brimmer Street and Chub's office in the State House was at the top of Beacon Hill.

He was very tolerant of my lack of skill and I suspect he was generous and probably let me win some of the time. I did make one contribution to his term in as Governor (1963-1965). One afternoon after squash we talked at length and I focused on the attractiveness of Massachusetts, especially Boston, for young people. It is even more so today. A high percentage of the graduates of the numerous major colleges and universities in the area choose to stay (as I did) after graduation. A huge 2017 study by the Wall Street Journal and the Times showed 26 of the 500 top-rated colleges in the country are in the small state of Massachusetts, and Harvard and M.I.T are frequently at the very top.

The City is magnificent, a well-handled mixture of antique buildings and skyscrapers, and there are loads of things to do to suit every style and taste, from playing sports to being a spectator. Some of the teams have declined in statue, but most of the time I was there the Celtics and the Bruins were at the top of their leagues. At that point the Patriots were embarrassing and the beloved Red Sox had not won a World Series since 1918. The Red Sox were still great to watch, especially when the game was in Fenway Park.

Anyway, I was pleasantly surprised to read in the news and see on TV that Chub had used a long list of the points I had made to him in a speech he gave the next day. Today, most people outside of the Ivy League hardly know Harvard football exists but, when there, Chub had made All-American and is in the College Football Hall of Fame. Imagine a Harvard player today being selected as an All American. Most friends I knew in Boston were amused to cite all of the nicknames Chub had. The joke was that he was the only US Governor to have three cities in his state named after him. The obvious ones were Endicott, Peabody and Marblehead, but Athol was frequently added.

JOHN F. KENNEDY

I just barely met and talked with JFK. He came to my college graduation ceremony in June of 1959, at which time he was still a Senator representing Massachusetts. At that point he had no Secret Service, so I was able to walk up and introduce myself. I have no story to tell about this one so it is very short. All I did was meet him and talk briefly. We were standing in front of Memorial Church across from Widener Library, the beautiful area in which Harvard commencement ceremonies are held.

A few years later, when I went to his Presidential inauguration it was nice to have that small memory. I got a picture of him but not one with him. I also took great pictures from our seats up close to the podium for his inauguration. This was back when inaugurations were held on the east front of the Capitol, so you could sit much closer to the podium where Kennedy gave his inspiring Inaugural Address. Sarah Lingham's and my seats were fabulous. Today, much larger crowds are accommodated by having the ceremony face west across the expanse of The Mall. The picture I snapped at the perfect moment included the Kennedys, the Johnsons, Eisenhower and Supreme Court Chief Justice Earl Warren.

Kennedy's love of sex was widely known, but he was nowhere near as flagrant about it as his younger brother, Teddy. In those days, before there were 24-hour TV news channels, it was much easier to conceal what a major official was doing than it is today. These days, a political celebrity's screwing around without getting caught has become almost impossible. Few get away with it but, as you often read in the press, this does not prevent it from happening.

There is one widely known revelation about JFK that most readers of this will not have heard about. A woman, Mimi Alford, waited more than forty years before she allowed Random House to publish a book about her affair with JFK. Interestingly, Mimi had gotten her job in the White House as a result of having graduated from Miss Porter's School, where both Jacqueline Kennedy and her press secretary had studied. JFK had met her a year earlier and spotted her working as an intern in the White House press office. When she showed up at a small party in the White House with the President, he offered to give her a personal tour of the great building. Innocent and overwhelmed by such an invitation, on only her fourth day at work in the White House, Mimi would have had to accept even if she had not been thrilled by the opportunity.

In her book, she writes that upon arrival in the President's bedroom he grabbed her, threw her onto the bed and climbed on top of her. Later in the book she acknowledges that she did not resist and that the relationship grew into an affair that lasted over a year, including having sex in Jacqueline Kennedy's bed. This is probably the biggest single example of a situation in which the "victim" cannot think of complaining to the authorities, no matter how heinous the offense was in the beginning. It may have been improper for JFK to seduce her, but it is difficult to claim she was a victim.

To those who think all of the stories about Kennedy's carousing are fabricated, this one includes too many facts that simply could not be fiction. Ms. Alford kept her mouth shut until the story emerged from someone else. A Presidential Historian, Robert Dallek, learned from a White House staffer of a "tall slender and beautiful nineteen-year-old college sophomore" who had been with JFK many times and observed by many of the staffers. Alford's book names five of the women known to have been involved with Kennedy. Interestingly, the staff referred to two women as "Fiddle and Faddle," and the actual identification of Fiddle was not revealed until Ms. Alford's book.

A newspaper, the New York Daily News, dug into the story's description of the young intern and uncovered the fact that the unnamed beauty was Mimi Alford. One publication, seeking the rights to publish her book, slipped an envelope full of cash under her door. She immediately donated it to the church where she worked. Mimi turned down loads of money for her story, including a one million dollar offer for the film rights, before finally giving in and revealing her relationship. Had she been making up her story to make money she would not have donated it to charity or passed up the million.

Does this remind you of a story about a girl named "Monica?" I had wondered if Monica would be invited back to the White House by the countries first "First Gentleman" but this possibility was eliminated when his wife lost the election. The name of Hillary's book was "What Happened?" As they say, it was the first time that a question and its answer are on the cover of a book.

JOHN MICHAEL KING

Here is another example of a person whose name you almost certainly will not recognize. Pat and I didn't when we met him. The first year we sailed down the east coast of the United States, the territory was all new to us. Every turn we took gave us a new view. Sailing around Rhode Island, through the long but beautiful stretch of Long Island Sound, past the skyscrapers of Manhattan, down the coast of New Jersey, up the Delaware River and through the surprisingly large expanse of Chesapeake Bay we rarely saw the same boat twice.

This all changed abruptly once we entered "The Big Ditch" at Norfolk.

Once you are confined to "the ditch" that is more properly called the Atlantic IntraCoastal Waterway, or just the ICW, you have many boats you are passing or motorboats that are much faster and are passing you, all in close proximity. Because boats were so close together in the narrow channel you could examine boats and wave at the people as the pass was made, frequently talking for a moment on the radio.

Our first stop south of Norfolk was at a place we have never heard of, Coinjock, North Carolina, just south of the Virginia state line. It was well known to boaters and a favorite stop heading south for the winter. There are long face docks you can tie up to at marinas on both sides of the ICW without having to make tight maneuvers into slips, but it was apparent back then that everybody southbound in the fall went to the one on the left, the Coinjock Marina. It had a good restaurant filled with a lively group of boat owners served by cute waitresses.

Aboard Eagle en route south from Norfolk to Coinjock, we had passed through the one and only lock on the ICW astern of an antique Huckins motor yacht named "Billie." The couple aboard were very friendly. Pat talked with them about our friend in Marblehead, Massachusetts who owned a small Huckins runabout boat. The Kings could travel much faster than our sailboat, so they disappeared ahead of us shortly after the lock opened and both boats got underway.

They may have gone faster, but they didn't travel as many hours each day, so when we tied up at Coinjock they were there in front of us. We got to talking, had dinner with them and ended up inviting them after dinner for drinks aboard *"Eagle."*

Since we had most of our possessions in storage and the company would not store alcoholic beverages, we had a large supply of great old single-malt scotch on board and that was what Michael King loved. This led to a most enjoyable conversation and, after several nights, a noticeable reduction in our scotch whiskey inventory. We learned that they headed south every fall and spent their winters on their boat tied up in the marina at Harbourtown, near the southern tip of Hilton Head Island.

The next morning, they again pulled far ahead of us, but once again we caught up with them for the night at Belhaven, where we both tied up at the River Forest Marina. The Kings knew the restaurant well and told us to order not just the "regular" oyster fritters on the menu but to get the "specials" that were not on the menu but would be made upon request by the outstanding chef....Alice. They were truly outstanding and led to the consumption of a good bit more scotch. Alice has since died, so I hope the restaurant has her recipe.

We continued on down the waterway and tied up again that night near the Kings in Oriental, North Carolina. We again made a big dent in our single malt scotch inventory again. My wife, Pat, was puzzled that the King's had learned so much about us but we had, despite several attempts, not been able to learn much about them, except for the fact that she had a been a Senior VP in the Trust Department of Manufacturers Hanover Bank in New York.

Michael was noticeably silent; Pat eventually just asked him point blank. He finally, and somewhat reluctantly, said he had been an actor. When he didn't elaborate, Pat asked him if he had been in movies. His "no" obviously led to Pat's question about what kind of acting and his response was "on stage." Nothing more was disclosed. Pat pushed ahead again and Michael finally got to the point of saying he had been on Broadway. Having gone that far it was not long before he said he had been in what I think might well be voted the all-time best musical... *"My Fair Lady."*

Michael hadn't just been in the show, He had played the young man madly in love with Eliza Doolittle, played by Julie Andrews. He had sung the delightful song "On the Street Where You Live." It began with the lines "I have often walked down this street before, but the pavement always stayed beneath my feet before." He also sang an amusing duet with Julie Andrews, "Show Me,' but it was nowhere near as memorable as his solo.

Michael said it had been a very quiet period in his life. Because he had to be prepared to sing perfectly every night, he could not take risks that might hinder his performance. There was no drinking; he had had to get a good night's sleep every night for years. He never said why it had taken us so long to get that key bit of information out of him, but he did continue to enjoy good scotch.

ADLAI STEVENSON

Thanks to Alabama Governor Gordon Persons, I got to sit and chat for over an hour with Adlai Stevenson in the study of the Alabama Governor's Mansion on Perry Street in Montgomery. This was back when I was attending Montgomery's Sidney Lanier High School, where I was a writer for the school newspaper.....the *Blue and White*. The newspaper put our picture on the front page and published my interview with Adlai. Unfortunately, someone made a bad mistake and put a paragraph from somewhere in the middle of my copy at the start of the piece, so the article seemed very strange.

The article focused on education, but our conversation covered many topics. My impression was that Adlai was a truly extraordinary and knowledgeable gentleman. He was something that would not be acceptable, much less electable, in today's highly-partisan environment. He was a brilliant moderate. Adlai had a massive resume of experience, but that did not come close to having him win against the great war hero, Dwight David Eisenhower, shortly after the end of World War II.

One comment attributed to Adlai resurfaced at an appropriate time just after Romney was walloped by Obama in 2012. During his 1956 presidential campaign, a woman had called out to Adlai Stevenson with a question. She supposedly stated that "Senator, you have the vote of every thinking person!" to which Stevenson responded: "That's not enough, madam, we need a majority!" Truer words were never spoken. Certainly that might be said by liberals in 2016.

CLIFFORD and VIRGINIA DURR

I knew Cliff and Virginia fairly well when I was dating their daughter, Lucy, throughout my junior year in high school. Because at the time I was an old-fashioned super-conservative white person, it was extremely awkward and, at the end, frequently embarrassing. My upbringing prevented me from understanding, much less accepting, the incredible contributions the Durrs were making to the civil rights movement in the United States. To put it mildly, they were disliked by most of my friends, intensely by my dad.

In the 1953-54 period in Montgomery, prior to the Supreme Court's decision in *Brown vs. Topeka Board of Education*, segregation was still the law in Alabama and virtually all whites considered it to be the way things should be. Almost all whites thought it was the way things had been and it was the way they should continue to be. I always wondered why the word "Topeka" was deleted from the name of that landmark case.

One of the people dad hated the most was Supreme Court Justice Hugo Black, an Alabamian who many thought had betrayed their state. Hugo Black was probably the worst on the list, even ahead of Franklin Delano Roosevelt. The Durrs had become personally very close to Justice Black because Virginia's sister had married him. The numerous marches and sit-ins that resulted in bombings and beatings did not come until much later, but things were beginning to heat up in 1954.

Virginia Durr had gone to Wellesley long before I went to Harvard, but we experienced similar problems. Meeting blacks much smarter than I came as a shock. Virginia's experience was more difficult. She told me she had to be worried about what her friends and family back home in Alabama would think about the socializing with black girls. Virginia had brought her concern to the attention of the college and had been told in no uncertain terms that, if she wouldn't sit down with the black girls, she would have to leave school. The choice was clear and the decision was obvious.

Cliff was even more educated, having gone to Oxford after graduating from the University of Alabama. When he lost his job at a law firm in Birmingham, Alabama, Cliff had moved to Washington, DC in 1933, just as FDR and his "New Deal" were getting into full swing. Cliff and Virginia fitted right in with the ultra-liberal agenda. My belief today is that the vast amount of money doled out by the FDR administration was as necessary for avoiding financial collapse as Obama's stimulus was in 2009, the big difference being that the Roosevelt money was spent effectively. The far left (what little there was in Montgomery at the time) began to gather at the Durr home. In addition to the financial problems the country faced, this was a time when large businesses treated employees horribly and unions really were needed and beneficial for the country and their members (in contrast with the situation today).

ELEANOR ROOSEVELT

An amusing, at least from today's perspective, event took place in Birmingham when blacks and whites were expected to sit together in Boutwell Auditorium to discuss ideas. The stupid, highly-prejudiced police chief announced that this would be illegal. The result was that blacks and whites would be allowed to sit in the auditorium provided they were separated by a string strung down the aisle in the middle.

As a participant at the meeting, First Lady Eleanor Roosevelt sat on the "black" side of the string. The police ordered her to move to the "correct" side and, of course, she refused. At least the authorities had the sense to realize that arresting the country's First Lady would be an unworkable folly, but the story is that she at least compromised and sat in the middle *on* the string. Note, that is something I have been told and have read, but I do not know personally the facts of the story. Years later she was a guest at a Sitzundjiber dinner in Boston.

After World War II, when communism and the Soviet Union were replacing Hitler's Nazis as the most dangerous group in the world, stories began to surface about communists being discovered in our government. This brought outcries demanding that they be identified and thrown out, an attitude which made it easy for Senator McCarthy to hitch his star to the battle to eliminate communists from our government.

As Washington was transformed from a bastion of ultra-left ideas into a hornet's nest of haters of communism, the Durrs retreated from DC to Montgomery, where I first met them in 1953. Almost everyone I knew despised them, so being in love with their brilliant and beautiful daughter was, to say the least, extremely awkward.

It was at this point that my terribly embarrassing moment occurred. I was guilty of violating my old beliefs that "A closed mouth gathers no feet" and that you should be sure to "Turn on your brain and wait a minute before you open your mouth."

A BAD DAY IN NEW ORLEANS

Virginia had been subpoenaed to appear in court in New Orleans. At a time when so many of the far left were being threatened into admitting who among their friends had been members of the communist party, the oft-repeated phrase had been "On the advice of counsel, I decline to answer in accordance with the rights granted to me under the Fifth Amendment." I suspect that after all these years too many young kids do not even know what that means. If you are one of those, you should know that, under the Fifth Amendment to the US Constitution, it is the right we all have to refuse to say anything that could get us into legal jeopardy. It would be "self incrimination." The implication, certainly when used by the IRS' Lois Lerner, was that you wouldn't claim the right to refuse to answer a question if you didn't have something to hide.

The court demanded that Virginia supply the names of those she knew to have belonged to the Communist Party. Paul Krouch became agitated and forceful in his verbal attack on Virginia, causing Cliff to leap over the railing in the courtroom and physically attack him. It was all over the radio immediately (this was when TV was not yet widespread in the country, certainly not in Alabama). I happened to be parked in my old Ford on Felder Avenue with Lucy in front of her house. We made the mistake of listening to the radio and, of course tuned in the news. Lucy immediately burst into tears. I had no clue as to what to say, but as I have been told she remembers and frequently tells it, I said "Your father shouldn't have done that." I had simply blurted out what I thought.

It got even worse. Cliff suffered a heart attack. It was after the end of my relationship with Lucy. There was, however, one good result. I think that hearing contributed to turning the tide against the incredibly obnoxious bully, Senator Joe McCarthy. Today, McCarthyism is a dirty word, justifiably so.

People at the time were not aware that a sizeable number of the far left did belong to the communist party or *had* belonged. The party represented their views of many far-left liberals during the thirties. Membership in the party back in the twenties and thirties did not include the pro-Soviet anti-American attitude which it conveyed in the early fifties

Just a year later Cliff went on to be intimately involved with some of the key events of the Civil Rights Movement. One of the biggest names in the movement was Rosa Parks who, on December 1, 1955, precipitated Montgomery's bus boycott by refusing to give up her seat to a white man who demanded that she move to the back of the bus. Virginia Durr had been using Rosa Parks as a seamstress, making clothes for her daughters. I had first met Rosa at the Durr's home. When the highly-regarded civil rights leader, E.D. Nixon met with Rosa at the jail, he called Cliff to serve as counsel for Rosa. Here again I am not sure of the facts, but I had always heard that Cliff posted Rosa's bail.

SELMA TO MONTGOMERY MARCH

After the famous Selma to Montgomery march, leaders of the group went back to talk in the Durr home. There is now an historic marker in front of the house on Felder, the side of which is on South Court Street, close to where Lucy and I had gone to high school.

There is one interesting bit of information that many may not know about that march from Selma. I had always been led to believe that thousands, possibly ten thousand or so, had marched from Selma to Montgomery. I have driven the route many times and seen the markers at the fields where the marchers camped each night en route to Montgomery. I was amazed at the logistics that must have been required to move everything from tents to port-a-potties and meals each day from campsite to campsite for such a large number of people. The press made it sound bigger than it was by saying that thousands had "participated," a word that implies that they took the march. Only recently did I learn that thousands participated in only the final segment through Montgomery up Dexter Avenue to the Alabama State Capitol, where they listened to the speech by Martin Luther King, but that very few actually walked the 53 miles of the march.

To some extent the legal authorities had to be concerned about a large number of people walking on what had to remain open as a highway, actually US Highway 80 that runs from Tybee Island, Georgia to San Diego, California. Now, with the Interstate Highway System, US80 is very rarely used for transcontinental driving, but at the time it was a busy highway.

A very intelligent and reasonable man, Judge Frank Johnson, had to make a decision. He knew that he could not issue an injunction prohibiting the march and creating another dangerous confrontation, but he recognized that a huge crowd would be.unsafe. His ruling was that 200 people could march *beside (not on)* the highway to Montgomery. It was the reduction to this much smaller number that made the logistics feasible

Atlanta claims to be the home of Martin Luther King, but it is interesting to know that his church, now the Martin Luther King Memorial Church on Dexter Avenue in Montgomery, was the only church King presided over in all of his years as a minister. As the marchers approached the state capitol, they passed that brick church on their right just two blocks before reaching the long steep steps up to the front of the Capitol.

King stood at on the back of a truck to address the thousands who were standing in the street below. There is a bronze star only a few feet from where some stories claim King stood that day. Ironically, the bronze star commemorates the spot where almost a century earlier Jefferson Davis had been sworn in as the President of the Confederate States of America. I am told that another irony is that Davis really did not stand there. Historians say Davis was sworn in on a platform below. It is an interesting story, but the facts indicate that neither stood near, much less on, the bronze star at the top of the steps.

There is another ridiculous bit of irony in the story. The highway has several historic signs along the route from Selma to Montgomery. That stretch of Highway 80 also bears another name…the Jefferson Davis Highway. That is as awkward as the fact that many of the blacks in Montgomery graduate from either Jefferson Davis High School or Robert E. Lee High School. Given the current trend in the country, those names won't last long.

CAROL DODA

You won't know her unless you're old, from San Francisco and probably male. Even then you may not remember this name. The subject of this section is a highly-disreputable woman who achieved international fame. I just had dinner with her one evening in San Francisco.

Carol was a stripper. She had become famous as a shocking, topless, dancer at a nightclub, the Condor, in the North Beach section of San Francisco. Her notoriety stemmed from her being the first topless dancer. She was also an early "enhancer." The articles say 44 inches, but she told me had increased her tits from 34 to 46 inches. There may have been predecessors in private clubs throughout the world, but she was the first to appear topless in the United States in a place open to the public. It doesn't sound like much these days, but it was considered memorable enough to justify one of those metal historic markers on the sidewalk where the club had operated. The headline on the marker reads "The Condor, where it all began."

Carol's act at the Condor began with her dancing while descending from the ceiling standing on top of a grand piano (more on that piano later). Her performances, begun in

1964, became an instant success. She was a big attraction for delegates to the Republican Convention in 1964. A large mountainous area looms over San Francisco named the "Twin Peaks." Carol became known as "San Francisco's New Twin Peaks." She led the way again in 1969 as the first bottomless dancer.

Along with the owner of the Condor, Carol was arrested in 1965, but the judge ruled that lewd behavior and indecent exposure were in the eye of the beholder and subject to a person's opinion. When she was acquitted, San Francisco's leading newspaper, the San *Francisco Chronicle*, ran a huge bold-type headline across the top of its front page that read "TOPLESS ACQUITTED." She had become well known enough there is a section about her in the 1968 book, "The Pump House Gang" by the famous author Tom Wolfe. Many years later she is now a subject in a new book.

During my years in the travel agency business one of my primary areas of involvement was negotiating rates with the hotel industry. I was invited to speak many times at senior management meetings of a number of the world's largest hotel chains....chains such as InterContinental, Four Seasons, Sheraton, Hyatt, Best Western and Marriott. My meeting in San Francisco was with Paul Handlery, owner of Handlery Hotels, a small chain of older hotels throughout California.

One of his hotels was noted for having the first all-glass elevators. Paul told me he had arranged for me to go to dinner at his favorite spot, Vanessi's, with his friend, Carol Doda. Carol was two weeks younger than I. She did have a very large pair of famous tits, and was quite attractive looking in a surprisingly nice way. Her attire was by the current standards of movie stars and models, quite middle of the road. Conservative, yes; but they did show off a lot of her two biggest assets.

Carol was more intelligent than I had expected and made an interesting dinner companion, even though it was difficult to avoid the subject of the job for which she was known. At the end of the evening she gave me a large poster of herself, autographed on her left tit. It was more exposed than the tit on which the model, Elle McPherson, autographed a message to me on a poster many years later. Obviously, now that I am married, both posters are relegated to the attic. I don't even know where.

The piano became famous in 1983 when the club's assistant manager, Jimmy Ferrozzo, screwed a naked stripper, Theresa Hill, on top of the piano as it sat on the stage. In order to allow for Carol's dancing while the piano descended, the mechanism had to operate quite smoothly, with the piano pushed up by a hydraulic column beneath it. Jimmy must have accidentally hit the switch that caused the hydraulic lift to make the piano rise slowly and gently through the ceiling, crushing the two together to death. To say the least, it was an unusual way to go.

YO YO MA
Yo Yo isn't just a world-famous musician, he is an extraordinarily nice person. When he performed with the Savannah Symphony, we hosted a small party for him downtown on Broughton Street. We could exchange stories about more than his beautiful cello performance because he had gone to Harvard, living in Lowell House a couple of blocks from where I had lived in Adams House. As President of the Symphony, I signed his paycheck. Wish I had kept that canceled check, but it would have just been stamped.

I thought he must have had any musical talent driven out of him by the awful Russian bells that hang in the beautiful tower of Lowell House. They were a gift from the country and cast using the weird Russian tonal scale, for which there appears to be no decent music. I think it involved notes on something like a ten-or-twelve-note scale instead of the "normal" eight-note octave. Some of the guys in Lowell used to go up and ring the bells in late afternoon, forcing many on the campus around them to cover their ears.

Yo Yo said that the story about his jumping out of his New York taxi and forgetting that he had left his extremely valuable cello in the trunk was a fact. What is truly remarkable is that the cab driver located him and returned Yo Yo's precious instrument. On that subject, Yo Yo said he could not describe how relieved he was to get his cello back.

ITZHAK PERLMAN
The Savannah Symphony had to pay what for the orchestra's audience thought was a lot of money to get Itzhak to perform with the Savannah Symphony. His normal rate was deeply discounted as a result of his friendship with our conductor, Philip Greenberg. As a result, we could make money on the evening by filling the seats with 2,350 people in Savannah's Civic Center where our orchestra performed.

The audience loved him. It was sad to see him have to come on stage in his wheelchair, but it added to his mystique. My personal opinion was that his performance was no better than several other name violinists we had as soloists in Savannah, especially Eugene Fodor and Rachael Barton.

STUART WOODS
This is a strange one because, at the time, I did not have any idea of who he was. A lady who wanted to visit our boat and talked with Pat brought Stuart aboard "Eagle" one night when we were in Vero Beach. Only years later did I discover his great fiction. Stuart has written many-dozen works of fiction, including about four dozen involving the cop/lawyer named Stone Barrington. All of his latest more-than-two-dozen books have

been on the New York Times Bestseller List. I love the incredible plot of his book, *"Santa Fe Edge."* At least Pat, a voracious reader of fiction, knew who he was.

It was a fun evening aboard *"Eagle,"* but I wish I had known who he was at the time.

IDI AMIN

This segment illustrates the difference between gambling limited to slot machines on Indian Reservations in Alabama and gambling in major, elegant casinos in many parts of the world, especially Western Europe. It is also an indicator of my having met many people. I did not remember this one until about 40 years later when I had stumbled across notes on my first visit to Cairo.

I was lucky enough to be the guest of the President of Sheraton Hotels at a time when the Sheraton was the first-choice hotel in the city. It wasn't just first choice; it was the first by a mile. Our travel agency frequently had trouble getting a reservation for a VIP, despite our close relationship with our client, Sheraton. The hotel had a beautiful view up and down the Nile and was simply "the place to be." I was given two connecting suites overlooking the Nile and three almost-full-time "keepers" during my four-day visit, one to drive the limo, one as an English speaking guide and one to pay all of the bills. It was a great way to travel.

I had flown to Beirut to meet Sheraton's President and carried with me all of the solid gold gifts that were to be given to the Sheik who was investing in a new Sheraton to be built on the coast south of Beirut down toward the airport. I hate to think of what all that gold must be worth today.

On my third night they took me to a casino. I didn't gamble except when far away on a business trip, at which times I was usually alone and bored. I never really gambled for the sake of gambling. The "payer"even bought me a stack of chips. Roulette was my choice because it did not require skill and in country's other than the US, had just one "0" meaning about a 3% stake for the casino contrasted with a "0"plus a double "00" at US casinos, increasing their gross take to about 6%. Your cost per hour was low.

I always sat on the corner farthest from the employee who spun the wheel, called out the winner and racked in the money from those who had gambled and lost. I had developed a habit of betting on #31 as it was right there in the corner where I sat. What made the evening interesting was the arrival of the notorious Idi Amin, the brutal head of a ruthless government, President of Uganda (he was known as "PaPa Doc").

Neither of us had anyone else to talk with so we did get to talk for a good while (until my money limit had run out). Amin was an extremely tough and haughty character. It was interesting getting to talk with him but he was certainly not a fun person with whom to spend an hour.

JAMES MACARTHUR

Here is another example of one you probably don't know until you hear his stage name. During my years, Harvard had elitist "Final Clubs" and just one fraternity, SAE. I had joined SAE, a fraternity born at the University of Alabama, that died at Harvard in the 60s. A fellow member just told me it had risen from the dead, but currently in the news is the announcement by the far-left President of Harvard, Drew Faust, that she plans to close all social clubs. In contrast with the very elite "Final Clubs," SAE was the liveliest and by far the least expensive. SAE still had an orientation toward southerners. The richest guys belonged to Porcellian, which was through the wall on the second floor of the adjacent building on Massachusetts Ave. If you looked as the elaborate window directly over the door to Porcellian, the three windows of SAE were to the right.

While most of the clubs had large stand-alone buildings, it was an amusing coincidence that the poorest and the richest were next to each other on the second floors of two contiguous buildings. You might also say (I would) that ours was the most fun and theirs was the least. Back in those days a million dollars made you a wealthy man. The story, to my knowledge unfounded, was that if you did not have your first million by the age of forty, the Club would give it to you. How's that for charity? I was always led to believe most members had a million when they joined.

SAE, in contrast to the Clubs, allowed women and had great parties while most of the Clubs were sedate and, except at rare special occasions, men only. Having the club for entertaining on Saturday nights made dating economically feasible for those of us who could not afford the pricey restaurants around the city. A few of the "Pork" members (the elite sounding name, Porcellian, really came from their logo, which was a pig) would, upon rare occasion, come next door to visit. The visitor I remember who became the most famous was Karim Khan, who at the time was called just "K." He left Harvard for a year to undergo the unexpected process of becoming Aga Khan IV. Karim was Class of '58, but he graduated with me in 1959. He is the leader of 15 million Shia Muslims. He has been a great leader, eschewing the black garb and beard for standard business attire. By tradition, he was given his weight in precious jewels annually.

The Porcellian guy who was much more fun was James MacArthur, a name you probably have not recognized but will when you read that on the long-running TV Show *"Hawaii Five-O"* he was "Danno." This is not the new version. In the long-running and very-popular weekly TV show when they caught the bad guys McGarrett, the head of *Five-0* always said "Book'em, Danno!" That line is not used in the current show. So much for tradition.

James was the adopted son of famous actress Helen Hayes, and had been in a wide variety of shows before even getting to college. During his career, he performed in a list of plays and movies, none as memorable as *Five-0*. Amusingly, he co-starred with his mother in *"Invitation To A March"* and with her again when she made a guest appearance on *"Hawaii Five-0."* It is funny that I don't remember what we called him back then. I have trouble remembering any name but "Danno."

Despite being far above us socially and a member of Porcellian, MacArthur was very relaxed and fun loving. He once became somewhat of a celebrity, dating Jane Fonda when she was in Boston performing in a play that opened with her lying down near the front of the stage clothed, but appearing to be naked. He dropped out of college in his sophomore year. As in the case of Bill Gates, it must pay to drop out of Harvard early.

There was one very memorable evening during our sophomore year when James had a good bit too much to drink. At a party at Katie Gibbs School (officially "Katherine Gibbs," but nobody called it that), he became irate, believing that the punch had been loaded with salt peter, the ancient potion that some believed to reduce the chances of improper sex by preventing a man's "equipment" from becoming operational.

James grabbed a fire extinguisher and sprayed some of the faculty present. My roommate, Robby van Tienhoven, and I got him out the door onto Newbury Street and into Robby's car before security could catch him. The TV shows phrase might have been changed to "Book Danno." Sadly, James died in 2010 at age 72.

PAUL SAMUELSON

Most of you probably will not recognize this name, but if you studied economics in college, you probably used his textbook. Experts cite the fact that his book has the widest circulation of any economics textbook, with over 4 million copies sold worldwide in more than 40 languages.

Paul was an "Institute Professor," the highest rank in the faculty at the Massachusetts Institute of Technology. One of the fun things about my years of involvement with Heritage Travel was our claim that we handled travel for more Nobel Prize winners than any other travel agency.

Serving as the official travel agency for both Harvard and MIT, when the Nobel prizes were announced we usually learned that we would be handling travel to Stockholm for at least one winner to receive his or her prize. Twice we had two winners in one year. One of these was Paul, who was awarded the Nobel Prize in Economic Sciences. The *New York Times* rated Paul as "the foremost academic economist of the 20th century."

I dated his assistant, Joan Thompson, played tennis with him occasionally at his club in Belmont and visited his interesting home several times, once with my wife, Pat. Paul was brilliant, but he certainly was a friendly and charming person (although he usually did beat me at tennis, even though he was about 22 years older than I). Sadly, Paul died in 2009 at age 94. Too many friends are dying.

WOLF BLITZER

One of those strange treats received as a result of my job was being invited twice to have lunch with Wolf Blitzer. I have no idea how much a celebrity is paid to be stuck having lunch with people he doesn't know or have any reason to care about. Wolf was very interesting, even many years ago, but I got the impression he was bored stiff having to have lunch.

It certainly wasn't an interesting experience for him. At least all of the sports figures hired to dine with major customers were very enthusiastic, but because they were nowhere near as intelligent as Wolf, frequently boring. You can read about these in the next chapter. Wolf used to be the news anchor we watched the most, but now that CNN has become almost as far left as MSNBC, we rarely see him anymore.

STEVE FORBES

A few times, the Air Travel Card had Steve Forbes for lunch, but each time I sat across a big round table from him and did not get to talk with him much; he talked to the table. You didn't need to talk, because listening to him was always very interesting and educational. Steve was very smart and knowledgeable, but I could not imagine him as a Presidential candidate; he did not have the personality be a politician.

There was a funny story about Steve's grandfather that was in the September 22, 2017 Wall Street Journal. Forbes Magazine was run for many years by Steve's father, Malcolm. Before that came his grandfather, B. C. Forbes, who had started the magazine in 1917. B.C had gotten a job as a business writer and took a second job with another financial publisher using a "nom de plume," so that this double role would not be known. He was so good that the editors of both publications began boasting about what a good writer they had, without realizing they were both bragging about the same person.

EMMETT KELLY

Here is another example of a name you probably will not recognize unless you are very old, like me. Emmett was probably the world's best-known clown. Born in 1898, he worked for the Ringling Brothers and Barnum and Bailey Circus, becoming by far their star clown in 1931. As "Wee Willie," Emmett's stick was his incredibly sad expression. He had many acts, but his most amusing was using a broom trying to "sweep up" a puddle of light that was shining on the floor of the huge circus tent. Emmett also acted as "Willie" in Cecil B. DeMille's movie "*The Greatest Show On Earth.*"

In many respects I was very lucky as a kid growing up in Montgomery. The social editor of the *Montgomery Advertiser* newspaper, Esther Mahoney, was a friend of my mother, resulting in my being in the newspaper a ridiculous number of times. One year when the big circus was coming to town Esther asked me to be in a feature about the circus. She drove me and the paper's photographer to the big field where the workers, aided by elephants to do the pulling, were finishing raising the huge tent.

Emmett was the real star of the feature in the paper. I was just the little kid being shown the circus. They took pictures of us with Emmett's holding my hand as he showed me around and introduced me to a dozen of people in the different parts of the circus. The photos of Emmett and me were at every spot. For a little kid, it was an great experience. I loved the circus. I just wish that the section of the newspaper had been saved somewhere in all of "the stuff" accumulated over the years.

CARL ICHANN

Here is another bit of evidence re how much the travel industry recognized the brilliance of Don Sohn. Possibly the most feared takeover artist in the country, even today, is Carl Icahn. He is notorious for taking over companies and making money by splitting them up or doing things that made him millions while damaging the company, focusing on short term gains while damaging any long-range potential. Carl came to Boston to meet with us at Heritage Travel twice in the late 1980s, about both TWA and Eastern Airlines.

Don told him in spades how bad the problems where with both big name carriers. In these two cases, I knew enough to make several meaningful contributions to the discussion. These airlines were similar in that both were operating ancient computer systems and airplanes and had essentially unsolvable problems with tough unions. Especially in the case of Eastern, the weaker their employer became the more aggressive their unions became, making demands that exceeded what could be accepted.

TWA desperately needed to earn profits and, with this proving to be so difficult, Carl sold what was arguably TWA's biggest asset, their US to London routes. I had tried working with TWA and, as a result was invited to fly first class on their inaugural flight on their first Boeing 747 from JFK to London.

Eastern was short on funds, also had antique IT systems and planes, suffered from having to negotiate with a recalcitrant union, and did not have the expansive route system to compete as the industry rapidly evolved under deregulation. Carl asked a long list of questions, but Don and I gave him nothing but negative answers. Carl must have been very displeased by all he heard that day, which probably contributed to my thinking he was not a very pleasant guy. He must have been quite disappointed in both of his entries into the airline business. Note, even Donald Trump did not succeed with his airline.

CAROLL EDWIN SPINNEY

Here is another name I can almost guarantee you will not recognize. We used to handle his travel many years ago when Heritage Travel was the official agency for WGBH TV, the great TV station in Boston that still produces many of the best shows, constituting about a third of all the prime time shows on Public Television.

You may not know the actor, but bet you know the character he played on TV. Caroll was much better known as "Big Bird" on Sesame Street. He told me he could not see out of his costume. He had to look at a screen inside that showed him the audience in front of him via a small camera embedded in his costume. His right arm went up through the neck of Big Bird to control the head and his little finger operated the eyebrows.

The amusing part of the story is that, for a variety of reasons, we always reserved seats for Caroll, his wife, Debra, and one for Big Bird to sit next to them. Caroll, still alive at 86, lives in Woodstock, Connecticut. Debra called me on January 15, 2017 to verify that I had all the facts straight.

It was quite amusing when she added that Heritage was able to buy Big Bird a child's ticket at a big discount because Big was under six years old. Traveling as a passenger insured that Big Bird would be there when they got to their destination and it would have required lots of money and been less convenient to have to have him crated and shipped as cargo.

81 SPORTS STARS I KNEW
Some I Knew Fairly Well

JOHN McENROE
John became the best tennis analyst on TV. He was both articulate and extremely knowledgeable. He became quite a gentleman, but when he first started, he was what was called an "enfant terrible," the fancy French words for a horrible, obnoxious little bastard. It was the first time I had the pleasure of being the guest of Avis at the US Open tennis, way back when the Open was still held at Forest Hills, with a stadium much much smaller than the one used today at the National Tennis Center.

We were seated in folding chairs on the edge of the court directly in line with the service line. It was a fabulous location just a few feet from the players. When a player ran for a shot, they would almost land in your lap. John was a terrible brat that evening, both obnoxious and quite loud. He was brand new on the tennis scene, and his attitude came as a terrible shock to the staid old fans. We got to observe his temper tantrums from as little as five feet away. He was a disgusting person. Boy, how times change.

For those of you who watch tennis on TV, you get no comprehension of the speed at which the pros' serves are traveling. For a US Open match a year or two later in the new huge stadium, five of us were seated in a little triangular area at the corner of the court, actually out on the playing surface. Nobody gets seats like that anymore. We were lucky that Avis had passed out Avis seat cushions because we had to use them to fend off "faults" (I hate having to provide definitions for those of you who don't know sports, but a fault is a serve that lands outside the service area so the player set to receive the serve does not even try to hit it).

We had to hold up our cushions and be ready every time the serve was coming toward our corner of the court. Even back in those days when a hundred miles per hour was fast, you got no sense of how fast the balls where going until they were coming straight at you. TV and even being in the stadium do not adequately convey the speed of the balls. The balls came so fast that they hit our cushions with a loud whack. If a ball had hit one of us in the face it could have caused injury.

McEnroe became one of the very-best commentators of tennis.

BEN HOGAN
In contrast to most of the others, even as a very young kid, my impression of Ben Hogan was that he was not a nice guy. I did get the autograph, but no good memories to go with it. He was, to say the least, not a very likable guy, and I had been told his fellow golfers

shared my impression of him. He was unnecessarily abrupt and quite unpleasant, attributes recognizable even by a young kid.

My mother introduced me to him when he was playing at the Montgomery Country Club, and she had done most of the talking.

JACK KRAMER and BOBBY RIGGS

These were two of the great names in tennis in the middle of the twentieth century. They went on tour, playing each other in "exhibition matches." I got to ball boy one of their matches, a great memory of my tennis days. If you are a young tennis player, try to get to be a ball boy. I guess we now have to say "ball person," but I think the old term became so common that young females with this responsibility should be called female ball boys.

It is a little like comparing the old days when airlines had beautiful or at least very-good looking stewardesses. I don't know what to call the ugly stewardesses today but. As I said in an earlier chapter, the men in this job should be known as "male stewardesses." Yes, I believe in equal rights, but I don't think Hooters restaurants should be required to hire male "Hooters girls."

Serving as a ball boy gives you an excellent "up close and personal" view of the match and gives you an interesting relationship with the players. I still have the program that includes the page with the pictures of Jack and Bobby autographed to me. Jack was a much-more pleasant man than Bobby.

CARL YASTRZEMSKI

In the late sixties, Carl was one of the most-widely acclaimed players in the world, winning baseball's "Triple Crown" in 1967, the year of Boston's "Impossible Dream." Even if your do not follow baseball, you will recognize how few players had won the title. To give you some perspective, the very short list of names includes Lou Gehrig, Ted Williams, and Mickey Mantle. It has been such a tough accomplishment to achieve that Carl in '67 had been the last player to reach this pinnacle until Detroit's Miguel Cabrera in October of 2012. As O.J. had been for Hertz, local Boston hero Yastrzemski had been paid by Portland Printing as their celebrity PR person. In another one of those lucky times for me, he had committed to having lunch with Portland's customers at Boston's Pier Four Restaurant the day after the season ended in 1967.

As luck would have it, the Red Sox had a great end of the season, winning the American League Pennant. Everyone brought their copies of that morning's Boston Globe front page to get Carl's autograph on his picture, a great reminder of what, at the time, was one of Boston's best seasons in many years. I got to sit with Carl at lunch and imposed too much on him, coming away with a stack of autographed Globes.

Yaz spent his entire 23-year career playing for Boston, starting in left field the year after Ted Williams retired. Yaz was the league MVP, almost unanimously, with just one vote going to someone else. He had a .326 batting average, hit 44 home runs and 121 RBIs and was named "Sportsman of the Year" by *Sports Illustrated.* I think it sad for fans that players no longer stay playing for the same team during their careers. At least I hope Tom Brady stays with the Patriots.

It was amusing and most people don't remember that many years ago the long-time owner of the Red Sox, Tom Yawkey, insisted for years that he would have to move the Red Sox to another city if Boston didn't give him a better stadium. Fenway Park continues to this day as a truly historic place and a great place to enjoy a game, even though old fashioned and small. At least they were able to add lots of seats over "The Green Monster" wall in left field and several floors of seats and luxury boxes around the infield and, remarkably, they still sell out essentially every game.

In contrast with some of the sports stars in this section, Carl was an extremely nice guy.

BABE DIDRIKSON ZAHARIAS

Some of you, unless you are old like me, may not even recognize this name. "The Babe" was not just good at one sport. She was very good at many sports, from the Olympics to golf. When Patty Berg was trying to start up golf tournaments for what was then a relatively small number of female professional golfers, the Babe wrote Berg a letter saying she was not interested because she could make much more money touring the country playing exhibition matches and getting all the money for herself.

One of those matches was in Montgomery, so I was able to get her to sign my ticket to the match. Unlike the hastily scribbled "autographs" given by too many sports heroes today, the Babe took the time to sign her name with every letter of her three names clearly legible.

My mother got to play against her in a tournament in Texas in the late forties. We still have the trophy Mom won in Texas that is engraved "WWGA," the Womens Western Golf Association. At the time, before the US Open, it was considered the most important tournament in women's golf.

Of all the people in this category, The Babe and Ben Hogan were probably the ones with whom I got to talk for the briefest period. I mostly just stood there while mom talked with them. From that extremely brief encounter I did get the impression that The Babe was as nice as Ben Hogan was nasty.

BOBBY ORR

For those of you who do not live in ice hockey territory, this may be an unknown name, but Orr was the star of the Boston Bruins for many years. When National Rental Car would bring him to Heritage Travel, he brought along photos showing him horizontal in midair driving home the winning goal. This was clearly his most famous photo.

Of all the sports figures written about here, he was the nicest, willing to stand for his picture to be taken with many of our employees and talk with them for a while as well. Bobby would sit for an hour with a few of us in the conference room. He also took the time to write a little something personal with his autograph for each delighted guest. As I said, he was and extremely-friendly guy.

His ranking as the greatest in ice hockey may have been taken by Wayne Gretsky but, in my day. he was by far the biggest name in the sport, and he played for Boston.

PETE ROSE

Pete is known for being a truly-outstanding baseball player who should have, had he not had a stupid addiction to gambling, been admitted years ago to the Baseball Hall of Fame. Personally, I think Alex Rodriguez's taking performance enhancing drugs was much worse than gambling on baseball games, especially when it appears that Rose's betting was always betting for his team to win, never against them.

When the bicycling world was finally able to get Lance Armstrong to admit to having taken performance-enhancing drugs for years, he and his team were stripped of all their wins in the Tour de France. Why shouldn't the Yankees have to forfeit every baseball game in which Rodriguez scored a run that made the difference in a win have to forfeit every game they won?

One year Pat and I were flown by America West Airlines to Phoenix to sit in their luxury box and watch our New England Patriots play Arizona. I was seated next to Pat but on her other side she was next to Pete, so she did most of the talking with him throughout the game. It was an interesting experience, but there was little interesting conversation because you could not bring up the only subject of interest.

He clearly deserved to be banned from baseball and he should continue to be denied the honor of being in the Baseball Hall of Fame. Once he dies, he should be admitted immediately. He was certainly a friendly and charming guy. Sad that he was such a gambler when he had to accept the rules that he not gamble. Once again, why wasn't Rodriguez given the same punishment?

ARTHUR ASHE

The afternoon with Arthur Ashe was another example of the numerous benefits of belonging to the Sitzundjibers. Long ago, the Longwood Cricket Club in Brookline, Massachusetts (on the west side of Boston) hosted the annual US Pro Championships. This was before the inception of the US Open, so we got to watch the top pros play in what, by today's standards, was a truly tiny stadium, squeezed into the corner of Hammond Street and Boylston in Newton, Massachusetts in Greater Boston. The grass courts were beautiful and almost all viewable from the veranda of the clubhouse. There was actually nothing to make it deserve the title of stadium, it was just a few rows of wooden-seated stands to sit on.

One of the more active members of the Sitzundjibers and of Longwood was Sally Hurlbut, and she had the advantage of having her family's home directly behind Longwood's courts. By the way, the cricket club name came from long ago, the club has had only tennis courts for many years. As a long-time member but an embarrassingly-infrequent user of the club, I still got to play one evening with the iconic TV commentator, Bud Collins. He was a true character and great fun to be with.

The Sitzundjibers invited Arthur to spend time with us one afternoon at Sally's home after tennis. It was in theory a lesson, but it quickly evolved into a party. Stupidly, not many people took advantage of the opportunity to meet, talk and party with Arthur. At the time, black tennis players were almost non-existent. He was truly highly-respected pioneer. Arthur was quite willing to offer advice to everything from beginners to very-experienced players. I have met insufferable sports stars. Arthur was just the opposite, an extraordinarily nice congenial person.

I got to watch Arthur and meet him the first time when he was playing at Longwood, winning the National Amateur Championship in 1968. Longwood has quite a place in tennis history, having been the home club of Dwight Davis, who established the Davis Cup. He was a student at Harvard at the time.

His tournament now involves competition between men's teams representing countries throughout the world. The first Davis Cup matches were held at Longwood. Another early Longwood member, Hazel Wightman, created the Wightman Trophy, the trophy for a tournament between women's teams.

For years, I was reminded of Arthur every September when my wife and I watched all of the big matches of the US OPEN in the massive Arthur Ashe Stadium. His contributions to the sport of tennis clearly justified naming the largest tennis stadium in the world after him.

ORENTHAL SIMPSON

Once again, I bet some of you do not recognize this name. I had dinner with him twice, both times in California, both times as the guest of the Hertz Corporation. Orenthal is best remembered, not as Orenthal James, but as O. J. Simpson. He seemed so nice. Jovial. Charming. Lots of good adjectives. Wikipedia cited his "amiable persona and natural charisma." Those attributes he had in spades.

It wasn't just the lengthy trial for the murder of his ex-wife Nicole Brown Simpson and her friend Ronald Goldman, O.J. was involved in several cases on several different charges. In the civil suit regarding the murders he was found guilty and was ordered to pay the Brown family $33.5 million but never paid but a ridiculously small amount. He was also convicted of an armed robbery and kidnapping that occurred in Las Vegas in 2007 and went to prison. There are, however, four funny stories about O. J. For many years I have used the phrase "He's as innocent as O.J. Simpson" to define the status of someone who is obviously guilty. You don't need to reread all the stories here.

O. J. loved golf. When acquitted, he had sworn to search for and find "the real killers." The joke was that he must have thought the killers were golfers because he spent so much time on golf courses.

O. J. was paid as a spokesman or celebrity image for some major companies, the best known by far was his "running through airports" TV commercials for Hertz. Frank Olson, Hertz CEO, was a big fan of O. J. and it was through Hertz that I had dinner twice with O J. Hertz used many Olympic names, but O.J.'s was the best-known star and the only one I remember.

Frank had sponsored O. J. for membership in a very exclusive New Jersey club, the Arcola Country Club, which at the time was an elite men-only club just west of the Garden State Parkway, northwest of Manhattan. The design of the Garden State Parkway had to take am easily seen loop around the eastern side of the club in Paramus, New Jersey. Frank got O. J. elected. Frank told me that after the murders he had a lot of members furious at him for having pushed so hard to have O.J. voted in as a member.

Fake News?

Pat and I were sailing south from Boston in the fall of 1994 and missed (thankfully) most of O. J.'s trial that was watched every day by millions. We had sailed up the Delaware River, passed through the Chesapeake-Delaware Canal and, on the afternoon of October 3, 1995, were entering the upper end of Chesapeake Bay when a man's voice called out on VHF Channel 16. This channel is reserved for ships and boats needing to hail another vessel or the Coast Guard and most sailors left their radios on Channel 16. When hailing on 16 you are required to give your FCC Radio License call numbers, state the name of your vessel and request that the vessel or location you are hailing respond. If that vessel responds, you are to agree immediately upon a different channel and switch to it to conduct your conversation. *No* chatting on 16.

This time the voice on Channel 26 just blurted out "O. J. acquitted." Nothing else. A moment later another man's voice broadcast "You gotta be kidding." A third voice came on 16 and said "No, it's true." Finally, after only a couple of seconds, a fourth man, who must have had a great sense of humor, came on 16. He said "OJ acquitted; whites in LA riot." This was so memorable that it is one of the few times I remember the exact words.

In an unbelievable coincidence, LA magazine in its July, 1994 issue had printed a long, detailed article titled "Court Jester" deriding the L.A. District Attorney, Gil Garcetti, accusing him of incompetence in prosecuting many major very-high-profile murder cases in which the prosecution failed to get a conviction. These cases included the police beating of Rodney King, in which the acquittal led to the massive riots in L.A. Another example was the acquittal of the Menendez brothers for murdering their parents. There was never any question that they had done the deed, but they still got an acquittal, something for which critics blamed Garcetti for the inept prosecution by his the team.

The subtitle of LA Magazines article was "Gil Garcetti has achieved in just over a year what it took Ira Reiner eight years to achieve: the public perception that the D.A. is an office of incompetent bureaucrats, incapable of winning the big cases.

There are two events relevant to the prosecution of O.J. First was the timing of the article, written just before the O.J. murders on June 12, 1994 and published in June in an issue dated July. Amazingly, the article came out just before the O.J. murders, so it blasted the Attorney General for incompetence *before* the O.J. trial became a part of the list of failures. The major part of the story. the existence of that long and detailed blast was, to my knowledge, never mentioned once the O.J. trial commenced and resulted in an acquittal for which the prosecution was, once again, given the most blame. How could you lose when so many pieces of evidence clearly pointed to O.J.? Amazingly, this article got little publicity, essentially none.

TED HOOD

Ted was for years the biggest name in sailing. He was the world's leading designer and manufacturer of sails and was a highly-accomplished sailboat skipper, winning dozens of major races. Later, he went into designing excellent, top-of-the-line, cruising boats, both power and sail. Later, he went into building top-quality yachts at his "Little Harbor" company. It was in his "Little Harbor Boatyard" in Marblehead that my fiberglass IOD hull had sat next to Ted Turner's America's Cup hull under construction (in an earlier chapter. The huge trophy case in Ted Hood's living room of his home overlooking Marblehead Harbor was filled with sterling silver.

One Saturday afternoon, standing on the porch of the Corinthian Yacht Club after a race, Ted presented me with a "trophy," while people having a drink after the race laughed. Racing my antique wooden boat, I had always called Etchells racing sailboats "Eggshells" because they were made of fiberglass. The Etchells was a very fast boat that, without question, should have been selected in the competition in the late sixties to pick a new boat for the Olympics. Trials were held in Kiel, Germany among boat with a maximum waterline length of 22 feet. Shillalah, designed by Skip Etchells, won 8 of the 10 races. Even so, the selection committee could not agree upon a choice. Ridiculous.

More trials were held a year later in Travemunde and a fiberglass twin, named "Shillalah II," won an incredible 10 of the 13 races. It was a fabulous design and clearly should have been the choice for the Olympics. The Europeans shamelessly voted for a much slower and less attractive (I would risk using the word "ugly") looking boat named "Soling," designed by a Norwegian. The committee, consisting largely of Europeans, selected the boat designed by the Norwegian over the Etchells, designed by an American, a highly-questionable decision that many Americans complained about for years, and rightly so. The Soling went on to be in the Olympics from 1972 through 2000. The Soling, despite being an Olympic Class, never caught on in the great sailing port of Marblehead, where most of the new boats were Etchells.

A lady, Mary Lou Grinnell, had a husband, Jim, who raced an Etchells. Mary Lou had constructed a "trophy" consisting of a slice of tree trunk as its base, a branch that resembled a tree with it leaves stripped and replaced with little pieces of fiberglass cloth that had been cut in the shape of leaves. The base had a brass plaque that included what at the time were popular words among wooden boat sailors: "If God had intended for people to sail in fiberglass boats, he would have given us fiberglass trees." The trophy was presented to me on the porch of the Corinthian Yacht Club by Ted Hood, accompanied by much laughter. Unfortunately, the trophy was fragile and impossible to pack so sometime over the years it was lost or thrown out.

After the ceremony I went to the Club's men's room and was standing at a urinal with my "equipment" in my hand. A voice from behind, Jim Grinnell's, said "Thornton, what is it you call my boat." As usual, I responded that it was an "Eggshell." As I turned around, to my embarrassment, Jim said "I'd like to introduce you to Skip Eggshell." At least Skip could laugh at it.

Ted did, in those days, occasionally have too much to drink. The Eastern Yacht Club in Marblehead, Massachusetts, was only about 900 feet north on the road from Ted's home.

Each year, a north shore hospital held a benefit dance called "The Merry Mixers" at the Eastern Yacht Club.

One of the most beautiful women in the area at the time was the wife of Jim Marks, who had followed me as Treasurer of the Corinthian Yacht Club, also in Marblehead. Carol was dancing with me in the middle of the dance floor at the Eastern when Ted tapped me on the shoulder to cut in.

Here is where the best of the story had been written. After much deliberation I decided it had to be omitted; not because it wasn't true, but because it would embarrass his family. You may guess, correctly, that a story so bad it had to be edited out, was hilarious.

BART STARR

Arguably the most recognized name in Alabama football nationwide is Joe Namath, winning quarterback of the third Superbowl. Actually, the term Superbowl was not used to describe the pro championship before then. Only at the time of the third game did the first and second playoffs between the National and the American Football Leagues became known as Superbowls I and II. The first two Superbowls had been won by the Green Bay Packers of the National Football League, so Namath's "guarantee" that his American Football Conference New York Jets would win the next game was considered a ridiculous boast. The Colts were the big betting favorites, giving up 18 points to anyone foolish enough to bet on the Jets. The heavily-favored Colts ended up losing 16-7, a staggering 27 points worse than the betting spread. Despite the victory by the New York Jets, the game is more known for Namath's guarantee than for the game itself or Namath's performance in the game.

Here is where the subject of the Superbowl becomes so involved with football in Alabama. Joe Namath had played quarterback for Alabama. The winner of the first two Superbowls also had played quarterback for the University of Alabama and, prior to that, played for my school, Sidney Lanier High School, in Montgomery, Alabama. Bart Starr, quarterback for the winning Green Bay Packers in Superbowls I and II, grew up in the Ridgecrest neighborhood of Montgomery. When asked, most people think his name is Bart. It is not. I did a lot of asking before finding one person who knew his name and how he had been given it. How the great Bart Starr got his real name is an interesting story, especially for people in Montgomery who know other people in this story.

NAMING A KID

Back during the Depression in the 1930s, when a family could not afford to pay the doctor for delivering their kid, it was common practice for a family to thank and honor the doctor by naming the kid after him. The funny story, that I did not discover until 2010, is that I knew the doctor after whom "Bart" is named.

Two childhood friends of mine are children of the doctor and bore the same last name as Bart's middle name (the one from which his nickname was derived).

The man who delivered "Bart" Starr was Montgomery's Doctor Haywood Bellingraph Bartlett, so Bart's full name, as told to me by Bart, is Bryan Bartlett Starr. Today's Dr. Haywood Bellingrath Bartlett, Jr. is known as "Woody" Bartlett," who has a beautiful home squeezed onto a tiny little 4,000 acre lot in Pike Road, just east of Montgomery. Woody's sister, daughter of Dr. Haywood Bellingrath Bartlett, is now Mrs. James Inscoe. The Inscoes live on Allendale Road in Montgomery and own a beautiful open-to-the-public garden northeast of Montgomery called Jasmine Hill.

Of course, the family is the source of the well-known Bellingraph Gardens south of Mobile.

77 A VERY FAST LARGE BOAT
Octopussy

Sorry. No. This is not about a character in a famous book; it was an incredible boat worth mentioning. I only got to drive her once, but it was a helluva experience. A wealthy owner of car dealerships in New York City and Miami, John Staluppi, loved to build yachts and name them after James Bond books. The early ones were named *"Moonraker*" and *"Thunderball*."

Staluppi had recognized quite early the potential of a then-new-to-the-US make of car called "Honda." His headquarters may be in North Palm Beach, but he made his many millions as the owner of what eventually became about twenty large car dealerships throughout the western Long Island area, now offering ten different brands of automobile. His New York dealerships operate as "NY Auto Giant."

Heritage Travel had an extremely important prospective client, Procter & Gamble, coming to check us out in Cambridge at a time then the boat owner wanted Heritage's officers to see his boat so we could recommend it to potential charter customers. We could have the boat for free and entertain the prospect. My wife, Pat, was delighted to be included in the trip.

Octopussy was far from what would today be one of the largest powerboats, but she was known as the fastest megayacht. Three stories tall and 130 feet long, she was an incredible machine. We had to go slow motoring out of Boston Harbor, but opened it up once we passed Boston Light and headed up the Atlantic.

Standing at the helm of *Octopussy*, you had on earphones so that engineering specialists standing on your right and left constantly monitored instruments and alerted you to any problems. When we had been having cocktails near the stern of the boat, *"Octopussy"* ran calm and steady. I was given the helm once we were out of the harbor.

The Atlantic in that area is full of lobster pots (brightly-painted-wooden-chunks of wood that hold up the end of a rope that is attached to the lobster trap on the ocean floor). The paint on the floats in applied in designs that are registered with the state and tell the fishermen which are their traps These floating pieces of wood are grabbed to get hold of the line used to pull the trap to the surface so that lobsters can be transferred to the small boat. Dodging these traps in what was then my 43-foot sailboat at 10 miles per hour was no big deal. Even if you brushed one, the wide hull of the boat usually pushed the line aside, keeping it from entangling the propeller that was aft of amidships and further protected by the keel of the boat.

"Octopussy" had two engines, both huge waterjets, that had large water intakes under the hull. I was cautioned to dodge the lobster traps so that they would not get into the engines, but I had no clue how to do this. It was a very large boat and, at high speed, the traps came into view ahead so fast and were so close together that I could not turn left and right rapidly enough to keep the boat from inhaling one of those floats. Also, I had no idea how to deal fast enough with the fact that if you turned the boat to the left the rear part of the boat turned out behind you to the right at high speed. It was very embarrassing. When I went back down to the party everyone commented that when I took over the helm, the aft end of the boat was swinging back and forth so fast that people could not stand up. I do claim that it was a little bit unfair because we had been travelling in Boston Harbor in the ship channel that had no traps and after we got out to sea and into deep water *"Octopussy"* again did not have to weave through lobster pots.

This large boat could go about 67 miles per hour. That is not fast on a highway, but it is very fast in a large yacht trying to weavc bctween obstructions. The punch line that reveals how ridiculous the boat was asking someone to guess how much fuel she consumes at full speed. It is much-more difficult pushing through water than rolling on wheels, but think of how much it would take to move a heavy three-story house at high speed. I knew it was going to be a large number, but I did not expect the boat's fuel consumption at full speed to be 750 gallons per hour.

By the way, when you charter a boat like this, the contract normally calls for the boat and crew to be supplied but you pay for the fuel. If you drove for five hours at close to full speed you would use 3750 gallons which, at 2018 prices would be about $8,500. Not many people can afford to pick up that kind of tab, so it is remarkable how many people charter yachts like this.

THE REMARKABLE FOLLOWUP

In 2012 there was a TV special on spectacular yachts, the most beautiful of which was the antique "Delphine." The next long segment was about incredible fast large yachts. That segment started with a picture of Octopussy, but moved quickly to focus at great length on Staluppi's new boat named "The World Is Not Enough." This time he built and even larger and faster boat. "TWINE" is 140 feet long and has engines totaling 20,000 horsepower, enabling it to achieve a top speed of 75 miles per hour. At least that is the speed Staluppi stated on the TV show. Staluppi alluded to it on the TV show but did not disclose the boat's fuel consumption.

BAD NEWS

We did not win the Proctor & Gamble account.

78 EXTREMELY LARGE SAILING YACHTS
The Mirabellas

Joe Vittoria let Pat and me sail on his "*Mirabella 1"* shortly after he had her built in Thailand. I could not believe it years earlier when he explained to me his plan to build a series of 135 foot sailboats in Thailand and sell them. "Mirabella I" was the first of what ended up being four almost identical boats.

It was as guests of Joe and his wife, Luciana, for dinner in the Avis reception a couple of years earlier that had been Pat's and my first date. Joe was President of Avis which, at the time in the late 1980s, was the sponsor of the final Thursday night of the US Open Tennis, the night that was always the men's semis. At the time, I was president of Woodside, that booked by far the largest number of reservations with Avis worldwide.

When Joe's first Mirabella came to Boston, we were invited to sail aboard her. When "*Mirabella 1"* entered Boston Harbor she caused an uproar, not because of her size per se, but because of something that happened. I heard about it only because of my long involvement with the airport.

The ship channel heading out of Boston harbor hugs the downtown, skyscraper, side leaving the in-bound lane much closer to Boston's Logan Airport when entering the harbor. In order to be long enough, all of Logan's runways were built on filled land that takes up most of what had been Boston Harbor.

Harbor Pilots bringing tankers and other large cargo ships know that they are required to notify by radio the airport's control tower to alert them that their vessel exceeded the height that might obstruct planes landing on the runway to the north northeast (Runway 4 R). Runways obviously can handle takeoffs and landings in two directions. For 4 R, a pier holding a line of approach lights extends 700 feet out into the harbor, forcing boats to stay at least that distance from the land and the start of the runway, but you do go by very close to the end of that long pier of lights.

The skipper of "*Mirabella I"* did not know this requirement. A large American Airlines jet, coming in low over Boston's Pleasure Bay and then over the harbor channel to touch down near the start of runway 4, had to abort its landing suddenly to avoid colliding with "M*irabella I's"* mast. The mast just happened to be approaching the line of the runway as the plane was nearing that point. "*Mirabella 1"* had a cute little sitting area for two people ahead of and higher than the main helm location. that included an ultra-modern little iddy-biddy "Joy Stick" about the size of a short pencil that electronically transmitted your steering to the boats rudder. Today, Joy Sticks on large boats are quite common.

"MIRABELLA V"

There are two funny stories about the newest "*Mirabella*" that were not mentioned in the articles about her. This ship (it's too big to call it a boat) is known for being the world's largest sloop. Again, for those non-sailors, this means a sailboat with just one mast. She is 245 feet long and her beam (width) is 48 feet, a little narrower than the entire length of what we considered a large sailboat on which Pat and I lived for a year and a half.

"*Mirabella V*" is an incredible design because her mast is so tall, 290 feet. This prevents her from getting under the Verrazano Bridge, maximum clearance 228 feet. and the Golden Gate Bridge, 220 feet, so she cannot visit New York or San Francisco. Her keel extends down in the water an incredible 33 feet, but the keel is retractable so she could get into Palm Beach where the Vittorias live. Joe sold her to Rodney Lewis, who shortened her name to just "M5." If you wanted to charter *"Mirabella V"* she was just $420,000 per week, but you could get a discount if you wanted her longer. Pat and I would be happy to come along if you have room for extra guests.

STUPIDITY

The other story about "*Mirabella V*:" involves stupidity, negligence on the part of its highly-paid professional captain. When anchored in the Med off the coast of Beaulieu-sur-Mer (a beautiful town about 4 miles east of Nice), France, the skipper of "*Mirabella V"* went to sleep when a severe storm with strong winds was forecast. They could have (in my opinion *should* have) left the engines running and there should have been a highly skilled crewmember on watch that night. There was not. "*Mirabella V's"* enormous hull provided a large area against which the wind could blow. "*Mirabella' Vs"* huge anchor did not hold and began to drag along the bottom. As the beautiful yacht began to be moved by the wind, the crew did not have time to get the engines running. Putting the engines in forward would have taken the strain off the anchor and kept the boat safe. "*Mirabella"* was blown onto sharp rocks and incurred major damage. Pictures of the yacht on the rocks appeared in most of the major yachting publications, something that must have been very irritating and embarrassing for Joe. I trust Joe fired the captain.

I have an old friend in Marblehead, Massachusetts, Robbie Doyle, who made the sails for " *Mirabella V* The mainsail is so large and heavy that it has to be brought to the boat in parts on large trucks and loaded onto the boat by a crane. The top portion or the sail has to be fed into the track on the mast, hoisted up a bit to the point where the second section is zippered to its predecessor and the process is repeated for each section.

THANK YOU

In 2017, I talked with Joe and thanked him for Avis' role in Pat's and my relationship, our first date, that led to our getting married.

79 ANOTHER FOOTBALL STORY

I Lied Before, This Really Is The Last One

HARVARD

In the early days of American Football, Harvard was a powerhouse; hard to believe, but true. When my wife attended her first Harvard football game, she laughed, saying it reminded her of high-school football. Pat had obtained a masters degree in earth science from the University of Oklahoma when their football team was at its peak and another masters, an MBA, from SMU in Dallas when its football team was in top form. Ivy League football is true amateur football, real students playing football as opposed to football players masquerading as students.

Harvard did play in, and win, a number of the early Rose Bowls and had a player I knew who was chosen as an All American (in a previous chapter), but the most amusing story is not about the team, but about its stadium.

Construction of Harvard Stadium, built in 1903, was the first concrete-reinforced stadium constructed for collegiate sports in the United States. Unlike huge new stadiums that today take years to construct and cost hundreds of millions, the elegant design of Harvard Stadium cost just $310,000 and was finished in less than five months.

Because it was the first example of a stadium using reinforced concrete construction people questioned its strength and safety. Rebar metal had been used to strengthen flat concrete pourings but had not been used in vertical construction. Could it really hold up the weight of so many people? Harvard became concerned when word circulated that spectators would be afraid to sit up in the stands. The construction contract had gone to Aberthaw Construction, still a major contractor a century later, headquartered in Lowell, Massachusetts. Supposedly, the contract required Mr. Aberthaw to stand beneath the stands for the first quarter of the first game, so nervous fans would see that he was confident that his new construction technique could withstand the weight.

THE NEW ENGLAND PATRIOTS

In addition to hosting Harvard's football team for over a century, the stadium was used by the Boston Patriots for a season during the construction of their first stadium in Foxboro, (the move that resulted in their name change to the New England Patriots).

The first game was to be in Boston on Boston University's Nickerson Field, designed for baseball, when on September 9, 1960 they played the Denver Broncos in the very first game of the new American Football League. There were to be more AFL games on the weekend, but this game was on the Friday night of that first weekend. The Patriots lost to the Denver Broncos, 13-10.

MAJOR CHANGE TO THE GAME

Harvard Stadium's impact on the game of football was quite large, possibly having a greater long-term effect than any other factor. The stadium is great for watching a game; the concrete stands are steep and were designed to have the fans very close to the field. They didn't see the need for much space between the sideline of the actual playing field and the front rows of the stands. The stands are so close that during one game the quarterback, an SAE fraternity brother of mine named Ron Johanson, when facing a sack got rid of the ball by throwing it far out of bounds. The stands are so close to the field that, against ridiculous odds, I caught my friend's pass. The stadium may be old fashioned, but it certainly makes the fans close to the action. This is what resulted in the huge impact on the game of football.

In 1905, there were many injuries during games, even 11 deaths in high school and 7 in college football. The practice at the time was for offensive linemen to stand with arms interlocked to each other so defensive players could not get through. Players frequently ended up bloody and seriously injured.

Football was gaining a bad reputation and this was increasing interest in rugby. There was talk of eliminating football as a sport. President Teddy Roosevelt called a meeting of coaches to address the problem (can you imagine that today?). In those days, the rules of the game of football were determined by an annual meeting of the coaches (much like the NCAA operates today). According to an article in the Wall Street Journal, the meeting with Roosevelt on October 9, 2005, included just Harvard, Yale and Princeton.

Here it becomes confusing, but my interpretation is that there was a subsequent meeting of 62 coaches in early 1906, at which they voted to accept the changes. The other story is that the game was boring, and the majority of the coaches thought a wider field, as in soccer, would make the sport more exciting. One of the most respected coaches in all of college football was Yale's Walter Camp. His proposal was to widen the field by 40 feet and the majority of other coaches arrived at the meeting favoring this change. Making the field wider for American football would reduce the injuries in the lines.

The obstacle to this change was Harvard Stadium. Widening the field would have made Harvard's brand-new stadium obsolete, something that simply could not be done. As an alternative, the coaches ended up voting for their second choice, the forward pass. They also made changes such as giving a team just three tries to move 10 yards for a first down instead of 5. Fatalities dropped in 2006 and injuries fell substantially.

Few of even the most ardent football fans know that Harvard Stadium is the reason the forward pass is part of football today. I hope this story is not "Fake News.".

80 GOLF

Life Is Just A Game, Golf Is Serious

When we were living in a house overlooking the Marshwood Course at The Landings, south of Savannah, one of the six 18 hole golf courses at The Landings, I used to play golf four or five times a week, gradually went from very poorly to playing fairly poorly.

One day I happened to be playing in a group of eight golfers, a foursome ahead of us and the foursome I was in. We were playing on a course designed by "The Shark," Australia's Greg Norman. The residential development was named the "Woodyard," but years later the name was changed to "Savannah Quarters." The course wound its way through many marshes that included muddy water and tall weeds. You didn't want to hit your ball into one of them.

The course's eleventh hole was a par-four dogleg left with marsh to the left of the entire fairway and behind the right hand side of the second part of the dog leg. The normal practice, especially among those who are not pros, is to hit safely to the turn and hit the second shot from there toward the green.

Golf courses are usually designed with about seven par 4 holes and seven par fives, par meaning the number of strokes a good golfer should take to hit down the fairway, get to the green and sink the putt. In addition, there are usually about four par 3 holes on a golf course, meaning you should hit from the tee, land on the smooth grass of the green and putt your ball into the hole using two putts, one to get near enough to the hole to sink the ball on the third shot. When you hear of someone's scoring a "Hole in One" it is almost always on a par three hole.

One player and I took the easiest option, hitting straight down the first stretch of grass fairway to the turn. We were pleased to land in the grass rather than the muddy marsh.

Frank King, who had been a college classmate of mine, stepped up next, announcing that he was going to try the very-risky long shot over the entire marsh, skipping the first and second legs of the dogleg. He aimed at the green, belted the ball and sent it flying over the marsh. The foursome of friends we knew ahead of us had finished putting, walked off the green, and were getting in their golf carts to ride to the next hole. When they heard Frank's successful shot land, having cleared the marsh, they cheered. We knew Frank had made a great shot just by clearing the marsh. It was quite a feat to fly over the marsh and his ball was bouncing onto the green. Moments later, their cheers turned to screams. Frank's shot had cleared the marsh, landed on the grass, rolled over undulating grass on the long green, reached the far end of the green and dropped into the hole.

Once again for those non-golfers, players like me usually hit bogies, meaning we had required one more shot than we should have. For me, on this hole, that would mean taking five strokes. Poor players frequently hit double bogies, taking two shots more than the desired "par" and I all-too-frequently did that. For most of us, shooting par on a hole is very good and, unfortunately, rare. If you can get your ball into the hole in one stroke less than par it is called a "birdie." These are quite common in professional golf. Getting your ball into the hole in two shots less than par is called an "Eagle." Even with professional golfers playing in the biggest tournaments you only see a few Eagles and these are usually on par fives. Frank had shot a hole in one where the par was 4, a feat called a "Double Eagle," something that is extremely rare even among professional golfers.

Frank determined that the actual direct flight his ball took that day before landing was 265 yards. For an amateur it was quite a hit even if it had not fallen into the cup.

The owner's paid Greg Norman to re-design the course, so if you go looking for the place this happened, it no longer bares any resemblance to the way it looked that day.

PLAYING GOLF IN THE DARK

The title of this story sounds ridiculous, even worse than the time I went water-skiing in the dark. Golf is a game you simply do not play in the pitch-black dark. Pat and I were having drinks after playing with a large group of social golfers who would play 9 holes (half of a normal round of golf) before gathering for drinks and dinner at the Oakridge Clubhouse of The Landings. One of the ladies had shot a hole in one, taking just one shot from the tee to the hole where the par was 3. The accomplishment among casual golfers is unusual and many players play golf their entire lives without getting a hole in one.

It is not in the actual rules of golf, but the accepted practice is designed to keep a player from going out and hitting many shots at the same hole before sinking one. To be counted as a hole in one, the shot has to be in an actual 18 holes of golf, it requires witnesses. The lady's shot was not going to count.

Pat came up with the idea of organizing a bunch of people after dinner to drive their golf carts around the remaining 9 holes of the golf course with some of us using our headlights to illuminate the tee, others to light the area of the fairway at which the player should aim. Once the first shot had landed, the carts at the rear would drive ahead to light the next target area so that the hitter could see where to aim.

It worked well and the lady was playing fast. It didn't make any difference how many shots it took, she just had to play those nine holes. I knew, however, that people living in the houses that overlooked each hole of the course would suspect kids were out destroying the course. Someone, probably many people, would call security.

After just two holes were played the blinking blue lights could be seen approaching our location. In the rear of the group of people in carts, I was the first person to meet the security guys. I went to the first security guard and explained what was happening and why. The immediate result was great laughter. They went back and knew how to answer the many phone calls that must have kept reaching them. Because she was the only player and could just hit each shot without worrying about her score, she completed the nine holes (which would usually take two hours) in just 42 minutes. She, officially, got her hole in one.

SURPRISE!

Golf is a game you have to play a lot to get to be any good. Most of the world's best golfers start at a very early age. I did get off to a very good start at the required very early age. As you have read, my mother was an avid golfer. She got me my first set of clubs and I still have a picture of me in a ridiculously formal looking all white golf outfit, holding a club at the age of three.

After college there was no time for golf; I had to travel much of my working career. Also, golf was an extremely expensive sport, even if you did not belong to one of the better clubs. As a result, I never played more than an occasional, dreadful, round of golf until we retired. Even then, playing four or five times a week, it took several years for me to become a halfway decent golfer. I usually shot in the 90s, sometimes down in the high 80s. A round in the 80s was a great day for me. I could only dream of playing in the 70s and at my age, 65 at the time, getting that good was highly unlikely.

One day everything began to go OK. We were playing Eagle Pointe, a course in South Carolina on the highway to Hilton Head, a course I did not like because my all-to-frequent slice would spin the ball right and into the water on a course where there were many water holes and it always seemed that most were along the right hand side of the fairways. One day, after the first nine holes, I knew I was playing unusually well because I had managed to stay out of the water and the traps. My cartmate, who had been keeping score, said something like "Wow, do you know what you shot on the first nine?" I said "no" and asked him not to tell me.

I just wanted to focus on continuing to hit well, focusing on one shot at a time. I stayed lucky, to the point where it became ridiculous. My luck just kept going. It may have been a small part skill because I could not have hit where I did without some skill, but the results of the day were clearly dependent upon luck. I ended up shooting a 79, breaking the 80 barrier just once in my life.

AN EARLY END TO MY GOLFING

At age 17, I was lucky enough to have made it to the final round of the junior championship at the Montgomery Country Club. It was "match play," which means you won or lost each hole by beating your opponent on that hole, regardless of how many strokes difference there was on that hole. I was essentially unbeatable, up 3 and 3, meaning I was ahead by 3 with just 3 holes left to play. All I had to do was win one hole or halve (tie) any one of the remaining three. It was a sure thing.

Because people who belong to the Club today had corrected me when telling the story, I have to interject that we had played the back nine (holes 10 through 18) first and were finishing our 16th, 17th and 18th holes by playing the holes that are still numbered 7, 8 and 9. To make the story understandable, I am going to tell it as the holes we were playing. As my opponent and I were walking up 16, the green was very close to Carter Hill Road. In those days there was no fence and my mother had just parked on Carter Hill and walked onto the golf course. She got me flustered and I lost hole 16. Still up 2 with just 2 to play. The 17th, (really number 8), starts along Narrow Lane Road. Having won hole 16, my opponent had "the honor" so he drove first off the tee.

He hit a lousy drive, curving to the right into the bushes and trees beside the road. He was ready to concede the match until my mother talked him out of it, telling him to hit a "provisional" ball that could be played if his first ball could not be found. That got me so flustered, and mad, that I blew the 17th, giving him another win. I was still up 1 with 1 final hole to play. As you can guess, obviously I continued to be so upset that I lost that hole, losing the championship in the extra hole that followed. My mother never understood how most mothers should cheer for their son and not help his opponent. I gave up golf for four decades.

Interestingly, and at least to me, my mother won the Club's tournament that year, 1955, and we have her silver tray trophy that reads "MCC Winner 1955" to my goddaughter as a wedding present in 2016.

BEST QUOTE ABOUT GOLF

My radio acquaintance, Paul Harvey, once sadly, but all-too-accurately, said "Golf is a game in which you yell 'fore,' shoot six, and write down five."

81 THE SAVANNAH SYMPHONY
A Complex Story

It was an honor so I was most pleased when asked if I would serve on the Board of the Savannah Symphony. I quickly learned that the Board had several people who were very powerful in the city, some whose families had been prominent in this beautiful old city for generations, others who were remarkably knowledgeable about the various composers and much of their work and one who was the largest donor by a considerable amount.

For several meetings, I sat in one of the chairs along the wall, behind the powerful bunch around the conference table. I became increasingly puzzled by the President's usually-brief comments about the finances. After a variety of unimportant subjects were reviewed, he would just end meetings with a comment that essentially said: "all the finances were in order." This was the most important subject and it was being ignored.

After only about a half dozen of the monthly board meetings, it became time to appoint a nominating committee to develop a slate for the following year's board and officer positions. I vividly remember sitting at dinner in the Oglethorpe Club when I was told that there was an urgent call holding for me on the club's phone. I was truly astonished to hear the Symphony's Conductor ask if I would accept the nomination to be the next president. He said I had already contributed to the Board, asking questions when needed. It did not take long to say "yes."

I guess I should have questioned the situation more, but I couldn't resist the honor and I did not have any time to consider why one of the experienced board members who had been serving on the board for years had not been chosen. I was guilty of "answer first, ask questions later." It became apparent that many of the board members had already served a term or two as president and would not accept again. I like the great old classical music by the traditional composers, but knew very little (that should read "almost nothing) about a large professional orchestra's operations.

I learned very quickly about the problems any symphony orchestra in the United States faces because of being unionized. There are very few community orchestras where the musicians are unpaid volunteers. In Savannah, the cost of musician's salaries and medical insurance comprised more than half of the expense side of the annual budget and income from tickets accounted for only about a third of the total required income. This was typical of many symphony orchestras in the country. You had to raise lots of money.

Later, In Montgomery, I learned that the good symphony orchestra was almost entirely staffed by volunteers. They were not "professional" because the musicians were not paid and the symphony job was not their principal source of income. Most were highly-respected music teachers in colleges around the area who were willing to perform as volunteers. My dentist was a violinist in the orchestra. There was very little staff and the conductor, who had been there for years, was paid a small salary.

Under the Savannah Symphony's contract with the union (which was printed in a sizable, bound book), we were required to keep on the payroll a minimum of 38 musicians. This line item only accounted for about $800,000. The medical insurance added a huge amount to that number. The symphony hired "per-service" musicians to fill in all the slots where an instrument was required for the performance of a particular work. The 38 in the "core orchestra" played the standard instruments and per service musicians were hired to increase the number of violins, violas, cellos, basses and the major horn instruments and, on many occasions, you also had to hire musicians to play unusual instruments that were not required on a regular basis but had to be there for a particular composition.

BUDGETS

It became obvious to me that the finances were a dangerous mix of counting income for next season as income in the current season. The orchestra adhered to a schedule that began in the fall and ended in late spring, standard for any symphony anywhere. In order to get subscriptions for the following season, the renewal effort kicked off in January. It was obvious that moneys received on subscriptions for next season were being counted as income in the season that was still going on. There was no accrual of income.

You would not have had enough cash to get through the current season if you did not operate on a cash basis as opposed to an accrual basis. The financial statements were not considering any of that subscription money received in this operating year as *unearned* income to pay for the expenses of the following season. This had been going on for years. The longer this went on, the tighter the finances became. The President, at the end of board meetings, may have kept saying "everything is fine" but it certainly was not. The orchestra was in deep trouble and clearly was going to run out of money soon. New to the responsibility, that was a devastating surprise.

The longer it was allowed to continue, the deeper the hole from which you would have to dig out. The finances were not in "fine shape;" they were approaching disaster. I was surprised that the auditors had not, *at the very least,* footnoted this practice in the official annual reports. It was clearly improper accounting.

THE LIBRARIAN

When taking my first look at how to save money, one of the things I questioned was the need for a Librarian. After a few laughs from the staff at my ignorance, I learned that a librarian controls all of the printed music. It is complicated because music has to be ordered well ahead of time and you had to be sure all of the required bound sheets were received in time for distribution to the musicians, as required by the union contract, a minimum number of days before each concert so they could practice.

One part of this subject baffled me, and still does. If you have attended a classical concert or seen a concert on TV, you have probably noticed that in the string instrument sections the bows always go up in the air at the same time and start down at the same time. The tops and bottoms of the bows' movements do not show on the printed sheet music, but this does not happen by accident. There have to be little marks that indicate on what note the bow starts up and where it starts down. The long technical book on the process reveals how complex the process is.

No big deal, right? These little symbols are called "Bowings." The problem is that they have to be written on each musician's sheets of music in pencil so that they can be seen clearly but later erased. Where the bows start up and down is determined, not be the composer, but by the Concertmaster, the first violinist. The Librarian didn't have to receive the music from the rental company the two weeks before each concert; she had to obtain it is time to give one copy to the Concertmaster for determining his or her personal preference regarding the bowings, these symbols had to be copied onto the music of every other musician in each of the string sections. It is time consuming and, to my mind, ridiculous. The composer should determine the desired bowing so that it can be printed on the sheet music.

UNUSUAL PRODUCTION COSTS

Another area about which I had no knowledge whatsoever was the actual sheet music that the musicians read. A symphony orchestra rents music, usually from a company specializing in this and most US sources are in New York City. You pay that company to rent the actual pieces of paper. Depending upon what is being performed, you also pay the composer or the composer's representative who owns the rights to perform the music. That makes Pops concerts more expensive than music written by the great old composers, all of whom are long dead.

SOLOISTS

According to the 2010 US census, Savannah had a population of 136,268, compared with Montgomery's 296,764. Savannah may have many more very rich people living in the city and in major retirement places such as "The Landings", but the obvious discrepancy is the fact that Montgomery has to work to support a largely volunteer orchestra and Savannah, with less than half the population, supported a professional orchestra with a budget more than four times the size of Montgomery's.

Some of that was made possible by the large number of highly-sophisticated and wealthy retirees in the area. They are used to seeing and hearing some of the great soloists of the world. As a result, the Savannah Symphony was able to attract musicians of worldwide fame, such as Itzhak Pearlman, Andre Watts and Yo Yo Ma on the classical side. The comment about cost is misleading, because out of respect for Savannah's Conductor, Philip Greenberg, most came for much less than they could normally command. Some came for a quarter of what they would earn in other venues and two played for free.

With the core musicians being paid a salary whether they performed or not, it was necessary to schedule a lot of concerts, classical about once a month and Pops a little less than every month. Basically, the more concerts you performed, the more you earned. In addition, there were Pops outdoor concerts during the summer. There were other costs, but the primary costs were the salaries and benefits of the musicians and you could have them perform more often without paying them any more money.

We even had a big-name Guest Pops Conductor, Skitch Henderson. When critics looked for places to reduce our expenses, his name would frequently come up. Why do we need him? What people did not realize was that Skitch brought with him the musical arrangements from his great New York Pops without charge, and that music was not just routine arrangements of popular songs, they were Skitch's excellent personal arrangements. Although he could be a curmudgeon, he was an amusing gentleman with loads of appropriate anecdotes that livened up a performance.

One of the most enjoyable aspects of being the orchestra's president was accepting the obligation (certainly the wrong word) to have dinner with a soloist before or after a performance. We usually had these dinners after the rehearsal, the night before the actual performance. Dinners with Skitch were always most enjoyable

THE UNION

What a shock this was. I had made it through life without ever having to deal with a union. Dealing with the elected leaders of the local chapter of the American Federation of Musicians was a highly disappointing, to a large extent disgusting experience. Their involvement had increased costs, but they were still underpaid.

These were highly intelligent people, almost all of whom had masters degrees. They were making on average just about $60 a day. Assuming that they had to work at practicing, rehearsals and concerts 8 hours a day, they were making about minimum wage, but they did not work anywhere close to that much time. The problems with the union leadership were not salary costs; they were in unnecessary disruption of the ability to manage the business and insistence upon work rules that made things more expensive for their employer without providing any benefit to their fellow Savannah Symphony musicians.

THE UNION CONTRACT

Whenever I would raise an issue that would help the Symphony financially, the head of the union would say that the terms I was asking be amended had been agreed to by previous Boards and were in the union's contract. I could not ask the union to help management, which they clearly believed was their enemy. Over the years, the Board had repeatedly had to concede on some dumb points in order to avoid another strike.

My study indicated that in all too many cases the Board had not understood the ramifications of the concessions that they had been asked to accept. The musicians had struck four times in the recent past before my arrival and long-time members of the board told horror stories about the strikes. The musicians, had been very loud and angry during each strike. One board member, a *grande dame* of Savannah, related an awful story of how she and her husband and feared for the safely of their young daughter.

Anyway, the Board had, in some cases unknowingly, agreed to terms with the union that simply ran up the cost. When you hired a per service musician you at the time had to pay the union rate for rehearsal and the actual performance about $464 per concert. If you needed to have an extra dozen musicians, that meant $5,568 for a night's concert.

The inexcusable problem, on which the union refused to budge despite my pleas, was the treatment of per-service musicians for outdoor Pops concerts. The orchestra was subsidized for many outdoor concerts by the City or County, each of which required the performance to be at least 45 minutes for us to be paid. Big summer thunderstorms were common in Savannah in the late afternoon and management had thought it be risky to look at the forecast and be confident the concert would not be stopped by rain before performing the minimum time.

When outdoor concerts were scheduled and announced, they typically had a rain date of the next evening, normally a Sunday. By contract, we had to give 24-hour notice to the per-service players (typically from other cities) if we were not going to need them on the rain date. If we didn't cancel that far ahead, we had to pay them for the extra day, essentially doubling the cost to the Symphony, without providing any benefit or income to the orchestra's actual employees.

If the contract had allowed us to cancel with 23hour notice, we could have known we had made it through the minimum time to get the income and could have avoided the extra cost. The union contract was helping the out-of-town musicians but hurting the finances of their own employer, the business that had to break even to continue as their employer.

Those musicians brought in for a concert were members of the American Federation of Musicians, so our local union fought for them rather than helping their own employer survive. This was one of many issues on which the union's incredibly-tough leadership would not budge.

THE CONDUCTORS

Conducting a symphony orchestra can be a highly satisfying vocation. Conducting a major symphony orchestra for the few that have the top jobs can be very rewarding financially. Our Conductor in Savannah for many years was Philip Greenberg. We had another salaried conductor, Chelsea Tipton, Associate Conductor (who conducted most of the many POPS and outdoor concerts, and New York's Skitch Henderson, who conducted some of the POPS concerts in the Civic Center. Skitch, who had celebrity status from his conducting on the Johnny Carson Show and later the New York Pops, was a great character.

Most music lovers are aware of the piano portion of the annual Tchaikovsky Competition in Moscow, getting lots of publicity in the States when it was won by pianist Van Cliburn. There is a similar international competition in Copenhagen for young conductors named for a highly regarded conductor, Nikolai Malko. In 1977 the Malko Competition was won by Philip Greenberg. There is a very interesting and enlightening additional fact about that result.

Sadly, in too-many US symphony orchestras the musicians hate their conductor. The leaders of the musicians union in Savannah complained incessantly and loudly about how dreadful our conductor was, saying that he did not even "understand music." The Malko has two parts, an official award made to a conductor by the team of jurors after observing all of the conductors entered in the competition, and an award based upon the rating by the musicians in the orchestra. For the first time in the history of the event, and I am told is still the case, both the expert jurors and the musicians picked the same conductor ....Philip Greenberg.

In complaining about Philip, the union leaders would cite their previous conductor, Christian Badea, as an example of how excellent and likeable a conductor could be. There is an interesting story about Badea after he left his job conducting in Savannah that made me question their complaints. About that time a highly-respected young black conductor, Calvin Simmons, died, drowning in a canoeing accident out west. The supposedly-beloved former Savannah conductor, Badea, had moved to Columbus, Ohio. The musicians there "loved" him so much that they purchased and, in the dark of night, placed a canoe on Badea's front porch as a somewhat less-than-subtle hint that he, too, should take up canoeing. The union also printed bumper stickers that read "Do the Christian thing, fire a musician."

Not knowing the truth, I called a wide variety of big-name soloists who had performed for Philip. They all praised his skill. They were not just favorable; they thought Philip was a marvelous conductor. I was careful to phrase questions so as not to be given the answers the renowned musicians thought I would want to hear. Stories about specific instances supported the basic responses. Savannah was lucky to have such an accomplished conductor.

I also learned several other things. Despite the union's professed love of Badea and hatred of Philip, the union had hated Badea when he was their conductor. Badea appears to have pushed his board to increase musician's salaries beyond what a small orchestra could afford. Several musicians, of the few that had worked for Badea before I arrived on the scene, told me that the flamboyant Badea had made a practice of firing musicians and replacing them with better, more expensive ones. This matched the thought in the bumper sticker two paragraphs earlier. I subsequently learned that it was extraordinarily difficult to fire a musician, almost impossible. One should have been fired, but I found there were huge barriers to firing him if he was president of the union.

Since losing his job in Savannah after 49 years (because the orchestra had to declare bankruptcy), Philip has been conducting in France, Germany, the Ukraine, Bulgaria, Spain and Italy. From my observation, the European musicians all greatly appreciated his conducting. Instead of looking at their watches and demanding that, according to theis contract) it was time to quit rehearsing and head home, the European musicians frequently would say that wanted to stay and work some more to be sure they got it right. What a contrast.

SELECTING MUSICIANS

Another sad story about the impact of the union on the quality of the music is the process whereby musicians perform in competition for a job opening. The contract requires that the orchestra's management involve the musicians union in the selection process. Competitors enter and sit behind a large screen so their music can be heard but they cannot be seen. Sounds good, what is wrong?

The problem lies in the union leaders' desire to attract more of their union buddies who would join their fight against management. The process sounded good until you heard that musicians signaled to their buddies by noises such as the notes they played upon entering the room or a series of coughs. I learned that many conductors also use a technically-improper way of identifying prospective members of their orchestra. When they call for references, in addition to the typical questions about musical skill, they ask the applicant's current conductor if the applicant is a "good citizen." That was an obvious way of avoiding troublemakers, but I heard some references lie in their answer in order to "lose" troublemakers to some other orchestra.

Philip said he had always wanted to attract the best musicians and he did that without regard for their union activities. Several sources told me that as a result, Savannah had an overabundance of the country's toughest union members.

"POPULAR" CLASSICAL MUSIC

In surveying the audience by a one-page written list of questions, I found that the vast majority agreed with my taste in classical music. I liked the traditional classical music greats, especially Rachmaninoff and Tchaikovsky violin and piano concertos. The orchestra's paid Executive Director complained that in my list of rating options offered on the survey of our audience re "modern" classical music I had as the final option "hate," and this was checked almost unanimously by the respondents.

Many wrote additional negative comments about their dislike. I suspect this is true of most audiences; it just doesn't get through to the musicians, conductors, managers and boards. George, the Executive Director at the time, insisted that the questionnaire's option should have been "Do you prefer the traditional classical music?" This would have resulted in a much milder response but it would have been misleading....the audience really did hate the modern junk that was all too often foisted upon them.

An orchestra faces some interesting conflicts on this subject. It was clear that the audience dwindled when the evening's program featured a modern composer. This was applied to the music that sounds like kids in the alley smashing garbage can lids together. It even applied to a widely accepted moderately-old composer such as Gustaf Mahler. Even season ticket holders who paid whether they came to a concert or not stayed away from concerts in which the major segment was going to be Mahler. From my perspective, there was another negative about Mahler. His works included many unusual instruments or required a large number of standard instruments, making the cost of performing Mahler considerably more expensive than more-traditional composers. With one result of performing Mahler being reduced income and another being considerably higher cost, the decision to avoid his works was pretty obvious except for two reasons.

First, and understandably, the musicians like to add to their resume having performed as many works as possible. Musicians do not want to keep having to perform the most famous works over and over again. Secondly, sticking to what were known as the "old warhorses" was considered very *de classe.* Many conductors try to force their audience to sit through music they hate by putting it between two popular works in a strategy known as "bookending." You put loved works before and after what you want to force on them. Should customers really like to listen to what they don't like?

From my marketing background, I still believe that to be successful in any business, even classical music, should endeavor to give the customer what they want, not try to force customers to take what they don't want, even if it is what you think they *should* want. It was also apparent that some of the most devoted lovers of symphony orchestras believed that those who liked only the old-fashioned music were intellectually beneath them. I guess I was in that category.

ONE GREAT SEASON

Trying to get the orchestra back to breaking even financially, I convinced the Board and, with greater difficulty, the conductor, to try a season consisting entirely of the greatest masterpieces. The extremely knowledgeable board members on the Artistic Committee spent weeks holding meetings and discussing various works trying to agree upon the best three dozen works, for the orchestra to perform, based upon performing an average of four a night for nine Masterworks Series performances.

It worked. Ticket sales went up. We raised a lot more money from major donors. To accomplish this, I had to promise the major donors that, in return for their donations, all in the $25,000 to $200,000 range, that having streamlined the operation and improved attendance we could operate at breakeven financially from this point on. From what I had learned running the day to day operations for almost two years I was confident that it could be done from that point on. Sadly, it only lasted that one season.

FINANCIAL OBSTICLES

The worst financial shock I faced as President was a huge increase in the rental fee the City of Savannah charged the Symphony for holding its concerts in the City's Civic Center Auditorium. The rental fee had been $1,000 per concert. I received notice that the city was increasing the charge. We could have lived with a 10% increase or a gradual increase, but the increase was to be an astounding 400%, effective immediately.

A meeting with the city's director responsible for the Civic Center was scheduled and I was confident he would not insist upon such a massive increase, especially all at one time. In a city the size of Savannah, having to sell enough subscriptions and raise enough in grants and donations to enable a $3.2 million annual budget took a huge amount to time and effort by many dedicated board members. 400% was simply much too much.

The most generous donor was understandably insistent upon a balanced budget and I had been confident I could keep my promise. He had donated several hundred thousand dollars and gotten his friends to give a total of $1.2 million. It was a shock to be told that the 400% increase was going to stay because the Mayor, Floyd Adams, had ordered the increase. Floyd Adams, a black, made a racist comment, saying that the City needed to support black music and that the Symphony was "whitie's plaything."

All of a sudden the cost of venue for the season's Masterworks and Pops concerts jumped from $19,000 to $76,000 a year. We had already scheduled, promoted and sold subscriptions based upon financial projections that had seemed feasible but were now impossible to achieve. I pled for a reduction or at least a phased-in increase over four years but the city officials said they simply would not do anything; the Mayor had ordered it.

THE EXECUTIVE DIRECTOR

As I had written, we fired the existing General Manager and I stepped into that role for a couple of years while we searched for an appropriate qualified person, planning to give the new employee the more powerful title…Executive Director.

When a man applied for the job, we thought we had found a good potential employee. The interview went very well. A Board member, the previously mentioned "Grande Dame" of Savannah, agreed to call the applicant's previous employer to check his references. We should have been suspicious, but we were too eager to fill the spot. I was, by this time, tired of working a second year full time as a volunteer. I was too eager to quit "my day job." We closed our eyes to the obvious. The man had been the Executive Director of the Atlanta Symphony. It does not take much thinking to wonder why a man who had held a much more important and lucrative job would apply to work in a much smaller job. I'm sure you agree with me; we were stupid.

As the season started, I began to have problems once again trying to figure out what was happening. One of our wealthiest and most successful board members told me that our new Executive Director had much more experience than I did and that I should let him run things his way. I gave in, reluctantly, because the Executive Director wanted to change our entire accounting system. Instead of an expense category, he wanted to allocate every single expense to each concert. This meant that if you issued a one hundred-dollar check, it had to be spread $4 and change being entered for each concert.

This resulted in Excel spreadsheets that were so wide that they consumed several computer screens. It was extremely difficult to figure out because when you looked at the numbers on the computer screen you could not see the labels of the expense categories that were several screens to the left out of sight. George insisted upon scrolling back and forth so fast that there was no way I could see what was being shown, much less understand it. There was no way I could compare how we were doing to how we had done the previous year. I began to express concern at board meetings, but the problem just became worse and worse. Even given my experience, it was impossible to tell what was going on.

CASH FLOW

We once again began to be short of cash. It got so bad that the Board needed to know whether our cash flow was sufficient to get us through the year. The Executive Director, who attended Board meetings, agreed to do a cash flow analysis that we could review at an emergency meeting of the Board the following week. I offered to help and a very experienced lady on the board who serving as our Treasurer offered to help. Both of our offers were refused repeatedly. The Director said he was making "fine progress" and did not need help. As the days slipped by,I kept asking to see what he had accomplished. He refused. It shouldn't have taken anywhere near this long to look at cash flow.

When we got down to the last couple of days before the big Board meeting, I became desperate to see some preliminary numbers. Still 'No." Finally, the day of the meeting arrived. When called to order at 6pm the Board was there but the Executive Director was not. I called and learned that he was running off copies for every Board member and would drive to the meeting in a few minutes. We sat patiently until he finally showed up carrying a very large box full of numbers on legal size paper printed in landscape format so that the lines were extremely long. He began by announcing that he had the reports but he did not want to pass them out because they still contained some errors that needed to be corrected. I couldn't believe it. We had waited a week and desperately needed to know where things stood. That was the reason for the meeting. I could have done a thorough cash flow analysis in a day or less. He had had a week.

I asked to see a copy to find out if we could at least get an idea of where we stood. It only took a few seconds to recognize that we could ignore the entire document. It was simply not a cash flow analysis. He did not even know what "cash flow" meant. Instead of cash flow, the report was full of accrued expenses in many dozens of categories. We needed to know the expenses that would have to be paid and the cash income we could expect in the next few months.

When I stated what I had seen and asked the Director why all of these accrued expense items were in there even though they did not need to be paid and were not part of cash flow, he responded that you could not just develop the numbers without allowing for the all the accruals. He simply did not know what cash flow is.

The Board was in shock. A board member who had been one of the ones insisting that I had to let the Executive Director do everything his way, Ron Kronowitz, immediately raised his hand and moved for the Board to go into an executive session, meaning the Executive Director had to leave the room. As soon as the door was closed, Ron made a motion that the Executive Director be fired immediately. This passed with essentially no debate and I found myself once again thrust back into the role of running the place. It was much worse this time because the financial accounting system was in total disarray.

REFERENCES
It was not the most important issue, but board members wanted to know how he had been selected and hired in the first place. One Board member had contacted our Executive Director's former employer, the Atlanta Symphony, and reached their paid President, Allison Vulgamore. Our original questioning should have been much tougher. The one key question needed to ask why a person would leave a large and thriving job in Atlanta to take a much lesser job in Savannah. I did not see how our new hire could have gotten a good reference.

Because I was mad about why our sister symphony orchestra in Georgia would lead us to hire a man who proved to be such a disaster, I called Atlanta and spoke at some length with Allison. How could she have done this to us? The key part of her response, which did include an apology, was that she had thought telling our reference checker that the man was "good at education and outreach" was a subtle way of signaling us that those were the only positive things she could say. I don't remember most of the conversation, but I still think that the failure to give us enough information and endanger a sister organization was inexcusable.

It is interesting to note that after 16 years in Atlanta, Vulgamore quit to become the head of the Philadelphia Philharmonic, beginning there on February 1, 2010. That 110 year old orchestra, one of the renowned "Big Five" in the US, filed for bankruptcy in April of 2011. I thought that the correct spelling of her name should begin with "Vulgermore."

ACOUSTICS
One problem symphony orchestras frequently face is having to perform in venues that were not designed for that purpose. The most common need is for a tilted acoustic ceiling over the stage that reflects the sound from the instruments toward the audience on a stage that accommodates performances that have vast empty space above the stage to accommodate the storing, lowering and raising of various backdrops and curtains required. Adding a tilted ceiling helps the sound projection and when budgets are in trouble enables an orchestra to pay for fewer musicians. I talked the City of Savannah into buying such a foldable ceiling with lights installed in it. To get the Mayor to approve this expenditure of $37,000 I had to make a commitment that the orchestra would stay in the City's auditorium. The Mayor wanted to block any chance that the orchestra might decide to move to the smaller but elegant Lucas Theater which was under renovation. This was a commitment he demanded *before* raising the rent 400%.

The ceiling arrived and was installed on lifts above the stage. Mayor Floyd Adams scheduled a celebration to be on the stage of the auditorium so that the symphony's board, city officials and other guests could observe the first lowering of the acoustic ceiling. Inadvertently, the celebration'was scheduled on a day that became infamous......September 11, 2001. Nobody was in the mood for a celebration so that I requested that it be delayed, assuming this would be allowed. The the Mayor refused to delay the party. Very few people showed up.

SUPPORT FOR THE ARTS

A problem resulting from 9/11 was one that few outside the arts community heard about and or cared about. The next year, 2012, the IRS reported that donations to all of the arts in the US, both visual and performing arts, plummeted by just over 26% in one year. Most arts organizations had been operating at break even or less and the loss of a full quarter of their normal expected income from donations was more than many could survive. Our budgeted donations plummeted by more than $400,000.

Savannah lost its symphony a few years later. The demanding musicians union refused to recognize what was happening and would not budge to help. They had agreed to a salary reduction but demanded that their compensation had to return to its previous level. I met with the Chairman of the Charleston Symphony who was being tougher than I was with his union. He had proposed an 18% salary cut for Charleston, a plan that faced fiery opposition.

Only when the union leaders in Charleston saw that Savannah had gone under did they agree to the much-needed austerity plan. Even with that savings, Charleston's orchestra went under. The staggering surprise came when Philadelphia, one of the oldest and greatest symphony orchestras in the world gave up and went out of business. Remember that Savannah's population was just 136,268. Metro Philadelphia had a population of more than 5 million about 37 times that of Savannah.

The other part of the equation is the ability to sell tickets for Pops concerts that usually include arrangements of hit popular songs, themes from movies, and the great hits from Broadway shows. What attracted, and continues to attract, a large audience, is Andrew Lloyd Weber's '*Phantom of the Opera"* and "*Cats*," Claude-Michel Schonberg's *"Les Miserables,"* and movie themes composed by Boston's great pops conductor: Roger Williams. To a lesser extent this is true of *"My Fair Lady," "South Pacific"* and "*The Sound of Music*." How are you going to make POP's-style orchestral arrangements of all the rap style music that we have to listen to today? It does not bode well for the future of orchestras throughout the country, except for those in the very largest cities.

IT'S A BIRD, IT'S A PLANE

The symphony's POPS schedule one year included an evening of Broadway and Movie musical themes. Included was the theme from "Superman." Drew, the symphony's operations director, asked me if I would agree to be Superman during the performance. Of course, my answer was "yes." Drew's idea was for me to fly from behind the orchestra up into the rafters wearing a Superman blue costume with the red and yellow "S" on the front. In addition to the cloth costume with cape, the outfit came with a fantastic looking artificial chest insert and huge fake biceps. The part of the cable that was to carry me through the air was not professionally designed and constructed. There was no "seat." The rig was nothing more than two rings of wire cable at the end of the cable that was to lift me into the air. It had no padding whatsoever. At the rehearsal I learned that hanging in the cables was very painful. We also discovered that, were I to tip forward, I would fall out of the rig and probably fall head first. So much for OSHA and safety. The solution was for me to fly with my arms straight overhead, holding the cable with my fingers. Having my arms straight up looked like Superman would fly, but it also had a crucial function. These discoveries made having a rehearsal unusually important.

The Superman theme was to be the last piece before intermission, and upon completing the rehearsal of the piece, the musicians all started to walk around taking a break, pretending to forget that I was hanging up there out of sight in the rafters. After some yelling at them they laughed and lowered me down. Their "failure" to remember I was up there had become extremely painful.

Drew did an excellent job of designing how the flying would be incorporated with the music. I was to stand with my legs spread and my hands on my hips behind a translucent white curtain with a bright spotlight behind me projecting my shadow much larger than life onto the curtain between me and the audience. Near the end of the music, as the curtain was pulled up, I raised my arms to grasp the cable above my head and assumed the Superman appearance of flying. I had worn the costume over my suit, so I was able to rip off the costume and appear in the Green Room for intermission before some of the major-donor guests reached the room that was only a few feet from the stage. They couldn't believe I had been up in the air above them just moments before they saw me in a suit in the Green Room.

THE AFTERGLOW

For at least a year, I had amusing moments when little kids would come up to me in a supermarket or some place and ask "My mother says you are Superman; is that really true?" I got incredible reactions when I would say "yes." Maybe I wasn't really Clark Kent, but at least my name was Clark. I got even more acceptance of my great but grossly-exaggerated title when I would say "Yes, just call me Clark."

Now, about 20 years later, I still leave the Superman costume hanging in the hall guest closet, evoking amusing reactions from people who see it and don't know why I have it.

82 A EUROPEAN TV COMMERCIAL
It Could Never Be Shown In The US

One of the most interesting things about the Internet is the number of amusing performances that can be seen by millions of people all over the world. I'm sure that everyone has their favorites and many may be better than the ones I suggest here. By the time you read this, some of these may no longer be on YouTube, but if they are still there, you should take a look.

The first one, a German TV commercial, does include nudity, but it is not the least bit pornographic, just funny. What is most interesting for Americans is that this commercial for Siemens dishwashers could air on TV in Europe. Are Americans incredibly prudish or are Europeans too lax?

The store that distributes Siemens appliances in the town of Flensburg in northern Germany is Fleggard. It is just over the border from Denmark south of Copenhagen and northwest of Kiel, Germany. I mention that because you will see at the end it is their commercial. If you look at any of these videos be sure to have your sound turned on.

The most viewed ad is one you should be able to see on YouTube at

http://www.youtube.com/watch?v=BEDiKo5S-xA

Can you imagine seeing that ad on US TV? When you watch it you can agree that it is obviously directed at a male audience, even though it does end up being amusing. The main point is that it illustrates the vast difference between the conservative attitude of many Americans contrasted with the acceptance of sex by Europeans. Women who think that ad is too sexist and aimed only at men should look at the version designed for women

adsoftheworld.com/media/tv/fleggaard_what_women_really_want

There are a few other sites worth looking at. These include:

The Incredible Fountains in Dubai. On the website below, be sure to have your sound on.

http://www.wimp.com/dubaifountain

All of you have probably viewed the earth-shattering first performance of the unheard of little old lady, Susan Boyle, on *Britains Got Talent*. It has not been viewed on youtube more than 300 million times. Incredible. Even if you have seen it, it is worth looking at again. The best version is at

https://www.instagram.com/p/Byqx9gdBcaQ/?utm_source=ig_embed

.

83 HOMELESS

No House On Land, Our Boat Was Our Home

Pat and I have sailed all over the place, northern Europe, the Mediterranean, to Bermuda from Jost van Dyke, the coasts of Brazil, Croatia, Thailand, and many places throughout the United States. We sailed the Virgin Islands with the Eastern Yacht Club's Winter Cruise man times.

As I mentioned earlier, when golfing buddies in Savannah read an article about Pat's and my living aboard our sailboat for a year and a half, they could not believe it. All said they would have trouble talking their wives into sailing for a week. How in the world did I do it?

The answer was simple….it was her idea!

When the company I had worked for in Cambridge, Massachusetts was sold to American Express, I was laid off first. My specialty had been taking major corporate accounts away from American Express. They had a great credit card, but had a lousy reputation at serving as managers of corporate travel. The only job options were in places we did not want to live, especially the cold of Minneapolis. The only big advantage of being first was that I was given a big party: cocktails, dinner, presents from corporations, dancing and speeches. A hotel chain, Marriott, knowing we were going sailing, gave us a large ice sculpture of our boat, including details such as the mast and sails. The party went on into the wee hours of the morning.

We sold the large house we had built on the Charles River in Dover, Massachusetts. We assumed we would probably move to Florida, but looking along the east coast had not resulted in our identifying a place we would choose. We made an offer on a house on the water in Satellite Beach, Florida, but when the owner countered we did not raise our offer. Pat finally said, since we don't know where to go, why don't we just put our stuff in storage and go sailing.

Most people were surprised to learn that we had no home ashore. We had to use a Mail Boxes, etc.in Ft. Lauderdale to forward our mail to us by Fedex each week. It was a challenge to figure out where we would be to meet the packages every time, especially once we got out of the US. Being homeless was interesting, but difficult in many ways.

David Hooks, the boat broker we had used before, found us a fabulous sailboat in Ft. Lauderdale. It was long and fat, providing lots of comfortable interior space, but managing to do so without looking ugly. At 55 feet, it was unusual to have just two

staterooms. The master bedroom was wide enough to allow walking around a queensize double bed. The custom teak and leather sofas were elegant.
One thing I used to hate about most of the boats we chartered was having to use a hand held shower while standing over the sink and john in the bathroom. This boat had a sizeable walk-in shower. The galley had a microwave oven and a full "house size" and style refrigerator/freezer and a generator to keep it operating when sailing. The "living room" had an oriental carpet with Italian leather sofas on either side of a standard glass-top coffee table. We had two zone heating and air conditioning and two TV sets. The boat had been customized to include a remote-controlled opening transom (stern) that had a fold- down section that served as a swim platform off the stern and allowed storage of a propane tank connected to the grill, Scuba gear and other supplies inside the compartment.

"Eagle" was very easy to operate. The mainsail had electrically-powered roller furling, which meant that at the touch of a button, the person steering the boat could pull the sail out the boom or retract it entirely into the mast. The large Genoa jib also had roller furling onto the headstay, and even though it had to be cranked out by a hand-turned wench, it was pretty easy to do. I used to be able to set the sails or take them "down" without having to wake Pat if she was asleep below.

The funniest thing about the boat was a second steering station. There was the normal big stainless steering wheel in the cockpit. We had great fun telling people that the boat had a nice safe well-protected steering station inside the main cabin. Even very experienced boaters and boatyard employees could spend minutes looking and not find it. The steering "wheel" was disguised as a large wooden salad bowl sitting on the kitchen counter. It had a gearshift lever and throttle hidden next to it but they were hard to spot behind the salad bowl. Pat kept fruit in the bowl as camouflage. Standing at the inside wheel you could see straight ahead out of the forward "windshield" but because you could not see the water it would not have been safe if you used it where you might need to be able to dodge anything in the water. We only used it once, but it was a source of frequent amusement.

THE EAST COAST OF THE UNITED STATES
What appears to be a lot of boats motor down the coast to Florida, the Bahamas or the Caribbean for the winter and back north in the spring. At the time, we read that there were usually about 1,200 boats making the trip in the IntraCoastal Waterway southbound in the fall and most do it about the same time of year. You can go out in the Atlantic and travel 24 hours a day (which is what we did heading north the first time) or take the safer, protected and much more scenic route down the Intracoastal Waterway, known as the "ICW," or, disparagingly, "The Big Ditch." It is a very interesting trip.

Except for the trips around Manhattan Island, the route does not pass through any large cities, but there is much of interest and beauty. Almost all of the trip is beautiful and parts, some stretches such as the northern Chesapeake and the relatively short coastlines of Georgia and South Carolina are largely natural and gorgeous. Nevertheless, the entire trip is very interesting and there is lots of beautiful coastline to see, followed by lots of mansions along the ICW, especially once you reach the middle of Florida. I have sailed places with much more beautiful natural coastlines throughout the world, but our country's coastline is something that Americans will enjoy doing.

For anyone with an appropriate boat and time to make the excursion it is a highly-recommended experience. The navigation is very easy, the miles of the ICW are identified by numbered signs and there are many floating and stationary aids to navigation making it easy to tell where you are (except in very few instances). Some people anchor at every opportunity. Pat and I enjoyed going into marinas and visiting many of the cities along the way.

Conversely, we had a great time exploring many little rivers on both sides of the Chesapeake and anchoring for the night. If you stay in the channel down the middle of the Chesapeake you don't even see land on either side. It pays to have time to explore both sides of the Chesapeake. The route through North Carolina is surprisingly uninteresting and the ICW through South Carolina and Georgia is largely natural beauty with loads of quiet creeks in which to anchor for the night. Sometimes a bunch of boats will anchor in a popular spot, but we had loads of evenings where we had a peaceful anchorage all to ourselves.

The actual Intracoastal Waterway is generally considered to be the thousand miles between Norfolk, Virginia and the southern tip of Florida. In Key West, you are just 94 miles from Cuba. There is an inland waterway stretch through New Jersey but it is suitable only for small power boats. With the exception of the Cape Cod Canal and the trip through Long Island Sound, for large boats the entire length of the New Jersey coast is entirely in open water, but there are harbors big enough for most boats within easy reach of safety should a storm approach.

RUSH HOUR

Southbound in the fall you are going with the flow, encountering very few boats going the other direction. There is certainly no traffic jam, but you typically see a lot of boats every day. Faster power boats are passing you (knowledgeable ones know to pass on your left) and you are passing some remarkably small and what must be frustratingly-slow sailboats. We found eleven miles per hour a very enjoyable speed for several reasons. It was much safer and you can easily keep track of where you are on your chart.

A slow speed allows you to enjoy the scenery and stop at interesting places you would pass by if you were going much faster.

MAINE

The coast of Maine is one of the most beautiful and interesting shorelines in the world, dotted with rocky islands, and interesting rivers. You can visit charming little towns and see the harbors and the rocky coastline that you simply cannot see in a car. The numerous peninsulas all point south like long fingers with water between each one, so you have to drive south down one and then back north and across to get to the next one and repeat the process. The result is that very few tourists really see much of the coast.

More importantly, you simply cannot reach the most beautiful spots from the road. This is obviously true of the hundreds of islands. More than most other places on earth, to see and enjoy Maine you *must* be in a boat. Look at a map and you will be amazed to learn that, as a result of all those points of land and islands the coastline of Maine, just 225 miles as the crow flies, is longer than the coastline of California, not by much (51 miles), but, at 3,478miles, it is still longer. Most cruisers go only as far as Bar Harbor and turn around. Up near the Canadian border we enjoyed anchoring out of sight of any other boat in beautiful Mistake Harbor and at Roque Island. Sailing to Mistake is no mistake.

THE ROUTE ALONG THE COAST

In Massachusetts, Manchester Harbor and Marblehead Harbor must be seen If you have not been there, Boston Harbor has great buildings and fun dining right along the waterfront. Seeing Plymouth Rock is best done by automobile; it could just be skipped. In a boat, it is a long way into Plymouth to see that rock. Remember, the Pilgrims really first landed near Provincetown, at the very tip of Cape Cod.

Newport, Rhode Island is very interesting both from the water and prowling on foot around the town. It is out of the way, but Nantucket, Martha's Vineyard and the back side of the Elizabeth Islands could easily consume weeks of cruising without making much progress down the coast. Martha's Vineyard is more active and much easier to reach but, as a result, has many more tourists. Smaller and less developed Nantucket is much more charming. On Martha's Vineyard, we much prefer Edgartown, usually near the action on Water Street, but we twice took a mooring in front of Walter Cronkite's home and beside his sailboat in Katama Bay.

NEW YORK TO NORFOLK

Long Island Sound is interesting but not naturally beautiful. You need to switch sides of the Sound several times to visit the most interesting harbors. Entering New York is one of the most exciting parts of the entire journey, through Hells Gate and down the East River. It is quite an experience. Sailing past the Statue of Liberty is inspiring, but you have to be careful because of the boat traffic in New York Harbor. Boats and ships come at you from every direction. Technically, there is a waterway through New Jersey, but it is only usuable by small boats. We did the length of New Jersey northbound one time at night. There is little danger and the lights on shore are very pretty.

CHESAPEAKE BAY

Most boaters have heard about cruising Chesapeake Bay. There are loads of places to explore. One year we were invited by Dr. Tulloch, then the Commodore of the Gibson Island Yacht Club, to join their annual cruise in the Chesapeake. Wish we had had the time to do that.

It is similar to Long Island Sound because the best route involves the eastern shore from the Chesapeake and Delaware Canal down to just before the Bay Bridge, then to the west side for Annapolis, going back to the east to St. Michael's, then south for thirty miles before crossing to the western side from Solomon Island down to Norfolk. If you go down the middle you see nothing.

With dock space tight and anchoring not allowed in Annapolis per se, we have stayed twice across the river far up Mill Creek. The entrance to Mill Creek is so narrow and well hidden that you feel as if you are going onto someone's beautiful grass lawn just before you cut hard left into Mill Creek.

The first time we sailed through the Chesapeake we spent a month prowling and still missed some great spots that we discovered heading north the next year. At Annapolis, go over the eastern shore and prowl the beautiful creeks, starting at St. Michael's and continuing south for thirty miles before crossing back to the western shore the rest of the way south to Norfolk.

Norfolk is tricky in the daytime, *very* tricky at night. One night we met head on in the channel a barely-visible huge submarine heading out into the Atlantic. We dodged it, but not by much. At night the thousands of lights and welding machines make it hard to see anything else when you pass the huge aircraft carriers and numerous other ships undergoing repairs. North Carolina, to our surprise, was the least interesting state.

In South Carolina, except for the city of Charleston and the large development on Hilton Head Island, the ICW route takes you through long stretches of natural beauty. Charleston itself is very interesting and frequently cited as being the most hospitable city in the country. Its City Marina is most welcoming. Charleston's restaurants are truly outstanding. Despite the proximity to all of the beach towns facing the Atlantic, there are miles of beautiful natural stretches where the waterway winds its way through secluded rivers in South Carolina.

GEORGIA
Savannah is 8 miles off the ICW, up the Savannah River, but it should not be missed. To visit the city, River Street is the place to stay. The best place to tie up is the Hyatt, and you better call for a reservation. Savannah's historic district is beautifully preserved and the restaurants are outstanding. All are within walking distance of River Street. To give you an idea of Savannah as a tourist destination, note that it has 31 companies offering many kinds of tours of the historic district, everything from trolleys to Segways and hearses. Our favorite restaurant by far is Garibaldi.

South of Savannah is where you find many deserted little creeks meandering through the serenity of the large marshes. We frequently found ourselves anchoring in creeks with no other boat in sight. In tidal creeks, we always used two bow anchors, one upstream and one downstream, both running to the bow, to keep us away from the sides of the creek when the current reversed. Using two anchors was a bother but a necessity in a large boat.

FLORIDA
Entering Florida, we recommend a stop in Fernandina, with its charming little main street. Once you reach Cape Canaveral, the ICW becomes heavily populated on both sides. There are no beautiful little creeks and few places where you can anchor, but you get to see the "backyards" of many mansions that simply are hidden from view from the street. It is totally different but very interesting and, here again, the only way to see it is from a boat. There are many interesting cities to visit and, if you haven't been there, Cape Canaveral.

Next is an amusing story about passing between Titusville and Cape Canaveral.

"EXTREME CAUTION"
Our most amusing moment on the entire trip was as we approached Titusville, on the mainland west of the northern end of Cape Canaveral. At the time, the Coast Guard published the *"Notice to Mariners."* It alerted boaters to problems at points up and down the coast and there were frequent publications, each covering small sections of the route. You could pick up a copy at most marinas along the way. Because I had read the current issue, I radioed the Coast Guard on Channel 16.

I don't think it is there any longer, but at the time there were very high-tension cables carrying electricity from the mainland to NASA's Space Center at Cape Kennedy. The unusual design relied upon the weight of the long cable spans on either side of the ICW channel to pull tight the short lengths of the cables that were on rollers up on towers fairly close together on either side of the channel. The *Notice to Mariners* alerted boaters to a serious problem at this point. The rollers had not functioned properly and the cables with the huge amount of electricity had sagged and were hanging much too low over the waterway. The Coast Guard's Notice read that boaters with masts of 55ft or more were to "exercise extreme caution" when passing under these high-voltage cables. Our mast was 59 feet and our VHF and single side band radio antennae stuck up to 69 feet.

When the Coast Guard answered Channel 16, I cited the warning in their notice and its date, asking how I was supposed to exercise extreme caution and not risk getting electrocuted. The officer on the radio had me read him the whole section and put me on hold while he checked. It was surprising that the local Coast Guard station was not familiar with the big warning that had put out to boaters.

Finally, having put me on hold twice, the radio operator came back on and assured me that the problem had been corrected and passage was now safe. For days after that boats seeing our boat's name, *"Eagle."* and realizing we were the one whose conversation with the Coast Guard they had listened in on thanked me profusely, acknowledging that they had not read the Notice to Mariners and were shocked (no pun intended) by the high voltage warning.

The Coast Guard is badly needed. Too many times we encountered couples on small powerboats with signs indicating they were "Coast Guard Auxiliary. Usually, they frequently caused stupid problems due to lack of knowledge of sailboats. The volunteer-staffed Auxiliary boats were a true pain in the neck.

THE BAHAMAS

We had not realized how long that string of islands is, stretching south almost five hundred miles from the Abacos up about as far north as Central Florida. We island hopped all the way to the last of the Bahamas, just before the Turks and Caicos Islands down near the Dominican Republic. Unless you are in a fast sportfisherman, it takes a long time to work your way down the Exumas and back up the string of islands along the east that head back north to the Abacos. There is great variety in the islands and they are laid out so that you can take a loop down one string of beautiful islands and back up the other. Nassau is the only city with big hotels and lots of people. The prettiest islands are far to the south and east. Don't miss the Exumas.

I had considered going to the Bahamas with some fear and trepidation because they are known for having very few aids to navigation and none in the little remote islands. Accustomed to sailing in places where there were many marks out in the water to guide you, the Bahamas are essentially bereft of any such help. We learned very quickly that dark water meant deep water and it was very shallow where you could see the white sand through the clear water. Even though we were accustomed to going from navigation mark to mark wending our way through the rocks of Maine, the sailing was surprisingly easy in the Bahamas except for one notorious spot called "The Devil's Backbone."

I will mention just a few stories of events that occurred during our 21-month odyssey.

GREEN TURTLE KEY TO BEAUFORT, NORTH CAROLINA
When it got to be May we had spent a good bit of time in the Abacos, the islands in the northeast sector of the Bahamas, and decided to sail the 430 miles in the Atlantic straight to Beaufort, North Carolina, rather than making the long sail west back to Florida and traveling in the daytime slowly up the ICW through Georgia, South Carolina and most of the coast of North Carolina, which would have taken six weeks.

At Green Turtle Key we met up with sailors on two sailboats planning to do the same thing the next day. We were the fastest boat and left first, so at the end of the first day we were already far ahead of them. During the night at the helm, I spent a good bit of time talking with a cargo ship that had left Havana and was now heading across our bow toward Europe. This had happened years earlier far out in the Atlantic.

When at sea, Pat and I took turns at the helm, changing the time on watch every two hours. Yes, I know, the normal is three to six hours, but it is my opinion that on deck alone you can't stay focused that long. By the end of the first night our radar had quit working and our lights had dimmed. Then we lost our GPS. We had no way of telling where we were and no way of communicating with other boats. It was not a fun discovery. Our electrical system had quit working.

We figured our best option was to turn around, head back east, try to spot and intercept the other boats and sail with them to North Carolina. Luckily, we had left the engine running the night before for extra speed and electricity for the refrigerator. We needed the engine to go directly into the wind in search of the two other boats, so we did a 180 degree turn and headed toward where the sun would rise. A few hours later we saw a white sail far away on the horizon and headed toward it. It was our friends from Green Turtle.

After considerable conversation, they urged us not to go with them, especially since we would be a dark boat all night each night. They insisted that we should head west toward Florida where we supposedly could "easily spot" the huge launch tower for the Space Shuttle. The problem was that we would have no way of knowing if our actual course was taking us north or south of Cape Canaveral, which was one of the very few places deep enough for a boat that drew seven feet to entire the ICW along this long coast. Also, we would have to be crossing the strong northward flow of the Gulf Stream, making it more difficult to guess where we were headed. Reluctantly, we said goodbye and turned and again headed west toward Florida.

I was, to say the least, not happy being out there with no lights, no navigation systems and no normal ship's radio. We sailed west for three hours that morning before I decided I had to try something. The problem was that our diesel engine, via the alternator was not sending current to charge our array of a half dozen heavy-duty batteries. The batteries were dead, far from strong enough to restart the engine if we stopped it, so I had to leave it running. In any event, we would have to have it to enter the canal just south of Cape Canaveral, and that would require the engine. I moved the furniture, opened up the floorboard access to the engine and climbed down in beside the hot, running engine.

It did not take long to figure out what had happened. We had had the stuffing box, the sealed tube through which the propeller shaft runs from the engine inside the hull to the water, worked on by the highly-regarded Albury's Marine on Man-O-War Cay before getting underway. Their man, lying beside the engine with his head toward the stern, must have pushed with his foot, disconnecting all the connections in the junction box that connected all of the wires that ran from the alternator on the engine to the six batteries tucked up under the deck. The control panel had shown everything working when we left Green Turtle, but now they were just lying there.

Our boat carried an unusual collection of stuff, including everything from a tux and long evening gown to ski clothes. I put on my thick ski gloves and used rubber-handled pliers and a screwdriver to put the connections back together, all with the engine running. Instantly, all the power came on.

We did another turn, this time to the northeast, estimating the course we would need to follow to intercept the other boats. We caught up to them by mid-afternoon. This time we could use the regular radio to communicate. Our batteries had completely recharged. We went on ahead, sailing north toward Beaufort, which lies just west of Cape Hatteras.

The last night was pretty scary in the dark. The wind was from the northeast, causing steep seas as it blew against the strong current of the Gulf Stream, which at this point was flowing northeast. I quickly learned not to look over my shoulder. Even in the moonlight, I could see the crest of each swell looming way over my head each time the boat surfed down into the trough of the swell. It is hard to imagine a boat that big and heavy surfing so steeply down that leading edge of a swell. It was quite difficult keeping the boat going straight down each swell so you did not get spun sideways and risk getting capsized by the huge swells.

Because it was so dangerous, I let Pat sleep below and stayed five hours at the helm for the time it took to get through the Gulf Stream and back into calmer waters. Something that happened in the middle of all that was irritating and dangerous. Far ahead off to my right I saw a flare in the sky. Even though it was not red, I assumed that it was, or at least could be, and attempt to signal from a boat in distress out there in the ocean. I called for another boat but got no response. I tried the Coast Guard in the United States, but they were still out of radio range. I called repeatedly on Channel 16, the "hailing" channel for communicating with another boat, to no avail. Getting no response from anyone, I felt I had to alter course in the direction I had seen the flare to offer assistance if needed.

After an hour or so the Coast Guard answered my calls, but I could still barely understand them. They had received no call for help. They did, however, say that the flare might have been part of a Navy practice operation. If that were the case, I was surprised that someone on a navy ship had not radioed me that I did not have to worry and respond to the flare. When I got close enough to determine that there were many ships I knew that it was the Navy, but found it hard to believe that they had put me in danger by refusing to answer my calls. The man at the Coast Guard said that it was Navy policy not to talk on the radio during such a practice. I thought that was inexcusable, taking me far off course, and costing me hours of sailing.

Pat came to the helm and I went below to get some much needed sleep. She said it was a delightful dawn. Some dolphins came near the boat on each side to say good morning. The seas were much less, but still high enough for the boat to tilt steeply down the face of each swell. The dolphins gathered together on each side of the boat and surfed along beside us for quite a while. Pat had a beautiful experience. After that trip, we were happy to get through the nasty breakers at he entrance into Beaufort, North Carolina, clear customs and get some sleep.

CAPE MAY

One day in our second year aboard we were sailing down the coast approaching Cape May at the southern tip at the southern tip of New Jersey.

Up ahead I saw a mass of small boats, at least a hundred of them, mostly outboard powered open fishing boats all clustered fairly close together. Later I looked at the chart and found there is a strange long pointed spot on the sea floor which must have made for fantastic fishing. I weaved our way through all the boats, planning to round Cape May and continue up the Delaware River. As I emerged from the cluster of boats I saw a large Coast Guard "mother ship" of some sort with a pack of what must have been at least a dozen large inflatable boats headed toward the point we were headed. I had been boarded by the Coast Guard several times in New England, but could not comprehend why there would be so many headed for me.

As expected, on radio channel 16 a voice hailed "the sailboat headed south toward Cape May." This confirmed their interest in *Eagle*. The only reason for coming at us would be to board and inspect the boat. To my surprise, the voice on Channel 16 in a plaintive tone said that he knew I had right of way but asked if I would slow down and let the Coast Guard's practice maneuvers pass in front of me. With great relief I said "sure." At least I had just cleared the mass of little boats so I could head into the wind enough to slow down, letting the swarm of Coast Guard boats pass.

Rounding Cape May is treacherous because there are shifting shoals with shallow water and no aids to navigation.....not a single mark. This is ridiculous. The Coast Guard must have expected everyone to go all the way to the cargo ship entrance far south in the middle of Delaware Bay before turning west toward the Delaware River.

We developed four GPS points that appeared to indicate a safe path through the shoals so we could use those points on future trips. We were delighted and flattered when the dean of all cruising, Tom Neale, wrote down our GPS points to use on future trips. We had a very nice relaxing sail up the middle of the uninteresting Delaware River. When the Bay begins to narrow, you turn south into the Chesapeake-Delaware Canal, well before reaching Philadelphia. If you look at a standard map, you probably will not notice that there is a canal at this point.

NAVIGATION

One of the very first things you learn about boating is the way to understand the two most common aids to navigation. These are red marks and green marks, some lighted, most floating, sometimes firmly attached to a rock or solid ground underwater and sometimes on the shore. The basic rule is that the channel that it should be safe for you to travel in (assuming it is deep enough for your boat) is that when you are returning from the ocean to a harbor you keep the reds on your right and the greens on your left, hence the saying "Reds, right, returning." Obviously, the greens are on your left.

BEAUTIFUL BOATING

Without any question, the most beautiful boating we had was aboard a sailboat we chartered in the spectacular Phang Nga Bay off the Andaman Sea east of Phuket, Thailand. The tall small-in-area stone islands with vegetation growing out of the rocks rise straight out of the water.

The most stunning is Ko Topu, popularly known as James Bond Island, because it had been in a Bond movie. The water has eroded the base so that the island is much wider up in the air than it is at its base. Most of the flatter islands have beautiful white sand beaches. The most remarkable fact is the way the sea has eroded several tall islands at water level, one of which you could actually go "under" the island in a small boat.

Arguably the most beautiful, Maya Bay on Ko Phi Phi Le, has become overrun with people on the beach and boats tied up to each other in rows just off the beach. It was much more beautiful when we were there.

Sadly, several of the beaches we visited were hit hard by the great tsunami, wiping all of the people off the face of the earth. We enjoyed anchoring by ourselves off a beautiful beach and taking the inflatable into a small wooden structure on the beach and having a good dinner for $4 per person. Saying "very inexpensive" is an understatement. Notice that I wrote "boating" rather than sailing. That was because there was little wind and, even if there had been, you wanted to weave around and explore the islands, so you had to be under power.

CROATIA

One year we sailed northwest out of Dubrovnik, one of our favorite little cities, and visited many of the islands along the Dalmation Coast. The largest island city of Hvar has a harbor full of big yachts and an upscale downtown full of ritzy clientele. Our favorite cities on the mainland Dalmation Coast were Trojir and Split.

One of the funny things about the area is that dividing the coast of Croatia there is a narrow 58 mile bit of Bosnia Herzegovinia, about 40 miles up the coast from Dubrovnik. We had an amusing time there because one of our crew, Ali Muhammad Nasr, was a direct descendant of the Prophet. His name attracted extra attention from customs and border control people. While the rest of us got whisked through border control promptly, he got stopped twice and had his passport very-carefully scrutinized.

A LONG SAIL WITH NO SCENERY

Leaving one of our favorite islands, Jost Van Dyke in the British Virgin Islands, we sailed due north (literally 0 degrees on the compass) on the beautiful schooner *"Ashanti of Saba"* to our favorite island, Bermuda. There is nothing in between. It is 981 miles north with the US coast about a thousand miles to the west. My most amusing time was when I was at the helm late one night. We spotted the lights of a ship far to the west, looking as if it would cross fairly close ahead of us. I talked on the radio with the Russian ship's captain who said he was en route from Havana around the north cape of Norway to Murmansk, similar to what the Russian ship had been doing when aboard *Eagle* we passed it in the Atlantic between Green Turtle and Beaufort, NC. Turned out he, too, wanted to practice his English, so we stayed on the radio for about four hours until he went over the horizon to the east.

At the time I was a member of the Royal Bermuda Yacht Club, so we got a good mooring and had a fabulous time on the extremely-sophisticated and magnificent island. The most dangerous moment was dodging a large floating container that must have fallen off a cargo ship a few hundred miles south of Bermuda. It must have held heavy cargo because the air kept it just barely visible above the seas. If we had hit it, we probably would have sunk far from radio range of the US or Bermuda.

A FRIEND IN TROUBLE

One of our good friends in Marblehead, Dick Robie, was sailing with his wife, Ann, on the annual Eastern Yacht Club Cruise along the coast of Maine. When we left Northeast Harbor, in the middle of Mt. Desert Island, our next anchorage down the coast for several dozen boats on the cruise was in Pretty Marsh Harbor on the west side of the island. Dick anchored his beautiful, antique, wooden Concordia sailboat about 200 feet east of the western shore of the harbor and we dropped anchor about a hundred feet east of him.

While enjoying evening cocktails, we looked over and saw a commotion on board Dick's yacht, *"Christie."* The boat appeared to be rising out of the water. How could that be? They had managed to anchor directly above the one small rock on the bottom and, as the tide went out, the rock began to lift the boat. They must have radioed the Race Committee Boat for assistance because a small rubber dinghy with several members of the Race Committee aboard came speeding past us toward them.

The solution was to take the halyard from the top of the mast and attach it to the stern of the dinghy. They raced the dinghy's large outboard motor, pulling from the side of the sailboat, causing *Christie* to heel over far enough for the boat's keel to rise higher in the water, freeing the boat from its perch atop the rock.

The story's funny part occurred when *Christie's* keel became free of the rock. The very heavy lead keel caused the boat to return instantly to vertical, jerking the halyard with the dinghy attached. The startled looks on the faces of the Race Committee were hilarious as they were jerked backyard unexpectedly and quite hard. All's well that ends well. Bet they had a drink (maybe even two) after that.

84 TIDBITS BASEBALL
Some Short Ones

MUFFINS

It is very difficult adjusting to living back in the hometown where you grew up after living in New York and Munich and spending most of your life in Boston, cheering for the Red Sox. Montgomery has a strangely-named baseball team, the Biscuits. Don't laugh, that's really their name. I have never been able to get a definitive answer from anybody about how this name was chosen, but it was honored as the best name in minor league baseball in 2014.

ANOTHER MONTGOMERY TEAM NAME

The high school from which I graduated in 1955 was named Sidney Lanier High School. Today, I bet few of the students there even know the reason for the name of their teams. How would you like to be a big tough football player and have to say you were a "Poet." Lanier was an extraordinary gentleman, a lawyer, a flautist (bet some of you don't know what that means), a writer but best known as a poet. To my surprise, when writing this I learned that he had belonged to my college fraternity: SAE. He is the reason the school's teams are called the "Poets." Lanier also played the organ in what is now the oldest surviving church in Montgomery, the First Presbyterian.

THE HERO'S LAST GAME

Ted Williams may have had a nasty personality throughout his playing career, but he was a hero for the Red Sox, nonetheless. His 400-season-batting average still sits at the top of baseball achievements. It was a great record, as of this writing, still unmatched.

It was fun watching him play in Fenway Park and sad to know he would be retiring at the end of the season. A good college friend from Connecticut, Chris Larsen, and I planned far ahead to see Ted's last games. We bought tickets to his final game in Boston and for the Red Sox final game of the season in Yankee Stadium against the Damn Yankees.

It was great fun sitting in Fenway Park and seeing Ted hit a home run that day the last time he came to the plate to bat. The fans went bananas. Just like moments such as hearing of Kennedy's assassination, you remember where you were sitting when it happened. Chris and I had a great time, but got ready to drive to New York for the final Red Sox game of the year. It wasn't just going to be Ted's last game, it was against the hated Yankees. The feeling was illustrated by numerous Boston bumper stickers that read "I love New York, I just hate the Yankees."

We got to Yankee Stadium only to learn that Ted would not play. The team's management, probably joined by Ted, wanted that great homerun in Fenway Park to be his last at bat. Quite a memory; delighted we were there to witness it.

SPORTS ILLUSTRATED

It was amusing two dozen years after it happened to read in Sports Illustrated an article about steroids in baseball that mentioned something I had done. The article did not mention my name, but my amusing accomplishment. I always had a very-deep-pitched voice that carried in a crowd. A co-worker, Dave Smith, and I had tickets from American Airlines right behind the visitor's dugout, near home plate on the third base line.

Jose Canseco, looking terribly bloated from all the steroids, was at this point still denying that he took banned drugs. He was playing right field, so when the first inning ended and he had to jog to his team's dugout, he had to come straight toward us. I started chanting "Steroid, steroid" Given his admission and book years later, he must have known the truth, but he had a fierce scowl on this face when he got near us. The fun thing was that we got the stadium to join in the chant, making Jose even more mad. He stopped and glared at me for several seconds before ducking into his team's dugout. That chanting that day was in a Sports Illustrated article on performance enhancing drugs years later.

DRUGS IN BASEBALL

Does anybody believe that the suddenly massive Roger Clemens was not on something? He had been a fabulous pitcher for the Red Sox, but management caught up in the drug debate years later commented that they had determined he was past his prime and would begin to go downhill. They let him go. What caused the sudden reversal and rapid growth to massive proportions? Could it have been the used of banned steroids?

It is funny to read years later about the inadequacy of testing for drugs in many sports, but the worst examples in a major sport were clearly American baseball, and the stubborn barrier to meaningful testing was for years the player's union. Unions had to fight for members, the players, even though they must have known this was wrong. So sad.

When it finally came out that Lance Armstrong, despite years of strong claims to the contrary, had for years taken performance enhancing drugs he had to forfeit all of his Tour de France championships and his team was stripped of its wins.

Alex Rodrigues in 2013 was caught having used drugs to improve his playing. Shouldn't the Yankees have to give up all their wins, including World Series Championships in which he played unfairly against the other teams? Turnabout should be fair play."

85 GROUNDHOG DAY
Déjà Vu, All Over Again, And Again And Again

Groundhog Day, always celebrated in the United States on February 2, began in the U.S. way back in 1887, having evolved from a tradition in Europe dating back several hundred years. As you know, the groundhog is supposed to come out of his hole, look around and, if he sees his shadow, forecasts six more weeks of winter. Not the most scientific weather forecast, but fun. Punxsutawney Phil, lives as you might guess, in Punxsutawney, Pennsylvania, 64 miles northeast of Pittsburgh.

In 1993 a hilarious movie entitled "Groundhog Day" came out. This is one of my stories because, for a ridiculous combination of reasons, I have watched the movie (or, as you will read, at least *most* of the movie) eight times. It may be a very funny story, but why in the world watch it so many times?

The plot of the movie is based on an obnoxious weatherman from a TV station in Pittsburgh who believes it is beneath his dignity to be assigned to drive out to Gobbler's Knob (just outside the southeastern city limits of Punxsutawney) to do the show, broadcasting live the emergence of the groundhog and the announcement of his forecast.

A FRIEND IN THE MOVIE

One of the scenes is about his sitting in the TV room of the hotel with elderly people who are amazed that he knows the question to go with every answer on the classic TV show *"Jeopardy."* I had been told that, during this scene, the movie shows the TV screen briefly showing a contestant who was a friend in the travel industry, Mark Pestronk.

Mark was a lawyer and highly knowledgeable expert on travel law, based in Washington, DC. He won *Jeopardy* several times in 1991, winning $67, 000, which was worth a lot back in those days. He went on to be a semi-finalist in Jeopardy's "Tournament of Champions." Every time I watched the movie *something* happened to make me miss that scene. I was like Bill Murphy in the movie, repeating over and over again.

One time I was sure that at long last I was going to see Mark in the movie. I was sitting in the right window seat in first class on a long flight with *"Groundhog Day'* showing on the small screen over the aisle. I told the man on my left the story about missing that scene so many times. Finally, I had to go to the bathroom. Picking a point in the film where it appeared highly unlikely that the *Jeopardy* scene would come on, I dashed under the movie screen into the men's room as quickly as I could.

As I emerged, the man pointed violently at the screen but by the time I could get past it and turn around the *Jeopardy* scene, once again, had gone. Like the movie, it had reached the point of being ridiculous.

Yes, I did finally get to see the infamous scene. The movie initially got fairly-poor reviews but over the years began to the rated as a true classic, one of the top movies ever. Fairly recently, in 2016, the story was used in the Broadway Musical *"Groundhog Day."* One strange and unfortunate fact about the film is that it was not filmed in Punxsutawney; for some reason it was filmed in Woodstock, Illinois. Why?

"Groundhog Day" may sound ridiculous and you now know the basic plot, but it you have not seen it, do see it. The scenes and the way they take place are hilarious and should not be missed. Despite having seen most of it so many times, I still enjoy when it comes on TV every few years. I still watch the great "*Forrest Gump"* and *"Notting Hill"* when on.

Mark, can I bill you for all the hours I spent because of you?

86 TRAVEL TIDBITS
Great Meals

Even after traveling the world and dining in thousands of restaurants, there are a few that stand out. Some were obscenely expensive for Americans, even before the fall of the dollar's purchasing power. Some were very good despite being inexpensive. Some were just delightful experiences. Here again, if you have a chance to go to some of these, do.

ITALY

My most memorable surprise occurred in mid-January of 1982 in the northwest corner of Italy. I had finished business in Turin and stayed Saturday to explore the city. Because I had read about Alba's being the center of Italy's white-truffle region and the highly-rated Hotel Savona, I stopped in Alba for lunch en route back to Milan.

The dining room was filled with families, including loads of kids dressed up for church. I was seated by myself at a table for four near the center of one side of the large dining room. I was familiar with Black Truffles and loved the way their aroma enhanced flavor, but had never experienced white truffles. I talked to the manager about wanting to try their specialty white truffles and accepted his recommendation that the exquisite taste was most enjoyed when served on a relatively simple pasta with a white cream sauce.

As I started my meal, a young boy who had heard me talking with the manager walked up, said that he was studying English in school, and asked if I would mind letting him practice his English talking with me. His parents a few tables away were beaming at me and waved vigorously. It was not long before my table was surrounded by kids from other families, all eager to speak with me. The parents all watched from their tables, with their faces covered with smiles. Their generation had not been taught English, and they were obviously delighted with the skill that their young children were learning

The manager was delighted that his regular guests were having such a great time. He was most generous, shaving very expensive truffle repeatedly onto my pasta what must have been many times the amount of truffle I suspect would normally have been provided for a moderate amount of money. The manager had been sitting in the bar, talking with a man who turned out to be the distributor for one of the best of the delicious and powerful Barolo red wines indigenous to the area. I was given a bottle of 1961 Giacomo Conterno Barolo Monfortino Riserve. It was fabulous, as good as the truffles and its strong flavor was a perfect match. I kept eating truffles, drinking Barolo and talking with the kids.

In all my travels, I had eaten at many more-expensive restaurants and ones that were much more highly rated by the "expert" critics, but this was by far the best meal for the money I ever had the pleasure of eating. My expense account showed $22 for lunch. On the front page of the Life&Arts Section of the February 12, 2018 Wall Street Journal there was an excellent article on truffles, in which they reported that the current wholesale price of Italian White Alba Truffles now runs in the $3,000 to $4,000 range per pound. At today's prices, I must have been given about a thousand dollars worth of white truffles plus an expensive bottle of wine. I did not know at the time that Barolo claims to be "The King of Wines, the Wine of Kings."

A great meal and a great wine are much better when combined with a delightful experience.

LA TOUR D'ARGENT

One of these, La Tour d'Argent, is frequently criticized as being a tourist trap, but it is well worth a visit for a tourist. Dining there at sunset can be a truly fabulous experience. The specialty is pressed duck, with the elaborate preparation named after the restaurant, the Tour d'Argent. Each duck is numbered, and you are given a card with the number of the duck you were served. The ornate silver press in which the ducks are prepared is, in itself, quite beautiful.

My wife's oft-proven belief is that restaurants with great views rarely have good food to justify their high prices. This is not true in the case of La Tour d'Argent, where the view across the Seine to the rear and side of Notre Dame is truly exceptional. Having gone there fairly often many years ago, I was able on several occasions to be offered a window table and once, for Bastille Day (July 14, for those who don't know), the great corner window. The French jets trailing red, white and blue smoke flew up the Seine barely above window level. What a sight.

One evening I had the pleasure of having Claude Terrail dine with me. He was the son of the original owner, Andre Terrail, and the father of the next in line, another Andre Terrail. In my collection of framed favorite menus from throughout the world, I have two from La Tour d'Argent, one special silver one autographed to me by Claude on the night he sat with me. He was great company, making it a most enjoyable dinner, and he donated the wine, a well-aged Chateau Petrus..

TAILLEVANT

This restaurant has outstanding French haut-cuisine, even by the highest French standard. It is certainly not touristy. It is the reverse. Taillevent (pronounced Tie-eh-vahnt) is the beloved enclave of top Paris executives and high-ranking government officials at lunch, which can run hours. It is extremely "clubby," quite formal in style. The rooms are surrounded by great old antique paneling (although it has been gimped up in recent years by too much modern art), but nowhere near as badly as the great old dining room of the Helmsley Palace in New York City. The service at Taillevant is impeccable.

Several years ago, it was painful to watch an American TV show feature a totally inept American couple being told about the restaurant and the menu by the manager. They were being treated to a fabulous meal despite asking the most ignorant questions imaginable. It was not educational for the vast majority of the audience, 99.9999% of whom will never be able to see this restaurant, much less dine there.

My framed item from Taillevent is not their menu, it is their wine list, dating back to days when the recent vintages of France's greatest wines were available at what today seem to be ridiculously low prices. One of my favorites, a 1962 Chateau Haut-Brion, was just $15. Today, a complete lunch for two is likely to run at least in the $400 range; that's with several courses and wines, but can run much more than that if you drink top-rated wines. The guidebooks usually advise that if you want to dine at Taillevant you must reserve far in advance, but that is insufficient information for people who are accustomed to calling a restaurant a few days ahead. "Far Ahead" in this case means weeks and for some dates, months. If you can afford this fabulous restaurant, it's worth it. Needless to say, I can't go there anymore.

LASSERRE

Lasserre may not be ranked for the most highly rated French cuisine, but the food and service are excellent and, if you are seated in the right area at the right time of year, it is one of the most romantic dining rooms in the world. There are restaurants such as The Jules Verne, 400 feet up in the Eiffel Tower or the famous old "Windows on the World" that used to look out over Manhattan from high atop The World Trade Center, but Lasserre is romantic in a totally different manner. Be sure to try to get a table in the center underneath the retractable roof. On beautiful nights when the weather permits, the two sections of the roof glide almost silently apart, opening the view to the sky.

The last time I was there, my wife and I spent much of the evening barely speaking because we eavesdropped on the conversation at the next table where Art Buchwald, the famous political satirist with the Washington Post (and syndicated throughout the world), regaled the people at his table with a long list of great stories.

Both Taillevent and Lasserre are on the "right bank" in the ritzy 8th Arrondissement on side streets off the Champs Elysee. Tour d'Argent is on the left bank, on the Seine just upstream from Notre Dame. If you can afford it, try to go to all three of these in Paris, but do not go to any of these if you are not the kind of person who appreciates antique elegance and haut cuisine. The Hotel Savona is, by European standards, relatively inexpensive. The three in Paris are, even by European standards, extremely expensive, and for Americans spending their dollars, horrifyingly expensive.

PAUL BOCUSE, Collonges au Mont D'Or, Lyon, France
In the days I was in the travel agency business, airlines gave agents (the people who actually made reservations) trips of various descriptions. The largest travel agencies got more than their share. Working for what at the time was the seventh largest agency in the US, I was offered many great trips and, later when I was President of The Woodside Group of Travel Agencies, I was usually given free first class travel whenever I wanted.

Some of the "inaugural" flights offered to travel agents were a bit of an exaggeration. Airlines were allowed by the authorities to invite guests on an "inaugural," the first flight that an airline operated between city A and city B. I had been flown to Paris for the opening of Charle de Gaulle Airport, but the funniest one I took was an Air France inaugural from Paris to Lyon, France. Of course, this gave Air France an excuse to fly me first class from Boston to Paris. I flew eastbound 3,438 miles over the Atlantic one night, connected to the 248 mile "inaugural" flight south to Lyon on the morning I landed, had dinner and spent the night in Lyon before flying back to Boston the next day.

What made it worthwhile was an invitation to have dinner at the famous restaurant of Paul Bocuse on the river in Collonges au Mont D'Or five miles north of Lyon. At the time, Bocuse was known as the biggest-name chef in the so-called "Nouvelle Cuisine," which really was new at the time. Years later, he would be called "The Chef of The Century." This style of cooking was very rich and tasty French cooking, usually served in very-small portions, delicately presented on the plate and devoid of the heavy sauces that had for centuries been customary in French cuisine.

Air France had arranged for me to be introduced to Bocuse and he very graciously sat with me for a brief time, suggesting dishes and offering wines. It was fabulous. Most of the reviews today in TripAdvisor.com pan the restaurant as a very-expensive tourist trap, but those who know great cuisine still rave about it. I suspect that for most people who respond to TripAdvisor, it is much too expensive. Today, it would be for me. Nicer when you don't have to pay.

I happened to love truffles, so I was lucky to accept Bocuse's recommendation and start with his Black Truffle Soup. It is probably too strong for many people's taste, but I thought it was magnificent.

7,124 miles was a lot of traveling just to have dinner, but it was a marvelous experience. I frequently wished I had time to stay and see more of a place, but I had to get back for a meeting in Boston.

87 AMUSING MEALS
And Related Stories

THE RITZ, the original one in Boston

This tidbit is under restaurants and great meals, but it is really about a meal that was *not* served. This one is about great but stuffy old Ritz Carlton hotel in Boston, the original one on Arlington Street at the corner of Newbury (unfortunately, now The Taj). There are now Ritz Carltons all over the world, but for many years, there were only the two top-rated Ritzs in the Western Hemisphere, Montreal and Boston.

The one in Boston, overlooking the Public Garden, was known for a strange sign over its revolving door. The large red sign reads "Not an accredited egress." What in the world is that? The required notice was the result of a famous fire, one of the worst back when it happened, at a nightclub called The Coconut Grove in Boston. 400 people died that night, many of whom could not get out through a revolving door when too many people jammed the door. It was a tragic night, but it did result in more strict fire codes throughout the country. The resulting fire law is the reason that the Ritz had to label its revolving door as an exit that does not count as a legal exit.

Despite the addition of many elegant hotels and restaurants throughout the city, the main dining room at the Ritz remained for many decades as one of the finest places to dine in Boston. It was quite formal and had a dress code to match.

Years ago, I had a good friend and Vermont ski house roommate, Erling Lagerholm, who was a Vice President of Cabot Cabot and Forbes in Boston. The firm, headed by Gerry Blakely, owned the Ritz in Boston. The manager of the Ritz reported to Erl, who loved to tell the story about the day Jackie Kennedy was turned away by the Maitre d' at the Ritz, even though she had a reservation, the dining room had tables available and Jackie had recently been First Lady of the United States, arguably the most famous ever.

Remember the dress code. Many men have fond memories of the days when the fashion fad was "Hot Pants." They were usually tight fitting and always extremely short. When worn with high heels, women's legs never looked more stunning (if you were a female with well-shaped legs in the first place). Jackie was known for her high-fashion taste in clothes and hers were not cheap hot pants. Nevertheless, she was denied the right to have lunch in the Main Dining Room at the Ritz. She was "improperly attired."

Her rejection made headlines all over the world, bringing what today would be valued at millions of dollars of free publicity for the hotel, strengthening its reputation for conservative atmosphere and their insistence that "proper attire" be worn by everyone, *without* exception.

THE MOST EMBARRASSING MEAL, ***Locke Ober, Boston***

As head of the company called Woodside, I got to pick the location of the office. The truth was that it was above the Tremont Street subway station at the intersection of the main east west and the main north south subway lines. This was a superbly convenient spot for the vast majority of employees. I lived on Mt. Vernon Place, next to the State House (in other states this would be called the state capitol), just a six-minute walk across the Boston Common from the office.

Many of the Woodside offices around the country and, in a few instances, Europe, brought their major corporate client prospects to visit our complex central reservations office. We usually took them to lunch at Locke Ober, my old favorite restaurant from the sixties when I was working for State Street Bank. Locke Ober was on Winter Place, just a few hundred feet down Winter Street from the Woodside headquarters on Tremont Street. We went to Locke's frequently, often enough that when I had three or four guests we were awarded what I considered the prime table, the large round table in the L corner of the antique bar. It was a great spot for a "power lunch."

One day, the publisher of several Ziff Davis travel magazines in New York called asking me if I would "host" a lunch at Locke Ober. Dick Friese would pay for everyone, but I would perform as master of ceremonies. Dick was bringing to Boston a former member of the Mexican government's Cabinet, explaining that he was the man who had the foresight to create Cancun, the resort that triggered the development of Mexico's Gulf Coast and all of the tourism that resulted.

When we arrived at the restaurant, Dick assigned the seats, asking me to sit next to the Minister (wish I had written down his name) on my left. After a round of drinks, Dick asked me to discuss for the honored guest the specialties on the extensive menu. At the end of the discussion, I added the fact that my dad's favorite had been something you rarely, almost never, found on a restaurant menu…..Honeycomb Tripe. For those of you who do not know, this is the lining of a cow's stomach. In preparation, it has to be cleaned very carefully and cooked a long time. I think that the result is still tough enough that it should be deemed inedible, which is why I said that I had nicknamed Locke's dish "Honeycomb Tripe a la BF Goodrich." It truly did resemble chewing on a piece of car tire. I went on to say how bad it is for a restaurant to offer such a dish, much less consider it a specialty, because some unknowing people might make the mistake of ordering it.

Unfortunately, it is difficult to imitate the response I received and even less effective to attempt to do so in writing. Basically, the Cabinet member said something like "I beg a thousand pardons and hope you will forgive me, but Honeycomb Tripe is my absolute favorite dish and I can almost never have it. Would you be offended if I ordered it now?" Oh, man, what a blunder. I did manage to get my foot out of my mouth.

BANGKOK

Bangkok became one of my favorite cities in the world, but my first trip there was amusing. As President of Woodside, I was met by the manager of the Woodside offices in Thailand and Malaysia and his assistant for lunch. They took me to a large restaurant up near the famous American designer, Jim Thompson's, house. I don't remember the name but the large red words on the side as you entered just read in English "The Seafood Restaurant."

My hosts ordered in Thai. The first dish was a large steel bowl of shelled shrimp. They were delicious. When they arrived, my host took pains to caution me about the sauces that arrived in tiny little plates. Each had three compartments, one he said was mild, one hot and one so incredibly hot that an American shouldn't touch it.

With my first few shrimp I had consumed all of the super-hottest Thai sauce. My host was in shock; he simply could not believe I had eaten that sauce. The waitress brought me a little bowl of the superhot. When I finished that, it was causing a bit of a commotion. When I finished that, she brought out a soup bowl filled with the superhot. My host was now really in shock when I drank that with a soup spoon. It was a large restaurant, probably at least a hundred people, so when the manager let the waitresses gather around to see the crazy American, they circled the table two deep.

I like and am usually not bothered by very spicy food, but I have to admit this was a bit too much. When I finished that soup bowl and they brought another bowl, the word had spread and they had to let a bunch of the kitchen staff come out to watch the crazy American.

BERMUDA

At our summer house overlooking Marblehead Harbor, one of our friends was David Phillips, Mayor of Lynn, Massachusetts, who wore SCUBA gear and dove for lobsters. The price, free, was hard to beat, and one night I had eaten eleven pound-and-a-half lobsters.

When racing sailboats in Bermuda, I stayed once at the home of an English gentleman who took me for dinner at his favorite restaurant. You can see where this is headed....their specialty was lobsters. Somehow, my host's conversation with the owner/manager got around to talking about a huge lobster he had in the kitchen, an 18 pounder. When I told the story of my having eaten so many lobsters one night in Marblehead, my host bet me $500 I could not eat that one giant lobster.

When the owner came to the table, he brought a half of a lobster cut down the middle. I finished it off and was ready for the second half. Embarrassed, the owner had not cooked the other half, knowing that I would be unable to finish the first half and not wanting to waste the second half. I finished the whole lobster, had a great dinner, and won $500 in the process. I have one very bad memory of this friend's home. While racing there one year a friend asked me to change rooms and sleep out in the pool house so he and another friend's wife could share the bed I had been in. Awkward.

CLAM CHOWDER

Every year, and maybe still going, Boston used to conduct a Chowder Fest, at which people in City Market tasted various clam chowders and voted for the one they considered best. This information should be a great benefit for diners, especially for tourists from out of town. Right? Wrong!!!

I couldn't figure out how the Westin at Copley Place kept being selected as having the best chowder. In my opinion, the Sail Loft on Atlantic Avenue had by far the best chowder, even better than the highly-acclaimed Legal Seafoods. The husband of a lady working at Heritage Travel was the manager of the Westin. Bodo Lempke laughed and told us that he gave all of his employees, something like nine hundred people, an extra hour off for lunch on chowder competition day to go to City Market and vote for the Westin's clam chowder. Good way to win, but it illustrates how such "popular vote" by the people can be ridiculous and misleading. The Westin Copley Place, by winning in 1984,1985 and 1986, moved into the "Hall of Fame" and therefore out of the annual competition.

THE DANGEROUS MEAL

Probably about fifty years ago I had a cute little plant about two feet tall that was covered in tiny tomatoes. It was very pretty in my apartment. The fruit looked exactly like any other tomato, just much smaller…probably about 3/8 inch in diameter. They were essentially tiny cherry tomatoes. I tried adding them to salads for dinner and they worked fine. Sometimes I would put a dozen in a salad. Not much taste, but they livened up the appearance of the green salad.

At the time, I was dating a girl, Prentiss Gauld, who had been business manager for Horticulture Magazine. It turned out that, to my surprise, my tomatoes were not tomatoes. The article went into detail about the plant being avoided in homes with children because the "tomatoes" were poisonous. Preparing to write this, I looked up Jerusalem Cherry, technically named "Solanum." Here is a partial list of the symptoms: vomiting, diarrhea, fever, delirium, hallucination, low body temperature, paralysis, shock and damage to the nervous system. Doesn't sound too enticing.

88 A FEW LAST TIDBITS

"Misplaced" Places

It probably doesn't make sense to say a place isn't where it is. There are many examples of places that commemorate some event that did not occur there. These are some of places that simply are not where they really are. If I happened across this many, how many more must there be out there in the world?

EQUADOR

Equador is named Equador because it sits on the Equator. That much is true. The first time I traveled to Equador on business I wanted to see some of the country, especially the well-known tourist spot a few miles north of Quito where there is a monument and a painted line that is the Equator. People come to this spot from all over the world and usually have a picture taken facing east while they pose with their left foot in the northern hemisphere and their right foot across the line in the southern hemisphere with a large globe behind them.

Only problem is that the place for the line, established many years ago, is in the wrong place. All those tens of thousands of photos have shown people with both feet in the southern hemisphere. Equador should move the line and its park to the correct place, but they don't want to be bothered (and incur the cost). It's time to fix it.

The actual equator is several hundred feet on up the road to the north. Having heard the story, on my second trip to Quito I drove there once again and found the small correct "hand painted" sign on a fence where it should be, where the equator *really* is. Today, GPS systems make it easy to find the exact spot.

SPAIN

Pat and I went to Gibraltar by ship. It is a well-known spot and its "Rock of Gibraltar" is clearly identifiable by anyone who has seen the thousands of Prudential ads claiming to be as strong as the rock. I guess it is defensible to have the narrow bit of water between the Atlantic Ocean and the Mediterranean Sea be known as the Straits of Gibraltar, but the famous rock does not stand at the narrowest point where continental Europe is closest to Africa. The real "tip" of Spain, the entrance to the Mediterranean, is a few miles west at a place called Punta de Tarifa. It is very close to being at exactly 36 degrees north latitude and it reaches down to just 9.4 miles from Morocco at the northwestern corner of Africa. Nobody ever mentions Punta de Tarifa. By the way, in our opinion Gibraltar "ain't worth going to (sic)." If you do go, beware of the monkeys.

Just east of that spot in Morocco is a tiny island that brought two countries to the brink of war. If you know where the Falkland Islands are you will have a good perspective on how ridiculous the Spanish Moroccan problem was. The Falklands are a group of small islands with one fairly-large island where most of the residents live and where Stanley, the capital, sits. In 1982 the British sent ships to the island to take them back from the Argentines.

If you look at a map you may think the Falklands are very small, but the islands do comprise 4,700 square miles and the 3,000 residents are mostly of British decent. It may have been costly, but stopping Argentina from taking the islands made sense. It would, however, make more sense geographically for them to belong to Argentina. That is not true of Parsley Island. Bet you don't know where this one is. Parsley sits close to the southern edge of the Strait of Gibraltar. It belongs, illogically, to Spain. This rock is only the size of a few football fields and it is uninhabited. It sits only 765 feet off the coast of Morocco. Parsley, barren with cliffs surrounding the coastline, sits 50,280 feet from the nearest point in Spain. That is 9.6 miles. I happened to go by there. Don't bother.

Morocco decided to send a half dozen guys out to Parsley Island to claim ownership of the island for Morocco. Spain was so furious that they almost went to war. They called on the United States to intervene on their behalf. When Secretary of State Colin Powell was contacted by Spain his immediate reaction, as written in his excellent autobiography, was that this problem should be resolved with a bilateral treaty between the two nations. Colin's writing about the involvement of the US is something that should be read by all Americans. It provides great insights into the role that the United States plays in the world, whether we like it or not.

Spain did not trust Morocco and Morocco did not trust Spain. They both trusted the United States, which is why we had to end up in the middle on such a local and obscure dispute. There is another funny story about a city in Spain. Just up the Mediterranean Coast from Barcelona is what might be the worst name for a major city in the entire world. As I was driving north up the Catalonian Coast from Barcelona, I laughed at the sign as we entered the city. How would you like to live there, be in the United States and have to say you were from Peniscola? Doubtful it will compete with Coca Cola.

THE BATTLE OF BUNKER HILL

Some details in the history may differ, but millions of American students read about the Battle of Bunker Hill in Charlestown, just across the harbor from downtown Boston. There is a tall Bunker Hill Monument on top of the scene of the battle. Only problem is that the Battle of Bunker Hill did not take place on Bunker Hill.

The most credible story is that the American fighters had to establish their position in the dark and went past Bunker Hill to Breed's Hill, much closer to Boston Harbor, leaving them within range of the guns on the British ships. The rebels retreated when they ran out of gunpowder.

THE TENNESSEE RIVER

Atlanta Georgia is facing a massive water problem and has been in a legal battle with Alabama and Florida for many years. Atlanta is built on a huge granite dome and the city has expanded far beyond their ability to get an adequate supply of water, taking so much water out of the Coosa River that an inadequate amount is reaching Alabama and Georgia is taking so much from the Chattahoochee River that it is harming the great Apalachicola oysters where the Apalachicola River meets the Gulf of Mexico in Florida. Searching for a solution, Georgia discovered an interesting fact (maybe) involving the surveyors' placement of the state line between Tennessee and Georgia in the absolute northwest corner of Georgia right next to the boundary with Alabama. That line originated with the original gift by the King to Oglethorpe, who founded Savannah. If the state line here was just 223 feet farther north Georgia would touch the Tennessee River and be able to claim the right to extract some of this water. Even if the evidence proves that a mistake was made, it is too late to change it now.

THE DIOMEDE ISLANDS

When she was the Republican nominee for Vice President, everybody laughed at Sarah Palin for claiming you could see Russia from her home state of Alaska. It was considered hilarious and ridiculous. Democrats scoffed at her statement. Problem is: it's true. I never saw the facts in the press. Russia's Big Diomede Island is just 12,302 feet west of Alaska's *inhabited* island of Little Diomede. You can easily see Russia from Alaska. The United States citizens who live on the westernmost point of Little Diomede Island can look out their windows and see Russia from their homes. Bet very few Americans know that our country is just a little more than two miles from Russia.

HOHENZOLLERNSTRASSE

Here is another example of a story that doesn't fit here but there is no better place for it. When I had finished selecting a country and a city in which State Street Bank should locate its first foreign office, I had to spend a lot of time making sales calls in major financial cities throughout Europe. I stayed a good bit of time in a hotel several blocks north of where we had ended up picking for that first office on Leopoldstrasse in Munich. A brand new hotel, the International at 5 Hohenzollernstrasse let me leave all of my clothes in the closet of a room when I was away on a trip. They charged me only for the nights that I stayed in the room. That location is now the Cosmopolitan Hotel.

I would get funny looks or reactions from taxi drivers when I would tell them my destination. Hohenzollernstrasse 5 (as it is written in German) had been a well-known brothel for many years.

89 TRAVEL
The Places You Really Should See Before You Die

There is a best seller that lists one thousand places to see before you die. As you might guess, that number is more than all but a miniscule number of people in the world would ever have a chance of seeing and many of the places are truly second or third choices in the categories they are in, maybe fifth or even tenth…….just not ones you really should see.

That book was followed by a more sensible approach, listing just ten places to see. It is very difficult to name the ten most interesting places in the world and that book names ones that should not be in the top twenty five, much less the top ten. The normally dependable National Geographic Magazine in the spring of 2012 must have decided it needed to be cute. In a big article about the best national parks in the U.S. they put in ones even I had not heard of, put in some that should be far down the list and ignored the one that is arguably the most powerful single natural wonder in the world, Arizona's Grand Canyon of the Colorado River.

The Grand Canyon is truly grand, it's 277 miles length is so long that the only way you can see the enormity is from high in the air or down in the river. At its widest point, the canyon is 18 miles wide. You don't realize until you ride down on a mule that it is a full mile deep, showing geology dating back two billion years. It is simply ridiculous for a highly-reputable organization to make a big deal out of their feature article and do such an absurd job of picking what to include.

If you are a naturalist, you could be interested only in places that display great scenic beauty and interesting wildlife. If you are a big city person, you should still see some of the beauty of nature, especially the spectacular valleys and mountains of the world.

The book with the list of ten includes the Golden Pavilion in Japan, the island of Bimini (that I would not even put in the top one-hundred islands, much less the most recommended in the world. Santorini or Kauai should rank far above Bimini. Loch Ness, known for its fictitious monster (which you won't see) and not much else. Loch Ness is certainly not high on the list of beautiful lakes of the world and the "monster" is obviously fiction. As a matter of fact, Loch Ness is fairly drab, with the exception of ruins on its western shore. That list of ten does include a couple of places, such as the Pyramids at Giza and the whole area of northern Italy (not really a "single place"), and it leaves out the largest cities in the world, including New York.

It is disappointing to encounter so many wealthy Americans who are able to spend money on travel, have traveled to foreign countries, but have not even seen The Grand Canyon in their own country. Pat and I love Santorini; the huge old volcano crater and Santorini's white buildings with bright blue trim are beautiful. Stonehenge is interesting, but most people would consider an hour of looking at it to be enough. I considered it plenty. There are many more interesting and spectacular examples of construction by ancient man than Stonehenge. Put the Pyramids of Giza at, or at least near, the top of that list, along with places such as the beautiful Acropolis and the extremely long Great Wall of China (several thousand miles). You can see only a small re-built portion of the Great Wall just north of Beijing, but it is flooded with tourists.

Lots of lists include Machu Picchu and it *is* beautiful. The ruins are largely rebuilt but the view of the mountain that shows in essentially all of the photographs of Macchu Picchu is interesting and climbable. The route is hairy, scary in some places, but not terrifying.

One list of the top twenty five includes a couple of places that are truly magnificent. The easy one for American's to visit is Antelope Canyon, just a few miles east of Page, Arizona. It is quite small, but its elegant curves are magnificent. The spectacular natural area that is extremely difficult to reach is China's Tianzi Mountain area, several hundred miles north of Hong Kong. Tianzi might well be voted the most beautiful place in the world, but there just isn't much to do. The mountains that point like needles straight up into the air are truly spectacular, especially from their bases looking up. The only problem is that getting to Tianzi is extremely difficult, so it is mobbed by Chinese tourists and few from elsewhere.

There are some great places that you should see, and this medium-sized list will describe those that you really should make an effort to visit. When you are talking about natural beauty, there are many incredible mountains, rivers, lakes, valleys and coastlines throughout the world. Several that you should see are in the United States. It is amusing, or unfortunate, that books and TV shows have to address some unknown or "new" place to get the public's attention. The most recent example of that was the TV show "Good Morning America" in August of 2011 announcing their choice of Sleeping Bear Dunes along the shore of Lake Michigan west of Traverse City, as the single most beautiful place in the United States. No mountains, no waterfalls, no great beach, just light brown sand and a couple of large steep dunes overlooking Lake Michigan. Ridiculous.

Yes, I know I am about to be guilty in a subsequent chapter of naming a single most beautiful place in the world, but my choice has spectacular cliffs, mountains that are snowcapped all year, a very fast flowing river, 72 waterfalls, and beautiful villages with a vivid array of flowers. Yes, this is a personal choice and I acknowledge that there are many others that could claim this distinction. I will attempt to describe those cities and places of natural beauty that should be considered the most interesting in the world.

CITIES

First, in the category of cities, it is not just an American position that New York is the most incredible city in the world for a wide variety of reasons, but it is far from the most beautiful. There can always be disagreement, certainly if you make a slight change to the definition. Paris usually is credited with being the most beautiful city in the entire world, and it also commands the title of most romantic. Those titles are widely acclaimed by most people. Venice is a close second as romantic and I am prejudiced toward it because of all the boats and the absolute absence of cars. San Francisco is beautiful, but just not up there with Paris. London is more historic than the others (especially for Americans), and some relatively new cities, such as Hong Kong and Dubai, are spectacular in their own way. In both, the recent construction is what is truly amazing.

Yes, I know Shanghai is technically not "new," but it is new as a stunning metropolis. Dubai has a small antique area and old town, but it is the remarkable new construction that make it so spectacular, and it clearly sits atop the list in the category of cites that have had the fewest world travelers in relationship to its incredible man-made construction. Rome wins in the category of historic cities and is, of course, quite interesting, especially for Catholics. There are a few cities that have an exaggerated reputation, such as Buenos Aires, which is a big city without the natural beauty or the great architecture found in some others.

THE TWENTY FIVE PLACES YOU SHOULD NOT MISS

CITIES

New York, Paris, Venice, London, Dubai, Shanghai, Washington, D.C., Hong Kong, Rome, Amsterdam, St. Petersburg, Istanbul, and Bangkok.

NATURAL BEAUTY

The Grand Canyon, Niagara Falls, Lauterbrunnen Valley, The Serengeti, The west coast of Ireland,

MAN MADE STRUCTURES

The Pyramids of Giza, The Eifel Tower, The Golden Gate Bridge, The Acropolis, Machu Picchu, Angkor Wat, Chichen Itza.

90 THE WORLD'S MOST BEAUTIFUL PLACE

A Place I Bet You have Never Heard Of

When planning our wedding my soon-to-be wife, Pat, asked where I wanted to go on our honeymoon in August. When I said it should be her choice, she suggested that we go to some place I would like to see but to which I had not traveled. The only place I could think of was Tierra del Fuego at the southern tip of South America. We went there on a trip to Antarctica years later, but you should not go there in their winter and our wedding in the heat of summer would be winter in the southern hemisphere.

Pat then asked where I thought was the most beautiful place in the world. Without hesitation, my response was the Lauterbrunnen Valley, just seven miles south of Interlaken, Switzerland. Yes, it is a place few Americans have even heard of, much less visited. It is an incredibly beautiful place with a wide array of natural features. It is that remarkable combination of nature and civilization that makes it such an enjoyable place.

THE VALLEY

First, for Americans, Lauterbrunnen is in several key respects similar to Yosemite Valley in California. The sides of both valleys are steep and have huge granite cliffs. One big difference is that the majestic snow-capped-year-round peak of the Jungfrau dominates the end of Lauterbrunnen Valley, surrounded by a long stretch of jagged snowcapped peaks. At 13,642 feet, the Jungfrau stands 11,000 feet above the valley floor. That's more than two miles up in the sky.

It must be indicative of the type of people who visit or live in the valley; the three towns are clean as a whistle, graffiti and litter free. Both of the towns on the cliffs above the valley, Murren and Wengen, do not intrude upon all of the natural beauty of the area. They provide a number of high-quality places to stay while you explore the region.

WATERFALLS

The largest waterfall is Staubach but the most unusual is Trummelbach which you can't see from the valley because it flows fairly far back *inside* the rock and that is what makes it so beautiful. Over millions of years, the fast flowing water has eaten back into the mountain. As the waterfall cut its way into the rock, it began to leave beautiful undulating harder rock on either side through which you can walk on wooden stairways as you climb higher and higher inside the cliff. Don't miss it.

RIVER

The river that flows through the valley is the Weisse Lutschine, or White Lutschine River. For its entire length it is fast flowing white water, making it a great haven for kayaking, especially in the stretch downstream from the town of Lauterbrunnen.

HIKING

The easily accessible trails offer a wide variety of views and degrees of difficulty from quite easy to pretty difficult. From Kliene Scheidegg, you can take an expensive train to the Jungfraujoch, the highest railroad station in Europe. The view of the huge glacier and the peak of the Jungfrau from the train station is magnificent. Unfortunately, the cog railroad climbs over four miles up the *inside* of the Eiger mountain in total darkness, circling around and around as it climbs through the mountain.

The famous Eiger, the central point at the end in the movie "The Eiger Sanction," looms above Kleine Shiedegg, which is easily reachable by the cog railroad that runs up from Lauterbrunnen through Wengen, The first early attempts at climbing the North Face of the Eiger are powerfully displayed in the 2009 movie, "North Face."

PARAGLIDING

The flight is clearly one of the most, if not the most, thrilling experiences I have ever had. We strongly recommend the flight from Murren. You get several hundred feet of flying high over the town of Murren several hundred feet below before you suddenly find yourself passing over the cliff, and suddenly looking down at the valley floor about two thousand feet beneath your feet. It is an incredible sensation.

PLACES TO STAY

You should stay up on one of the cliffs. Wengen (pronounced Ving'-n) lies 4,000 feet about the valley floor on the eastern side of the valley or in the much smaller town of Murren on the west. On my first two trips to the valley I stayed with friends in Murren and the third time a short distance away in Grindelwald (which is a city).

On our honeymoon, Pat and I stayed in Murren, which is the smallest and least touristy, having a great view of the Monch and an up-close view at the large stone cliff, the Schwanchwald, that is directly across the narrow valley. Take the gondola and get a spot on the right that offers fabulous views of the huge stone cliff and of the tiny bridge near the top of the gondola ride. The Wengen side has much more to do so, for a first time visitor, it is the place to stay.

91 DUBAI

Because It Is An Incredible Place So Few Know

Dubai is spectacular. That one word says it all. Dubai is still very rarely on anyone's list of the great cities of the world to visit. It should be. The manmade structures are what make Dubai so interesting.

When I went to Dubai the first time it was on business in the seventies, when the entire area was largely just sand…lots and lots of flat sand extending for many miles. Everything of interest in the country today is in the city, and oh what a city it is.

The brand-new city was laid out with extra-wide boulevards and highways, making it easy to get around in a vehicle. It is *not* a city for walking. Taxis in Dubai are quite cheap. Be sure to get a good map instead of the official Dubai City Map. There is an excellent map by Explore called "Dubai Mini Map," Buy before you leave home.

BURJ KHALIFA

The Burj Khalifa (for now, the world's tallest building, by a lot), is the top spot. The ride to the top is expensive, but it gives you a fantastic view which is a good way to start. It will give you the best view of The Palm, built out in the Gulf. The nearby fountain, as it true of much of what you see in Dubai, is beyond belief. It is remarkably large, with hundreds of jets of water coming up in elegant patterns set to music in the lake beside the Burj Khalifa. Be sure to get the schedule and be there for a performance. The style of music is different for each performance, so you might want to check and determine what best suits you. Personally, I think the classical music is better accompaniment for the elegant fountains. You can look down at it from far above at the top of the Burj Khalifa, but you should not miss it from ground level, where you can hear the accompanying music.

.

BURJ Al ARAB

This hotel is a sight-seeing attraction. The aquariums on each side of the escalator up to the lobby are huge and beautiful. The small water fountains between the escalators cost $20 million. The round fountain with geyser in the middle of the lobby is quite something. Ask for its schedule. Its initial spout goes up (as I remember) something like 18 stories, but it is designed so that when all that water falls back to where you are standing, almost all of it falls within the round dish at the base of the fountain. I still suggest you don't stand too close when the water starts to fall a little splatters out.

The hotel itself is (at this writing) the world's tallest and the atrium lobby is the world's highest. When Pat I were in a taxi headed to the hotel I looked at the sailboat-shaped building and clearly saw the mast, the sail and what looked like two little "spreaders" on the mast near the top. When we were having lunch in a very large dining room up high, I walked over to the large windows and looked up and down trying to see the "spreader."

The manager came over, asked what I was looking for, and told me I was standing in one of the spreaders. The other one houses the bar. Go to the bar, as the food is pricey but not that good. If you can, take a brief tour and see some of the rooms, that would be well worth it. They also have an underwater restaurant. Their cheapest single room is $1,900.

GOLD MARKET
The Gold Souk is a safe place to shop because it is a major crime for a gold store to sell you anything that is not of the karats they claim. The sheer volume of gold hanging in the store windows is blinding in the sunlight. Pat likes to spell Dubai "Do Buy!"

HOTELS
As stated earlier, you can't miss the Burj Al Arab from the outside and you should go inside. If you have time, I also suggest you go see The Atlantis and the Fairmont out on The Palm. For most Americans, these are *not* the places to stay. I suggest the much less expensive, more-conveniently located, with more American décor the J.W. Marriott. Of course, if you have the really big bucks, try the One and Only, which is $1,400 and up. There are so many super hotels under construction that you should check the current choices.

92 CONCLUSION

That's Just A Fancy Word For "The End." Hope you enjoyed it.

Made in the USA
San Bernardino, CA
28 August 2019